The Vegan Cookbook

Gordon Baskerville and Alan Wakeman have been writing articles and recipes for vegan and vegetarian magazines for more than a decade, and have taught cookery courses for organizations as varied as the Vegetarian Society and local government training departments. They have also given many vegan cookery demonstrations to groups ranging from the mammoth *Here's Health Exhibition* at Olympia to local vegan societies all over the country.

Alan Wakeman's other published work includes an English language course, a book of poems, a collection of short stories and a book for children, *Tim, Willie and the Wurgles* (Abelard, 1976). His most recent publication is a new translation of Saint-Exupéry's *The Little Prince* (Pavilion Books, 1996).

Gordon Baskerville now works as a freelance production manager in film and television, and occasionally lectures in Film Studies at the University of North London.

The Vegan Cookbook

Over 200 recipes
all completely free from animal produce

ALAN WAKEMAN *and* GORDON BASKERVILLE

faber and faber

First published in 1986
by Faber and Faber Limited
3 Queen Square London WC1N 3AU
This new edition published in 1996

Photoset by Parker Typesetting Service, Leicester
Printed in England by Clays Ltd, St Ives plc

A CIP record for this book
is available from the British Library
ISBN 0-571-17804-9

10 9 8 7 6

For the many friends
who field-tested these recipes for us.
No more prohibitions on making changes,
no more tiresome questionnaires to fill out –
just good food to enjoy.

Contents

Introduction

When the first edition of this book was published in 1986 nearly all our reviews came from groups such as Compassion in World Farming and the Vegan Society. Most mainstream reviewers ignored us or assigned us to the 'lunatic fringe'. In those days vegan meant nothing to most people and it was virtually impossible to get anyone interested in the mistreatment of calves or the cruelty of battery henhouses. Now the word 'vegan' is routinely used in television news broadcasts where ordinary people are to be seen, almost daily, demonstrating against the cruelty of factory farming and the transport of live animals, while MPs, MEPs and even government ministers actively campaign for the abolition of veal crates in the European Union. Clearly this represents an important change of consciousness.

But it's still only a beginning. For the reality is that *all* factory farming is morally reprehensible. Even if the European Parliament succeeded in passing legislation to make veal crates or battery hen cages a bit bigger, it wouldn't make the rearing of animals in such conditions less despicable. *All* veal production involves the removal of newborn calves from their mothers and this is only one of a score of ways in which the meat and dairy industries are interdependent. The sad truth is that you cannot drink cow's milk, or eat butter, eggs or cheese, without making a small but significant contribution to the persecution of animals on a scale that dwarfs all previous examples of human tyranny. Yet, as the pioneers of the Vegan Society first established over fifty years ago, *a total boycott of the produce* is one of the most effective ways of opposing these monstrous practices.

So our chief objective in this latest edition of our book remains the same: to facilitate this boycott by providing a wide spectrum of recipes, from the everyday to the celebratory, for people who enjoy good food, have no desire to eat anything that isn't delicious as well as healthy and who have decided to become vegan for this, or for any other, reason. (See Appendix 2, *Seven Reasons to be Vegan*, page 270.) To this end we have added more than a dozen new recipes, improved a few old ones and revised and updated the information sections.

When the first edition of this book was published we had scant competition. Now, many bookshops have vegan sections in their cookery departments. So it is doubly gratifying to find our book still very much in demand and we would like to take this opportunity to thank the many readers who have sent us testimonials from all over the world – particularly the delightful one from the Australian outback.

Important Notes

If you are new to veganism, please read the *Notes on Vegan Nutrition* on page 265 before converting to an exclusively vegan diet.

We've used a few unusual ingredients so if you come across any you're not familiar with, please refer to the *Glossary* on page 285 for more information.

Please note that the word 'margarine' in the recipes should be taken to mean '*vegan* margarine' throughout. For more information and notes on where to buy vegan margarine, see page 230.

The nutritional analysis values are based on *McCance and Widdowson's The Composition of Foods* by A. A. Paul and D. A. T. Southgate (4th revised edition), Her Majesty's Stationery Office, London, 1978 and on *Food Composition Table for Use in East Asia*, FAO, Rome/US Dept. of Health, Education & Welfare, Bethesda, Maryland, USA, 1972. But please note that the figures given should be treated as an *approximate* guide only. The exact nutritional content of foods varies widely with the season, the prevailing weather conditions, the soil, the fertilizers used and so on. Note also that the nutritional values given for salads include the full value of the dressings in the calculations; bearing in mind that some people leave most of the dressings on their plates while others mop up every last drop with bread, the critical factor is not how much of the dressing you put on the salad, but how much of it you put in your mouth!

Soups

Soups

A good soup can be the basis of a simple, nourishing lunch, a light evening meal, a quick snack at any time, or it can be the starter for something big. But please don't be tempted to use *tinned* soup, even if you're short of time. The simple recipes from early in this section take hardly a moment or two longer than it takes to open a tin, pour the contents into a saucepan, heat them up and transfer the mixture to a bowl (time yourself if you don't believe us!) and a home-made soup is, of course, from a different dimension. Besides, tinned soups are full of chemicals – preservatives to increase their shelf-life, artificial flavourings and colouring agents and sugar, and are seldom vegan, even the vegetarian ones. (Close scrutiny of the list of ingredients usually reveals the presence of animal products of the factory farming industry.)

An electric blender makes a soup-maker's life easier and we have assumed that you have one. (If you haven't, you can still make most of the soups using a hand-mouli or by simple sieving – indeed, some dedicated cooks insist that the resultant purées are superior and claim not to mind the extra work and washing up.)

We've given you lots of recipes to start you off but why not try *inventing* your own? You can start by dicing any root vegetables you happen to have and sautéing them in oil or margarine with herbs and a bay leaf, or you can work from the basis of almost any leftovers, including the final stages of a stockpot.

To provide the basic liquid, or for thinning, use vegetable water or stock, liquidized tomatoes or tomato juice, soya milk, red or white wine, stout, beer, or grapefruit, apple or orange juice.

To thicken, use flour or arrowroot (dissolve it in a little cold water before adding it to the saucepan), rolled oats or oatmeal, pulses (lentils are particularly good because they cook so quickly), potatoes, agar flakes or carrageen.

To season or flavour, use herbs, spices, yeast extract, Vecon vegetable stock, miso, tomato paste, salt and pepper.

To make a soup more nourishing and attractive, add any of the following just before serving: fresh chopped herbs, *croûtons* (see below), *Vegan Yoghurt* (page 240) or try adding diced or blended tofu.

To make *croûtons*, dice a slice of wholewheat bread (or toast) and fry the pieces in oil with a clove of crushed garlic added to the pan. Drop them into the soup straight from the pan just before serving and they will make the most appetizing sizzling sound, look gorgeous and taste wonderful.

To turn a simple soup into a complete meal, serve it with slices of wholewheat bread or toast spread with nut-butters, tahini, yeast extract, or one of the many spreads from the *Spreads* section or dips from the *Starters* section, or with *croûtons* as described above; follow it with a salad and round it off with fresh fruit and coffee and you have a nutritionally-sound, delicious and healthy meal. Add a bottle of wine and you have a spread that can be set without shame before your favourite friends, vegan, vegetarian or omnivore.

Although a hot soup is a perfect way to start a winter meal, don't forget about *cold* soups in summer. There's no more appetizing way to start a summer dinner-party than with a home-made, chilled soup. Again we have given a number of recipes to get you started.

Tomato Soup

To Serve 3–4
Allow 5–10 minutes to prepare
Each serving (of 4) provides: 38 kcal, 3 g protein, 5 g carbohydrate,
1 g fat, 2 g fibre

Metric		Imperial/American
½ kg	fresh or tinned tomatoes	1 lb
¼ litre	soya milk	½ pint/1¼ cups
1 tsp	mixed spice	1 tsp
1 tsp	salt	1 tsp
1 tsp	freshly-ground black pepper	1 tsp

1 Skin the tomatoes (page 255).
2 Put all the ingredients in a blender and blend to a smooth frothy cream.
3 Transfer the blended mixture to a saucepan and warm through over a medium heat, stirring continuously. Serve very hot.

If you use tinned tomatoes this recipe is so quick, cheap and delicious that you may well wonder why anyone would ever bother to buy tinned tomato soup with all its chemical additives but perfectionists, of course, will prefer to use fresh tomatoes and this takes a little bit longer.

For extra bezaz add *croûtons* (page 3) or stir in a tablespoon of *Vegan Yoghurt* (page 240) just before serving.

Mushroom Soup

To Serve 4
Allow about ¼ hour to prepare
*Each serving provides: 102 kcal, 8 g protein, 7 g carbohydrate,
3 g fat, 3 g fibre*

Metric		Imperial/American
¼ kg	mushrooms	½ lb
¾ litre	soya milk	1½ pints/3½ cups
1	clove garlic	1
1 tsp	salt	1 tsp
1 tsp	freshly-ground black pepper	1 tsp

1 Wash and coarsely chop the mushrooms and put them in a large
saucepan with the soya milk. Bring quickly to the boil, then reduce
heat and leave to simmer, uncovered, for 10 minutes, stirring often.
2 Meanwhile, skin and crush the garlic, add it to the pan and stir
well in.
3 Remove pan from heat, transfer the mixture to a blender, add the
salt and pepper and blend to a smooth, frothy liquid. Return to pan,
reheat gently and serve.

We've put this recipe early in this section because it is so quick and
simple to make – but this doesn't mean that it wouldn't do as the starter
to a special-occasion dinner-party. Indeed, one of our circle of friends
who sampled it during our field trials rated it 'Triple A', asked for
second and third helpings and claimed that it was the best recipe we'd
come up with. While we couldn't agree with that, it was a useful
reminder that making things more complicated doesn't necessarily
make them taste better.

Adding wholewheat *croûtons* (page 3) at the last moment before
serving gives the soup extra dash and verve.

Cauliflower Soup

To Serve 6
Allow 20 minutes to prepare
Each serving provides: 54 kcal, 5 g protein, 4 g carbohydrate, 12 g fat, 3 g fibre

Metric		Imperial/American
1	large cauliflower	1
1 tsp	salt	1 tsp
¾ litre	soya milk	1½ pints/3½ cups
60 ml	sunflower oil	4 tbs
1 tsp	ground nutmeg	1 tsp
	salt and pepper to taste	

1 Cut the cauliflower into the smallest possible florets and dice the stems and outer leaves. Plunge into fiercely-boiling salted water until tender (about 5 minutes). Remove from heat and drain.
2 Put the cooked cauliflower into a blender together with the soya milk, sunflower oil and nutmeg and blend to a creamy (though still granular) texture.
3 Transfer the mixture to a saucepan, add salt and pepper to taste, reheat gently and serve. (If it seems too thick, add more soya milk till you get the consistency you prefer.)

Cauliflower has a subtle, delicate flavour which is easily smothered if you use too many herbs and spices but nutmeg complements it perfectly. Although we have put this recipe in the everyday section because it is so easy to make, it is a perfect way to start a dinner-party because you can prepare the soup hours in advance and simply reheat it just before your guests arrive, or you can leave making it till the last moment.

Onion Soup

To Serve 4–6
Allow 40 minutes to prepare
*Each serving (of 6) provides: 139 kcal, 1 g protein, 6 g carbohydrate,
13 g fat, 1 g fibre*

Metric		Imperial/American
65 ml	olive oil	4½ tbs
½ kg	onions	1 lb/2 large
¾ litre	water	1½ pints/3½ cups
45 ml	soya sauce	3 tbs
1 tsp	freshly-ground black pepper	1 tsp

1 While the oil is heating in a large saucepan, peel and slice the onions into thin rings.
2 Add them to the pan and cook gently, stirring occasionally, till they are completely soft (about 15–20 minutes).
3 Add the water, soya sauce and pepper and simmer for a further 10 minutes and serve.

This simple clear soup is a perfect starter for a substantial meal. Try adding *croûtons* (page 3) to it just before serving. Delicious!

Lentil and Tomato Soup

To Serve 4–6
Allow 50 minutes to prepare
Each serving (of 6) provides: 180 kcal, 10 g protein,
27 g carbohydrate, 4 g fat, 7 g fibre

Metric		Imperial/American
30 g	margarine	1 oz/2 tbs
1	clove garlic	1
½ kg	onions	1 lb/2 large
1 kg	fresh or tinned tomatoes	2 lb
180 g	red lentils	6 oz/1 cup
	salt and pepper to taste	

1 Put the margarine in a large saucepan over a low heat.
2 While it is melting, skin and crush the garlic, skin and chop the onions, add them to the pan and sauté till transparent.
3 Skin the tomatoes (page 255) and liquidize them.
4 Add them to the pan together with the lentils and stir continuously over a medium heat till the mixture boils, then reduce heat and simmer, partially covered, for 30–40 minutes. Stir from time to time and add a little water if necessary to prevent the mixture from becoming too thick. When the lentils are soft, add salt and pepper to taste and serve.

This nourishing soup makes a good starter to any winter meal and as it will keep well for several days, provided it is brought to the boil at least once a day, it makes sense to prepare a lot and use it for a range of meals.

Green Pea Soup

To Serve 6
Allow 1¼ hours to prepare
*Each serving provides: 260 kcal, 13 g protein, 32 g carbohydrate,
9 g fat, 8 g fibre*

Metric		Imperial/American
¼ kg	green split peas	½ lb/1 cup
60 g	margarine	2 oz/4 tbs
2	cloves garlic	2
½ kg	leeks	1 lb
¾ litre	water	1½ pints/3½ cups
1	lemon	1
45 ml	soya sauce	3 tbs
25 ml	wine vinegar	1½ tbs
¼ litre	soya milk	½ pint/1¼ cups

1 It's preferable to pre-soak the split peas (see page 257) but, if you haven't, put them in a saucepan, cover with boiling water and set aside.
2 Melt the margarine in a large saucepan over a low heat. Skin and crush the garlic and add it to the pan. Carefully wash, trim and chop the leeks, add to the pan and sauté till tender, increasing the heat as necessary (about 10–15 minutes).
3 Drain the split peas, stir them into the pan, add the water, bring to the boil then reduce heat and simmer, partially covered, till soft (about 40–50 minutes).
4 Meanwhile, squeeze the lemon, set the juice aside and get all the other ingredients ready.
5 As soon as the peas are soft, remove the pan from heat, add the lemon juice, soya sauce, vinegar and soya milk, then transfer to a blender and blend to a smooth, thickish liquid. (You'll probably have to do it in two stages.)
6 Return the blended soup to the saucepan, warm through and serve.

This provides an almost perfect balance of essential nutrients so you can feel virtuous as you tuck in!

It's also excellent chilled – though you'll probably need to thin it down with a little extra cold soya milk just before serving.

Cream of Parsley Soup

To Serve 4–6
Allow ½ hour to prepare
Each serving (of 6) provides: 145 kcal, 5 g protein, 10 g carbohydrate, 10 g fat, 4 g fibre

Metric		Imperial/American
60 g	margarine	2 oz/4 tbs
1	medium onion	1
1	clove garlic	1
¼ kg	potatoes	½ lb
¾ litre	water	1½ pints/3½ cups
¼ kg	tofu	½ lb/1 cup
1	large bunch parsley	1
	salt and pepper to taste	

1 Put the margarine in a large saucepan over a low heat.
2 While it is melting, skin and chop the onion, add to the pan and leave to cook gently. Skin and crush the garlic, add it to the pan and sauté until the onion is transparent. Don't let the mixture brown.
3 Wash and dice the potatoes (peel them if you wish), add them to the pan and stir continuously for a few moments before adding *half* the water. Bring quickly to the boil then reduce heat, cover and leave to simmer.
4 Put the rest of the water into a blender and crumble in the tofu. Now coarsely chop the parsley, set a few sprigs aside to use as a garnish and add the rest to the blender with the salt and pepper. Blend to a smooth pale green cream.
5 As soon as the potatoes are completely cooked and beginning to break down, remove pan from heat, combine the two mixtures and blend again thoroughly.
6 Return the blended soup to the saucepan and reheat gently for a few minutes. Check the seasoning and adjust if necessary, garnish with the sprigs of parsley and serve.

Parsley is much too good to use only as a garnish for other things. This flavoursome soup is full of vitamins and nutrients as well as being a delight to the eye. The perfect way to start a special dinner.

Apple and Parsnip Soup

To Serve 6–8
Allow ½ hour to prepare
*Each serving (of 8) provides: 125 kcal, 2 g protein, 14 g carbohydrate,
7 g fat, 4 g fibre*

Metric		Imperial/American
60 g	margarine	2 oz/4 tbs
½ kg	parsnips	1 lb
1½ tbs	mustard powder	1½ tbs
½ kg	cooking apples	1 lb/2 large
1 litre	water	2 pints/5 cups
25 ml	soya sauce	1½ tbs
1 tsp	caraway seeds	1 tsp
	salt and pepper to taste	

1 Put the margarine to melt in a large saucepan over a low heat.
2 Peel and chop the parsnips.
3 Stir the mustard powder into the melted margarine and when it has
   completely dissolved add the chopped parsnips and stir till they are
   all well coated. Cover and leave to cook gently.
4 Meanwhile, core and chop the apples (peel them if you wish) and
   add them to the saucepan together with the water. Bring quickly to
   the boil then reduce heat and simmer, partially covered, till the
   apples begin to break down (about 5–7 minutes).
5 Remove from heat and transfer the mixture to a blender. Add the
   soya sauce and blend to a smooth, rich, thick texture.
6 Put the mixture back into the saucepan, add the caraway seeds and
   salt and pepper to taste, reheat gently and serve.

Do try this satisfying, fruity, winter soup even if you don't usually like
parsnips. You may be pleasantly surprised.

It keeps well, provided it is brought to the boil at least once a day.

For variety, try fennel seeds instead of caraway, or try adding ¼ tsp
chilli powder.

Celery and Coconut Soup

To Serve 4–6
Allow ½ hour to prepare
Each serving (of 6) provides: 100 kcal, 2 g protein, 2 g carbohydrate, 9 g fat, 6 g fibre

Metric		Imperial/American
1	large head of celery	1
¾ litre	water	1½ pints/3½ cups
1 tsp	salt	1 tsp
90 g	creamed coconut	3 oz/⅓ cup
½ tsp	freshly-ground black pepper	½ tsp

1 Break the celery head up into individual stalks and wash thoroughly.
2 Chop the stalks into bite-sized lengths, including the green leaf tips, unless these are badly discoloured, and put them into a large saucepan together with the water and salt. Bring quickly to the boil then reduce heat and simmer, partially covered, till tender (about 15 minutes).
3 Meanwhile, dissolve the creamed coconut in a little hot water taken from the saucepan.
4 As soon as the celery is tender, take some more water from the saucepan and add it to the dissolved coconut until it is fairly thin, then pour the mixture back into the saucepan and stir well in. Add the pepper, check the seasoning and adjust if necessary.
5 The soup may be served immediately, just as it is, or you may wish to liquidize it first.

The soup is attractive enough, with its pale green celery pieces floating in creamy white coconut milk, to serve without liquidizing; it's a matter of taste. But in the unlikely event that your guests leave you any, liquidize it, store it in the fridge and serve it chilled. It's so good like this that you may prefer it this way in the first place, especially in summer.

As an added feature, try sprinkling celery seeds over the soup just before you serve it.

Chick Pea and Rosemary Soup

To Serve 6
Allow 2 hours to prepare (if you have pre-soaked the chick peas)
*Each serving provides: 156 kcal, 10 g protein, 6 g carbohydrate,
9 g fat, 22 g fibre*

Metric		**Imperial/American**
¼ kg	chick peas (dry weight)	½ lb/1½ cups
¼ kg	onions	½ lb/2 medium
3 tbs	rosemary (preferably fresh, chopped)	3 tbs
1½ litres	water	3 pints/7½ cups
25 ml	soya sauce	1½ tbs
1½ tbs	miso	1½ tbs
1	lemon	1
	salt and pepper to taste	

1 Drain the chick peas of their soaking water and put them in a large saucepan.
2 Skin and chop the onions and add them to the saucepan together with the rosemary and water. Bring quickly to the boil, then reduce heat and simmer, partially covered, till they are quite tender (about 1–2 hours).
3 Transfer the cooked chick peas and any remaining water to a blender and add the soya sauce.
4 Finely grate the lemon rind and add it to the mixture, then squeeze the lemon and add the juice. Blend to a rich, smooth, thick consistency.
5 Return the blended soup to the saucepan, warm through, stir in the miso, add salt and pepper to taste and serve.

This is substantial enough to make a simple meal in itself, served with lots of wholewheat bread or a salad. Add a glass of wine each and round it off with fresh fruit and coffee and you have a satisfying and delicious everyday meal.

Asparagus Soup

To Serve 5–6
Allow 20 minutes to prepare and cook
*Each serving (of 6) provides: 167 kcal, 7 g protein, 5 g carbohydrate,
12 g fat, 2 g fibre*

Metric		Imperial/American
½ kg	asparagus	1 lb
¾ litre	soya milk	1½ pints/3½ cups
4 tbs	sunflower oil	4 tbs
	salt and pepper to taste	

1 Wash and chop the asparagus spears, discarding only damaged or woody ends.
2 Place in a saucepan together with half the soya milk, bring to the boil then reduce heat and simmer, uncovered, till tender (about 10 minutes).
3 Put the remaining (cold) soya milk in a blender together with the sunflower oil. Now scoop the cooked asparagus from the saucepan using a straining spoon or tongs, set aside a few tips for use as a garnish, add the rest to the blender and blend to a smooth foamy cream.
4 Return the blended mixture to the saucepan, stir into the (hot) soya milk, and warm through. Season with salt and pepper to taste, garnish with the cooked tips, and serve.

Although quick and easy to prepare, this pastel green soup is certainly sumptuous enough for our 'special occasions' section. For even more flavour and bezaz, use *walnut* instead of *sunflower* oil.

Lentil and Apricot Soup

To Serve 4–6
Allow ½ hour to prepare
Each serving (of 6) provides: 261 kcal, 11 g protein,
37 g carbohydrate, 9 g fat, 11 g fibre

Metric		Imperial/American
¼ kg	onions	½ lb/2 medium
45 ml	oil	3 tbs
¼ kg	red lentils	½ lb/1¼ cups
¼ kg	cooking apples	½ lb/1 large
125 g	dried apricots	¼ lb/1 cup
1 litre	water	2 pints/5 cups
¼ tsp	chilli powder	¼ tsp
	salt to taste	

1 Skin and chop the onion, put in a large saucepan and sauté in the oil until transparent.
2 Add the lentils and fry gently for a few minutes, turning continuously.
3 Peel, core and chop the apple and add it to the saucepan with the apricots and water and bring the mixture quickly to the boil, then reduce heat and simmer, partially covered, until the lentils soften (about 20 minutes). Stir the mixture from time to time to prevent sticking.
4 Remove from heat and add the chilli powder and salt to taste. Be careful not to overdo the chilli powder – a quarter of a teaspoonful should suffice!
5 Transfer the mixture to a blender, liquidize and serve.

This fruity soup is guaranteed to cheer you up on a freezing cold and wet winter day but it is also good in summer with the chilli omitted.

Watercress Soup

To Serve 6–8
Allow ½ hour to prepare
*Each serving (of 8) provides: 103 kcal, 3 g protein, 9 g carbohydrate,
7 g fat, 4 g fibre*

Metric		**Imperial/American**
60 g	margarine	2 oz/4 tbs
1	medium onion	1
¼ kg	potatoes	½ lb
1 litre	water	2 pints/5 cups
2 bunches	watercress	2 bunches
1	lemon	1
2 tsp	soya sauce	2 tsp
¼ litre	soya milk	½ pint/1¼ cups
	salt and pepper to taste	

1 Put the margarine in a large saucepan over a low heat.
2 While it is melting, skin and chop the onion, add to the pan and sauté until transparent. Don't let it brown.
3 Wash and dice the potatoes (and peel them if you wish), add to the pan and stir continuously for 2–3 minutes.
4 Now add the water and bring quickly to the boil, then reduce heat and simmer, uncovered, for 5 minutes.
5 Finely chop the watercress and set about a quarter of it aside to use as a garnish. Add the rest of the chopped cress to the pan and simmer for a further 5 minutes.
6 Meanwhile, grate the lemon rind and stir the grated peel into the mixture.
7 Squeeze the lemon and add the juice to the mixture.
8 Remove pan from heat and stir in the soya sauce. Transfer the mixture to a blender and liquidize thoroughly.
9 Return the blended soup to the saucepan, stir in the soya milk and reheat gently for a few minutes before seasoning with salt and pepper to taste. Garnish with the rest of the chopped cress and serve.

This delicate soup has a subtle flavour that is the perfect way to start a dinner-party, but don't try serving it after something with a strong taste. The recipe provides enough for 6 generous servings, or 8 if it is to be followed by a substantial meal.

Carrot and Orange Soup

To Serve 6–8
Allow 40 minutes to prepare
Each serving (of 8) provides: 154 kcal, 2 g protein, 15 g carbohydrate, 10 g fat, 5 g fibre

Metric		Imperial/American
1 kg	carrots	2 lb
½ litre	orange juice	1 pint/2½ cups
1 tsp	salt	1 tsp
1	large orange	1
1	lemon	1
75 ml	oil	5 tbs
¼ litre	soya milk	½ pint/1¼ cups
	pepper to taste	

1 Wash, top and tail the carrots (or peel, as necessary) and slice them very thinly. Put them into a large saucepan with the orange juice and salt, bring quickly to the boil, then reduce heat and simmer, covered, till very tender (about 15–20 minutes).
2 Meanwhile, coarsely grate the orange peel and set aside.
3 Squeeze the orange and the lemon and set the juice aside.
4 Remove the carrots from heat as soon as they are soft, add the oil, orange peel, juices and soya milk, transfer to a blender and blend to a smooth, creamy (though still granular) mixture. Transfer back to the saucepan and reheat gently. Add pepper to taste and serve.

This soup has a gorgeous colour and is equally good hot or chilled.
Serve it hot as a starter to a winter meal, with curry and rice to follow, or chilled, in summer, followed by a cold flan and salad.

Pear and Ginger Soup

To Serve 6–8
Allow 40 minutes to prepare
*Each serving (of 8) provides: 108 kcal, negligible protein,
14 g carbohydrate, 6 g fat, 3 g fibre*

Metric		Imperial/American
60 g	margarine	2 oz/4 tbs
1½ tbs	freshly grated ginger	1½ tbs
	(or ¾ tbs dried ground ginger)	
1 kg	pears	2 lb
1	lemon	1
½ litre	water	1 pint/2½ cups
	salt and pepper to taste	

1 Put the margarine to melt in a large saucepan.
2 Grate the ginger into the melting margarine and leave to cook gently over a low heat.
3 Slice the pears in half and remove the pips and stalks then chop them up and add them to the saucepan, stirring each time you add more till they're all done.
4 Squeeze the lemon and add the juice to the pan.
5 Now add the water, bring quickly to the boil, reduce heat and simmer, covered, till the pears are cooked right through (about 20–30 minutes depending on how ripe they are).
6 Transfer the mixture to a blender and blend to a rich, smooth, creamy liquid.
7 Return the blended soup to the saucepan, add salt and pepper to taste, reheat gently and serve. (If the soup seems too thick, add a little water to get the consistency you prefer.)

Although we have given a quantity for dried ginger, the soup is only really worth making if you can get fresh.
 It's also good chilled.

Gazpacho (Spanish Chilled Cucumber and Tomato Soup)

To Serve 6

Allow 2 hours to prepare (including 1½ hours to chill)

Each serving provides: 150 kcal, 2 g protein, 7 g carbohydrate, 13 g fat, 3 g fibre

Metric		Imperial/American
½ kg	fresh or tinned tomatoes	1 lb
1	large cucumber	1
1	medium green pepper	1
1	small onion	1
2	cloves garlic	2
75 ml	olive oil	5 tbs
75 ml	wine vinegar	5 tbs
25 ml	lemon juice	1½ tbs
1 tsp	dill	1 tsp
¼ kg	whole tomatoes	½ lb/3 large
	salt and pepper to taste	

1 Put the skinned tomatoes (page 255) in a blender.
2 Wash the cucumber and pepper, cut off a quarter of each and set aside, and remove the seeds and pith from the pepper. Coarsely chop the remainder and add to the blender. (It isn't necessary to peel the cucumber.)
3 Skin and coarsely chop the onion, skin and crush the garlic and add to the blender.
4 Add the oil, vinegar, lemon juice and dill and blend to a thick, smooth liquid. Transfer to a tureen or suitable serving-bowl.
5 Chop the remaining cucumber, pepper and the whole tomatoes as finely as possible, stir them into the soup and season with salt and pepper (only if you think it needs them!). Chill for at least 1½ hours before serving.

This is a wonderful soup to serve outdoors on a hot summer's day: add some ice cubes from time to time to keep it chilled and follow it up with a salad and *Savoury Summer Tart* (page 75) and you have the perfect alfresco meal.

Beetroot and Apricot Soup

To Serve 6
Allow ½ hour to prepare, 1 hour to cook
*Each serving provides: 183 kcal, 3 g protein, 27 g carbohydrate,
7 g fat, 12 g fibre*

Metric		Imperial/American
½ kg	raw beetroots	1 lb
¾ litre	water	1½ pints/3½ cups
1	medium onion	1
3 tbs	sunflower oil	3 tbs
¼ kg	dried apricots	½ lb/2 cups
¼ litre	orange juice	½ pint/1¼ cups
	salt and freshly-ground pepper to taste	
	fresh dill (as a garnish)	

1 Wash, peel and dice the beetroots and put them into a large
   saucepan with half the water. Bring quickly to the boil, then reduce
   heat and simmer, partially covered, until soft (about 45 minutes).
   Remove from heat and set aside to cool.
2 Meanwhile, skin and chop the onion, put it in another large
   saucepan and sauté in the oil until transparent. Add the apricots and
   orange juice and bring quickly to the boil, then reduce heat and
   simmer, partially covered, till the apricots soften (about 15 minutes).
3 Blend the apricot mixture with the remaining cold water till smooth
   and return it to the saucepan.
4 Put the cooled beetroot mixture into the blender (it doesn't need
   rinsing) and blend with its cooking water till smooth.
5 Combine the two mixtures in the saucepan and warm through,
   stirring often. Season to taste, garnish with the dill and serve.

For a really classy touch set 6 tbs of the apricot mixture aside at step 3
then, just before serving, pour 1 tbs onto each bowl in a crescent shape
and draw a knife across four or five times to make a decorative fan
design.

Don't buy expensive whole apricots for this dish. Broken ones are not
only cheaper but better – because of their sharper taste.

Vichyssoise (French Leek and Potato Soup)

To Serve 6
Allow ¾ hour to prepare
*Each serving provides: 184 kcal, 6 g protein, 18 g carbohydrate,
10 g fat, 5 g fibre*

Metric		**Imperial/American**
60 g	margarine	2 oz/4 tbs
½ kg	leeks	1 lb
¼ kg	potatoes	½ lb
400 ml	water	¾ pint/2 cups
45 ml	soya sauce	3 tbs
½ litre	soya milk	1 pint/2½ cups
	salt and pepper to taste	

1 Melt the margarine in a large saucepan over a low heat. Meanwhile, trim, carefully wash and chop the leeks. Now sauté them in the saucepan till tender (about 15 minutes).
2 Wash and chop the potatoes (peel them if you wish) and add them to the pan with the water. Bring quickly to the boil, then reduce heat and simmer, partially covered, till the potatoes are soft (about another 15 minutes). Remove from heat.
3 Transfer the mixture to a blender, add the soya sauce and soya milk and blend to a smooth consistency.
4 The blended soup can now either be returned to the saucepan and warmed through if you wish to serve it hot, or chilled in the refrigerator till needed if you wish to serve it cold (the traditional French way). Season with salt and pepper to taste just before serving.

This is good for a special occasion supper-party as it can be made well in advance, is equally good hot or cold and, although it's so easy to make, always seems to impress people.

Try serving it as a substantial starter, followed by *Bulgur Bake* (page 49) or *Ratatouille* (page 54), or use it as the centre-piece of a light lunch with lots of wholewheat bread and serve with a light, dry wine.

Wine and Walnut Soup

To Serve 4
Allow ½ hour to prepare
*Each serving provides: 441 kcal, 8 g protein, 12 g carbohydrate,
36 g fat, 3 g fibre*

Metric		Imperial/American
180 g	walnuts	6 oz/1½ cups
¼ litre	water	½ pint/1¼ cups
60 g	margarine	2 oz/4 tbs
2	cloves garlic	2
1½ tbs	wholewheat flour	1½ tbs
175 ml	sweet white wine	6 fl oz/¾ cup
¼ litre	soya milk	½ pint/1¼ cups
25 ml	soya sauce	1½ tbs
25 ml	lemon juice	1½ tbs
1 tsp	mixed spice	1 tsp

1 Bring a pan of water to the boil, plunge in the walnuts and boil for 2–3 minutes. Remove from heat and drain.
2 Put the blanched walnuts in a blender with ¼ litre (½ pint/1¼ cups) fresh cold water and blend to a thick, smooth consistency. Set aside.
3 Put the margarine to melt in a large saucepan. Skin and crush the garlic, add it to the pan and cook gently for a few minutes.
4 Stir in the flour and cook for a couple of minutes before adding the walnut purée. Mix thoroughly.
5 Now add the remaining ingredients a little at a time, stirring continuously till well heated.

This spectacular and substantial soup is best followed by a light main course such as *Savoury Summer Tart* (page 75) or *Carrot Flan* (page 60).

Starters

Starters

The starter is the prologue to the meal, setting the scene, giving a sense of occasion. It should *look* good enough to arouse a general glow of pleasurable anticipation at the prospect of the meal ahead, *taste* good enough to stimulate the taste buds and so whet the appetite but be *small* enough not to fill you up before the play begins.

Dips are particularly good for breaking the ice at a meal where some of the guests don't know one another so we've put them in this section too, but we've also included a number of other recipes that have the right attributes for perfect starters: they can be prepared well in advance (leaving you free to concentrate your energies on the main course) and they are visually attractive enough to be conversation-pieces. But don't forget that *soups* also make excellent starters so if you're planning a meal it's always worth having a look in the soup section first.

Although many of our starter recipes take quite a lot of time and care to prepare remember that it is precisely this that signals to your guests that you hold them in esteem and that the meal is going to be a worthwhile and pleasurable experience. Everyone knows that sinking feeling in an unknown restaurant when you realize that the starters on the menu are all of the slice-of-melon, half-a-grapefruit variety. Don't make this mistake! To continue the theatrical analogy – if your starter is the curtain-raiser *grab your audience in the first act!*

Savoury Tomato Jelly

To Serve 6
Allow 1½ hours to prepare (including cooling and setting time)
*Each serving provides: 42 kcal, 2 g protein, 6 g carbohydrate, 1 g fat,
4 g fibre*

Metric		Imperial/American
2	lemons	2
1 kg	fresh or tinned tomatoes	2 lb
45 ml	soya sauce	3 tbs
1 tsp	freshly-ground black pepper	1 tsp
4 tbs	agar flakes	4 tbs
12	stoned black olives	12

1 Cut one of the lemons in half and set aside 6 very thin slices to use as a decoration.
2 Squeeze the lemons and put the juice in a blender. Add the skinned tomatoes (page 255), soya sauce and pepper and blend till smooth.
3 Transfer the blended mixture to a saucepan, bring quickly to the boil, then reduce heat, stir in the agar flakes and simmer, uncovered, for 5 minutes, stirring continuously.
4 Remove from heat and pour into individual serving-dishes.
5 Refrigerate when cool.
6 Decorate the individual jellies with the slices of lemon and the halved black olives. Serve chilled.

If you really want to impress your friends, set the jelly in a ring mould and make a *Pepper Salad* (page 116) to put in the centre. If you have trouble getting the jelly out of the ring mould, proceed as follows: first tip and rotate the mould to loosen the jelly then place the serving-dish on top of the mould, invert the whole thing and, bringing it sharply downwards, stop suddenly. Be sure to position the mould carefully because once the jelly has dropped you won't be able to move it again.

Savoury Carrot Jelly

To Serve 4–6
Allow 1½ hours to prepare (including cooling and setting time)
Each serving (of 6) provides: 29 kcal, 1 g protein, 7 g carbohydrate,
negligible fat, 3 g fibre

Metric		Imperial/American
1	lemon	1
3 tbs	agar flakes	3 tbs
650 ml	carrot juice	1¼ pints/3 cups
25 ml	soya sauce	1½ tbs
	freshly-ground pepper to taste	

1 Cut thin slices of lemon (to use as a decoration), then squeeze the rest and set the juice and slices aside.
2 Put the agar flakes in a small saucepan together with about a quarter of the carrot juice and bring quickly to the boil, then reduce heat and simmer for 5 minutes, stirring continuously.
3 Remove from heat, stir in the rest of the carrot juice, the lemon juice, soya sauce and freshly-ground black pepper to taste, and pour into individual serving-dishes.
4 Refrigerate when cool.
5 Decorate the individual jellies with the slices of lemon or halved black olives. Serve chilled.

This delicious jelly also makes a good tart filling: simply make a pre-baked pastry shell (see page 203) and pour the jelly into it instead of into individual dishes. The result is good enough to serve as a main course.

For variety, try using a combination of carrot and mixed vegetable juices.

Pepper Jelly

To Serve 4–6
Allow 1½ hours to prepare (including cooling and setting time)
Each serving (of 6) provides: 46 kcal, 2 g protein, 8 g carbohydrate, 1 g fat, 2 g fibre

Metric		Imperial/American
½ kg	red, yellow or green peppers	1 lb/2 large
1	lemon	1
45 ml	soya sauce	3 tbs
½ tsp	freshly-ground black pepper	½ tsp
2 tbs	agar flakes	2 tbs
125 ml	water	¼ pint/½ cup

1 Wash and chop the peppers, taking care to remove all the seeds, and put them in a blender.
2 Squeeze the lemon and add the juice to the blender.
3 Add the soya sauce and ground pepper and blend to a smooth (though granular) paste.
4 Put the agar flakes and water into a small saucepan, bring quickly to the boil, then reduce heat and simmer for 5 minutes. Remove from heat.
5 Add the blended peppers to the saucepan and mix thoroughly before pouring into individual serving-dishes. Refrigerate when cool.
6 Decorate the individual jellies with slices of lemon or halved black olives. Serve chilled.

Note that if you *peel* the peppers (see page 256) you'll get a richer, deeper colour and a smoother texture but you'll lose some of the crispness and taste.

If you are cooking for a really special occasion, make this recipe three times over using a different coloured pepper each time and set each separately in a ring mould. You could substitute *Savoury Tomato Jelly* (page 28) for the red layer and pile *Asparagus Salad* (page 131) in the middle.

Curried Lemon Dip

To Serve 6–8
Allow 40 minutes to prepare (including ½ hour to chill)
*Each serving (of 8) provides: 26 kcal, 3 g protein, 1 g carbohydrate,
1 g fat, negligible fibre*

Metric		Imperial/American
¼ kg	tofu	½ lb/1 cup
1	clove garlic	1
1	lemon	1
75 ml	soya milk	5 tbs
25 ml	soya sauce	1½ tbs
2 tsp	*Garam Masala* (page 253)	2 tsp

1 Chop the tofu up and put it in a blender.
2 Skin and crush the garlic and add it to the tofu.
3 Squeeze the lemon and add the juice.
4 Now add the other ingredients and blend to a smooth cream.
5 Chill for at least ½ hour before serving.

Serve this simple, but delicious, dip as a starter with sticks of fennel, celery or raw carrot in summer, or with *Plain Oatcakes* (page 216) in winter.

Savoury Peanut Dip

To Serve 6–8
Allow 40 minutes to prepare (including ½ hour to chill)
*Each serving (of 8) provides: 213 kcal, 9 g protein, 3 g carbohydrate,
19 g fat, 2 g fibre*

Metric		Imperial/American
½ kg	tofu	1 lb/2 cups
2	lemons	2
75 ml	olive oil	5 tbs
5 tbs	peanut butter	5 tbs
75 ml	soya milk	5 tbs
45 ml	soya sauce	3 tbs
1 tsp	mustard powder	1 tsp
2 tsp	freshly-grated ginger (or 1½ tsp dried ginger)	2 tsp
1 tsp	freshly-ground black pepper	1 tsp
½ tsp	cayenne pepper	½ tsp

1 Dice the tofu and put it into a blender.
2 Squeeze the lemons and add the juice.
3 Now add all the other ingredients and blend to a smooth cream.
   (Add a little water if it seems too thick.)
4 Chill for at least ½ hour before serving.

This can be served with sticks of celery, fennel or carrot as a starter to a summer meal, with *Plain Oatcakes* (page 216) for a winter meal, or any time as a snack. It is also good for buffet parties and as a sandwich filling.

Guacamole (Mexican Avocado Dip)

To Serve 6–8
Allow 20 minutes to prepare
*Each serving (of 8) provides: 130 kcal, 3 g protein, 2 g carbohydrate,
12 g fat, 2 g fibre*

Metric		Imperial/American
3	large ripe avocados	3
2	lemons	2
4	cloves garlic	4
1 tsp	salt	1 tsp
¼ tsp	chilli powder (more or less to taste)	¼ tsp
¼ tsp	paprika (optional)	¼ tsp

1 Scoop out the flesh of the avocados and put it in a blender.
2 Squeeze the lemons and add the juice.
3 Skin and crush the garlic and add it to the blender together with the
  salt and chilli powder and blend to a smooth cream.
4 Transfer the mixture to a suitable serving-bowl, sprinkle the top
  with paprika and serve.

For variety, try stirring in very finely chopped raw vegetables such as
celery, fennel, radishes, red or green peppers or tomatoes.

Carrot Dip

To Serve 6
Allow 50 minutes to prepare (including ½ hour to chill)
*Each serving provides: 342 kcal, 1 g protein, 10 g carbohydrate,
33 g fat, 5 g fibre*

Metric		Imperial/American
1 kg	carrots	2 lb
4	cloves garlic	4
125 ml	sunflower oil	¼ pint/½ cup
45 ml	olive oil	3 tbs
125 ml	wine vinegar	¼ pint/½ cup
1½ tsp	salt	1½ tsp
2 tsp	freshly grated ginger (or 1 tsp dried ginger)	2 tsp
½ tsp	paprika	½ tsp
	pinch cayenne pepper	
2 tsp	cumin seeds	2 tsp
	chopped chives or parsley to garnish	

1 Peel and chop the carrots and plunge them in a large pan of fiercely boiling water. Reduce heat and continue cooking till tender (about 8–10 minutes).
2 Skin and crush the garlic and put it in a blender with all the other ingredients.
3 Drain the carrots, add them to the blender and reduce to a smooth cream.
4 Transfer to a suitable serving-dish and chill for at least ½ hour before serving, garnished with chopped chives or parsley.

Serve this dip as a starter with thin slivers of raw carrot, fennel or celery or with *Plain Oatcakes* (page 216). It is also good for buffet parties and has such an attractive colour that if you set it out among other dishes, your guests will make a beeline for it.

Hummus

To Serve 6
Allow 1–2 hours to prepare (if you have pre-soaked the chick peas –
see page 257)
*Each serving provides: 298 kcal, 10 g protein, 4 g carbohydrate,
25 g fat, 22 g fibre*

Metric		Imperial/American
¼ kg	chick peas (dry weight)	½ lb/1½ cups
2	lemons	2
2	cloves garlic (or more to taste)	2
75 ml	olive oil	5 tbs
3 tbs	tahini	3 tbs
	salt to taste	
	parsley or paprika as garnish	

1 Rinse and drain the pre-soaked chick peas, return them to their
  saucepan, cover with clean water and bring quickly to the boil, then
  reduce heat and simmer, partially covered, till tender (about 1–2
  hours).
2 Grate the lemons and put the grated peel in a blender, then squeeze
  the lemons and add the juice.
3 Skin and crush the garlic and add to the blender together with the
  olive oil and tahini.
4 As soon as the chick peas are tender enough, add them to the
  blender together with enough recipe water to blend all the
  ingredients to a smooth paste. Add salt to taste and blend again.
5 Decorate with a little chopped parsley or sprinkle with paprika.
  Refrigerate till needed.

Hummus is an ideal starter to a meal. Serve it as they do in the Middle
East on individual plates, decorated with black olives, or as a dip with
fennel or celery. It will keep for several days in a fridge so if you have
any left over you can use it as the basis for snacks for days after your
dinner guests have departed.

Roasted Red Peppers

To Serve 4
Allow 1½ hours to prepare
Each serving provides: 102 kcal, 1 g protein, 6 g carbohydrate,
8 g fat, 1 g fibre

Metric		Imperial/American
2	large red peppers	2
2	tomatoes	2
2	cloves garlic	2
1 tbs	freshly chopped basil	1 tbs
30 ml	olive oil	2 tbs
	salt and pepper to taste	

1 Cut the peppers in half lengthways (including the stems so that each has half a stem remaining). De-seed and wash them and place them in a shallow oven-proof dish.
2 Skin the tomatoes (page 255), cut them in quarters lengthways and arrange two quarters in each half pepper.
3 Skin and crush the garlic and spread it equally over each half pepper. Next sprinkle with chopped basil and olive oil and season with salt and freshly ground black pepper.
4 Bake in the middle of a fairly hot oven (190°C/375°F/gas mark 5) for ¾–1 hour till the tops start to blacken.

This is the way to start a meal with a true taste of the Mediterranean. And they're even better served cold, with a crisp dry white wine – if you can resist eating them long enough to chill them. For variety, sprinkle a few drops of lemon juice over the top.

Falafels

To Serve 4–6
Allow 1–2 hours to prepare (if you have pre-soaked the chick peas –
see page 257)
*Each serving (of 6) provides: 175 kcal, 11 g protein, 9 g carbohydrate,
9 g fat, 23 g fibre*

Metric		Imperial/American
¼ kg	chick peas (dry weight)	½ lb/1½ cups
2	medium onions	2
2	cloves garlic	2
1	bunch parsley	1
1 tsp	ground coriander	1 tsp
1 tsp	ground cumin	1 tsp
½ tsp	turmeric	½ tsp
¼ tsp	chilli powder	¼ tsp
1 tsp	baking powder	1 tsp
3 tbs	wholewheat flour	3 tbs
4 tbs	wheatgerm	4 tbs
	oil for frying	

1 Put the soaked chick peas into a large saucepan with enough water
  to cover, bring quickly to the boil, reduce heat and simmer till tender
  (about 1–2 hours).
2 Meanwhile, prepare the other ingredients in a large mixing-bowl:
  skin and finely dice the onions, skin and crush the garlic, finely chop
  the parsley and add everything to the bowl together with all the
  remaining ingredients except the wheatgerm and the oil. Mix
  together thoroughly.
3 As soon as the chick peas are tender transfer them to a blender
  together with enough recipe water to blend to a thick, crunchy
  paste. Transfer the paste to the mixing-bowl and combine with the
  other ingredients. Set aside for an hour.
4 Put the wheatgerm in a shallow dish, drop spoonfuls of the falafel
  mixture into it and shape into small, coated balls (for deep-frying or
  baking) or into shallow cakes (for frying in a pan).
5 The falafels can be deep-fried in vegetable oil till golden brown (lay
  them on kitchen paper to remove surplus oil before serving), baked
  in a moderate oven (20 minutes at 177°C/350°F/gas mark 4) or fried
  in a pan in olive oil till brown on both sides.

Serve these nutty, savoury cakes in the authentic Middle Eastern
manner, a few each on a dish of *Hummus* (page 35). They also make
good snacks, served with a salad. They are good both hot and cold.

Savoury Crunchies

To Make about Two Dozen
Allow 1 hour to prepare (if you have cooked the soya beans)
Each Savoury Crunchy provides: 138 kcal, 9 g protein,
12 g carbohydrate, 6 g fat, 1 g fibre

Metric		Imperial/American
½ kg	soya beans (dry weight)	1 lb/2½ cups
	(cooked according to the method on page 257)	
45 ml	soya sauce	3 tbs
1	large onion	1
45 ml	oil	3 tbs
2	cloves garlic	2
1 tsp	rosemary	1 tsp
1 tsp	thyme	1 tsp
1 tsp	mixed herbs	1 tsp
90 g	wheatgerm	3 oz/1 cup
60 g	wholewheat flour	2 oz/½ cup
60 g	buckwheat flour	2 oz/½ cup
1 tsp	baking powder	1 tsp

1 Put the cooked soya beans and any remaining water in a blender, add the soya sauce and reduce to a crunchy paste (add more water if necessary to assist with the blending). Transfer to a bowl and set aside.
2 Skin and finely chop the onion and sauté in a frying-pan with the oil until transparent.
3 Skin and crush the garlic, stir it in with the onion and continue heating for a few more minutes.
4 Put the herbs, flours, baking powder and half of the wheatgerm into a bowl and mix together thoroughly.
5 Now add the onion and garlic and the blended flours to the soya bean paste and mix thoroughly. Set aside for half an hour.
6 Put the rest of the wheatgerm on to a large plate and drop spoonfuls of the mixture on to it and, using your fingers, form into small, coated balls.
7 Arrange the balls on a greased baking-tray and bake in a hot oven (218°C/425°F/gas mark 7) for 20 minutes.

These are splendid served straight from the oven, but they're also good cold. They can be served as a main dish – try *Creamed Mushrooms* (page 97) or *Grated Courgettes with Garlic* (page 88) or *Baked Parsnips* (page 102) as side dishes – or they make delicious snacks. Try putting two or three in pitta bread with some salad, hot or cold.

Pepper Mousse

To Serve 6
Allow 1½ hours to prepare (including cooling and setting time)
Each serving provides: 73 kcal, 6 g protein, 7 g carbohydrate, 3 g fat, 2 g fibre

Metric		Imperial/American
1	lemon	1
½ kg	skinned or tinned red peppers	1 lb/2 large
¼ kg	tofu	½ lb/1 cup
125 ml	soya milk	¼ pint/½ cup
1 tsp	salt	1 tsp
1 tsp	ground white pepper	1 tsp
2½ tbs	agar flakes	2½ tbs
125 ml	water	¼ pint/½ cup

1 Squeeze the lemon and put the juice into a blender.
2 Skin the peppers (see page 256) and add them to the blender together with the tofu, soya milk, salt and pepper and blend to a smooth foamy cream.
3 Put the agar flakes and water into a large saucepan, bring quickly to the boil then reduce heat and simmer for 5 minutes. Remove from heat.
4 Now add the blended pepper foam to the saucepan and mix well in. Pour into individual moulds or serving-dishes. Refrigerate till set and chilled.
5 Decorate the individual mousses with thin slices of lemon, halved black olives or chopped parsley.

If you can't be bothered with skinning the peppers yourself – and it is a bit of a performance – tinned ones are perfectly acceptable and in this case you can use the liquid from the tin to boil the agar flakes in.

For really special occasions, set the whole mixture in a ring mould and make a *Pepper Salad* (page 116) to pile in the centre.

Celery and Coconut Mousse

To Serve 6–8
Allow 1½ hours to prepare (including cooling and setting time)
*Each serving (of 8) provides: 75 kcal, 1 g protein, 2 g carbohydrate,
7 g fat, 4 g fibre*

Metric		Imperial/American
1	large head of celery	1
¾ litre	water	1½ pints/3½ cups
90 g	creamed coconut	3 oz/⅓ cup
2½ tbs	agar flakes	2½ tbs
	salt and freshly-ground white pepper to taste	

1 Wash and finely chop the celery (including the green leaf tips unless
  they are badly discoloured) and put it into a large saucepan with the
  water. Bring quickly to the boil, then reduce heat and simmer,
  partially covered, till tender right through (about 15 minutes).
2 Meanwhile, dissolve the creamed coconut in a little hot water taken
  from the saucepan until it is thin enough to mix in with the cooked
  celery. Before mixing it in, however, spoon out enough water from
  the saucepan to dissolve the agar. Transfer the celery and coconut to
  a blender and blend till smooth and creamy.
3 Put the agar flakes and the reserved water in a small saucepan, bring
  quickly to the boil then reduce heat and simmer for 5 minutes.
4 Pour the dissolved agar into the celery and coconut mixture and stir
  well in. Season with salt and pepper to taste and transfer to
  individual serving-dishes.
5 Refrigerate when cool.
6 Decorate the individual mousses with halved green olives or thin
  slices of lemon. Serve chilled.

Serve this exotic mousse as a starter to *Savoury Avocado Tart* (page 72)
or *Mushroom Pie* (page 76).

Beetroot Mousse

To Serve 6
Allow 2 hours to prepare (including 1 hour to set and chill)
*Each serving provides: 96 kcal, 6 g protein, 12 g carbohydrate,
2 g fat, 4 g fibre*

Metric		Imperial/American
½ kg	raw or cooked beetroot	1 lb
¾ litre	soya milk	1½ pints/3½ cups
30 ml	soya sauce	2 tbs
2½ tbs	agar flakes	2½ tbs
125 ml	water	¼ pint/½ cup

(Note: if the beetroot are already cooked, peel and chop them and proceed from step 2.)

1 Wash, peel and dice the beetroot and put them in a large saucepan with the soya milk. Bring quickly to the boil then reduce heat and simmer, partially covered, till tender (about 45 minutes).
2 Put the cooked beetroot and the soya milk and soya sauce in a blender and blend to a smooth, foamy cream.
3 Put the agar flakes and water in a small saucepan, bring quickly to the boil then reduce heat and simmer for 5 minutes, stirring continuously.
4 Combine the agar solution with the beetroot mixture, mix thoroughly, pour into individual serving-dishes and leave to set. Refrigerate till needed. Serve chilled.

This looks spectacular – especially if you set it in a ring mould – tastes wonderful and has the added bonus of providing an almost perfect balance of essential nutrients. What more could you ask of any dish?

It makes the perfect starter for really special occasions. Individual mousses can be decorated with slices of lemon, stuffed green olives or juniper berries. A mousse set in a ring mould can have a *Pepper Salad* (page 116) piled in the middle.

Baba Ganush (Aubergine and Yoghurt Dip)

To Serve 6
Allow 2¼ hours to prepare (including baking and chilling time)
*Each serving provides: 31 kcal, 1 g protein, 3 g carbohydrate, 1 g fat,
4 g fibre*

Metric		Imperial/American
1	large aubergine	1
1 tsp	oil	1 tsp
125 ml	*Vegan Yoghurt* (page 240)	¼ pint/½ cup
1	lemon	1
1	clove garlic	1
1 tsp	soya sauce	1 tsp
1 tsp	freshly-ground black pepper	1 tsp
2 tbs	chopped parsley	2 tbs

1 Thinly coat the whole aubergine with oil and bake for 1 hour in a moderate oven (177°C/350°F/gas mark 4). Don't remove the stalk, it will help you with the next stage.
2 Remove the baked aubergine from the oven and peel it under running cold water. The simplest way is to pick it up by the stalk using an oven glove, make a nick near the stalk using a sharp knife and simply tear off long strips of skin.
3 Chop the peeled aubergine and put it in a blender.
4 Squeeze the lemon and add the juice to the blender.
5 Skin and crush the garlic and add it to the blender.
6 Now add all the other ingredients and blend to a smooth, creamy consistency.
7 Check the seasoning and adjust if necessary, then transfer to a suitable serving-bowl, garnish with sprigs of parsley and chill for at least an hour before serving.

This is another dish from the Middle East. Serve it as a starter to a meal with a bowl of black olives, or at buffet parties with sticks of fennel or celery. For variety, try substituting 4 tablespoonfuls of tahini for the yoghurt.

Lemon Galantine

To Serve 6–8
Allow 2½ hours to prepare (including 2 hours to cool and set)
Each serving (of 8) provides: 37 kcal, 2 g protein, 8 g carbohydrate,
1 g fat, 3 g fibre

Metric		Imperial/American
¼ kg	broccoli	½ lb
¼ kg	tomatoes	½ lb
1	small cucumber	1
1	small yellow pepper	1
12	stoned black olives	12
¾ litre	water	1½ pints/3½ cups
4 tbs	agar flakes	4 tbs
2½	lemons	2½
1 tbs	concentrated apple juice	1 tbs
1 tbs	mustard powder	1 tbs
1½ tsp	salt	1½ tsp
1 tsp	freshly-ground white pepper	1 tsp

1 Wash the broccoli, cut off the florets and thinly slice the stems. Plunge them into fiercely-boiling, salted water till tender (about 5 minutes). Remove from heat, rinse in cold water and drain in a colander.
2 Skin the tomatoes (page 255) and cut them into halves or quarters (ornamentally shaped if you wish). Set aside. Peel and slice the cucumber. Wash the pepper and cut into thin rings, removing pith and seeds as you go. Set aside.
3 Carefully arrange all the vegetables in decorative layers in a suitable jelly mould. Put the peppers and olives first, followed by the tomatoes and broccoli, and the cucumber slices last. (Follow this order and they won't attempt to float when you pour in the jelly.)
4 Put the water and agar flakes in a large saucepan, bring quickly to the boil then reduce heat and simmer till the agar flakes have completely dissolved.
5 Meanwhile, squeeze the lemons and put the juice in a basin with all the remaining ingredients. Mix to a paste and stir into the pan once the agar has completely dissolved.
6 Carefully pour over the vegetables in the mould, taking care not to disturb them. Refrigerate when set.
7 Turn out onto a suitable serving-dish, garnish with olives or parsley. Serve chilled.

This looks stunning and tastes great. Serve it either by slicing with a thin sharp knife or by scooping with a spoon.

Main Dishes

Main Dishes

It may be a hangover from pre-vegetarian consciousness that even vegans tend to expect a meal to consist of the vegetarian equivalent of 'meat and two veg', but meals don't have to be constructed in this way – in fact in most parts of the world they aren't: in most of the Middle East and all the Far East, China and Japan, meals usually consist of lots of tiny, appetizing dishes, each of which provides the individual guest with only two or three mouthfuls at the most – but what a delicious way to eat! In the West few of us are willing to spend the hours and hours needed to prepare such complicated spreads (we're all so busy rushing about) but they are a useful reminder to us to be flexible in our approach to planning what we eat and how we present and serve it.

Thus, most of our soups, starters, salads and even side dish recipes could be the main course of a nourishing and satisfying meal. Indeed, some of the meals which have been best received by our friends during the testing of the recipes in this book have consisted of nothing else!

Nevertheless, the dishes we have gathered together in this section have a number of features in common that make them particularly useful as a centre-piece to build a meal around: they all provide adequate servings for at least four people; they are all visually attractive; they are all substantial and nourishing enough to leave guests feeling satisfied; and the 'special' ones are spectacular enough to give a meal a sense of occasion.

A word or two about flans and tarts. When we were trying out our creations we were struck by the different reactions we observed, depending on what we *called* our recipes. Thus when we first tried out 'Savoury Avocado Tart', we called it 'Avocado Flan'. Unfortunately it seems that people have expectations dependent on names and therefore 'a flan should be like an *egg* quiche', i.e. with a filling that has set firm. So, alas, our guests at this first tasting turned up their noses because the filling remained soft and creamy. Well, we learned our lesson. The next time we tried it out we called it 'Savoury Avocado Tart' and our guests were ecstatic. 'Delicious!' they cried. 'Wonderful! How do you do it?' The sad fact is that a rose by any other name would not smell as sweet.

So, we have called pastry shells with fillings 'flans' if the filling sets firmly enough to cut out a wedge that will retain its shape even when served hot, straight from the oven, and 'tarts' when the filling remains soft and creamy but slightly runny.

Remember that if you're too pressed for time to make a flan shell, any of the flan (and tart!) fillings can be made up, put in a shallow ovenproof dish and baked without the pastry. Serve them with wholewheat bread to compensate for the lost 'protein complementarity'.

Finally, a word or two to vegans who live alone: don't assume that these main course dishes aren't for you. Remember that, unlike their meat-based equivalents, they all keep well and even those that don't reheat well are good cold. So if you don't have the time or inclination to spend more than one afternoon a week cooking, why not spend it making a savoury flan (or tart!) that you can conveniently serve cold or put in a packed lunch, or making a large casserole or stew that can form the basis of many meals during the week that follows?

Bulgur Bake

To Serve 4–6
Allow 50 minutes to prepare
Each serving (of 6) provides: 156 kcal, 7 g protein, 30 g carbohydrate, 2 g fat, 6 g fibre

Metric		Imperial/American
180 g	bulgur	6 oz/1 cup
½ litre	boiling water	scant pint/2 cups
1 tsp	salt	1 tsp
¼ kg	courgettes	½ lb/2 medium
¼ kg	carrots	½ lb
1	large cooking apple	1
180 g	tofu	6 oz/¾ cup
¼ litre	water	½ pint/1¼ cups
45 ml	soya sauce	3 tbs
2 tsp	mustard powder	2 tsp
2 tsp	vinegar	2 tsp

1 Put the bulgur in a saucepan and pour the boiling water over it. Stir in the salt, cover and set aside for 10–15 minutes until all the water has been absorbed.
2 Wash, top and tail the courgettes, quarter them lengthwise and chop them into bite-sized chunks. Wash, top and tail the carrots (peel them if necessary). Wash and core the apple. Now coarsely grate the carrots and apple into a large mixing-bowl, add the chopped courgettes and the soaked bulgur and mix well. Transfer the mixture to an ovenproof dish.
3 Put all the remaining ingredients in a blender and blend till smooth. Pour over the bulgur mixture and leave to soak in for a few minutes.
4 Bake in the middle of a moderate oven (177°C/350°F/gas mark 4) for half an hour. Serve immediately.

The vegetables lend a crunchy texture to this light dish. Try serving it with *Fried Cucumbers* (page 90) or *Creamed Mushrooms* (page 97) and follow it up with *Baked Bananas* (page 142) or *Vanilla Dessert* (page 141).

Cashew and Mushroom Roast

To Serve 4
Allow 50 minutes to prepare
*Each serving provides: 404 kcal, 13 g protein, 47 g carbohydrate,
20 g fat, 11 g fibre*

Metric		Imperial/American
¼ kg	bulgur	½ lb/1 cup
½ litre	boiling water	1 scant pint/2 cups
1 tsp	salt	1 tsp
30 g	margarine	1 oz/2 tbs
2	medium onions	2
¼ kg	mushrooms	½ lb
125 g	cashew nuts	¼ lb/1 cup
1½	lemons	1½
	salt to taste	
	parsley for decoration	

1 Put the bulgur in a saucepan and pour the boiling water over it. Stir in the salt, cover and set aside for 10–15 minutes until all the water has been absorbed.
2 Meanwhile, put the margarine in a large saucepan over a low heat.
3 While it is melting, skin and finely chop the onions, add them to the pan and sauté until transparent.
4 Finely chop the mushrooms, add them to the pan and continue to sauté for a few more minutes.
5 As soon as the bulgur is ready, stir it into the pan together with the cashew nuts and continue heating gently.
6 Grate the lemon rinds and stir the grated peel into the mixture.
7 Squeeze the lemons and add the juice to the mixture, stirring continuously.
8 Remove pan from heat, check the seasoning and add a little salt if necessary, transfer the mixture to a shallow baking-dish and heat through in a moderate oven (177°C/350°F/gas mark 4) for 20 minutes.
9 Garnish with sprigs of parsley and serve.

Serve with a plain salad to make a light meal or with another main dish, such as *Mexican Beans with Chilli* (page 67), *Broccoli and Lasagne* (page 55) or a savoury flan or tart, to make a more substantial meal.

Courgette and Tomato Crumble

To Serve 4–6
Allow 1 hour to prepare
Each serving (of 6) provides: 318 kcal, 7 g protein, 32 g carbohydrate, 18 g fat, 7 g fibre

Metric		Imperial/American
¼ kg	courgettes	½ lb
¼ kg	mushrooms	½ lb
1	medium green pepper	1
½ kg	fresh or tinned tomatoes	1 lb
1 tsp	freshly-ground black pepper	1 tsp
1 tsp	salt	1 tsp
180 g	wholewheat flour	6 oz/1½ cups
60 g	rolled oats	2 oz/¾ cup
125 g	margarine	¼ lb/½ cup

1 Wash, top and tail the courgettes, quarter them lengthwise and chop them into bite-sized chunks. Wash and slice the mushrooms. Wash the pepper, remove the seeds, coarsely chop and mix with the courgettes and mushrooms. Place the mixture in a shallow baking-dish.
2 Put the skinned (page 255) tomatoes, pepper and salt into a blender and blend till smooth. Pour over the vegetables in the baking-dish.
3 Now combine the flour and oats in a bowl and cut and rub in the margarine.
4 Sprinkle the crumble mixture to cover the whole surface of the vegetables in the baking-dish and bake in a moderate oven (177°C/350°F/gas mark 4) for 40 minutes. Serve hot, straight from the oven.

This is light to the palate but substantial in nourishment. It could be served with a simple salad to make a light meal, or with another main dish, such as a savoury flan or tart. It's also good cold.

For variety try sprinkling sunflower or sesame seeds over the top before baking.

Mixed Vegetable Stew

To Serve 4–6
Allow 40 minutes to prepare
Each serving (of 6) provides: 245 kcal, 13 g protein, 31 g carbo-hydrate, 9 g fat, 9 g fibre

Metric		Imperial/American
45 ml	oil	3 tbs
2 tsp	whole cumin seeds	2 tsp
¼ kg	onions	½ lb/2 medium
2	cloves garlic	2
125 g	mushrooms	¼ lb
¾ kg	fresh or tinned tomatoes	1½ lb
¼ kg	red lentils	½ lb/1¼ cups
45 ml	soya sauce	3 tbs
¼ kg	courgettes	½ lb/2 medium
	salt and pepper to taste	

1 Put the oil and cumin seeds in a large saucepan over a low heat.
2 Skin and chop the onions and add them to the pan.
3 Skin and crush the garlic, add it to the pan and sauté the onions and garlic till transparent.
4 Wash and chop the mushrooms and add them to the pan. Leave to cook gently for about 5 minutes, turning occasionally.
5 Add the skinned (page 255) tomatoes, lentils and soya sauce, bring quickly to the boil then reduce heat and leave to simmer, partially covered.
6 Wash, top and tail the courgettes and chop them up into bite-sized pieces. Add them to the pan and stir well in.
7 Leave to simmer, still partially covered, till the lentils are completely soft (about 15–20 minutes).
8 Check the seasoning, add salt (if you wish) and pepper to taste, and serve.

Ring the changes on this stew by adding other vegetables, or use fewer tomatoes and add a glass of dry red wine, or stir in a tablespoonful of peanut butter just before you serve it.

It's filling and substantial enough to make a complete meal served with green vegetables or a salad, or serve it with one of the many side dish recipes.

Tofu Stir-Fry

To Serve 4
Allow 50 minutes to prepare
*Each serving provides: 216 kcal, 10 g protein, 11 g carbohydrate,
15 g fat, 8 g fibre*

Metric		Imperial/American
¼ kg	tofu	½ lb/1 cup
45 ml	soya sauce	3 tbs
45 ml	oil	3 tbs
1	medium onion	1
¼ kg	carrots	½ lb
6	sticks celery	6
1	medium green pepper	1
¼ kg	mushrooms	½ lb
¼ kg	bean sprouts	½ lb

1 Cut the tofu into 2 cm (¾ in) cubes, place in a small bowl and pour the soya sauce over. Set aside to marinate.
2 Put the oil in a wok (or large frying-pan) over a medium heat. Skin and chop the onion and add it to the wok. Wash, top and tail the carrots then cut them into long thin strips and add them to the pan. Stir thoroughly. Reduce heat to low, partially cover the vegetables (a saucepan lid will serve) and leave to fry gently for about 10 minutes, lifting the lid occasionally to stir.
3 Wash and chop the celery and stir it in with the other vegetables. Leave to cook for 5 minutes.
4 Wash the pepper, remove the seeds and pith and cut it lengthwise into thin strips. Stir into the wok and leave to cook for 10 minutes.
5 Wash and drain the mushrooms. (Leave them whole if they are small, or cut them in halves or quarters if they are large.) Stir them into the wok, add the tofu cubes and soya sauce and leave to cook for 5 minutes.
6 Wash and drain the bean sprouts, add them to the wok and stir-fry them for 2–3 minutes. Serve immediately.

This can be served just as it is, with rice, to make a simple meal. Or it can be turned into a more elaborate (and authentically Chinese) dish by serving it with *Sweet & Sour Sauce* (page 169) or given an Indonesian flavour with *Spicy Peanut Sauce* (page 170). If you're going to add a sauce, be careful to drain away any excess liquid from the vegetables as you remove them from the wok.

Ratatouille (Traditional Vegetable Stew from Provence)

To Serve 4–6
Allow 40 minutes to prepare
Each serving (of 6) provides: 276 kcal, 4 g protein, 18 g carbohydrate, 21 g fat, 7 g fibre

Metric		Imperial/American
125 ml	olive oil	¼ pint/½ cup
½ kg	onions	1 lb/2 large
2	cloves garlic	2
½ kg	green peppers	1 lb/2 large
½ kg	red peppers	1 lb/2 large
¼ kg	aubergine	½ lb/1 medium
½ kg	courgettes	1 lb/2 large
½ kg	fresh or tinned tomatoes	1 lb
	salt and pepper to taste	

1 Put just over half the oil in a large saucepan over a low heat.
2 Skin and chop the onions, add them to the pan and sauté for 5 minutes. Don't let them brown.
3 Skin and crush the garlic and add it to the pan.
4 Wash the green peppers, remove the seeds and pith, and cut them into strips. Add them to the pan and sauté for a few minutes, increasing the heat slightly if necessary.
5 Repeat with the red peppers.
6 Wash, top and tail (but don't peel) the aubergine and chop it into finger-thick chunks. Add to the pan together with the rest of the oil and continue to sauté for a further 5 minutes.
7 Wash, top and tail the courgettes, cut them into finger-thick slices and add to the pan. Stir them in and leave the mixture to cook for 5 more minutes, stirring occasionally.
8 Meanwhile, skin the tomatoes (page 255), coarsely chop them and add them to the pan. Stir in and bring the mixture to a simmer for at least another 5 minutes. Add salt and pepper to taste and serve.

The secret of this traditional Provençal dish is to add the vegetables in the sequence given. The resulting stew is a wonderful *mélange* of subtle flavours and colours which is equally good hot or cold. It keeps well – in fact it seems to *improve* if kept for a day or two and then reheated.

This recipe is how one of us was taught to make it in a little country restaurant in Provence. Serve it with lots of wholewheat bread and red wine.

Broccoli and Lasagne

To Serve 4–6
Allow 1 hour to prepare
*Each serving (of 6) provides: 408 kcal, 13 g protein, 29 g carbo-
hydrate, 27 g fat, 9 g fibre*

Metric		Imperial/American
8 lengths	wholewheat lasagne	8 lengths
90 ml	oil	6 tbs
¼ kg	onions	½ lb/2 medium
¾ kg	broccoli	1½ lb
½ kg	fresh or tinned tomatoes	1 lb
2 tsp	marjoram	2 tsp
	salt and pepper to taste	
¼ kg	tofu	½ lb/1 cup
45 ml	soya sauce	3 tbs
3 tbs	tomato paste	3 tbs
45 ml	oil	3 tbs
125 ml	water	¼ pint/½ cup
1 tsp	freshly-ground pepper	1 tsp

1 Fill a large saucepan with water, add a little salt and a few drops of
   oil and bring to the boil. Add the lasagne. Allow to come back to
   the boil then reduce heat and simmer till tender (about 12 minutes).
   Stir often to prevent the pasta from sticking. Drain, rinse in cold
   water and set aside.
2 Put 6 tablespoonfuls of oil in another large saucepan over a low heat.
   Skin and chop the onions and sauté them in the oil till transparent.
3 Meanwhile, wash the broccoli, then cut off the florets and set aside.
   Finely chop the leaves and stalks and add them to the onions. Sauté for
   about 5 minutes before adding the skinned tomatoes (page 255),
   marjoram, salt and pepper to taste. Cook for another 5 minutes, stirring
   often and then add the broccoli florets and cook till they are tender.
4 Crumble the tofu into a blender, add all the remaining ingredients
   and blend to a smooth, creamy sauce.
5 Arrange the vegetables, lasagne and sauce in alternate layers in a
   lightly-greased, ovenproof dish (a rectangular one is easiest). Finish
   with a layer of lasagne and sauce.
6 Heat through in the middle of a moderate oven (177°C/350°F/gas
   mark 4) for about 20 minutes and serve immediately.

This tasty dish is fairly substantial and filling, so it's best to serve it with
something light – green vegetables or one of the salad recipes, for
example.

Savoury Rice

To Serve 4–6
Allow 1 hour to prepare
Each serving (of 6) provides: 383 kcal, 7 g protein, 41 g carbohydrate, 22 g fat, 4 g fibre

Metric		**Imperial/American**
¼ kg	brown rice (dry weight)	½ lb/1¼ cups
90 g	margarine	3 oz/⅓ cup
2	cloves garlic	2
¼ kg	onions	½ lb/2 medium
¼ kg	red pepper	½ lb/1 large
¼ kg	courgettes	½ lb
125 g	cashew nuts	¼ lb/1 cup
45 ml	soya sauce	3 tbs
2 tsp	fresh chopped dill (or 1 tsp dried dill)	2 tsp
	freshly-ground black pepper to taste	

1 Put the rice on to cook (*Plain Rice*, page 84).
2 Meanwhile, melt the margarine in a large frying-pan (or wok), skin and crush the garlic, skin and finely chop the onions, put them in the pan and sauté till tender (about 10 minutes).
3 Cut the pepper in half lengthwise and remove any seeds before washing and finely chopping it. Add to the pan with the onions and stir well in. Leave to cook over a low heat, stirring occasionally.
4 Meanwhile, wash, top and tail the courgettes (and if they are big, quarter them lengthwise) and chop them into finger-thick chunks. Add to the pan, mix well in and sauté till just tender (about another 10 minutes).
5 Add the cashew nuts, soya sauce and dill and mix well in. As soon as the rice is ready, combine it with the cooked vegetables, add freshly-ground black pepper to taste and serve immediately.

Almost any vegetables can be used (at steps 3 and 4) to ring the changes on this dish which is substantial enough to turn plain boiled rice into a main course. Serve it with salads or green vegetables or, if your guests are really hungry, with one of the many savoury tarts or flans.

Spinach and Mushroom Tagliatelle

To Serve 4–6
Allow 1¼ hours to prepare
Each serving (of 6) provides: 337 kcal, 15 g protein, 35 g carbohydrate, 16 g fat, 11 g fibre

Metric		Imperial/American
75 ml	olive oil	5 tbs
2	cloves garlic	2
½ kg	fresh spinach	1 lb
	(or 300 g [10 oz] packet of frozen spinach)	
¼ kg	tofu	½ lb/1 cup
2 tbs	fresh chopped basil	2 tbs
	(or ½ tbs dried basil)	
¼ kg	onions	½ lb/2 medium
¼ kg	mushrooms	½ lb
¼ kg	wholewheat tagliatelle	½ lb

1 Put 2 tbs oil in a large saucepan over a low heat.
2 Skin and crush the garlic and add it to the pan.
3 Wash and add the spinach. Increase the heat a little and cook till soft (only a few minutes if fresh; about 10 minutes if frozen).
4 Transfer the cooked spinach to a blender, crumble in the tofu, add the basil and blend to a smooth paste. (A little water may be needed to assist in the blending depending on how much water was produced during cooking.) Set aside.
5 Put the remaining oil in a frying-pan over a low heat.
6 Skin and finely chop the onions, add them to the pan and sauté till transparent. Don't let them brown.
7 Wash and finely chop the mushrooms, add them to the pan and sauté till tender (about 10–15 minutes).
8 Meanwhile, add a teaspoonful of salt and a few drops of oil to a large pan of water, bring quickly to the boil, add the tagliatelle, bring back to the boil then reduce heat and simmer till cooked (about 10 minutes). Remove from heat and drain.
9 Now add the spinach sauce and the cooked onions and mushrooms to the saucepan with the tagliatelle and mix well by turning with a large spoon. Season with salt and pepper to taste, transfer to a suitable ovenproof serving-dish and heat through in a moderate oven (177°C/350°F/gas mark 4) for about 20 minutes. Serve immediately.

Serve with *Cabbage, Fruit and Nut Salad* (page 117) and *Spiced Potatoes* (page 86) for a substantial and nutritious meal.

Root Vegetable Crumble

To Serve 4–6
Allow 1 hour to prepare
Each serving (of 6) provides: 466 kcal, 8 g protein, 45 g carbohydrate, 27 g fat, 8 g fibre

Metric		Imperial/American
¼ kg	potatoes	½ lb
¼ kg	carrots	½ lb
¼ kg	parsnips	½ lb
3 tbs	olive oil	3 tbs
2 tbs	mustard powder	2 tbs
3 tbs	concentrated apple juice	3 tbs
	salt and pepper to taste	
180 g	wholewheat flour	6 oz/1½ cups
60 g	rolled oats	2 oz/¾ cup
125 g	margarine	¼ lb/½ cup

1 Scrub the potatoes, wash, top, tail and peel the carrots and parsnips, and chop all the vegetables into bite-sized chunks. Plunge them into fiercely-boiling water for 6 minutes (but no longer). Spoon 4 tbs of the cooking water into a small basin, then drain the vegetables and set aside.
2 Put the olive oil, mustard powder and apple concentrate in the basin with the cooking water and stir together thoroughly.
3 Arrange the blanched vegetables in a shallow baking-dish, pour the sauce mixture over and toss till they are all well covered. Season with salt and (preferably freshly-ground) pepper to taste.
4 Combine the flour and oats in a bowl and cut and rub in the margarine.
5 Sprinkle the crumble mixture to cover the whole surface of the vegetables in the baking-dish, dot with knobs of margarine and bake in a moderate oven (177°C/350°F/gas mark 4) for 40 minutes. Serve hot, straight from the oven.

This hearty crumble is filling and substantial, so serve it with something light such as a simple steamed vegetable or a *Basic Green Salad* (page 114).

Winter Vegetable Stockpot

To Serve 6–8
Allow 1 hour to prepare
Each serving (of 8) provides: 223 kcal, 4 g protein, 23 g carbohydrate, 13 g fat, 9 g fibre

Metric		Imperial/American
125 g	margarine	¼ lb/½ cup
4	cloves garlic	4
¼ kg	onions	½ lb/2 medium
1	head of celery	1
1½ kg	mixed winter vegetables (see note)	3 lb
	dried herbs to taste (see note)	
3 tbs	miso (or 1½ tbs yeast extract)	3 tbs

(Note: suggested vegetables to use in the order in which they should be added to the pan, after step 1: *carrots, potatoes, turnips, swedes, parsnips, Jerusalem artichokes, leeks, peppers, cabbage, cauliflower, mushrooms, tomatoes, etc.* Suggested dried herbs to try (in no particular order): *sage, tarragon, basil, parsley, thyme, marjoram, oregano, dill, etc.*; or try a few spices: *coriander, cardamom, turmeric, paprika, cumin, etc.*)

1 Melt the margarine in a large saucepan. Skin and crush the garlic, skin and chop the onions, wash and chop the celery. Sauté the garlic, onions and celery for 5 minutes, then leave to cook gently, turning every now and again, while you prepare the other vegetables.
2 Clean, trim and chop the remaining vegetables into bite-sized pieces, adding them to the pan as you do them.
3 Stir in the herbs and spices you've chosen and continue to cook gently for a further 5 minutes.
4 Now add enough water (or vegetable stock, left-over soup, tomato juice or other vegetable juice, wine, stout, or soya milk) to cover, and mix well in. Bring quickly to the boil, then reduce heat, cover and simmer till the root vegetables are just tender. Stir in the miso and serve.

The stockpot keeps well provided it is brought to the boil at least once a day. When it starts to get low, simply add extra vegetables. To make it thicker, add lentils or pre-cooked split peas, or dissolve 3 tbs wholewheat flour in a little of the stock and stir it back in. To make it thinner, add a little dry red wine, or liquidized tomatoes, or any vegetable stock you happen to have to hand, or water. Try also adding pre-cooked wholewheat berries, rice or any pulse.

In colloquial French, to shut up house is: *fermer la marmite*, which literally means 'shut down the stockpot' because a stockpot like this really can be kept going all winter.

Carrot Flan

To Serve 8
Allow 1 hour to prepare (if you have the pre-baked flan shell)
Each serving provides: 273 kcal, 7 g protein, 30 g carbohydrate, 15 g fat, 7 g fibre

Metric		Imperial/American
1	*Pre-Baked Flan Shell* (page 203)	1
1 kg	carrots	2 lb
2	cloves garlic	2
225 ml	soya milk	8 fl oz/1 cup
25 ml	wine vinegar	1 tbs
45 ml	soya sauce	3 tbs
1 tbs	sesame seeds	1 tbs

1 Bring a large saucepan of water to the boil. Meanwhile, scrub the carrots to remove any mud, then top and tail them and slice them thinly. (Peeling is only really necessary if they have injured or pitted skins.)
2 Plunge the sliced carrots into the fiercely-boiling water, bring back to the boil then reduce heat and simmer, uncovered, till tender (about 10–15 minutes). Remove from heat, drain, and transfer to a blender.
3 Skin and crush the garlic, add it to the blender together with the soya milk, vinegar and soya sauce and blend to a smooth consistency.
4 Transfer the filling to the pastry shell, smooth the top, sprinkle the sesame seeds over and bake in the middle of a moderate oven (177°C/350°F/gas mark 4) for 30 minutes.

Serve this hot with *Creamed Mushrooms* (page 97), *Fried Courgettes* (page 85) or *Cauliflower Bhaji* (page 93), or cold with *Mixed Sprout Salad* (page 118), *Avocado and Apple Salad* (page 119) or any salad that doesn't include carrots.

Tomato and Lentil Flan

To Serve 8
Allow 1 hour to prepare (if you have the pre-baked flan shell)
*Each serving provides: 407 kcal, 13 g protein, 45 g carbohydrate,
20 g fat, 8 g fibre*

Metric		Imperial/American
1	*Pre-Baked Flan Shell* (page 203)	1
¼ kg	red lentils	½ lb/1¼ cups
½ kg	fresh or tinned tomatoes	1 lb
	salt and pepper to taste	
1	medium onion	1
25 ml	lemon juice	1½ tbs
60 g	margarine	2 oz/4 tbs
1 tsp	*Garam Masala* (page 253)	1 tsp
60 g	wholewheat flakes	2 oz/1 cup

1 Wash the lentils and put them in a large saucepan.
2 Put the skinned tomatoes (page 255) in a blender with salt and pepper to taste and reduce to a thick cream.
3 Now add the blended tomatoes to the saucepan, stir well in and bring quickly to the boil, then reduce heat and simmer, partially covered, till they are completely cooked and beginning to break down (about 30–40 minutes). Stir from time to time and add a little water if necessary to prevent them from sticking.
4 Meanwhile, skin and finely chop the onion and assemble all the other ingredients.
5 When the lentils have absorbed all the liquid and formed a thickish paste, remove from heat, add the margarine, chopped onion, lemon juice, garam masala mixture and wholewheat flakes and mix thoroughly.
6 Transfer the mixture to the flan shell, smooth the top and bake in the middle of a moderate oven (177°C/350°F/gas mark 4) for 30 minutes.

Serve this attractive, copper-coloured flan with green vegetables in winter or one of the salad recipes in summer. It keeps well but tends to dry out if reheated, so it's best to serve it hot, straight from the oven, when you first make it and cold thereafter.

Olive and Potato Flan

To Serve 8
Allow 1 hour to prepare (if you have the pre-baked flan shell)
Each serving provides: 392 kcal, 7 g protein, 41 g carbohydrate, 23 g fat, 9 g fibre

Metric		Imperial/American
1	*Pre-Baked Flan Shell* (page 203)	1
¾ kg	potatoes	1½ lb
60 g	margarine	2 oz/4 tbs
¼ litre	soya milk	½ pint/1¼ cups
¼ kg	black olives	½ lb/2 cups
25 ml	white wine vinegar	1½ tbs
	salt and pepper to taste	

1 Scrub the potatoes and remove any blemishes but don't peel or scrape them, then cut them into thin slices and plunge them into fiercely-boiling water and cook till tender (about 8–12 minutes). Remove from heat and drain.
2 Meanwhile, stone the olives if necessary. This is easy if you have the right gadget – many garlic presses have one in their handles – or a messy job with a sharp knife if you haven't. They can also sometimes be bought already stoned.
3 Set a few of the stoned olives aside (to use as a decoration) and put the rest, together with all the remaining ingredients and the cooked potatoes, into a mixing-bowl and mash together until well mixed. The result will be a dark, rich, smooth cream, speckled with bits of olive.
4 Transfer the filling to the pastry shell, smooth the top and decorate with a few halved olives and bake in the middle of a moderate oven (177°C/350°F/gas mark 4) for 25 minutes.

This can be served hot, straight from the oven, or chilled. It is rich, substantial and filling and so is best served with a light salad or green vegetables.
For variety, try adding a clove or two of crushed garlic at step 3.

Fresh Parsley and Tomato Flan

To Serve 8
Allow 1 hour to prepare (if you have the pre-baked flan shell)
*Each serving provides: 373 kcal, 8 g protein, 42 g carbohydrate,
20 g fat, 10 g fibre*

Metric		Imperial/American
1	*Pre-Baked Flan Shell* (page 203)	1
¾ kg	potatoes	1½ lb
1	large fresh bunch of parsley	1
60 g	margarine	2 oz/4 tbs
125 ml	soya milk	¼ pint/½ cup
1	lemon	1
2	cloves garlic	2
3 tbs	tomato paste	3 tbs
25 ml	soya sauce	1½ tbs
	freshly-ground black pepper to taste	

1 Scrub the potatoes and remove any blemishes but don't peel or scrape them, then slice them thinly and plunge them into boiling water and cook till tender (about 8–12 minutes).
2 Meanwhile, finely chop the parsley and set aside.
3 When the potatoes are done, remove from heat and drain in a colander.
4 Put the drained potatoes in a large mixing-bowl and add the margarine and soya milk.
5 Squeeze the lemon and add the juice to the bowl.
6 Skin and crush the garlic and add to the bowl.
7 Add all the remaining ingredients (set some of the chopped parsley aside for decoration) and mash with a fork till smooth and creamy.
8 Transfer the filling to the pastry shell, smooth the top and bake in the middle of a moderate oven (177°C/350°F/gas mark 4) for 25 minutes.
9 Decorate with the remaining chopped parsley and serve.

This is delicious made with fresh herbs but not worth bothering with otherwise; but you don't have to use parsley – try mint, or any other fresh herb you like.

It's rich and substantial so serve it with green vegetables or a light salad. It's equally good cold and so is suitable for buffet parties.

Mung Bean and Courgette Casserole

To Serve 4–6
Allow 1 hour to prepare (if you have pre-soaked the beans – see page 257)
Each serving (of 6) provides: 336 kcal, 10 g protein, 18 g carbohydrate, 25 g fat, 11 g fibre

Metric		Imperial/American
¼ kg	mung beans (dry weight)	½ lb/1 cup
125 ml	olive oil	¼ pint/½ cup
	seeds from 4 cardamom pods	
1 tsp	cumin seeds	1 tsp
½ tsp	chilli powder	½ tsp
½ kg	courgettes	1 lb/2 large
1	lemon	1
½ tsp	oregano	½ tsp
	salt and pepper to taste	
2 tbs	fresh chopped parsley as a garnish	2 tbs
	(or 1 tbs dried parsley)	

1 Cook the soaked beans in a fresh change of water, partially covered, over a low heat till just tender (about 20–30 minutes).
2 Meanwhile, heat the oil in a frying-pan and add all the spices (except the salt, pepper and oregano) and leave to cook gently over a low heat.
3 Wash, top and tail the courgettes, quarter them lengthwise and then chop them up into finger-thick chunks. Now sauté them in the pan with the spices till they're just beginning to brown. Remove from heat, stir in the lemon juice and oregano and set aside.
4 Drain the beans and put them in a casserole dish (the type with a cover). Add the courgettes together with all the spices, oil and lemon juice, season with salt and pepper to taste and gently toss till well mixed. Cover and reheat in the middle of a moderate oven (177°C/350°F/gas mark 4) for 20 minutes.
5 Garnish with the chopped parsley and serve.

This light dish is best served with something substantial such as *Savoury Rice* (page 56), *Mushroom Pie* (page 76) or baked potatoes; or it can be served as a side dish.

For variety, try adding a chopped aubergine at step 3 or stir in 1½ tbs of tomato paste at step 4.

Fruit and Vegetable Curry

To Serve 4
Allow 1 hour to prepare
Each serving provides: 461 kcal, 6 g protein, 38 g carbohydrate,
33 g fat, 18 g fibre

Metric		Imperial/American
75 ml	sunflower oil	5 tbs
1½ tsp	whole cumin seeds	1½ tsp
1 tsp	whole coriander seeds	1 tsp
4 tsp	*Garam Masala* (page 253)	4 tsp
¼ kg	onion	½ lb/1 large
¼ kg	carrots	½ lb
½ kg	fresh or tinned tomatoes	1 lb
400 ml	water	¾ pint/2 cups
¼ kg	potatoes	½ lb
1½ tbs	freshly-grated ginger	1½ tbs
	(or ¾ tbs dried ground ginger)	
¼ kg	courgettes	½ lb
60 g	dried apricots	2 oz/½ cup
30 g	raisins	1 oz/1 tbs
90 g	creamed coconut	3 oz/⅓ cup

1 Put the oil in a large saucepan over a low heat, add the cumin and coriander seeds and the garam masala and cook gently for a few minutes.
2 Skin and chop the onion, add it to the pan and cook till soft (about
5–10 minutes). Meanwhile, wash, top and tail and slice the carrots
and skin the tomatoes (page 255) if necessary.
3 When the onion is soft, add the sliced carrots and skinned tomatoes
together with the water. (If you're using tinned tomatoes, only add ¼
litre [½ pint/1¼ cups] water.) Bring to the boil then reduce heat and
simmer, partially covered, for 5 minutes.
4 Wash and chop the potatoes (and peel them if you wish) and add to
the pan together with the ginger. Bring back to the boil then reduce
heat and simmer for a further 10 minutes.
5 Wash, top, tail and slice the courgettes into finger-thick pieces and
add them to the pan together with the apricots and raisins. Add the
creamed coconut and stir in till completely dissolved. Simmer for a
final 10–15 minutes, stirring often and serve.

Ring the changes on this fruity curry by adding or substituting almost
any vegetable of your choice. Serve with *Plain Rice* (page 84),
Cauliflower Bhaji (page 93) or *Cucumber, Yoghurt and Ginger Salad*
(page 133).

Winter Pie

To Serve 6–8
Allow 1½ hours to prepare
Each serving (of 8) provides: 302 kcal, 7 g protein, 42 g carbohydrate, 13 g fat, 12 g fibre

Metric		Imperial/American
¾ kg	mixed carrots and parsnips	1½ lb
½ litre	water	1 pint/2½ cups
125 g	margarine	¼ lb/½ cup
4	cloves garlic	4
¼ kg	onions	½ lb/2 medium
1	head of celery	1
1 tsp	juniper berries (or *Garam Masala* [page 253]; or mustard powder)	1 tsp
	salt and pepper to taste	
3 tbs	wholewheat flour	3 tbs
1 kg	potatoes	2 lb
125 ml	soya milk	¼ pint/½ cup
30 g	bread crumbs (or wheatgerm)	1 oz/3 tbs

1 Clean, trim and chop the carrots and parsnips into bite-sized pieces and put them in a large saucepan with (unsalted) water. Bring quickly to the boil, then reduce heat, cover and leave to simmer till just tender. Remove from heat, drain, and reserve the cooking water.
2 Melt half the margarine in another large saucepan. Skin and crush the garlic, skin and chop the onions, wash and chop the celery. Sauté the garlic, onions and celery till just tender, taking care not to let the vegetables brown.
3 Stir in the juniper berries, add a seasoning of salt and pepper and mix well over the heat before sprinkling on the flour. Stir well in and continue cooking gently for a few minutes before adding the cooking water from the carrots and parsnips a little at a time till you have a thinnish sauce. Allow to simmer gently to mature flavours and cook the flour before removing from heat and folding in the cooked carrots and parsnips.
4 Wash and chop the potatoes (peel them if you wish) and cook them separately till soft. Remove from heat, drain, add the rest of the margarine and the soya milk and mash till smooth and fluffy.
5 Pour the vegetable mixture into a suitable ovenproof dish, cover with the mashed potato, sprinkle the breadcrumbs on top, dot with knobs of margarine and bake in a moderate oven (177°C/350°F/gas mark 4) till golden brown on top (about 20–30 minutes).

Mexican Beans with Chilli

To Serve 6
Allow 2 hours to prepare (if you have pre-soaked the beans – see page 257)
Each serving provides: 368 kcal, 14 g protein, 40 g carbohydrate, 18 g fat, 15 g fibre

Metric		Imperial/American
¼ kg	red kidney beans (dry weight)	½ lb/1 cup
75 ml	oil	5 tbs
¼ kg	onions	½ lb/2 medium
1	medium green pepper	1
1	medium red pepper	1
6	stalks of celery	6
3 tbs	tomato paste	3 tbs
¼ kg	tinned or frozen sweetcorn	½ lb/1 cup
3 tbs	sultanas	3 tbs
60 g	cashew pieces	2 oz/½ cup
1 tsp	chilli powder (more or less to taste)	1 tsp
	salt and pepper to taste	

1 Drain the pre-soaked kidney beans and put them in a large saucepan with plenty of clean water over a high heat. Allow to boil fiercely for 10 minutes before reducing heat and simmering, partially covered, till cooked (about 1½ hours).
2 Meanwhile, put the oil in a large frying-pan (or wok) over a low heat. Peel and chop the onions, add them to the pan and sauté till soft.
3 Wash and chop the peppers and celery, add to the pan and continue to sauté till tender (about 10–15 minutes).
4 When the beans are cooked spoon out some of the water if necessary (or add some) so that there is just enough liquid to come level with the beans, then stir in the tomato paste, the cooked vegetables and the remaining ingredients. Mix well and heat for a further 10–15 minutes, stirring occasionally. Serve very hot.

This colourful dish reheats well – it actually improves if it's allowed to stand for a while – so it can be made well in advance and then complemented by *Plain Rice* (page 84), green vegetables, or other side dishes prepared just before your guests arrive.

Serve it with dry red wine (see page 262) or try *Lassi* (page 252).

Courgette and Cauliflower Casserole

To Serve 6
Allow 50 minutes to prepare
*Each serving provides: 165 kcal, 6 g protein, 14 g carbohydrate,
7 g fat, 7 g fibre*

Metric		**Imperial/American**
1	large cauliflower	1
½ kg	courgettes	1 lb
60 g	margarine	2 oz/4 tbs
¼ kg	mushrooms	½ lb
½ tsp	turmeric	½ tsp
1 tsp	whole cumin seeds	1 tsp
1½ tbs	wholewheat flour	1½ tbs
¼ litre	dry red wine	8 fl oz/1 cup
¼ litre	soya milk	8 fl oz/1 cup
	salt and pepper to taste	
30 g	wholewheat flakes	1 oz/½ cup
	or	
30 g	wheatgerm	1 oz/4 tbs

1 Cut the cauliflower into its main florets and plunge them into
fiercely-boiling water for 5 minutes. Remove from heat, rinse in cold
water and drain.
2 Wash, top and tail the courgettes and cut them into finger-thick
slices. Fry them in a pan with the margarine till they're golden
brown on both sides. Remove from pan and arrange in a large
casserole dish.
3 Wash and drain the mushrooms and remove the stalks. Set the stalks
aside and fry the caps in the same pan till golden brown on both sides.
Remove from pan and arrange in the casserole on top of the courgettes.
4 Arrange the cauliflower florets on top of the courgettes and
mushrooms with their stalks pointing downwards.
5 Finely chop the mushroom stalks and fry them for a few minutes in
the same pan before adding the turmeric, cumin seeds and flour.
Continue heating for a few more minutes, stirring continuously.
6 Add the red wine and soya milk and continue heating and stirring
till the mixture thickens. (Add more soya milk if necessary to
produce a thinnish sauce consistency.)
7 Remove sauce from heat, season with salt and pepper and pour over
the cauliflower.
8 Sprinkle the wholewheat flakes on top and bake in the middle of a
moderate oven (177°C/350°F/gas mark 4) for 20 minutes. Serve
immediately.

Carrot Curry

To Serve 4–6
Allow 1 hour to prepare
Each serving (of 6) provides: 162 kcal, 2 g protein, 22 g carbohydrate, 8 g fat, 6 g fibre

Metric		Imperial/American
1 kg	carrots	2 lb
1 tsp	salt	1 tsp
¼ litre	orange juice	½ pint/1¼ cups
60 g	margarine	2 oz/4 tbs
	seeds from 5 cardamom pods	
1½ tsp	ground turmeric	1½ tsp
4	whole cloves	4
1½ tbs	whole cumin seeds	1½ tbs
1½ tsp	mustard seeds	1½ tsp
¼ tsp	cayenne pepper	¼ tsp
2 tbs	fine cornmeal	2 tbs
3 tbs	raisins or sultanas	3 tbs
1	ripe banana	1

1 Scrub the carrots to remove any mud then top and tail them and slice them thickly on the slant. (Peeling is only really necessary if they have badly-damaged or pitted skins.)
2 Put them in a large saucepan with the salt and orange juice and bring quickly to the boil, then reduce heat, cover and simmer for 5 minutes. Remove from heat and set aside.
3 Melt the margarine in a separate large saucepan and add all the spices. Heat them gently for a few minutes, stirring from time to time, then add the cornmeal and stir well in. Heat for a few more minutes.
4 Add the carrots and the orange juice, a little at a time, stirring continuously. When all the carrots and juice are in, add the dried fruit and the thinly-sliced banana.
5 Cover and simmer over the lowest possible heat, stirring occasionally to prevent sticking, for ½ hour before serving.

We are indebted to Anna Thomas for this delicious curry. Unfortunately it is one of the very few vegan recipes in her otherwise excellent *The Vegetarian Epicure*.

Serve it with *Plain Rice* (page 84), *Cucumber, Yoghurt and Ginger Salad* (page 133) or with green vegetables. *Lassi* (page 252) makes a good accompanying drink.

Butter Bean and Mushroom Casserole

To Serve 6
Allow 2–3 hours to prepare (if you have pre-soaked the beans – see
page 257)
*Each serving provides: 420 kcal, 17 g protein, 41 g carbohydrate,
20 g fat, 16 g fibre*

Metric		Imperial/American
350 g	butter beans (dry weight)	¾ lb/2 cups
¼ kg	mushrooms	½ lb
125 g	margarine	¼ lb/½ cup
60 g	wholewheat flour	2 oz/½ cup
¼ litre	soya milk	8 fl oz/1 cup
¼ litre	dry white wine	8 fl oz/1 cup
1	lemon	1
30 g	wheatgerm	1 oz/3 tbs

1 Cook the soaked beans in a fresh change of water, partially covered, over a low heat till just tender (about 1–2 hours). Continue simmering gently while you prepare and cook the mushrooms.
2 Wash the mushrooms, separate the caps from their stalks and set the stalks aside. Now fry the caps, gills upwards, in half of the margarine over a high heat for a few minutes till they begin to brown. Remove from the pan and set aside.
3 Finely dice the mushroom stalks and sauté them in the same fat for a few minutes till tender. Reduce heat, sprinkle the flour into the pan and continue stirring for a few more minutes before adding the soya milk and wine. Continue heating gently and stirring till the mixture thickens. Remove from heat and set aside.
4 Grate the lemon rind and set the grated peel aside. Squeeze the lemon and set the juice aside.
5 As soon as they're done, remove the butter beans from heat, drain and put them into a suitable casserole dish. Now add the rest of the margarine and the lemon juice and stir (gently! – because the beans are easy to damage at this stage) until you're sure that every bean is coated.
6 Pour the sauce over, arrange the mushroom caps on top, sprinkle with wheatgerm and the grated lemon peel, dot with a few knobs of margarine, reheat for 20 minutes in a moderate oven (177°C/350°F/ gas mark 4) and serve.

This substantial casserole goes best with a simple *Basic Green Salad* (page 114) or try it with *Grated Courgettes with Garlic* (page 88).

Barcelona Bake

To Serve 4–6
Allow 1½ hours to prepare (if you have pre-soaked the lentils – see page 257)
Each serving (of 6) provides: 577 kcal, 14 g protein, 38 g carbohydrate, 40 g fat, 12 g fibre

Metric		Imperial/American
¼ kg	green lentils (dry weight)	½ lb/1¼ cups
1	large aubergine	1
125 ml	olive oil	¼ pint/½ cup
¼ litre	dry red wine	8 fl oz/1 cup
3	cloves garlic	3
¾ kg	onions	1½ lb/3 large
75 ml	sunflower oil	5 tbs
¼ kg	carrots	½ lb
1½ tbs	fennel seeds	1½ tbs
1½ tbs	pine kernels	1½ tbs
45 ml	soya sauce	3 tbs
¼ kg	tomatoes	½ lb/3 large
	salt and pepper to taste	
2 tbs	fresh chopped parsley as a garnish	2 tbs
	(or 1 tbs dried parsley)	

1 Cook the soaked lentils in a fresh change of water, partially covered, over a low heat till just tender (about ½–1 hour).
2 Meanwhile, cut the aubergine into finger-thick slices and fry them in the olive oil in a large saucepan till just brown on both sides. Add the wine and cook for 5 minutes. Remove from heat and set aside.
3 Skin and crush the garlic, skin and chop the onions and sauté together in the sunflower oil in a frying-pan over a low heat till the onions are just transparent.
4 Wash and peel the carrots if necessary and then grate them into the pan with the onions. Stir-fry together for 5 minutes, then stir in the fennel seeds, pine kernels and soya sauce. Remove from heat and set aside.
5 Drain the cooked lentils, add the carrot and onion mixture, season to taste and stir thoroughly before transferring the mixture to a suitable casserole dish. Arrange the aubergine slices on top and pour the remaining wine over them. Slice the tomatoes and arrange decoratively on top and bake in the middle of a moderate oven (177°C/350°F/gas mark 4) for 20 minutes.
6 Sprinkle the chopped parsley on top as a garnish and serve.

This substantial dish is best served with a green salad or green vegetables.

Savoury Avocado Tart

To Serve 8
Allow 40 minutes to prepare (if you have the pre-baked flan shell)
*Each serving provides: 333 kcal, 9 g protein, 23 g carbohydrate,
23 g fat, 4 g fibre*

Metric		Imperial/American
1	*Pre-Baked Flan Shell* (page 203)	1
¼ kg	tofu	½ lb/1 cup
2	large ripe avocados	2
¼ litre	soya milk	½ pint/1¼ cups
45 ml	soya sauce	3 tbs
	juice of half a lemon	

1 Coarsely dice the tofu and put it in a blender.
2 Spoon out the flesh of the avocados and add it to the blender
  together with the soya milk and soya sauce.
3 Squeeze the half lemon and add the juice to the blender. Blend to a
  thick, creamy consistency.
4 Pour the blended mixture into the flan shell, smooth the top and
  bake in the middle of a moderate oven (177°C/350°F/gas mark 4)
  for 30 minutes.

This is rich, substantial and filling and so is best served with a light salad
or green vegetables. It is also excellent cold and so is suitable for buffet
parties.

For variety, try adding a clove or two of crushed garlic or freshly-
ground black pepper at step 2.

Savoury Onion Tart

To Serve 8
Allow 50 minutes to prepare (if you have the pre-baked flan shell)
*Each serving provides: 289 kcal, 8 g protein, 23 g carbohydrate,
19 g fat, 4 g fibre*

Metric		Imperial/American
1	*Pre-Baked Flan Shell* (page 203)	1
30 g	margarine	1 oz/2 tbs
¼ kg	onions	½ lb/2 medium
2	cloves garlic	2
¼ kg	firm tofu	½ lb/1 cup
200 ml	soya milk	8 fl oz/1 cup
	salt and pepper to taste	
½ tsp	freshly-grated nutmeg	½ tsp

1 Put the margarine to melt in a frying-pan over a low heat.
2 Meanwhile, skin and finely dice the onions, add to the pan and sauté for a few minutes.
3 Skin and crush the garlic and stir it in with the onions.
4 Continue cooking till the onion is just transparent but not yet beginning to brown. Remove from heat and set aside.
5 Coarsely dice the tofu and put it in a blender.
6 Add the cooked onion and garlic to the blender together with the soya milk, salt and pepper to taste and blend to a smooth cream.
7 Pour the onion mixture into the flan shell, smooth the top, sprinkle with the ground nutmeg and bake in the middle of a moderate oven (177°C/350°F/gas mark 4) until the top begins to brown (about ½ hour).

This is equally good hot, straight from the oven, or chilled. In summer, try serving it with *Sweet Rice Salad* (page128), *Peach and Cauliflower Salad* (page 129) or *Potato Salad* (page 124). In winter try *Cauliflower Bhaji* (page 93), *Savoury Buckwheat* (page 96), *Whole Courgettes Italian Style* (page 92) or green vegetables.

Leek, Courgette and Tomato Tart

To Serve 8
Allow 50 minutes to prepare (if you have the pre-baked flan shell)
*Each serving provides: 355 kcal, 9 g protein, 27 g carbohydrate,
24 g fat, 6 g fibre*

Metric		Imperial/American
1	*Pre-Baked Flan Shell* (page 203)	1
75 ml	oil	5 tbs
2	medium leeks	2
¼ kg	courgettes	½ lb/3 small
¼ kg	tofu	½ lb/1 cup
¼ litre	soya milk	½ pint/1¼ cups
3 tbs	tomato paste	3 tbs
45 ml	soya sauce	3 tbs
45 ml	lemon juice	3 tbs
2 tsp	fresh chopped marjoram	2 tsp
	(or 1 tsp dried marjoram)	

1 Put the oil in a frying-pan over a low heat. Thoroughly wash and drain the leeks, then finely chop them and sauté in the oil for a few minutes.
2 Thinly slice the courgettes, add them to the pan and sauté till just browning. Remove pan from heat.
3 Coarsely dice the tofu, put it in a blender with all the remaining ingredients and blend to a smooth cream.
4 Transfer the leeks and courgettes to the flan shell, making sure that they're evenly distributed, pour the blended tofu mixture over and smooth the top.
5 Bake in the middle of a moderate oven (177°C/350°F/gas mark 4) till the top begins to brown (about 20–30 minutes). Sprinkle some more chopped marjoram on top and serve.

Serve this stunning tart hot from the oven as the centre-piece to a dinner-party accompanied with one or two light side dishes such as *Cauliflower Italian Style* (page 89) or *Spiced Potatoes* (page 86) or a green salad. It is equally good cold and so is suitable for buffet parties.

Savoury Summer Tart

To Serve 8–12

Allow 2 hours to prepare (if you have the pre-baked flan shell and including setting and chilling time)

Each serving (of 12) provides: 151 kcal, 4 g protein, 15 g carbohydrate, 9 g fat, 3 g fibre

Metric		Imperial/American
1	*Pre-Baked Flan Shell* (page 203)	1
¾ litre	water	1½ pints/3½ cups
¼ kg	broccoli	½ lb
1	large tomato	1
1½ tbs	yeast extract	1½ tbs
4 tbs	agar flakes	4 tbs

1 Put the water on to boil in a medium saucepan.
2 Meanwhile, wash the broccoli and cut off the florets to about 2½ cm (1 in) long. Discard any leaves and dice the green parts of the stems.
3 Plunge the broccoli into the boiling water and simmer till just tender (about 3–5 minutes). Remove from heat, drain, taking care to preserve the cooking water, and set aside.
4 Thinly slice the tomato and arrange decoratively in the flan case, leaving space around the outside edge for the broccoli florets.
5 Arrange the florets decoratively around the edge of the flan case and the diced broccoli stems in the centre. Set aside.
6 Dissolve the yeast extract in the broccoli cooking water, add the agar flakes, bring back to the boil and simmer for 5 minutes, stirring continuously. Remove from heat and cool by placing the saucepan in cold water for a while.
7 As soon as the agar solution is cool (but before it begins to set!) carefully pour it over the vegetables in the flan case taking care not to disturb your decorative arrangement.
8 Chill in a refrigerator for at least 1 hour before serving.

This looks so gorgeous that we've put it in the 'special occasions' section even though it isn't really difficult or complicated to make.

For variety, try cauliflower or asparagus or virtually any vegetable that is good raw or that can be easily blanched, or try adding a tablespoonful of lemon juice to the jelly.

Mushroom Pie

To Serve 8
Allow 1½ hours to prepare (if you have the shortcrust pastry)
Each serving provides: 362 kcal, 8 g protein, 21 g carbohydrate, 28 g fat, 6 g fibre

Metric		Imperial/American
1½ × qty	*Basic Shortcrust Pastry* (page 203)	1½ × qty
125 g	margarine	¼ lb/½ cup
2	cloves garlic	2
¾ kg	button mushrooms	1½ lb
¼ kg	tofu	½ lb/1 cup
1	lemon	1
	salt and pepper to taste	

1 Melt the margarine in a large saucepan over a low heat.
2 Skin and crush the garlic, add it to the pan and cook gently for a minute.
3 Wash and drain the mushrooms, add them to the pan (whole) and sauté till tender (about 15–20 minutes). Remove from heat.
4 Squeeze the lemon and put the juice in a blender.
5 Strain the juice from the mushrooms into the blender, add the crumbled tofu, salt and pepper to taste and blend to a smooth cream.
6 Pour the sauce over the cooked mushrooms, mix together thoroughly and set aside.
7 Roll out ⅔ of the pastry and line a greased, floured pie or flan dish. Fill with the mushroom mixture.
8 Roll out the rest of the pastry (moisten the edge of the base first) and use to form the pie-crust. Use your forefinger and thumbs to pinch the edges together to seal the lid to the base and form decorative scallops. Decorate the centre with pastry trimmings and cut a few slits with a sharp knife to allow steam to escape.
9 Bake in the middle of a moderate oven (177°C/350°F/gas mark 4) for 40 minutes.

This is rich and sumptuous and best served with green vegetables in winter or salads in summer. It doesn't reheat well but is excellent cold.

Cashew Loaf

To Serve 6–8
Allow 3 hours to prepare
*Each serving (of 8) provides: 433 kcal, 12 g protein, 36 g carbo-
hydrate, 29 g fat, 8 g fibre*

Metric		Imperial/American
90 ml	oil	6 tbs
3	cloves garlic	3
¼ kg	onions	½ lb/2 medium
¼ kg	mushrooms	½ lb
180 g	wholewheat flour	6 oz/1½ cups
125 g	rolled oats	¼ lb/1¼ cups
3 tbs	soya flour	3 tbs
75 ml	soya sauce	5 tbs
¼ litre	warm water	½ pint/1¼ cups
¼ kg	red pepper	½ lb/1 large
¼ kg	cashew nuts	½ lb/2 cups
2 tbs	mixed herbs	2 tbs
	freshly-ground black pepper to taste	

1 Put the oil in a frying-pan over a low heat. Skin and crush the garlic and add it to the pan. Skin and finely chop the onions and sauté till transparent.
2 Wash, drain and finely chop the mushrooms, add to the pan and sauté till tender.
3 Meanwhile, put the flour, oats and soya flour in a large bowl and mix well.
4 Tip the contents of the frying-pan in with the flour, add the soya sauce and water and mix thoroughly.
5 Wash the pepper, remove the seeds, finely chop it and add to the bowl. Add the cashew nuts, mixed herbs and pepper to taste and mix all the ingredients thoroughly.
6 Transfer the mixture to a greased, floured 1 kg (2 lb) bread tin and bake in a warm oven (163°C/325°F/gas mark 3) for 1 hour, then turn it on its side still in its tin (this will prevent a hole forming) and bake for a further 1½ hours at the same temperature.
7 Allow to cool on a rack before attempting to remove from the tin.

This protein-rich loaf may be served cold – slice it up and arrange it on a plate decorated with parsley – or hot – warm it through again by putting it in a moderate oven for 20 minutes. It's also good sliced and fried.

Layered Terrine

To Serve 8–12
Allow 1½ hours to prepare, 2 hours to cook
Each serving (of 12) provides: 266 kcal, 8 g protein, 19 g carbohydrate, 17 g fat, 6 g fibre

Metric		Imperial/American
½ kg	carrots	1 lb
375 g	broken cashew nuts	12 oz/3 cups
50 ml	carrot juice	2 fl oz/scant ¼ cup
2 tbs	cider vinegar	2 tbs
1 tbs	soya sauce	1 tbs
	salt and pepper to taste	
½ kg	leeks	1 lb
375 g	potatoes	¾ lb
2	cloves garlic	2
150 ml	soya milk	¼ pint/generous ½ cup
50 g	margarine	2 oz/4 tbs
2 bunches	watercress	2 bunches
	fresh parsley as a garnish	

1 Oil a 1½ litre (2½ pint) bread tin, line it with greaseproof paper and oil again (see notes below).
2 For the carrot layer, top, tail, peel and slice the carrots and plunge them into boiling water till just tender (no more than 6–8 minutes). Drain and set aside.
3 Put a third of the cashews in a blender with the carrot juice, cider vinegar and soya sauce and blend to a coarse mixture. Add the cooked carrots and continue blending until the mixture is perfectly smooth and creamy. Season with salt and pepper to taste, then transfer to the prepared bread tin to make a smooth layer one third its depth. Set aside. (Spare mixture makes a great dip!)
4 For the leek layer, wash and chop the leeks, drop them into fiercely boiling water and cook till just tender (about 5–10 minutes according to size). Drain and set aside.
5 Peel and chop the potatoes and cook till just tender in the same way (about 8–12 minutes depending on how small you cut them). Drain and set aside.
6 Skin and crush the garlic and put it in the (rinsed) blender together with half the remaining cashews and half the soya milk. Blend to a coarse mixture. Add the cooked leeks, a third of the cooked potatoes and 2 tbs of margarine and continue blending until the mixture is perfectly smooth and creamy. Season to taste, then transfer to the tin to make another layer as before. (It should now be

just under two thirds full.) Set aside.

7 For the watercress layer, wash and trim the watercress and put it in the (rinsed) blender with the rest of the cashews and soya milk. Blend until smooth and creamy. Add the rest of the cooked potatoes and margarine and continue blending until perfectly smooth. Season to taste and transfer the mixture to the tin to make the final layer. (Leave a gap for expansion!)

8 Bake in the middle of a warm oven (150°C/300°F/gas mark 2) for 1½ hours. Leave to stand for 5 minutes before carefully turning out onto a warmed serving-dish, and wait another 5 minutes before removing the paper. Garnish with fresh parsley and serve immediately.

This makes a tasty, colourful and spectacular centre-piece for a party, though it is a bit of a performance to make. It's also delicious cold.

The easiest way to line the tin at step 1 is to put it on a sheet of greaseproof paper and draw round the base with a pencil; then swing it onto each side in turn and draw along the sides and top to produce a Maltese Cross shape. Cut it out with scissors, fold along the base line and it will fit your tin perfectly.

Festive Savoury Loaf

To Serve 8–12
Allow 2½ hours to prepare
Each serving (of 12) provides: 491 kcal, 9 g protein, 35 g carbohydrate, 36 g fat, 7 g fibre

Metric		**Imperial/American**
125 g	wholegrain rice	¼ lb/½ cup
1½ × qty	*Basic Shortcrust Pastry* (page 203)	1½ × qty
75 ml	olive oil	5 tbs
½ kg	onions	1 lb/2 large
¼ kg	carrots	½ lb
½ kg	broken mixed nuts	1 lb/4 cups
90 ml	water	6 tbs
5 tbs	tomato paste	5 tbs
2 tsp	yeast extract	2 tsp
2 tsp	oregano	2 tsp
	pepper to taste	

1 Put the rice on to cook (see page 84).
2 Put the oil in a large saucepan over a low heat. Skin and finely chop the onions, add them to the pan and sauté till transparent. Set aside.
3 Clean and finely grate the carrots, add them to the pan with the onions and mix thoroughly.
4 Grind the nuts into small pieces. (Fold them up in a clean tea-cloth and crush them with a rolling-pin. You can try using a blender but there is a danger that it will reduce them to a powder.) Add them to the pan with the onions and carrots and mix well.
5 Put the water into a small saucepan over a low heat, add the tomato paste and yeast extract and stir till completely dissolved.
6 When the rice is well cooked add it to the pan with the onion, carrot and nut mixture, pour the dissolved yeast and tomato paste over, add the oregano and pepper and mix thoroughly.
7 Roll out ¾ of the pastry and line a 1 kg (2 lb) bread tin, taking care to seal it well at the corners. Fill to the brim with the mixture and smooth the top. Roll out the remaining ¼ of the pastry and make a lid, taking care to seal it all round. Turn it out on to an ovenproof dish, decorate with pastry trimmings and bake in the middle of a moderate oven (177°C/350°F/gas mark 4) till golden brown on top (about 40 minutes).

This stunning loaf can be served hot or cold and makes a perfect centrepiece for festive occasions such as Christmas or Easter.

Side Dishes

Side Dishes

In France every dish, including the simplest plain boiled vegetable, is served as a course in its own right and although this tends to prolong meals (sometimes to two or three hour sagas) it does mean that every single item is eaten with equal appreciation of its special qualities. (When did you last give your full, concentrated attention to the colour, smell, texture and flavour of a perfectly-cooked Brussels sprout?) So, although most of us in this country prefer to serve the main course of a meal as a combination of a centre-piece dish with accompanying side dishes, remember that there are other ways of doing things.

Having decided that you do want to serve a side dish, how do you pick a suitable one? Well, the very best way to eat vegetables is *raw*, of course, because then you get the benefit of their full complement of vitamins and minerals. So, always begin by looking in the *Salads* section. If you do wish to have a cooked side dish, remember that many vitamins are destroyed by prolonged exposure to heat and many minerals dissolve away in water, so *steaming* is by far the best way of cooking vegetables. If you haven't got a steamer or prefer boiling, *blanch* them – that is, cook them in a large pan of fiercely boiling water for the minimum possible period of time. The side dishes we've gathered together in this section are all based on this approach, but please treat our recipes as springboards for your own ideas. Remember that any steamed or blanched vegetable can be turned into a more elaborate side dish by the simple addition of a sauce from the *Sauces and Dressings* section.

Remember too, when choosing a side dish, to take advantage of vegetables that are in season because not only will they be cheaper but they are also likely to be fresher and of higher quality.

Finally, the perfect side dish complements its main dish both nutritionally and aesthetically. It goes without saying that a main dish that is substantial and protein-rich should be served with a light, delicate, side dish but don't forget to take account of colours and textures of your dishes as well. Usually it's good to *contrast* colours and textures and even temperatures (though one of our best-received meals was an essay in shades of green!). It's not a matter of rules, but of awareness of a whole meal as a pleasurable experience for your guests.

Plain Rice

To Serve 4–6
Allow 50 minutes to prepare
Each serving (of 6) provides: 148 kcal, 3 g protein, 31 g carbohydrate, 1 g fat, 1 g fibre

Metric		Imperial/American
¼ kg	wholegrain rice	½ lb/1¼ cups
600 ml	water	1¼ pints/3 cups
½ tsp	salt	½ tsp

1 Thoroughly wash and drain the rice and put it with the water and salt in a saucepan with a tight-fitting lid.
2 Bring quickly to the boil then reduce heat and simmer *without lifting the lid* for 45 minutes.
3 Remove from heat and leave to stand for another 5 minutes *still without lifting the lid.*

This is the simplest way to get perfectly-cooked, tender, but not sticky, rice every time.

Note that the amount of water is 2½ times the amount of rice *by volume.*

Serve it just as it is with stews or curries as a basic simple side dish, or liven it up with one of the many sauces from the *Sauces and Dressings* section.

Why not make a lot while you're about it – it can easily be reheated by pouring fiercely-boiling water over it, leaving it to stand for a minute or two and then draining thoroughly, or it can be gently fried in oil for a few minutes, or it can be used cold in salads.

Fried Courgettes

To Serve 4–6
Allow 20 minutes to prepare
*Each serving (of 6) provides: 178 kcal, 1 g protein, 6 g carbohydrate,
17 g fat, 3 g fibre*

Metric		Imperial/American
1 kg	courgettes	2 lb
90 ml	olive oil	6 tbs
1	lemon	1

1 Wash, top and tail the courgettes and cut them on the slant into
   finger-thick slices.
2 Put the oil in a frying-pan over a medium heat and fry the courgette
   slices till they go deep brown. Turn them and repeat.
3 Transfer them to a serving-dish. Squeeze the lemon, sprinkle the
   juice over and serve.

Courgettes can only really be served in this simple way when they are at
their best. Try serving them with something substantial, such as *Olive
and Potato Flan* (page 62), *Butter Bean and Mushroom Casserole* (page
70) or *Mushroom Pie* (page 76).

Courgettes that are past their best are still perfectly good in
Ratatouille (page 54), *Grated Courgettes with Garlic* (page 88) or
Courgette and Cauliflower Casserole (page 68).

Spiced Potatoes

To Serve 3–4
Allow 15 minutes to prepare
Each serving (of 4) provides: 218 kcal, 3 g protein, 26 g carbohydrate, 12 g fat, 6 g fibre

Metric		**Imperial/American**
½ kg	potatoes (preferably new)	1 lb
½ tsp	salt	½ tsp
60 g	margarine	2 oz/4 tbs
1 tsp	*Garam Masala* (page 253)	1 tsp

1 Wash the potatoes, quarter or halve them if necessary (and peel them if you wish) and drop them in a large saucepanful of salted boiling water. Bring back to the boil, reduce heat and simmer, uncovered, till tender (about 8–12 minutes, depending on their size). Remove from heat and drain in a colander.
2 Put the margarine in a small saucepan over a low heat and add the curry spices. Heat gently for a few minutes.
3 Add the cooked potatoes and toss them around till they're all well coated with spices and margarine. Transfer them to a (preferably hot) dish and serve immediately.

This is a quick easy way to give boiled potatoes a bit of bezaz.

Leftovers can be stored in the fridge till needed and are delicious served cold combined with salads.

Nearly all the vitamins in potatoes are just beneath the skin and most are destroyed by cooking so it's best to cook them as little as possible and only to peel them if the skins are badly-marked or injured. The skins also contain most of the fibre.

Brussels Sprouts Italian Style

To Serve 4
Allow 15 minutes to prepare
*Each serving provides: 142 kcal, 5 g protein, 3 g carbohydrate,
12 g fat, 5 g fibre*

Metric		Imperial/American
½ kg	Brussels sprouts	1 lb
½ tsp	salt	½ tsp
60 g	margarine	2 oz/4 tbs
2 tsp	lemon juice	2 tsp

1 Trim the base of each sprout and remove any injured or discoloured outer leaves. Cut a shallow cross into the base (to help the tougher core to cook as fast as the tender outer leaves).
2 Drop the sprouts in a large saucepan of fiercely-boiling salted water, bring back to the boil then reduce heat a little and cook till just tender (about 5–8 minutes). Remove from heat and drain.
3 Transfer the cooked sprouts to a hot serving-dish, add the margarine and lemon juice and toss gently till they are all coated. Serve immediately.

Perfectly cooked Brussels sprouts are bright green in colour. If they've lost their colour it's because you've *over*cooked them! Remember, small, fresh sprouts are delicious raw.

Grated Courgettes with Garlic

To Serve 6
Allow 15 minutes to prepare
*Each serving provides: 99 kcal, 1 g protein, 6 g carbohydrate, 8 g fat,
3 g fibre*

Metric		Imperial/American
60 g	margarine	2 oz/4 tbs
1	clove garlic	1
1 kg	courgettes	2 lb

1 Put the margarine to melt in a large (preferably thick) saucepan over a low heat.
2 Meanwhile, skin and crush the garlic and add it to the pan. Cover and leave over a low heat.
3 Wash, top and tail the courgettes and begin coarsely grating them. Add them to the pan as you do them and give the mixture a stir each time.
4 Continue heating gently for a further 5 minutes after you've added the last of the courgettes, and serve.

We are indebted to Bob Ames for this recipe, which provides an elegant solution for the problem of imperfect courgettes – those with injured or bitter-tasting skins – but tastes even better with perfect ones.

Cauliflower Italian Style

To Serve 4
Allow 15 minutes to prepare
*Each serving provides: 127 kcal, 2 g protein, 2 g carbohydrate,
12 g fat, 3 g fibre*

Metric		Imperial/American
1	medium to large cauliflower	1
60 g	margarine	2 oz/4 tbs
25 ml	lemon juice	1½ tbs
2 tbs	fresh chopped parsley (or 1 tbs dried parsley)	2 tbs
	salt and pepper to taste	

1 Bring a large pan of slightly salted water to the boil. Meanwhile, cut the cauliflower into its main florets and finely chop the remaining stems and any suitable leaves. Now plunge them into the fiercely-boiling water, bring back to the boil then reduce heat and simmer, partially covered, till just tender (about 5–6 minutes). Alternatively, the cauliflower can be steamed till just tender.
2 Meanwhile, melt the margarine in a small saucepan over a low heat, add the lemon juice, parsley and salt and freshly-ground black pepper to taste.
3 As soon as the cauliflower is done, remove from heat, drain and arrange in a suitable hot serving-dish. Pour the lemon juice and parsley mixture over and serve immediately.

This goes best with something substantial. Try *Spinach and Mushroom Tagliatelle* (page 57), *Mushroom Pie* (page 76) or *Carrot Curry* (page 69).

Fried Cucumbers

To Serve 4–6
Allow 25 minutes to prepare
Each serving (of 6) provides: 95 kcal, 1 g protein, 4 g carbohydrate, 9 g fat, 1 g fibre

Metric		Imperial/American
2	large cucumbers	2
45 ml	olive oil	3 tbs
25 ml	soya sauce	1½ tbs
2 tbs	fresh chopped dill (as a garnish)	2 tbs

1 Wash, top and tail the cucumbers and cut them on the slant into finger-thick slices.
2 Put the oil in a large frying-pan over a medium heat, add a batch of the cucumber slices and fry them, turning often, till they are just beginning to brown on both sides. Push the fried slices to the sides of the pan and add another batch. Continue in this way till all the cucumber is done.
3 Transfer the fried slices to a hot serving-dish, sprinkle on the soya sauce and toss around, then garnish with the chopped dill and serve.

It's surprising how few people seem prepared to experiment with cooking cucumbers though they make such a welcome change from more conventional vegetable side dishes. This simple recipe goes well with hot savoury tarts and flans or with more substantial dishes such as *Butter Bean and Mushroom Casserole* (page 70), *Winter Pie* (page 66) or *Cashew Loaf* (page 77).

Grated Carrots with Garlic

To Serve 6
Allow 20 minutes to prepare
*Each serving provides: 113 kcal, 1 g protein, 9 g carbohydrate,
8 g fat, 5 g fibre*

Metric		Imperial/American
1 kg	carrots	2 lb
60 g	margarine	2 oz/4 tbs
2	cloves garlic	2
	salt and pepper to taste	

1 Scrub, top and tail the carrots and set them aside. (Peeling is only really necessary if they have injured or pitted skins).
2 Melt the margarine in a large saucepan over a low heat.
3 Skin and crush the garlic and add it to the pan.
4 Begin coarsely grating the carrots and stirring them into the pan as you do so.
5 Continue heating gently for a further 10 minutes after you've added the last of the carrots, season with salt and pepper to taste and serve immediately.

This is a simple way to turn carrots into a colourful side dish. But beware of overcooking them – remember how good they are raw.

For variety, try stirring in the juice of a lemon just before serving, or adding 1 tbs of soya sauce instead of salt and pepper after step 4.

Whole Courgettes Italian Style

To Serve 4
Allow about 15 minutes to prepare
Each serving provides: 75 kcal, 1 g protein, 5 g carbohydrate, 6 g fat, 2 g fibre

Metric		Imperial/American
45 g	margarine	1½ oz/3 tbs
45 ml	water	3 tbs
	salt and pepper to taste	
1 kg	small perfect courgettes (see remarks below)	2 lb
2 tsp	lemon juice	2 tsp
2 tbs	fresh chopped parsley (as a garnish)	2 tbs

1 Melt the margarine in a large (preferably thick) saucepan and add the water, salt and pepper.
2 Wash, top and tail the courgettes and add them (whole!) to the pan. Cover and place over a low heat.
3 Remove cover and turn them occasionally till they are just beginning to soften. Start testing them with a skewer after about 5 minutes; as soon as it goes in easily, remove them from the heat. Above all don't overcook them – remember, courgettes are delicious *raw*. For this dish they are just as delicious and *just* not raw.
4 Add the lemon juice and toss them around a little to coat each courgette, then transfer them to a hot serving-dish and garnish with chopped parsley.

Courgettes are baby marrows and you may be astonished at how good they can taste prepared in this simple way. But note that this recipe is only suitable for tiny, unblemished, really fresh courgettes. Older, larger or injured ones need different treatment. For them, try *Grated Courgettes with Garlic* (page 88), *Ratatouille* (page 54) or *Courgette and Cauliflower Casserole* (page 68).

Cauliflower Bhaji

To Serve 4
Allow ½ hour to prepare
*Each serving provides: 117 kcal, 2 g protein, 2 g carbohydrate,
11 g fat, 3 g fibre*

Metric		Imperial/American
1	medium to large cauliflower	1
75 ml	oil	5 tbs
1 tsp	whole cumin seeds	1 tsp
1 tsp	black mustard seeds	1 tsp
½ tsp	ground turmeric	½ tsp
	salt to taste	

1 Bring a large pan of slightly-salted water to the boil. Meanwhile, cut the cauliflower up into bite-sized florets and finely chop the remaining stems and any suitable leaves. Now plunge them into the fiercely-boiling water, bring back to the boil then reduce heat and simmer, partially covered, till just tender (about 5–6 minutes). Remove from heat, drain and set aside. Alternatively, the cut cauliflower can be steamed till just tender.

2 Heat the oil in a large frying-pan, then add the seeds and turmeric and cook gently for 1–2 minutes to release the flavours. Add the cauliflower and toss gently around until it is all warmed through and well coated with the oil and spices. Serve immediately.

This goes particularly well with curry dishes. Or try the same routine with potatoes, carrots or parsnips. Courgettes and mushrooms are also delicious served this way and don't need the pre-cooking of step 1.

Latkes (Yiddish Potato Cakes)

To Serve 4
Allow ½ hour to prepare
*Each serving provides: 246 kcal, 5 g protein, 36 g carbohydrate,
10 g fat, 8 g fibre*

Metric		**Imperial/American**
½ kg	potatoes	1 lb
¼ kg	onion	½ lb/1 large
4½ tbs	wholewheat flour	4½ tbs
	salt and pepper to taste	
60–90 g	margarine for frying	2–3 oz/4–6 tbs

1 Wash and scrub the potatoes (or peel them if you wish), then coarsely grate them and put them in a mixing-bowl.
2 Skin and coarsely grate the onions and add them to the bowl.
3 Add the flour and seasoning and mix thoroughly.
4 Melt the margarine in a large frying-pan then drop the mixture in the pan a tablespoonful at a time. (Use a spoon or spatula to flatten and shape the spoonfuls into round cake shapes.) Fry till golden brown, then turn over and repeat on the other side. Transfer the latkes to a (preferably hot) serving-dish as you do them. Serve hot.

Latkes are traditionally served with *Savoury Apple Sauce* (page 166) and are at their best straight from the pan. But if you have too many guests to cope with this, or if you think you'll be too busy with the main dish, they can be prepared in advance and kept warm in the oven.

They're tasty enough just as they are but, for variety, experiment with adding herbs and spices (such as fresh chopped dill or paprika) at step 3.

They also make a good starter. But beware of serving too many of them or your guests will have no appetite left for the main course!

Lime, Coriander and Coconut Rice

To Serve 4–6
Allow 50 minutes to prepare
Each serving (of 6) provides: 187 kcal, 3.5 g protein, 32 g carbohydrate, 4 g fat, 2 g fibre

Metric		Imperial/American
¼ kg	wholegrain rice	½ lb/1¼ cups
400 ml	coconut milk	¾ pint can
200 ml	water	8 fl oz/1 cup
1 tsp	cumin seeds	1 tsp
½ tsp	salt	½ tsp
1	fresh lime	1
2 tbs	fresh coriander	2 tbs

1 Thoroughly wash and drain the rice and put it with the coconut milk, water, cumin seeds and salt in a saucepan with a tight-fitting lid.
2 Bring quickly to the boil then reduce heat and simmer *without lifting the lid* for about 45 minutes.
3 Remove from heat and leave to stand for another 5 minutes *still without lifting the lid*.
4 Juice the lime, chop the fresh coriander, add to the cooked rice, mix well and serve.

This is a recipe from the Far East which makes an ideal accompaniment to any curry – try it with *Carrot Curry* (page 69) or *Tofu Stir-Fry* (page 53) or any hot main dish. The lime, cumin, coconut and coriander blend together to produce a dish of wonderfully subtle flavours.

It is also good served cold with salad.

Savoury Buckwheat

To Serve 6
Allow ½ hour to prepare
*Each serving provides: 239 kcal, 5 g protein, 33 g carbohydrate,
9 g fat, 1 g fibre*

Metric		Imperial/American
¼ kg	roasted buckwheat	½ lb/1¼ cups
¾ litre	water	1¼ pints/3 cups
60 g	margarine	2 oz/4 tbs
¼ kg	onions	½ lb/2 medium
25 ml	soya sauce	1½ tbs
1	lemon	1
2 tbs	fresh chopped mint (or 1 tbs dried mint)	2 tbs

1 Put the buckwheat and water in a large saucepan over a high heat and bring quickly to the boil, then reduce heat and simmer for 5–10 minutes, partially covered, till the buckwheat is cooked and still chewy. Remove from heat and drain.
2 Put the margarine in a frying-pan over a low heat.
3 Meanwhile, skin and chop the onions, add to the pan and sauté till transparent.
4 Add the buckwheat and soya sauce and stir-fry over a low heat for a few minutes.
5 Squeeze the lemon and add the juice (and dried mint if you're using it) and continue to stir-fry for a few more minutes.
6 Remove from heat, stir in the fresh chopped mint and serve.

Buckwheat has a full nutty flavour and is good served plain. However, try this recipe when you're in the mood for something more extravagant and don't mind the extra preparation time.

It's fairly light with a delicate flavour so would go well with something rich and substantial; try *Savoury Avocado Tart* (page 72), *Baked Onion Surprise* (page 108) or *Cauliflower Catalan Style* (page 101).

Creamed Mushrooms

To Serve 4–6
Allow ½ hour to prepare
Each serving (of 6) provides: 158 kcal, 4 g protein, 4 g carbohydrate, 14 g fat, 3 g fibre

Metric		Imperial/American
90 g	margarine	3 oz/⅓ cup
1	clove garlic	1
½ kg	mushrooms (preferably button)	1 lb
3 tbs	wholewheat flour	3 tbs
400 ml	soya milk	¾ pint/2 cups
	salt and pepper to taste	

1 Put the margarine to melt in a large saucepan over a low heat.
2 Skin and crush the garlic, add it to the pan and cook gently for a few moments.
3 Wash and drain the mushrooms, add them to the pan and sauté till tender (about 15–20 minutes). (If you couldn't manage to get button mushrooms, chop them into bite-size pieces first.)
4 Stir in the flour and allow to cook gently for a few minutes before adding the soya milk, a little at a time, stirring continuously till the mixture thickens. Remove from heat, season and serve.

These are rich and sumptuous and go best with something light. Try *Bulgur Bake* (page 49), *Courgette and Tomato Crumble* (page 51) or *Savoury Crunchies* (page 38).

Braised Fennel

To Serve 4
Allow ½ hour to prepare
Each serving provides: 147 kcal, 8 g protein, 11 g carbohydrate,
9 g fat, 2 g fibre

Metric		Imperial/American
½ kg	fennel	1 lb
½ litre	soya milk	1 pint/2½ cups
1 tsp	fennel seeds	1 tsp
30 g	margarine	1 oz/2 tbs
2 tbs	wholewheat flour	2 tbs
	salt and pepper to taste	

1 Wash the fennel, cut off the green, fern-like tops, finely chop them
   and set aside. Clean and chop the rest and put it in a saucepan
   together with the soya milk and fennel seeds, bring quickly to the
   boil, then reduce heat and simmer, partially covered, till just tender
   (about 10–15 minutes).
2 Meanwhile, melt the margarine in a separate, small saucepan over a
   low heat. When it's completely melted but before it begins to bubble,
   add the flour and stir in. Continue to heat gently and stir for 2–3
   minutes.
3 As soon as the fennel is done, remove from heat and drain, reserving
   the liquid. Arrange the cooked fennel in a shallow, ovenproof dish.
4 Slowly add the cooking liquid to the roux, stirring continuously.
   Continue stirring after you've added the full amount until the
   mixture thickens. Add salt and pepper to taste (and a little extra
   soya milk if it seems too thick), pour over the cooked fennel and
   warm through in a moderate oven (177°/350°F/gas mark 4) for
   about 15 minutes.
5 Sprinkle the chopped fennel tops over and serve.

This has a delicate flavour but is quite filling. Try serving it with *Butter
Bean and Mushroom Casserole* (page 70), *Olive and Potato Flan* (page
62), *Savoury Onion Tart* (page 73) or any other casserole, flan or tart
and a green salad.

Brazil Nut and Cabbage Stir-fry

To Serve 4–6
Allow ½ hour to prepare
*Each serving (of 6) provides: 270 kcal, 5 g protein, 6 g carbohydrate,
25 g fat, 6 g fibre*

Metric		Imperial/American
¾ kg	white cabbage	1½ lb/1 small
75 ml	oil	5 tbs
2 tbs	black mustard seeds	2 tbs
125 g	Brazil nuts	¼ lb/1 cup
1	lemon	1
	salt to taste	

1 Wash the cabbage and remove any injured or discoloured outer leaves. Thinly shred the rest and set aside.
2 Put the oil in a wok (or large saucepan) over a high heat, add the mustard seeds and leave them to cook for about a minute.
3 Add the shredded cabbage and stir till the mustard seeds are evenly distributed through the mixture. Reduce heat to medium and leave to fry for a while, stirring from time to time.
4 Meanwhile, coarsely chop the Brazil nuts and stir them into the pan, then finely grate the lemon rind directly into the pan and squeeze the lemon and add the juice. Continue to stir-fry for another 5 minutes.
5 Transfer to a hot serving-dish, season with salt to taste and serve.

Try this with *Spinach and Mushroom Tagliatelle* (page 57), *Mung Bean and Courgette Casserole* (page 64) or *Fresh Parsley and Tomato Flan* (page 63).

Any leftovers can happily be served cold, for lunch, the following day.

For variety, substitute caraway seeds for the mustard seeds at step 2 or use cider vinegar instead of lemon juice at step 4.

Red Cabbage and Spiced Apple

To Serve 6
Allow 1 hour to prepare
Each serving provides: 137 kcal, 3 g protein, 15 g carbohydrate, 6 g fat, 7 g fibre

Metric		Imperial/American
1	medium red cabbage (about 1 kg/2 lb)	1
1	medium onion	1
½ kg	cooking apples	1 lb
3 tbs	margarine	3 tbs
400 ml	water	¾ pint/2 cups
2 tbs	brown sugar (or apple concentrate)	2 tbs
1½ tsp	whole cloves	1½ tsp
1 tbs	cider vinegar	1 tbs
	salt and pepper to taste	

1 Wash and shred the red cabbage, peel and chop the onion, wash, core and chop the apples (there's no need to peel them).
2 Melt the margarine in a large saucepan, add the cabbage, onion and apples and sauté over a medium heat for 10 minutes.
3 Add the remaining ingredients, cover and simmer gently for 40 minutes, stirring occasionally, until the cabbage is tender and the apples have virtually disintegrated.

This colourful Eastern European dish goes well with *Courgette and Tomato Crumble* (page 51) or *Mushroom Pie* (page 76).

If you don't like the idea of finding a whole clove in your mouth – or find the taste too strong – use 15 g (1 tsp) of ground cloves instead.

For variety, try adding a cinnamon stick and some ground nutmeg. Or add raisins about 15 minutes before the cooking is complete.

Cauliflower Catalan Style

To Serve 4–6
Allow 40 minutes to prepare
Each serving (of 6) provides: 142 kcal, 5 g protein, 3 g carbohydrate, 13 g fat, 3 g fibre

Metric		Imperial/American
1	large cauliflower	1
1 tsp	salt	1 tsp
125 g	tofu	¼ lb/½ cup
45 ml	sunflower oil	3 tbs
200 ml	soya milk	8 fl oz/2 cups
2 tsp	vanilla essence	2 tsp
1 tsp	mustard powder	1 tsp
30 g	pine kernels	1 oz/2 tbs

1 Cut the cauliflower into its main florets and finely dice the remaining stem. Plunge into fiercely-boiling salted water until just tender (about 5 minutes). Remove from heat and drain.
2 Coarsely dice the tofu and put it in a blender.
3 Add the oil, soya milk, vanilla essence and mustard powder and blend to a smooth cream.
4 Arrange the cauliflower in a shallow ovenproof dish and sprinkle the pine kernels over it. Pour the blended cream over and bake in a moderate oven (177°C/350°F/gas mark 4) for 20 minutes. Serve immediately.

It's encouraging to think that this vegan version of a traditional dish from Catalonia is actually better for you than its cholesterol-laden original which is made, of course, with masses of fresh dairy cream. Its attraction is that each of its three main ingredients – cauliflower, cream sauce and pine kernels – has a subtle, delicate flavour that is all too easy to swamp, but put together they complement each other perfectly.

It is extremely rich and filling and is best served with a *Basic Green Salad* (page 114) or green vegetables.

Baked Parsnips

To Serve 4–6
Allow 45 minutes to prepare
Each serving (of 6) provides: 187 kcal, 3 g protein, 21 g carbohydrate, 9 g fat, 7 g fibre

Metric		Imperial/American
1 kg	parsnips	2 lb
60 g	margarine	2 oz/4 tbs
1½ tbs	mustard powder	1½ tbs
45 ml	apple concentrate	3 tbs
	salt and pepper to taste	

1 Top, tail and peel the parsnips, then cut them into quarters lengthwise. Plunge them into fiercely-boiling water for 4 minutes (but no longer) then drain them and set aside.
2 Put the margarine to melt in a small saucepan over a low heat, then stir in the mustard powder and apple concentrate and season with salt and (preferably freshly-ground) pepper to taste. Remove from heat and set aside.
3 Put the parsnips in an ovenproof dish, pour the sauce mixture over and toss them around until they are all well covered. Bake in the middle of a moderate oven (177°C/350°F/gas mark 4) for ½ hour.

The combination of mustard and apple concentrate enhances the parsnip's positive qualities – its sweetness and delicate flavour – while subtly disguising the slight aftertaste that puts some people off them. We have known some self-professed life-long parsnip-haters to ask for second helpings of this dish!

Celery Fritters

To Serve 4
Allow ½ hour to prepare (if you have the *Batter Mixture*)
*Each serving provides: 418 kcal, 12 g protein, 27 g carbohydrate,
30 g fat, 8 g fibre*

Metric		Imperial/American
1	large head of celery	1
1 tsp	salt	1 tsp
30 g	margarine	1 oz/2 tbs
	Batter Mixture (page 254)	

1 Trim off the leaves and break the celery head into individual stalks
  and wash thoroughly, then chop the stalks into bite-sized lengths
  and drop them into a large pan of boiling salted water. When they
  begin to soften (but are still firm and crisp – about 8–12 minutes)
  remove them from the heat and drain thoroughly.
2 Put the margarine in a large frying-pan over a low heat.
3 Start dipping the celery pieces in the batter mixture. If the batter
  won't adhere, roll the celery in flour first.
4 Fry the battered pieces for a few minutes on each side till they're
  golden brown. Remove from pan and serve.

If you have a lot of mouths to feed it's probably simplest to prepare the
celery fritters about an hour beforehand and then keep them warm in a
casserole dish in the bottom of the oven; but if you have just yourself
(and perhaps a special friend!) to feed, they are at their most delicious
served straight from the pan and, provided you already have some of
the batter mixture made up, are really quite quick and easy to prepare.

Grilled Broccoli

To Serve 4
Allow 25 minutes to prepare
Each serving provides: 193 kcal, 9 g protein, 5 g carbohydrate, 16 g fat, 5 g fibre

Metric		**Imperial/American**
½ kg	broccoli	1 lb
180 g	tofu	6 oz/¾ cup
45 ml	oil	3 tbs
25 ml	soya sauce	1½ tbs
1 tsp	mustard powder	1 tsp
1 tbs	sunflower seeds	1 tbs

1 Wash the broccoli, cut off the florets, dice the stems and plunge it all into fiercely-boiling, unsalted water till just tender (about 5 minutes). Remove from heat and drain, retaining 125 ml (¼ pint/ 6 tbs) of the cooking water.
2 Crumble the tofu into a blender, add the retained cooking water from the broccoli together with the oil, soya sauce and mustard powder and blend till smooth and creamy.
3 Arrange the cooked broccoli in a heatproof serving-dish, pour the blended mixture over, sprinkle with the sunflower seeds and place under a hot grill until it's just beginning to brown on top. Serve immediately.

This is light and delicate and so is best served with something substantial such as baked potatoes or *Savoury Rice* (page 56); or try combining it with several light dishes such as *Savoury Crunchies* (page 38), *Cashew and Mushroom Roast* (page 50), *Mung Bean and Courgette Casserole* (page 64) or *Celery Fritters* (page 103).

Aubergine Fritters

To Serve 4
Allow about ¾ hour to prepare
Each serving provides: 372 kcal, 8 g protein, 23 g carbohydrate,
28 g fat, 8 g fibre

Metric		Imperial/American
	Batter Mixture (page 254)	
½ kg	aubergine	1 lb/1 large
2 tsp	salt	2 tsp
3–4 tbs	wholewheat flour	3–4 tbs
	salt and pepper to taste	
1	lemon	1
	oil for frying (preferably olive)	

1 Make up a thinner batter mixture than usual, using extra soya milk.
2 While the batter mixture is standing, wash (but don't peel) the aubergine and cut it into finger-thick slices. Place these in layers in a bowl, sprinkling each layer with salt, and set aside for ½ hour to sweat.
3 Sprinkle the flour over a plate, add a little salt and pepper if you like, and set aside.
4 Squeeze the lemon and set the juice aside.
5 Put 2–3 tbs oil in a frying-pan over a medium heat.
6 Rinse the aubergine slices in cold water, drain and pat them dry with kitchen paper or a clean tea-cloth.
7 Dip each aubergine slice in turn, first in the flour, then in the batter and finally lay it in the frying-pan and fry on both sides till golden brown. Transfer the fritters to a hot serving-dish as you do them. Add more oil to the pan as necessary.
8 Pour the lemon juice over the fritters and serve.

These are at their best served straight from the pan – though it's a bit of a sacrifice to be the one making them and not one of the ones eating them! But if you want to serve them as a side dish in the normal way, it's probably best to make them well in advance and keep them warm in a casserole in the bottom of a warm oven.

Creamed Spinach

To Serve 4–6
Allow 50 minutes to prepare
Each serving (of 6) provides: 270 kcal, 10 g protein, 5 g carbohydrate, 24 g fat, 6 g fibre

Metric		Imperial/American
½ kg	fresh spinach	1 lb
	(or 300 g [10 oz] frozen spinach)	
125 ml	oil	¼ pint/½ cup
2	cloves garlic	2
3 tbs	wholewheat flour	3 tbs
¼ litre	soya milk	½ pint/1¼ cups
¼ kg	tofu	½ lb/1 cup
25 ml	soya sauce	1½ tbs
1	lemon	1
	salt and pepper to taste	

1 Put 2 tbs of oil in a large saucepan over a low heat.
2 Wash and add the spinach. Increase the heat a little and cook till soft (only a few minutes if fresh; about 10 minutes if frozen). Remove from heat and set aside.
3 Meanwhile put 3 tbs of oil in another saucepan over a low heat. Skin and crush the garlic, add it to the pan and cook gently for a couple of minutes before stirring in the flour. Continue to cook gently for another few minutes.
4 Set 5 tbs of soya milk aside, then gradually stir the rest into the pan with the flour and garlic. Continue to heat gently and stir to make a thick sauce. Remove from heat and combine the contents of the two saucepans by adding one to the other and stirring gently. Set aside.
5 Put the reserved soya milk (5 tbs) in a blender and crumble in the tofu.
6 Squeeze the lemon and add the juice, 3 tbs oil, salt to taste (about 1 tsp), freshly-ground black pepper and blend to a thick cream. Check the seasoning and adjust if necessary then fold the cream into the spinach and pour the mixture into a lightly-greased ovenproof dish. Bake in the middle of a moderate oven (177°C/350°F/gas mark 4) for 30 minutes.

This goes well with *Winter Pie* (page 66), *Festive Savoury Loaf* (page 78), or any of the savoury flans or tarts.

Spiced Pease Pudding

To Serve 4–6
Allow 1½ hours to prepare
Each serving (of 6) provides: 204 kcal, 9 g protein, 24 g carbohydrate, 9 g fat, 5 g fibre

Metric		Imperial/American
¼ kg	yellow split peas	½ lb/1 cup
45 ml	oil	3 tbs
1 tsp	whole cumin seeds	1 tsp
1 tsp	ground turmeric	1 tsp
½ tsp	ground cinnamon	½ tsp
½ tsp	chilli powder	½ tsp
½ tsp	ground cloves (or 6 whole cloves)	½ tsp
½ tsp	ground nutmeg	½ tsp
2 tsp	soya sauce	2 tsp

1 Wash the split peas, put them in a large saucepan, cover well with water, bring quickly to the boil, then reduce heat and simmer, partially covered, till they have completely softened and are beginning to break down (about ½–1½ hours depending on how old they are). Check the water frequently and add more as required.
2 When the peas are almost cooked put the oil and spices (but not the soya sauce) in a small saucepan and heat gently for a few minutes, stirring often.
3 As soon as the peas are done, remove both pans from heat, drain the peas if necessary, add the oil, spices and soya sauce and mash to a smooth, thick cream with a fork. Transfer to a hot dish and serve.

The traditional pease puddings of the North-East of England have an extra two stages in which they are put into a buttered basin and steamed for an hour; but in the view of these two lazy cooks, they are tasty enough as they are.

They can be served hot with curries or cold with salads. Any cold left-over pudding can be sliced, fried in margarine and served on toast as a quick snack.

For variety, try green split peas, omit the spices and double the amount of soya sauce. Or, for a quicker dish, substitute lentils for the split peas and make an Indian 'dhal'.

Baked Onion Surprise

To Serve 4
Allow 1¼ hours to prepare
Each serving provides: 437 kcal, 10 g protein, 27 g carbohydrate, 29 g fat, 7 g fibre

Metric		Imperial/American
4	large onions	4
90 g	margarine	3 oz/⅓ cup
125 g	mushrooms	¼ lb
125 g	black olives	¼ lb/1 cup
30 g	breadcrumbs (or wheatgerm)	1 oz/3 tbs
2 tsp	fresh chopped marjoram (or 1 tsp dried marjoram)	2 tsp
	salt and pepper to taste	
	ingredients for *Red Wine Sauce* (page 167)	

1 Separately wrap the whole onions in foil (don't peel them first!) and bake till soft in a moderate oven (177°C/350°F/gas mark 4); start testing with a skewer after about 30 minutes. When they are soft right through to the centre, remove from oven, discard the foil and set aside to cool.
2 Put the margarine to melt in a frying-pan over a low heat.
3 Wash and dice the mushrooms, add to the pan and sauté till tender. Remove from heat.
4 Top and tail the onions and remove their outer skins. Slice off the top thirds and set aside, then scoop out the hearts with a teaspoon, dice them and add to the pan with the mushrooms.
5 Stone the olives if necessary, then finely dice them and add them to the pan together with the breadcrumbs, marjoram, salt and pepper. Mix thoroughly.
6 Stuff the onions with the mixture and replace their top thirds as 'lids'. There should be plenty of the mixture left over to make a sauce.
7 Replace the stuffed onions in the oven for a further 15 minutes at the same temperature.
8 While they are reheating, prepare a sauce from the remains of the stuffing mixture. (*Red Wine Sauce*, page 167).
9 Remove the onions from the oven, transfer to a hot serving-dish, pour the sauce over, sprinkle on some more of the chopped marjoram and serve.

These look sumptuous and are rich and filling, so they should be served with something light – try *Whole Courgettes Italian Style* (page 92) or *Savoury Buckwheat* (page 96) or a green salad.

French Beans on a Bed of Spinach

To Serve 6
Allow 30 minutes to prepare
*Each serving provides: 145 kcal, 8 g protein, 3 g carbohydrate,
10 g fat, 12 g fibre*

Metric		Imperial/American
1 kg	spinach	2 lb
¼ kg	French beans	½ lb
2	lemons	2
75 g	margarine	3 oz/6 tbs
2 tbs	black mustard seeds	2 tbs
2 tsp	mustard powder	2 tsp
	salt and pepper	

1 Carefully wash the spinach and remove stalks. Drain and set aside.
2 Wash, top and tail the beans and set aside.
3 Put some water on to boil for the beans.
4 Squeeze one of the lemons and set the juice aside.
5 Heat the margarine in the largest saucepan you've got. When very
   hot, add the mustard seeds and stir around until they start popping.
6 Stir in the mustard powder, a little salt and pepper and the lemon
   juice, then add the spinach to the pan and continue to heat and stir
   until cooked (about 4–5 minutes).
7 Drop the French beans into fiercely boiling water and cook till just
   tender (about 2–3 minutes). Drain and set aside.
8 Make a bed of the cooked spinach on a large serving-dish, arrange
   the French beans on top, garnish with slices of lemon and serve.

Spinach collapses down to almost nothing once it's cooked, so don't be
afraid to pile it all into the pan at once even though it looks as if it might
not fit in. No need to add extra water – there'll be more than enough left
on the leaves from washing them.

Jerusalem Artichokes with Juniper Berries

To Serve 6
Allow 1 hour to prepare
Each serving provides: 307 kcal, 7 g protein, 19 g carbohydrate, 21 g fat, 2 g fibre

Metric		Imperial/American
1 kg	Jerusalem artichokes	2 lb
150 g	margarine	5 oz/generous ½ cup
1	medium onion	1
2	cloves garlic	2
24	juniper berries	24
6 tbs	wholewheat flour	6 tbs
½ litre	soya milk	1 pint/2½ cups
	salt and pepper to taste	

1 Scrub the artichokes thoroughly (but don't peel them – see below) and blanch till barely tender – that is, plunge them in fiercely-boiling salted water for about 5–8 minutes depending on size. Drain, put them back in the saucepan and run under cold water for a few minutes and drain again. Cut into thin slices and dry with kitchen paper.
2 Melt half the margarine in a large pan, add the artichoke slices and sauté for 15 minutes, taking care to prevent sticking. Remove from heat, cover and set aside.
3 Meanwhile, melt the rest of the margarine in another small saucepan. Skin and finely chop the onion, skin and crush the garlic and add to the pan together with the juniper berries. Sauté for 10 minutes, taking care not to let the onion brown.
4 Sprinkle on the flour while stirring continuously and continue cooking gently for a few minutes before adding the soya milk a little at a time till you have a thinnish sauce. Allow to simmer gently to mature flavours and cook the flour before removing from heat and seasoning to taste.
5 Arrange the Jerusalem artichokes on a warmed serving-dish, pour the juniper berry mixture over and serve.

Jerusalem artichokes are so knobbly they can be a pain to clean, but use an old toothbrush and it's easier than cleaning your teeth.

If you can't get Jerusalem artichokes, or just for variety, try this recipe with cauliflower, broccoli or French beans instead. The delicate flavour of juniper berries will lift them all into the gourmet category.

Salads

Salads

Whatever your view of history it is clear that human beings lived for millennia on this planet before we ever began *cooking*; and that, whatever our primitive natural diet was, it was certainly eaten *raw*. But during the past few decades the digestive systems we developed during these prehistoric times have been confronted with a fundamental change of diet that has led to an alarming array of degenerative diseases. Surely it's obvious that for truly radiant health we should eat at least *some* raw food at every meal.

This needn't be as difficult as it sounds. A bowl of muesli with your breakfast can include seeds, nuts and fresh or dried fruits; a mixed salad can provide the basis for lunch; and dinner can include a green salad and be rounded off with fresh fruit. If the population at large were to follow this simple formula, there would be a radical improvement in the nation's health.

Why not make a *Basic Green Salad* for lunch every day, simply adding raw *bean sprouts, broccoli, cabbage, carrots, cauliflower, chives, courgettes, cucumber, dill, leeks, mint, mushrooms, parsley, peppers, radishes, spring onions, tomatoes, watercress*, etc., depending on what is in season and what you have to hand. We've given a range of combinations to get you started, but experiment with others – more than 6,000 plants have been identified as edible so the possibilities are literally endless.

Don't forget that salads can also be served as starters, side dishes and main dishes on their own, or they can provide the basis of a complete, delicious, satisfying and healthy meal with the simple addition of wholewheat bread spread with nut butters, tahini, yeast extract or one of the spreads from the *Spreads* section and fresh fruit to finish. Add a glass of wine and you have a feast.

Basic Green Salad

Per Serving
Allow 10 minutes to prepare
*Each serving provides: 200 kcal, 1 g protein, 2 g carbohydrate,
20 g fat, 2 g fibre*

Metric	**Imperial/American**
25 ml *French Dressing* (page 176)	1½ tbs
3–4 leaves Cos, Webb or similar lettuce	3–4 leaves

1 Put 25 ml (1½ tbs) of dressing per person in a large salad bowl.
2 Discard only the really damaged outer leaves of the lettuce as
  necessary (see below), then break off 3–4 leaves per person, wash
  them thoroughly and drain.
3 Fold them up in a clean tea-cloth (or kitchen paper) and pat them
  dry. (Or use a centrifugal hand dryer.)
4 Tear the leaves into bite-sized pieces, put them into the bowl, toss till
  they are all well coated with the dressing and serve.

If you are serving a big, rich meal, always include a simple green salad
as one course. It aids digestion and increases the fibre content as well as
contributing many essential minerals and vitamins to the diet. Raw
lettuce is particularly rich in vitamins A and C but note that cutting the
leaves with a steel knife destroys some of the vitamin C (by oxidation)
so always *tear* them. Note also that the darker green outer leaves
contain up to 50 times more vitamin A than the inner white ones.

Nearly all the calories are in the dressing so if you're trying to keep
down your calorie count, use *Yoghurt Salad Dressing* (page 180)
instead.

Lemon Carrot Salad

To Serve 6
Allow 15 minutes to prepare
Each serving provides: 41 kcal, 1 g protein, 10 g carbohydrate,
0 g fat, 6 g fibre

Metric		Imperial/American
1 kg	carrots	2 lb
2	lemons	2

1 Scrub the carrots to remove any mud, then top and tail them (peeling is only really necessary if they have badly-damaged or pitted skins).
2 Finely grate or shred them (the finer the better) and put them into a suitable serving-bowl.
3 Grate the lemons and set the grated peel aside.
4 Squeeze the lemons, add the juice to the bowl and mix thoroughly.
5 Sprinkle the grated peel on top and serve.

Considering how quick and easy it is to prepare, this simple salad is amazingly delicious to eat. It is also very good for you. Raw carrots are particularly rich in vitamins A and C – vitamin A is actually called *carotene* after them. Note that mature carrots contain twice as much of it as young ones.

Mixed Pepper Salad

To Serve 4–6
Allow 15 minutes to prepare
Each serving (of 6) provides: 301 kcal, 5 g protein, 18 g carbohydrate, 23 g fat, 5 g fibre

Metric		Imperial/American
½ kg	red peppers	1 lb/2 large
½ kg	green peppers	1 lb/2 large
½ kg	yellow peppers	1 lb/2 large
125 g	black olives	¼ lb/1 cup
125 ml	*French Dressing* (page 176)	¼ pint/½ cup

1 Wash the peppers and remove the seeds before slicing them into bite-sized pieces.
2 Put the dressing into a suitable serving-bowl, add the sliced peppers and toss till well mixed.
3 Stone the olives if necessary (some garlic presses have a gadget for the purpose in their handles), arrange them on top of the peppers and serve.

This quick salad is an attractive addition to any meal with its range of bright primary colours each of which has a different taste, the yellow being the sweetest.

Cabbage, Fruit and Nut Salad

To Serve 4–6
Allow 15 minutes to prepare
Each serving (of 6) provides: 356 kcal, 6 g protein, 17 g carbohydrate, 29 g fat, 9 g fibre

Metric		Imperial/American
1 kg	red cabbage	2 lb/½ large
½ kg	eating apples	1 lb
125 g	pecans (or walnuts)	¼ lb/1 cup
125 ml	*French Dressing* (page 176)	¼ pint/½ cup

1 Shred the cabbage as finely as possible and put into a suitable serving-bowl.
2 Wash and core the apples (but don't peel them), then dice and add them to the bowl.
3 Add the pecan nuts and salad dressing, toss till well mixed and serve.

This salad will look most attractive if you can buy *green* eating apples such as *Granny Smiths* to offset the rich red of the cabbage. For variety, try adding sultanas or chopped dates.

Mixed Sprout Salad

To Serve 6–8
Allow 20 minutes to prepare
Each serving (of 8) provides: 157 kcal, 4 g protein, 5 g carbohydrate, 14 g fat, 4 g fibre

Metric		Imperial/American
¼ kg	mung bean sprouts	½ lb
¼ kg	lentil sprouts	½ lb
125 g	alfalfa sprouts	¼ lb
¼ kg	red pepper	½ lb/1 large
175 ml	*Tahini Dressing* (page 178)	12 tbs

1 Put all of the mung bean and lentil sprouts and half of the alfalfa sprouts into a suitable serving-bowl and mix well together.
2 Wash the pepper and remove the pith and seeds. Cut off a few strips and set aside to use as decoration. Finely chop the remainder, add it to the bowl, together with the dressing and mix thoroughly.
3 Decorate the top with the rest of the alfalfa sprouts and the strips of red pepper and serve.

Any kind of bean sprout can be used to ring the changes on this delicious, crunchy salad. A wide range is available in most wholefood shops, but perfectionists will, of course, wish to sprout their own. (See page 258 for advice on how to proceed.)

Avocado and Apple Salad

To Serve 4–6
Allow 20 minutes to prepare
Each serving (of 6) provides: 486 kcal, 9 g protein, 13 g carbohydrate, 44 g fat, 6 g fibre

Metric		Imperial/American
2	large avocados	2
½ kg	eating apples	1 lb
1	bunch watercress	1
125 g	salted peanuts	¼ lb/1 cup
125 ml	*French Dressing* (page 176)	¼ pint/½ cup

1 Scoop out the flesh of the avocados and cut into finger-thick slices. Put them in a suitable serving-bowl.
2 Wash and core the apples (but don't peel them), then dice them and add to the bowl.
3 Chop the watercress into bite-sized pieces and add to the bowl together with the salted peanuts.
4 Add the dressing, toss till thoroughly mixed and serve.

This is a summery salad which you can serve all year, the fresh taste of the apples and watercress perfectly complementing the richness of the avocados. It looks best if you use *red* apples to offset the greens of the other ingredients. The peanuts are included to add a bit of protein and crunch.

Celeriac Salad

To Serve 4
Allow 20 minutes to prepare
*Each serving provides: 222 kcal, 4 g protein, 5 g carbohydrate,
19 g fat, 9 g fibre*

Metric		Imperial/American
275 ml	*Mayonnaise* (page 182)	1 jar
1	large celeriac	1
1 tsp	caraway seeds	1 tsp

1 Put the mayonnaise in a suitable serving-bowl.
2 Peel and slice the celeriac and then grate it as finely as possible directly into the bowl with the mayonnaise. Stop from time to time to toss the grated mixture to coat it with dressing.
3 Sprinkle the caraway seeds on top and serve.

Everyone likes the taste of the bottom bits of sticks of celery – the root part – yet few seem prepared to buy celeriac though it tastes similar and consists of nothing else. This recipe is simple to prepare and makes a delicious winter salad. Serve it with savoury flans and tarts, at buffet parties or as a simple starter to a hot meal.

Celeriac discolours very quickly once cut and although this does not affect its taste, it does reduce its visual appeal. Mixing it with the dressing as you go along, as suggested, solves this easily.

Carrot and Coconut Salad

To Serve 4–6
Allow 20 minutes to prepare
Each serving (of 6) provides: 150 kcal, 3 g protein, 14 g carbohydrate, 9 g fat, 7 g fibre

Metric		Imperial/American
½ kg	carrots	1 lb
60 g	chopped dates	2 oz/½ cup
60 g	desiccated coconut	2 oz/½ cup
2	lemons	2
25 ml	apple concentrate	1½ tbs
2 tbs	sesame seeds	2 tbs

1 Finely grate the carrots, put them in a suitable serving-bowl and mix them with the chopped dates and desiccated coconut.
2 Squeeze the lemons and add the juice to the bowl together with the apple concentrate. Mix thoroughly.
3 Put the sesame seeds in a dry pan over a low heat and stir them until the seeds are toasted and begin to pop.
4 Add the toasted sesame seeds to the bowl with the other ingredients, mix once more and serve.

The rich variety of flavours in this unusual salad makes it suitable for special occasions even though it is so quick and easy to prepare. Serve it with something substantial such as *Cashew Loaf* (page 77) or *Festive Savoury Loaf* (page 78).

Celery, Carrot and Sprout Salad

To Serve 6–8
Allow ½ hour to prepare
Each serving (of 8) provides: 178 kcal, 4 g protein, 6 g carbohydrate, 16 g fat, 5 g fibre

Metric		Imperial/American
1	head of celery	1
½ kg	carrots	1 lb
125 g	bean sprouts	¼ lb/2 cups
	Spicy Peanut Sauce (page 170)	

1 Break the celery into individual stalks and wash thoroughly before chopping them into bite-sized pieces. Put them in a suitable serving-bowl.
2 Wash the carrots (or peel, as necessary) then finely grate them into the bowl with the celery.
3 Add the bean sprouts and the peanut sauce, mix well together and serve.

This crunchy, spicy salad is delicious served by itself as a starter, or as an accompaniment to a hot main dish.

For variety, try *Tahini Dressing* (page 178) or, if it's a really special occasion, try gently heating the peanut sauce and pouring it over the top of the salad just before serving.

Any kind of bean sprout will do and many varieties can be bought in most wholefood shops but perfectionists will of course prefer to sprout their own. (See page 257 for advice.)

Avocado and Grapefruit Salad

To Serve 4–6
Allow 1¼ hours to prepare (including 1 hour to chill)
Each serving (of 6) provides: 187 kcal, 4 g protein, 6 g carbohydrate, 17 g fat, 3 g fibre

Metric		Imperial/American
2	large grapefruit	2
3	large avocados	3
1	lemon	1
3 tbs	fresh chopped mint (or 1 tbs dried mint)	3 tbs

1 Peel the grapefruit, divide them into their individual segments, then slice these into bite-sized pieces, taking care to remove any pips.
2 Scoop out the flesh of the avocados, cut into finger-thick slices and add to the bowl. (Don't mix yet!)
3 Squeeze the lemon, pour the juice over the avocado slices and then gently toss to spread the juice evenly through the mixture. (This will prevent the avocado from discolouring.)
4 Add most of the chopped mint, toss again to mix well, then sprinkle the rest on top as a decoration.
5 Chill for at least an hour before serving.

This wonderfully delicate, fresh-tasting salad is the perfect way to start a summer dinner-party.

Note that, despite the routine with the lemon juice, the avocado will gradually discolour and although this will not affect its nutritional value or its taste, it does spoil the appearance of the salad, so it's not a good idea to make a lot.

Potato Salad

To Serve 4–6
Allow 1½ hours to prepare (including 1 hour to chill)
Each serving (of 6) provides: 239 kcal, 3 g protein, 27 g carbohydrate, 13 g fat, 6 g fibre

Metric		Imperial/American
¾ kg	potatoes (preferably new)	1½ lb
275 ml	*Mayonnaise* (page 182)	1 jar
1	bunch chives	1

1 Scrub the potatoes and halve or quarter them depending on their size (and peel them if you wish). Drop them in a large saucepan of fiercely-boiling salted water. Bring back to the boil, then reduce heat and simmer, uncovered, till just tender (about 8–12 minutes depending on how small you've cut them). Remove from heat, rinse thoroughly in cold water and drain in a colander.
2 Put the cooled, drained potatoes in a suitable serving-bowl, add a jarful of mayonnaise and toss till well coated.
3 Finely chop the chives, add them to the bowl (saving a few for decoration) and toss again. Chill for at least an hour.
4 Sprinkle the rest of the chives on top and serve.

This keeps well, so why not make a lot and stash it in the fridge for the occasional, unexpected visitor?

Serve it as a side dish to cold savoury flans or tarts in summer or as a starter to a hot meal in winter. It's also suitable for buffet parties.

For variety, try *Tahini Dressing* (page 178) or *Spicy Peanut Sauce* (page 170) instead of the mayonnaise. Almost any fresh chopped herb can be used instead of chives.

Leek Salad

To Serve 4–6
Allow 1½ hours to prepare (including 1 hour to chill)
Each serving (of 6) provides: 226 kcal, 4 g protein, 10 g carbohydrate, 19 g fat, 6 g fibre

Metric		Imperial/American
1 kg	leeks	2 lb
1 tsp	salt	1 tsp
125 ml	*French Dressing* (page 176)	¼ pint/½ cup
2 tbs	fresh chopped mint (or 1 tbs dried mint)	2 tbs

1 Wash and chop the leeks and plunge them into fiercely-boiling salted water till just tender (about 5–10 minutes depending on their size). Drain and then immediately plunge into cold water. Leave them for a few minutes to cool before draining in a colander.
2 When the water has completely drained out transfer them to a suitable serving-bowl, pour the dressing over and toss gently till they are all well coated.
3 Sprinkle the chopped mint on top and refrigerate for at least an hour before serving.

This salad is particularly good served with cold savoury flans or tarts in summer, at buffet parties in winter, or as a starter to a meal any time.

Tabbouleh

To Serve 6
Allow 2½ hours to prepare (including 2 hours to chill)
Each serving provides: 254 kcal, 12 g protein, 21 g carbohydrate, 14 g fat, 2 g fibre

Metric		Imperial/American
¼ kg	bulgur	½ lb/generous cup
400 ml	boiling water	¾ pint/scant 2 cups
½	small cucumber	½
4	medium tomatoes	4
1	medium green pepper	1
2	cloves garlic	2
4 tbs	lemon juice	4 tbs
4 tbs	virgin olive oil	4 tbs
4 tbs	fresh chopped parsley	4 tbs
2 tbs	fresh chopped mint	2 tbs
	salt and pepper to taste	

1 Put the bulgur and a little salt in a large basin, stir in the boiling water, cover and set aside for 10–15 minutes until all the water has been absorbed.
2 Meanwhile, finely chop the cucumber, tomatoes and pepper and, when the bulgur is ready, stir into the basin. (If there's still a little loose water, strain the bulgur through a sieve before adding the chopped vegetables.)
3 Skin and crush the garlic and put it in a separate basin together with the lemon juice and olive oil. Wash and finely chop the parsley and mint, add it to the basin, season with salt and freshly-ground black pepper to taste and mix thoroughly.
4 Put the bulgur and chopped vegetable mixture into a suitable serving-dish, pour the dressing over, mix well in and refrigerate for a couple of hours.
5 Garnish with sprigs of mint or parsley and serve.

Tabbouleh is a classic Middle Eastern dish which is best prepared in advance and refrigerated for a few hours – to give time for the delicious contrasting flavours of the olive oil, lemon juice, garlic, parsley and fresh mint to seep into every grain. It's good as a starter, served with sticks of fennel and a bowl of black olives, and is also perfect for buffet parties.

For variety, try substituting chopped fresh coriander for the mint or, for extra crunch, add finely diced celery or carrots.

Wheatberry and Bean Salad

To Serve 8–10
Allow 1½ hours to prepare
Each serving (of 10) provides: 248 kcal, 10 g protein, 27 g carbo-hydrate, 12 g fat, 9 g fibre

Metric		Imperial/American
¼ kg	wholewheat berries	½ lb/1 cup
¼ kg	mung beans	½ lb/1 cup
1	head of celery	1
25 ml	soya sauce	1½ tbs
125 ml	*French Dressing* (page 176)	¼ pint/½ cup
1 tsp	ground cinnamon	1 tsp

1 Put the wheatberries in a large saucepan, well covered with water, bring quickly to the boil, then reduce heat and simmer, partially covered, till tender (about 1 hour). Check from time to time to see if the water needs topping up. Note that even when they are cooked, wheatberries are still firm and rather chewy.
2 Put the mung beans in a separate large saucepan, also well covered with water, bring quickly to the boil, then reduce heat and simmer till tender (about 20 minutes).
3 When the beans and berries are done, remove from heat and drain thoroughly before mixing them together in a suitable serving-bowl.
4 Wash and chop the celery into bite-sized pieces, add to the bowl together with the soya sauce, dressing and cinnamon, mix thoroughly and serve.

This unusual and attractive salad, with its shades of greens and browns, has the advantage of providing an almost perfect protein balance. It keeps well and so is suitable for buffet parties.

It's odd that people who habitually cook and eat rice – which has to travel a long way to get to our shops – never think of cooking and eating wholewheat berries – which grow right on our doorsteps.

Sweet Rice Salad

To Serve 4–6
Allow about 2 hours to prepare (including 1 hour to cool)
Each serving (of 6) provides: 311 kcal, 5 g protein, 44 g carbohydrate, 13 g fat, 2 g fibre

Metric		Imperial/American
¼ kg	wholegrain rice	½ lb/1¼ cups
¼ litre	orange juice	½ pint/1½ cups
¼ litre	water	½ pint/1½ cups
1 tsp	ground turmeric	1 tsp
60 g	sultanas	2 oz/2 tbs
1	red pepper	1
60 g	cashew pieces	2 oz/½ cup
125 ml	*Orange Juice Dressing* (page 177)	¼ pint/½ cup

1 Wash and drain the rice and put it together with the orange juice, water and turmeric into a large saucepan. Bring quickly to the boil, reduce heat, cover and simmer over the lowest possible heat without lifting the lid for 45 minutes. Remove from heat and leave to stand for 5 minutes before lifting the lid. (Don't worry if there's a little juice left in the bottom.)
2 Sprinkle the sultanas over the surface of the rice, re-cover and set aside to cool. (This softens the sultanas.)
3 Finely dice the red pepper, mix with the cashew pieces and set aside.
4 When the rice has completely cooled, turn it out into a suitable serving-bowl, add the chopped pepper and cashew pieces and the dressing, mix till you're satisfied that every grain of rice is coated and serve.

The simplicity of the dressing adds an agreeable lightness to this colourful and unusual salad which, as it may be prepared well in advance, is suitable for buffet parties as well as everyday use.

Peach and Cauliflower Salad

To Serve 6
Allow 50 minutes to prepare (including ½ hour to chill)
Each serving provides: 221 kcal, 8 g protein, 16 g carbohydrate,
14 g fat, 6 g fibre

Metric		Imperial/American
1	large cauliflower	1
6	peaches	6
1	carton mustard and cress	1
60 g	wheatgerm	2 oz/¾ cup
275 ml	*Mayonnaise* (page 182)	1 jar

1 Cut the cauliflower into bite-sized florets and put them in a suitable serving-bowl. Finely dice the remaining stems and add them to the bowl.
2 Stone and slice the peaches and add them to the bowl.
3 Cut the mustard and cress as near to the roots as possible and add to the bowl.
4 Add the wheatgerm and mayonnaise and mix all the ingredients thoroughly.
5 Chill for at least half an hour before serving.

This unusual salad is at its best in the late summer when the seasons for peaches and cauliflowers happily overlap. Raw cauliflower is particularly rich in vitamin C, but even lightly cooking it destroys more than two-thirds of it.

For variety, try nectarines instead of peaches, or broccoli instead of cauliflower.

Salsify Salad

To Serve 4–6
Allow 1 hour to prepare (including ½ hour to chill)
*Each serving (of 6) provides: 101 kcal, 4 g protein, 5 g carbohydrate,
7 g fat, negligible fibre*

Metric		Imperial/American
1 kg	salsify	2 lb
150 ml	*Mayonnaise* (page 182)	10 tbs
2 tbs	chives (preferably fresh, chopped)	2 tbs

1 Peel, top and tail the salsify and cut them on the slant into bite-sized pieces. (The simplest way is to hold them under cold water and use a potato peeler.)
2 Plunge the cut pieces into a large saucepanful of fiercely-boiling unsalted water until they begin to soften (about 8–12 minutes). Remove from heat, rinse in cold water and drain in a colander.
3 Put them in a suitable serving-bowl, add the mayonnaise and toss to mix.
4 Garnish with chopped chives and chill for at least ½ hour before serving.

This is a simple way to make an unusual salad. Salsify has a delicate flavour similar to asparagus but at only half the cost. Nevertheless it is still expensive and that is why we've put this recipe in the 'special occasions' section. Unfortunately it is only rarely seen in street markets but can be obtained in tins.

Asparagus Salad

To Serve 4
Allow 1 hour to prepare (including ½ hour to chill)
*Each serving provides: 149 kcal, 5 g protein, 4 g carbohydrate,
12 g fat, 4 g fibre*

Metric		Imperial/American
1	bunch asparagus spears	1
1½ tsp	salt	1½ tsp
45 ml	*French Dressing* (page 176)	3 tbs
½ kg	tomatoes	1 lb/4 large
12	stoned black olives	12

1 Prepare the asparagus spears by tying them in bundles of about a dozen. (They are often sold already prepared.)
2 Drop the bundles in a large pan of fiercely-boiling salted water. (Check before you boil the water that the pan is wide enough for the bundles to lie down flat – if it isn't and you have to cut off some of the fibrous ends, don't throw them away! See below.) Bring the water quickly back to the boil, then reduce heat and continue to simmer, uncovered. After about 10 minutes, begin testing the spears by pushing a thin, sharply-pointed knife into their bases. As soon as they begin to soften, remove from heat and drain. Cut the string and lay them out on a clean cloth or kitchen paper to cool.
3 Thinly slice the tomatoes and arrange decoratively round the edge of a large, flat serving-dish. Lay out the cooled asparagus spears in the centre and carefully pour the dressing over them, making sure that every spear is coated. Garnish with the olives and chill for at least half an hour before serving.

This is not a complicated or time-consuming recipe to prepare. The only reason we've put it in the 'special occasions' section is the price of asparagus!

For variety, try *Mayonnaise* (page 182) or *Yoghurt Salad Dressing* (page 180).

If you have a lot of the fibrous ends left over, you can make an agreeable asparagus soup by gently boiling them in soya milk for about 15 minutes and discarding them before serving it, seasoned with a little salt and pepper. (But for the real thing see *Asparagus Soup*, page 15.)

Aubergine and Tomato Salad

To Serve 4
Allow 2½ hours to prepare (including 1 hour to demoisturize the aubergine and 1 hour to chill)
Each serving provides: 349 kcal, 2 g protein, 7 g carbohydrate, 31 g fat, 6 g fibre

Metric		Imperial/American
½ kg	aubergine	1 lb/1 large
1 tsp	salt	1 tsp
½ kg	tomatoes	1 lb/4 large
125 ml	olive oil	¼ pint/½ cup
200 ml	dry red wine	7 fl oz/1 cup
1	clove garlic (crushed)	1
2 tbs	parsley (preferably fresh, chopped)	2 tbs

1 Peel the aubergine, remove the stalk and cut into finger-thick slices. Place in layers in a bowl with a sprinkle of salt over each layer. Set aside for an hour.
2 Skin the tomatoes (see page 255) and arrange round the edge of a large serving-dish.
3 Put some of the oil in a large frying-pan over a low heat. As you transfer each slice of aubergine to the pan, pat it dry with kitchen paper. Fry each slice just long enough on both sides to begin to colour, then push it to the side of the pan to make room for more. As you add each new batch of slices, add more oil. (They'll drink up enormous quantities, so if you prefer you can use a cheaper vegetable oil, but do put in at least 3 tbs of olive oil as this is important for the finished flavour.) When you've fried all the slices on both sides, add the wine, crushed garlic and parsley, mix everything together thoroughly and simmer for 5 minutes.
4 Remove the cooked aubergine slices and arrange them in the middle of the tomatoes on your serving-dish. Pour the contents of the pan over as a sauce.
5 Garnish with more fresh parsley and chill for at least an hour before serving.

This is a perfect starter for an alfresco summer dinner-party. As it can be prepared well in advance, it is also suitable for buffet parties, in which case you should double or triple the quantities and allow extra preparation time.

Cucumber, Yoghurt and Ginger Salad

To Serve 6
Allow 2½ hours to prepare (including demoisturizing and chilling time)
Each serving provides: 70 kcal, 4 g protein, 6 g carbohydrate, 2 g fat, 2 g fibre

Metric		Imperial/American
3	large cucumbers	3
1½ tbs	salt	1½ tbs
½ litre	*Vegan Yoghurt* (page 240)	1 pint/2½ cups
2 tbs	freshly grated ginger (or 1 tbs dried ground ginger)	2 tbs
	salt and pepper to taste	

1 Wash the cucumbers (or peel them if you wish) and cut them into quarters lengthwise. Slice them into finger-thick chunks, put them in a bowl in layers and sprinkle each layer liberally with salt. Set aside for an hour.
2 Rinse the cucumber chunks in cold water and drain. (If you're a perfectionist, dry them by patting between layers of kitchen paper.) Put them in a suitable serving-bowl.
3 Put the grated ginger and salt and pepper to taste in the yoghurt container and stir well in. Pour over the cucumber chunks and mix thoroughly.
4 Chill for at least an hour before serving.

This is a delightful, fresh-tasting summer salad which also goes well with hot curries.

Do try to use *fresh* ginger if you can – it lifts the flavour into a unique taste experience.

If the batch of yoghurt you're using is too bland in taste, add a few drops of lemon juice.

Marinated Mushroom Salad

To Serve 4–6
Allow at least 4½ hours to prepare (including 4 hours marination time)
Each serving (of 6) provides: 198 kcal, 2 g protein, negligible carbohydrate, 20 g fat, 2 g fibre

Metric		Imperial/American
½ kg	button mushrooms	1 lb
125 ml	olive oil	¼ pint/½ cup
75 ml	white wine vinegar	5 tbs
½ tsp	salt	½ tsp
½ tsp	pepper	½ tsp
1 tsp	mustard seeds	1 tsp
¼ tsp	cayenne pepper	¼ tsp
1 tbs	juniper berries	1 tbs

1 Wash, drain and slice the mushrooms and put them in a suitable serving-bowl.
2 Make a marinade from all the remaining ingredients (the easiest way is to put them all in a jam jar, seal and shake well) and pour over the mushrooms. Toss lightly for a few moments till every single slice of mushroom is coated.
3 Chill for at least 4 hours.
4 Toss again to remix and serve.

As the only problem with this salad is the marination time, it is particularly suitable for buffet parties, where it can be one of the first things you make. Note that during the marination the mushrooms will shrink to about half their volume.

For variety, try using capers instead of juniper berries.

Don't slice the mushrooms too thin. We did this the first time we tried it and as a result they produced too much juice which diluted the marinade and had to be drained off. Slice them about 60 mm (¼ in) thick and you'll be all right.

Desserts

Desserts

Fresh fruit is the healthiest everyday dessert as well as the simplest and cheapest, and a good habit we might acquire from Latin countries is the serving of a bowlful at every meal. It's odd that in this country many people seem to think of fresh fruit as an ornament to be displayed on the sideboard and eaten only as a snack between meals.

Nevertheless there are, of course, good reasons for making more elaborate desserts occasionally – indeed, if you want to give a sense of occasion to a meal, they are essential. And, it has to be said, just as many vegans as omnivores are gluttons. (It's a curious fact that few of the population at large can begin to comprehend that one can be a gourmet, a glutton and a vegan without difficulty!) But the unexpected bonus with vegan food is that the most sensual delights imaginable are *not* cholesterol bombs and indeed that, provided you do not over-indulge in them, they are often actually a good, healthy form of nutrition.

A word or two about trifles. All the ingredients for a delicious vegan trifle are given in this book but we haven't given a specific recipe. Simply use any of the biscuit or cake recipes that take your fancy as the base, add some fresh soft fruit, then make up a *Fruit Juice Jelly* (page 138) and top the whole thing with *Vanilla Dessert* (page 141), *Vegan Cream* (pages 235–6) or *Custard* (page 173). If you want to be really self-indulgent, pour some rum over the biscuit or cake base before adding the jelly, decorate the top with *Vegan Piping Cream* (page 237) and sprinkle with desiccated coconut or chopped nuts. Chill for at least two hours before serving.

Fruit Juice Jelly

To Serve 4
Allow 1½ hours to prepare (including setting and chilling time)
*Made with orange juice each serving provides: 43 kcal, 1 g protein,
11 g carbohydrate, 0 g fat, 0 g fibre*

Metric		**Imperial/American**
3 tbs	agar flakes	3 tbs
½ litre	fruit juice	1 pint/2½ cups

1 Put the agar flakes into a small saucepan and add about a quarter of
  the fruit juice. Bring quickly to the boil then reduce heat and simmer
  for at least 5 minutes, stirring continuously. Remove from heat.
2 Add the rest of the fruit juice and stir well. Pour into individual
  serving-dishes.
3 Refrigerate till set.

The individual jellies can be decorated with slices of fruit, topped with
Vegan Cream (pages 235–6), *Cashew Cream* (page 238) or *Coconut
Cream* (page 239), or simply served plain.

For parties and special occasions, make a layered jelly from two or
three different juices, set in a ring mould. You can pile a fruit salad in the
middle and decorate the whole thing with *Vegan Piping Cream* (page
237) and you will have an impressive party dish.

Fresh Fruit Fool

To Serve 4
Allow 40 minutes to prepare (including ½ hour to chill)
*Each serving (with eating apples) provides: 243 kcal, 1 g protein,
16 g carbohydrate, 19 g fat, 3 g fibre*

Metric		Imperial/American
1	lemon	1
125 ml	soya milk	¼ pint/½ cup
75 ml	sunflower oil	5 tbs
½ kg	any suitable fresh fruit (see below)	1 lb

1 Grate the lemon rind and set the grated peel aside.
2 Squeeze the lemon and put the juice in a blender.
3 Add the soya milk and sunflower oil.
4 Core and peel the fruit (as necessary), then coarsely chop it, add it to
  the blender and blend till smooth and creamy.
5 Transfer the blended mixture to individual serving-dishes, sprinkle
  the grated lemon peel on top and chill for at least ½ hour before
  serving.

Almost any fruit can be used to make this light, creamy fool – from
eating apples to mangoes – and although it's so quick and easy to make
it's succulent enough to serve at any gourmet meal – but note that fruit
with a high water content such as melons will produce more like a milk
shake consistency than a fool.

Creamed Apricots

To Serve 4
Allow 10 minutes to prepare (the day before serving)
*Each serving provides: 100 kcal, 4 g protein, 20 g carbohydrate,
1 g fat, 11 g fibre*

Metric		**Imperial/American**
180 g	dried apricots	6 oz/1½ cups
¼ litre	soya milk	½ pint/1½ cups

1 Finely chop the apricots, divide them equally between four
   individual serving-dishes, pour a quarter of the soya milk into each
   and refrigerate overnight.
2 Serve chilled.

This simple dessert works because the apricots gradually absorb liquid
from the soya milk, turning it into a rich, thick, apricot-flavoured cream
in the process. It's good just as it is, but try adding one of the following
as a topping: *Vegan Cream* (pages 235–6), *Vanilla Dessert* (page 141)
or *Fruit Juice Jelly* (page 138).

Vanilla Dessert

To Serve 3–4
Allow 1¼ hours to prepare (including 1 hour to chill)
*Each serving (of 4) provides: 121 kcal, 5 g protein, 18 g carbohydrate,
2 g fat, 2 g fibre*

Metric		Imperial/American
2 tbs	arrowroot powder	2 tbs
½ litre	soya milk	1 pint/2½ cups
60 g	dark muscovado sugar	2 oz/2 tbs
30 ml	vanilla essence	2 tbs

1 Put the arrowroot in a small saucepan, add a little of the (cold) soya milk and stir until completely dissolved. Gradually add the rest of the soya milk, stirring continuously.
2 Stir in the other ingredients and bring to a simmer over a medium heat, still stirring continuously until the mixture thickens. Remove from heat, pour into individual serving-dishes and set aside to cool.
3 Refrigerate till needed. Serve chilled.

Serve this simple dessert, just as it is, or pour it over sliced fresh fruit, muesli, chopped nuts, or use it as a topping for sweet flans, tarts or trifles.

For variety, add a tablespoonful of cocoa or carob powder at step 2. The addition of 3 tbs of rum or brandy lifts it into another category altogether.

Baked Bananas

To Serve 4
Allow ½ hour to prepare
*Each serving provides: 190 kcal, 2 g protein, 15 g carbohydrate,
13 g fat, 4 g fibre*

Metric		Imperial/American
4	bananas	4
1	lemon	1
60 g	chopped nuts	2 oz/3 tbs
30 g	margarine	1 oz/2 tbs
45 ml	red wine (optional)	3 tbs

1 Peel the bananas and lay them side by side in a shallow ovenproof dish.
2 Squeeze the lemon and pour the juice over the bananas.
3 Sprinkle the nuts over the bananas, dot with knobs of margarine and, if you wish, sprinkle with wine.
4 Bake in the middle of a fairly hot oven (190°C/375°F/gas mark 5) till deep brown (about 20–30 minutes).

This is a simple way to turn 4 bananas into a special treat. Serve just as they are or try pouring *Vegan Single Cream* over (page 235), or serve with chilled *Vegan Yoghurt* (page 240).

Baked Apples

Per Serving
Allow ¾ hour to prepare
*Each serving provides: 175 kcal, 1 g protein, 44 g carbohydrate,
negligible fat, 9 g fibre*

Metric		Imperial/American
1	large cooking apple	1
1–2 tbs	sultanas	1–2 tbs
1 tsp	maple syrup	1 tsp
½ tsp	lemon juice	½ tsp
	knob of margarine	

1 Wash and core the apples and make a shallow cut in the skin around their 'equators'.
2 Begin stuffing the hole left by the core with the sultanas; when it's about half full, pour in the maple syrup and lemon juice. Continue with the sultanas and press the filling in firmly, top with a knob of margarine and place on a baking-tray or ovenproof dish.
3 Bake in the middle of a moderate oven (177°C/350°F/gas mark 4) till the apples are just beginning to brown on top (about 30–40 minutes).

These are good served hot, straight from the oven, just as they are, or topped with *Custard* (page 173), *Brandy Sauce* (page 175) or *Vegan Single Cream* (page 235) but they are also good chilled and decorated with *Vegan Piping Cream* (page 237).

Peach Pudding

To Serve 6
Allow 1 hour to prepare
Each serving provides: 292 kcal, 8 g protein, 40 g carbohydrate, 11 g fat, 6 g fibre

Metric		Imperial/American
	Batter Mixture (page 254)	
90 g	raw demerara sugar	3 oz/5 tbs
6	large peaches	6

1 Make up a batter mixture, add the sugar and stir till thoroughly dissolved.
2 Wash, stone and coarsely chop the peaches and stir them into the batter mixture.
3 Preheat an oven to very hot (232°C/450°F/gas mark 8).
4 Lightly grease a shallow, ovenproof dish with margarine.
5 Pour in the fruit mixture and bake in the middle of the oven for 35 minutes. Serve hot or cold.

This is moist enough to serve on its own but try it also with *Brandy Sauce* (page 175), *Vegan Cream* (pages 235–6) or *Custard* (page 173). Any leftovers can either be served chilled or used in a trifle.

For variety, try fresh apricots, plums or any soft summer fruit instead of peaches.

Apple and Banana Crumble

To Serve 8
Allow 1¼ hours to prepare
*Each serving provides: 383 kcal, 7 g protein, 45 g carbohydrate,
20 g fat, 7 g fibre*

Metric		Imperial/American
½ kg	cooking apples	1 lb/2 large
2	bananas	2
60 g	raisins	2 oz/2 tbs
25 ml	apple concentrate	1½ tbs
¼ kg	wholewheat flour	½ lb/2 cups
60 g	sunflower seeds	2 oz/½ cup
1½ tbs	raw demerara sugar	1½ tbs
125 g	margarine	¼ lb/½ cup
2 tbs	sesame seeds	2 tbs

1 Wash, core and chop the apples (peel them if you wish) and put
  them in an ovenproof dish.
2 Peel and chop the bananas and add them to the dish together with
  the raisins and mix thoroughly. Pour the apple concentrate over the
  fruit mixture.
3 Put the flour, sunflower seeds and sugar into a separate bowl and
  mix them together. Cut and rub in the margarine till the mixture
  resembles coarse breadcrumbs.
4 Pour the crumble mixture over the fruit, dot with knobs of
  margarine, sprinkle with the sesame seeds and bake in a fairly hot
  oven (190°C/375°F/gas mark 5) for 50 minutes.

This makes a substantial dessert which is ideal as a warming winter
pudding especially if served with *Brandy Sauce* (page 175).

For variety, try *pear and banana* or *rhubarb and date* for the filling.

Apple Pie

To Serve 8–10
Allow 1 hour to prepare
Each serving (of 10) provides: 259 kcal, 4 g protein, 38 g carbohydrate, 11 g fat, 6 g fibre

Metric		Imperial/American
1½ × qty	*Basic Shortcrust Pastry* (page 203)	1½ × qty
90 g	chopped dates	3 oz/¾ cup
¼ litre	water	½ pint/1¼ cups
¾ kg	cooking apples	1½ lb/3 large
125 g	raisins	¼ lb/¾ cup
1 tsp	ground cinnamon	1 tsp
4	whole cloves	4
25 ml	apple concentrate	1½ tbs

1 While the pastry is chilling in the refrigerator, chop the dates and put them in a large saucepan with the water over a low heat and simmer till they begin to disintegrate.
2 Wash, core and finely chop the apples (peel them if you wish) and add them to the pan together with the raisins, cinnamon and cloves. Stir well, then partially cover and simmer gently for 15 minutes.
3 Remove from heat, stir in the apple concentrate and set aside.
4 Roll out ⅔ of the pastry and line a greased, floured pie or flan dish. Fill with the apple mixture.
5 Roll out the rest of the pastry and, after moistening the rim of the pastry base with cold water, use to form the pie crust. Use your forefingers and thumb to pinch the edges together to seal the lid to the base and form decorative scallops. Decorate the centre with the pastry trimmings and cut a few slits with a sharp knife to allow steam to escape.
6 Bake in the middle of a moderate oven (177°C/350°F/gas mark 4) for 30 minutes.

This is delicious served hot, straight from the oven, with chilled *Vegan Yoghurt* (page 240), *Vegan Double Cream* (page 236) or cold with *Hot Chocolate Sauce* (page 174).

Summer Fruit Compote

To Serve 6
Allow about 4½ hours to prepare (including 4 hours to chill)
Each serving provides: 45 kcal, 1 g protein, 10 g carbohydrate,
0 g fat, 10 g fibre

Metric		Imperial/American
1 kg	mixed summer fruits (strawberries, raspberries, blackberries, blackcurrants, redcurrants, etc.)	2 lb
2 tbs	brown sugar	2 tbs
4 tbs	water	4 tbs
5 cm	stick of cinnamon (or 1 tsp ground cinnamon)	2 in

1 Stem, stalk and wash the fruit.
2 Put the water and sugar in a large saucepan, bring to the boil and melt the sugar.
3 Add the fruits, turning gently so as not to break them. Add the stick of cinnamon, cover and simmer gently for 10 minutes until lightly cooked.
4 Allow to cool, turn into a serving dish, pick out the cinnamon stick, cover and refrigerate till needed.

The brilliant colours of this dish look even more sumptuous decorated with *Cashew Cream* (page 238) or *Vegan Piping Cream* (page 237). We like it slightly sharp but simply add more sugar if you prefer a sweet dessert.

For variety, try mixed spices or a dash of liqueur instead of cinnamon.

When summer fruits are not available try dried fruit compote. Use apricots, (stoned) prunes, figs, pears and peaches. Unlike fresh fruit they won't produce their own liquid, so cover them with water, bring to the boil and simmer till tender (about 30 minutes). Alternatively soak all the fruit overnight. A delicious taste of summer in mid-winter!

Caramel Cream Pudding

To Serve 6
Allow about 1½ hours to prepare (including 1 hour to chill and set)
Each serving provides: 108 kcal, 4 g protein, 17 g carbohydrate,
2 g fat, 2 g fibre

Metric		**Imperial/American**
125 g	raw muscovado sugar	¼ lb/5 tbs
45 ml	water	3 tbs
150 g	tofu	5 oz/⅔ cup
4 tsp	vanilla essence	4 tsp
½ litre	soya milk	1 pint/2½ cups
1½ tbs	agar flakes	1½ tbs

(Note: if you haven't made caramel creams before, read the remarks below before trying to turn them out of their moulds.)

1 Put the sugar and water in a small saucepan over a low heat, bring to the boil (stirring often) and simmer for 5 minutes, uncovered, to make a caramel mixture.
2 Crumble the tofu into a blender, add 1 tablespoon of the caramel mixture and the vanilla essence, and set aside.
3 Pour the rest of the caramel mixture equally into six individual moulds (or small bowls, or cups) and rotate each in turn to coat the base and sides. Set aside.
4 Pour the soya milk into the same saucepan, add the agar flakes, bring quickly to the boil then reduce heat and simmer for 5 minutes, stirring continuously.
5 Add the hot soya milk to the crumbled tofu in the blender and blend to a smooth cream.
6 Pour the blended mixture equally into each of the moulds and set aside to cool.
7 Refrigerate till set.
8 Turn out on to individual dishes (saucers are ideal) and serve chilled.

To get the puddings out of their moulds, proceed as follows: first tip and rotate each mould till the caramel mixture separates the filling from the side; then place your chosen dish on top of the mould taking care to position it exactly in the centre; invert the whole thing, raise it up to shoulder high, bring it down again to waist high and stop it suddenly. You should hear it drop on to the dish. Be sure to position the mould carefully in the centre of the dish because once the pudding has dropped you won't be able to move it again.

Orange and Chocolate Mousse

To Serve 6
Allow 1½ hours to prepare (including 1 hour to chill)
*Each serving provides: 282 kcal, 4 g protein, 11 g carbohydrate,
23 g fat, 1 g fibre*

Metric		Imperial/American
1	orange	1
2 tsp	lemon juice	2 tsp
½ litre	soya milk	1 pint/2½ cups
45 ml	maple syrup	3 tbs
1 tsp	vanilla essence	1 tsp
5 tbs	unsweetened cocoa powder	5 tbs
125 ml	sunflower oil	¼ pint/½ cup

1 Finely grate the orange and put the grated peel in a blender.
2 Squeeze the orange and add the juice to the blender together with the lemon juice.
3 Add all the remaining ingredients except the oil and blend till thoroughly mixed.
4 Slowly add the oil a little at a time while continuing to blend until the mixture thickens.
5 Pour into individual serving-dishes and chill for at least an hour before serving.

This is at its best on the day of its preparation, garnished with a twist of orange. If you have leftovers that begin to separate, stir with a spoon just before serving.

For variety, try carob powder instead of cocoa.

Avocado and Coconut Whip

To Serve 4–6
Allow 1¼ hours to prepare (including 1 hour to chill)
Each serving (of 6) provides: 240 kcal, 4 g protein, 7 g carbohydrate, 22 g fat, 6 g fibre

Metric		Imperial/American
90 g	creamed coconut	3 oz/⅓ cup
125 ml	boiling water	¼ pint/½ cup
2	large ripe avocados	2
125 ml	soya milk	¼ pint/½ cup
45 ml	maple syrup	3 tbs
2 tsp	fresh chopped mint (or 1 tsp dried mint)	2 tsp

1 Put the creamed coconut and the boiling water in a small bowl and stir till completely dissolved.
2 Scoop out the flesh of the avocados and put it in a blender together with all the other ingredients (including the melted coconut) and blend to a smooth rich cream.
3 Pour into individual serving-dishes and decorate each with sprigs of fresh mint. Chill for at least an hour before serving.

Avocados are unusual among fruit in being rich in both vegetable oils and protein so, as your guests indulge themselves in this sumptuous pale green dessert, they can comfort themselves with the thought that, unlike so many comparable non-vegan dishes, it isn't *bad* for them!

If you can't get fresh mint, use dried in the recipe and decorate with chopped nuts, pomegranate seeds or thin slices of lemon or orange.

Note that it doesn't keep well so don't make more than you need.

Peach and Apricot Puffs

To Serve 4–6
Allow 2 hours to prepare (including cooling time for the filling)
Each serving (of 6) provides: 263 kcal, 3 g protein, 39 g carbohydrate, 8 g fat, 9 g fibre

Metric		Imperial/American
90 g	dried peaches	3 oz/½ cup
90 g	dried apricots	3 oz/½ cup
300 ml	apple juice	12 fl oz/1½ cups
12 sheets	filo pastry	12 sheets
2 tbs	sunflower oil	2 tbs

1 Finely chop the peaches and apricots and put them in a saucepan with the apple juice. Bring to the boil, reduce heat and simmer, uncovered, for 30 minutes. Set aside to cool.
2 Take 15 leaves (3 spare in case you spoil some!) of filo pastry and cut into approximately 12 cm (5 in) squares (it usually comes in oblongs of this width). Place the cut sheets under a damp cloth to keep moist.
3 Pre-heat the oven to fairly hot (190°C/375°F/gas mark 5) and prepare a baking tray.
4 Take one square at a time and thinly brush the entire surface with oil. Repeat with 2 more squares, laying each on top of the other at angles to produce a 12-pointed star. Now spoon 3 tbs of the cooled fruit mixture into the centre of your star and carefully lift up the corners of the pastry and pinch them together to form a sealed parcel. Finally, lightly brush the outside with oil and place on the baking tray. Repeat with the remaining squares till you have 4 or 5 fruit puffs.
5 Bake in the middle of the pre-heated oven till golden brown (about 10–15 minutes). Serve hot or cold.

There's enough filling to make more of these delicious fruit puffs if you wish. Or you can use the spare filling to make tarts or fruit desserts with *Custard* (page 173) poured over. It's also good to eat just as it is.

Filo pastry can be difficult to handle if you're not used to it, but persevere and you'll soon get the hang of it. For variety, try different fillings such as sugarless marzipan (page 197), jams or thick custard and try experimenting with different shapes.

Fresh Fruit Tart

To Serve 8–12
Allow 2 hours to prepare (including 1 hour to set and chill)
Each serving (of 12) provides: 253 kcal, 4 g protein, 21 g carbo-hydrate, 17 g fat, 3 g fibre

Metric		Imperial/American
125 g	wholewheat flour	¼ lb/1 cup
125 g	ground almonds	¼ lb/1 cup
30 g	raw demerara sugar	1 oz/1 tbs
30 g	sesame seeds	1 oz/2 tbs
150 g	margarine	5 oz/⅔ cup
3	kiwi (or other soft tropical) fruit	3
¼ kg	black grapes	½ lb
½ litre	white grape juice	1 pint/2½ cups
3 tbs	agar flakes	3 tbs

1 Put the flour, ground almonds, sugar and sesame seeds in a bowl and mix thoroughly. Cut in the margarine and rub together till well blended.
2 Transfer the mixture to a greased, floured flan dish (about 23 cm [9 in] is the right size). Gently push down and smooth out the mixture till it lines the side and base of the dish, using your forefingers and thumb to shape the edge into decorative scallops. Bake in the middle of a moderate oven (177°C/350°F/gas mark 4) for 15 minutes. Remove from oven and leave to cool on a rack.
3 Meanwhile, peel and slice the kiwi fruit, and halve and pip the grapes. When the flan case is cool, arrange the fruit decoratively to cover the whole base.
4 Put 125 ml (¼ pint/½ cup) of the grape juice in a small saucepan with the agar flakes, bring quickly to the boil then reduce heat and simmer for 5 minutes, stirring continuously. Remove from heat, add to the rest of the grape juice and mix thoroughly.
5 Taking care not to disturb your artistic arrangement, slowly pour the grape juice into the flan case.
6 Refrigerate for at least an hour before serving.

This looks gorgeous and, unlike many of the things you see in cake-shop windows, isn't even bad for you! If you want to make it even more fancy, decorate it with *Vegan Piping Cream* (page 237).

For variety, try other combinations of juice or fruit. For example, peaches with red grape juice, or strawberries with apple juice; or use cherries instead of grapes (they need to be stoned, though).

Banana Tart

To Serve 8
Allow 1½ hours to prepare (if you have the pre-baked flan shell and including 1 hour to chill)
Each serving provides: 308 kcal, 6 g protein, 40 g carbohydrate, 14 g fat, 5 g fibre

Metric		Imperial/American
1	*Pre-Baked Flan Shell* (page 203)	1
3	large ripe bananas	3
5 tbs	fine cornmeal (or cornflour)	5 tbs
60 g	raw demerara sugar	2 oz/3 tbs
½ litre	soya milk	1 pint/2½ cups
1 tsp	vanilla essence	1 tsp

1 Slice one of the bananas and arrange the slices on the base of the pre-baked flan shell. Mash the other two and set aside.
2 Put the cornmeal and sugar into a saucepan and mix together thoroughly before slowly adding the soya milk and combining to a creamy consistency. Place over a low heat and stir continuously till the mixture thickens. Remove from heat.
3 Stir in the vanilla essence and the mashed bananas and mix well before pouring into the flan shell. Smooth the top and chill for at least an hour before serving.

The only reason we've put this tart in the 'special occasions' section is that it is a bit too rich for everyday use, but it is certainly not time-consuming or expensive to make. Try decorating it with chopped nuts or, for an exotic finish to a really special dinner-party, add a generous topping of *Coconut Cream* (page 239).

Chocolate Tart

To Serve 8
Allow 2½ hours to prepare (if you have the pre-baked flan shell and including 2 hours to chill)
Each serving provides: 344 kcal, 8 g protein, 46 g carbohydrate, 15 g fat, 5 g fibre

Metric		Imperial/American
1	*Pre-Baked Sweet Pastry Shell* (page 204)	1
60 g	cocoa powder (unsweetened)	2 oz/8 tbs
60 g	fine cornmeal (or cornflour)	2 oz/8 tbs
150 g	raw sugar	5 oz/1 cup
¾ litre	soya milk	1½ pints/3½ cups
1 tsp	vanilla essence	1 tsp

1 Put the cocoa powder, cornmeal and sugar into a large saucepan and mix thoroughly.
2 Add the soya milk a little at a time and mix to a smooth creamy consistency taking care to break down any lumps.
3 Stir in the vanilla essence.
4 Use a low heat to bring the mixture to the boil very, very slowly, stirring continuously. Simmer and continue stirring till the mixture thickens (about 5–10 minutes). Then as quickly as you can remove from heat and pour into the pastry shell. (With practice, you can get it to form attractive scallops by revolving the shell as you pour.) Set aside to cool for half an hour.
5 Chill for at least 1½ hours before serving.

Serve this delicious tart with *Vegan Cream* (pages 235–6), freshly-brewed black coffee and brandy to round off a special dinner-party and your guests will wonder where they ever got the idea that vegans were practising a masochistic form of self-denial!

For variety, use carob powder instead of cocoa or try piping the tart with *Vegan Piping Cream* (page 237).

Fruit Flan

To Serve 8
Allow 1½ hours to prepare (including 1 hour to cool and set but assuming you have the pre-baked flan shell and have pre-soaked the dried fruit: if not, see below)
Each serving provides: 321 kcal, 7 g protein, 45 g carbohydrate, 14 g fat, 15 g fibre

Metric		Imperial/American
1	*Pre-Baked Flan Shell* (page 203)	1
¾ litre	water	1½ pints/3½ cups
¼ kg	dried apricots	½ lb/2 cups
180 g	prunes	6 oz/1½ cups
¼ litre	soya milk	½ pint/1¼ cups
2½ tbs	agar flakes	2½ tbs
30 g	chopped nuts (for decoration)	1 oz/1½ tbs

1 Cover the apricots and prunes with the water and leave to soak for several hours or overnight.
2 Remove the stones from the now soft prunes and discard them. Put the prune flesh, the apricots, the soya milk and half of the remaining soaking liquid into a blender and blend to a smooth cream.
3 Add the agar flakes to the rest of the soaking liquid (adding a little extra water if necessary) and bring quickly to the boil then reduce heat and simmer for 5 minutes while stirring continuously.
4 Combine the blended mixture with the agar solution and stir thoroughly.
5 Pour into the flan shell, decorate with chopped nuts and refrigerate till set. Serve chilled.

The only complicated thing about this flan is remembering to soak the dried fruit the previous night. But even if you forgot, you can still make it: simply *stew* the fruit in the recipe liquid till it's soft and then proceed from step 2 above.

The filling is moist enough for the flan to be delicious served on its own, but try also serving it with *Custard* (page 173), *Brandy Sauce* (page 175), *Vegan Cream* (pages 235–6), *Cashew Cream* (page 238) or *Vegan Yoghurt* (page 240).

Banana Curd Cake

To Serve 8–12
Allow 3 hours to prepare (including 2 hours to set and chill)
Each serving (of 12) provides: 281 kcal, 6 g protein, 14 g carbo-hydrate, 23 g fat, 3 g fibre

Metric		Imperial/American
90 g	wholewheat flour	3 oz/¾ cup
90 g	ground almonds	3 oz/¾ cup
30 g	raw sugar	1 oz/1 tbs
125 g	margarine	¼ lb/½ cup
350 g	tofu	¾ lb/1½ cups
4	ripe bananas	4
¼ litre	soya milk	½ pint/1¼ cups
100 ml	sunflower oil	7 tbs
	juice of 1 lemon	
¼ litre	apple juice	½ pint/1¼ cups
3 tbs	agar flakes	3 tbs

1 Put the flour, ground almonds and sugar in a bowl and mix thoroughly. Cut in the margarine and rub together till well blended.
2 Transfer the mixture to a greased, floured cake or similar tin with a loose bottom, about 20 cm (8 in). Gently smooth out and push down the mixture till it evenly covers the base of the tin. Bake in the middle of a moderate oven (177°C/350°F/gas mark 4) for 15 minutes. Remove from oven and leave to cool in the tin.
3 Crumble the tofu into a blender, add the peeled and chopped bananas, soya milk, sunflower oil and lemon juice and blend till smooth and creamy.
4 Put the apple juice and agar flakes into a small saucepan and bring quickly to the boil then reduce heat and simmer for 5 minutes, stirring continuously. Remove from heat, add to the blended banana and tofu mixture and stir till thoroughly combined.
5 Now pour the mixture on to the pastry base in the tin and refrigerate till set and chilled (about 2 hours).

Serve this with freshly-brewed black coffee as a dessert course, or as a snack any time.

The top may be decorated with thin slices of lemon, chopped nuts or *Vegan Piping Cream* (page 237).

Lemon Cheesecake

To Serve 12–16
Allow 3 hours to prepare (including baking and chilling times)
*Each serving (of 16) provides: 225 kcal, 5 g protein, 18 g carbo-
hydrate, 15 g fat, 3 g fibre*

Metric		Imperial/American
1	*Basic Sweet Pastry Mix* (page 204)	1
4	lemons	4
575 g	firm tofu (see below)	1¼ lb/2½ cups
125 ml	soya milk	¼ pint/½ cup
125 ml	sunflower oil	¼ pint/½ cup
125 g	raw demerara sugar	¼ lb/¾ cup
25 ml	vanilla essence	1½ tbs

1 While the pastry is chilling in the refrigerator, finely grate the lemon
  rinds and put the grated peel in a blender, then squeeze the lemons
  and add the juice.
2 Add all the other ingredients and blend together till the mixture is
  smooth and creamy.
3 If you have a 23 cm (9 in) baking-ring, put it on an ovenproof plate,
  roll out the pastry and line the base with it. Otherwise a pie, flan or
  cake tin with a loose bottom may be used. Pour in the blended
  mixture, smooth the top and bake in the middle of a warm oven
  (163°C/325°F/gas mark 3) for 1¼ hours. The finished cake will be a
  rich, golden brown on top.
4 Allow to cool on a rack and then chill thoroughly before attempting
  to remove from the baking-ring.
5 Decorate the top with thin slices of lemon, chopped nuts or toasted
  sesame seeds.

You may need to adjust the timing for your oven to get the cheesecake
to cook through to the centre without the top burning. Also, be sure to
use *firm* tofu or your finished cake *may* ooze water. (This doesn't detract
from the pleasure of eating it but does complicate serving it.) If you can
only get ordinary tofu, remove as much excess water as you can before
beginning by pressing it between two boards for an hour or so.

This may all seem a bit of a performance but the end result tastes
wonderful and, unlike its non-vegan counterpart, contains nothing that
is bad for you. Nor does it sit heavily on the stomach if you succumb to
the temptation to eat too much of it!

Serve it as a dessert course with freshly-brewed black coffee and it
will turn a light meal into a feast.

Chocolate Chestnut Chalices

To Serve 6
Allow about 4½ hours to prepare (including 4 hours to chill)
*Each serving provides: 286 kcal, 5 g protein, 28 g carbohydrate,
17 g fat, 10 g fibre*

Metric		Imperial/American
1 jar	*Coconut Cream* (page 239)	1 cup
½ kg	sweetened chestnut purée	17½ oz tin/large can
90 g	margarine	3 oz/6 tbs
3 tbs	unsweetened cocoa powder	3 tbs
2 tbs	Grand Marnier or rum	2 tbs
6	glacé chestnuts as a garnish	6

1 Make up the coconut cream (page 239) and put it in the fridge to chill.
2 Put the chestnut purée, margarine, cocoa and Grand Marnier in a basin and cream together.
3 Set 90 g (6 tbs) of the coconut cream aside to use as a garnish. Add the rest to the chestnut mixture and whip to a firmish mousse.
4 Spoon into individual chalice style serving-dishes, pipe a decorative dollop of the remaining coconut cream onto each, top with a glacé chestnut and refrigerate till needed. Serve well chilled.

If you can't get glacé chestnuts, decorate with flaked almonds or any chopped nuts. But don't use glacé cherries which are *not* vegan.

These *Chocolate Chestnut Chalices* are quick and easy to prepare yet luscious, lavish and light to eat, and we readily admit an attack of alliteration is the only reason we've suggested 'chalice style' serving-dishes.

Rum and Chocolate Cheesecake

To Serve 12–16
Allow 3 hours to prepare (including baking and chilling time)
Each serving (of 16) provides: 368 kcal, 8 g protein, 19 g carbo-hydrate, 26 g fat, 3 g fibre

Metric		Imperial/American
125 g	wholewheat flour	¼ lb/1 cup
125 g	ground almonds	¼ lb/1 cup
225 g	raw demerara sugar	7 oz/1¼ cups
150 g	margarine	5 oz/scant ⅔ cup
¾ kg	firm tofu	1½ lb/3 cups
175 ml	sunflower oil	6 fl oz/¾ cup
175 ml	dark rum	6 fl oz/¾ cup
125 ml	soya milk	¼ pint/½ cup
60 g	unsweetened cocoa powder	2 oz/7 tbs
½ tbs	vanilla essence	½ tbs

1 Put the flour, ground almonds and 1 tbs of the sugar in a bowl and mix well together, then rub in the margarine to form a firm dough.
2 If you have a 23 cm (9 in) baking-ring, put it on an ovenproof plate. Flatten the dough between your hands, put it in the baking-ring and press it down firmly to form a smooth, thick base. Alternatively, use a pie, flan or cake tin.
3 Crumble the tofu into a blender, add all the remaining ingredients and blend together till smooth and creamy. (You may need to do this in two goes.)
4 Pour the blended mixture over the pastry base and bake in the middle of a warm oven (163°C/325°F/gas mark 3) for 1¼ hours.
5 Allow to cool on a rack and then chill thoroughly before attempting to remove from the baking-ring or tin.

This tastes wonderful just as it is without any decoration but you may wish to arrange halved strawberries around the rim and sprinkle chopped nuts in the centre. If you want to serve it as a spectacular finale to a really special meal, ice it with *Vegan Piping Cream* (page 237) as well.

Sauces and Dressings

Sauces

Dressings

Sauces and Dressings

Our object in this section is to demonstrate that it is perfectly feasible – even easy – to make a wide range of vegan sauces and dressings. Indeed, it's an area in which it is a pleasure to be inventive and imaginative. And it is well worth the effort, for a good sauce can turn any simple steamed or blanched vegetable into a memorable dish.

We've given a range of savoury and sweet sauces and dressings to get you started and advise you not to be put off by the mystique that seems in some quarters to be associated with sauce-making – as if they were in a different category from ordinary cooking. This is nonsense. They are as easy to make as anything else provided you're prepared to follow simple instructions. The only secret, if you can call it that, of smooth, lump-free sauces is *continuous stirring*. But they do spoil quickly so always make them last – just before serving the dish they are to accompany.

For the most part we have used 100 per cent wholewheat flour as a thickening agent. Why is *whiteness* in a sauce supposed to be superior? Sauces made with 100 per cent wholewheat flour are not only better for you but actually have an attractive, nutty flavour of their own.

We have also occasionally specified *arrowroot* when we wanted a thin or transparent sauce. This is available in most wholefood shops (sometimes for some mysterious reason labelled with its Japanese name '*kuzu*') and also in some grocery stores – though we suspect that chemical preservatives may have been added in this case.

Finally, a word or two about salad dressings. Vitamins A, D, E, and K are all oil-soluble. This means they are only assimilable if some oil is eaten at the same time, so there is a sound nutritional reason for serving a salad of raw vegetables with an oil-based dressing.

Sunflower oil has probably the most pleasant and unobtrusive flavour, is cheap and widely available and is completely free of saturated fat (unlike palm or coconut oils). So it's a good basis for most dressings where other oils aren't specifically mentioned. But cold-pressed olive oil is essential for some dishes for the unique taste it contributes. We have used it sparingly only because it is so expensive in this country. But if you should find yourself travelling in the Mediterranean region, don't forget to bring back as large a tin of it as you can carry and stash it away in your larder for a sunny day.

Basic Plain Sauce

To Make 4–6 Average Servings
Allow 5–10 minutes to prepare
*Each serving (of 6) provides: 61 kcal, 2 g protein, 3 g carbohydrate,
5 g fat, 1 g fibre*

Metric		Imperial/American
30 g	margarine	1 oz/2 tbs
3 tbs	100 per cent wholewheat flour	3 tbs
¼ litre	soya milk	½ pint/1¼ cups

(Note: if you haven't made a sauce before, read the introductory
remarks on page 163 before beginning.)

1 Melt the margarine in a (preferably thick) saucepan over a low heat.
2 When it has completely melted but before it begins to bubble, add
   the flour and stir in. Continue to heat gently and stir for 2–3
   minutes.
3 Add the soya milk a little at a time, stirring continuously. Continue
   stirring after you've added the full amount until the mixture
   thickens.
4 The sauce is now ready for the appropriate flavouring.

This makes a thick, plain sauce to which you can add flavourings as
desired. It forms the basis of several recipes. To make a thinner sauce,
simply use more milk.

Basil and Tomato Sauce

To Make 4 Average Servings
Allow 10 minutes to prepare
*Each serving provides: 80 kcal, 1 g protein, 5 g carbohydrate, 6 g fat,
2 g fibre*

Metric		Imperial/American
½ kg	fresh or tinned tomatoes	1 lb
30 g	margarine	1 oz/2 tbs
1½ tbs	wholewheat flour	1½ tbs
2 tbs	fresh chopped basil (or 1 tbs dried basil)	2 tbs
1 tsp	freshly-ground black pepper	1 tsp
1 tsp	salt	1 tsp

1 Liquidize the skinned tomatoes (page 255) in a blender and set
  aside.
2 Melt the margarine in a small saucepan over a low heat, stir in the
  flour and cook gently for a few minutes.
3 Stir in the liquidized tomatoes a little at a time. Now add the
  remaining ingredients, stirring continuously. Bring to the boil then
  reduce heat and simmer, still stirring, till the mixture thickens
  slightly. Serve immediately.

This strong, richly-coloured sauce is at its best made with fresh basil but
is still very good made with dried. Serve it with lightly-boiled new
potatoes, or any other steamed or blanched vegetable that takes your
fancy. It's also good with *Plain Rice* (page 84) or *Olive and Potato Flan*
(page 62).

Savoury Apple Sauce

To Make 4 Average Servings
Allow 25 minutes to prepare
*Each serving provides: 34 kcal, 1 g protein, 6 g carbohydrate, 1 g fat,
1 g fibre*

Metric		Imperial/American
1	medium cooking apple	1
125 ml	water	¼ pint/½ cup
2 tsp	celery seeds	2 tsp
125 ml	soya milk	¼ pint/½ cup
	salt and pepper to taste	

1 Peel, core and chop the apple, put it in a small saucepan together
  with the water and celery seeds, bring to the boil then reduce heat
  and simmer, uncovered, till the apple has gone to a mush (about 15
  minutes).
2 Remove from heat, stir in the soya milk, season with salt and pepper
  to taste and serve.

This light sauce goes well with simple steamed or blanched vegetables
such as cauliflower, broccoli, Brussels sprouts, or even potatoes. It is
also a good accompaniment to any main dish that seems a bit dry, such
as *Cashew Loaf* (page 77) or *Bulgur Bake* (page 49), or rice or any
cooked grain.

Red Wine Sauce

To Make 4–6 Average Servings
Allow 5–10 minutes to prepare
*Each serving (of 6) provides: 77 kcal, 1 g protein, 3 g carbohydrate,
4 g fat, 1 g fibre*

Metric		Imperial/American
30 g	margarine	1 oz/2 tbs
3 tbs	wholewheat flour	3 tbs
¼ litre	dry red wine	8 fl oz/1 cup
125 ml	soya milk	¼ pint/½ cup
	salt and pepper to taste	

1 Melt the margarine in a small saucepan over a low heat.
2 When it's completely melted but before it begins to bubble, add the flour and stir in. Continue to heat gently and stir for 2–3 minutes.
3 Add the red wine a little at a time, stirring continuously, then begin adding the soya milk a little at a time. Continue stirring after you've added the full amount until the mixture thickens.
4 Add salt and pepper to taste and serve.

This is a good, simple sauce just as it is, but try also adding finely chopped mushrooms, onions or mixed herbs; or stir in 2 tbs of peanut butter after step 3.

It goes well with any steamed or blanched green vegetable, sautéed mushrooms or any root vegetable to make an appetizing side dish.

Lemon Curry Sauce

To Make 4 Average Servings
Allow 10 minutes to prepare
*Each serving provides: 42 kcal, 3 g protein, 4 g carbohydrate, 1 g fat,
1 g fibre*

Metric		Imperial/American
¾ tbs	arrowroot powder	¾ tbs
¼ litre	soya milk	½ pint/1¼ cups
25 ml	lemon juice	1½ tbs
2 tsp	*Garam Masala* (page 253)	2 tsp
½ tsp	ground turmeric	½ tsp
½ tsp	salt	½ tsp

1 Put the arrowroot into a small saucepan, add a little cold soya milk
  and stir till completely dissolved, then stir in the rest of the milk.
2 Stir in all the remaining ingredients and bring the mixture slowly to
  the boil, stirring continuously, then reduce heat and simmer till the
  sauce thickens. Serve immediately.

This low-fat sauce is excellent with any steamed or blanched vegetable,
cooked grain or pulse, but is particularly good with boiled potatoes.
  Leftovers are good served chilled as a starter.

Sweet and Sour Sauce

To Make 4–6 Average Servings
Allow 10 minutes to prepare
*Each serving (of 6) provides: 74 kcal, 1 g protein, 4 g carbohydrate,
4 g fat, negligible fibre*

Metric		Imperial/American
25 ml	oil	1½ tbs
2	cloves garlic	2
2 tbs	freshly grated ginger (or 1 tbs dried ginger)	2 tbs
¾ tbs	arrowroot powder	¾ tbs
¼ litre	water	½ pint/1¼ cups
25 ml	cider vinegar	1½ tbs
1½ tbs	tomato paste	1½ tbs
25 ml	soya sauce	1½ tbs
45 ml	apple concentrate or raw demerara sugar	3 tbs

1 Put the oil in a small saucepan over a low heat. Skin and crush the garlic and add it to the pan. Finely grate the ginger and add it to the pan. Heat gently for a few minutes, stirring occasionally.
2 Meanwhile, dissolve the arrowroot in the cold water then add all the remaining ingredients and stir till well combined.
3 Pour the arrowroot mixture into the saucepan and bring to a simmer, stirring continuously, till the mixture thickens.

This can be poured over stir-fried vegetables to make the traditional Chinese dish, or over any steamed or blanched vegetable to turn it into a tasty and unusual side dish.

Perfectionists may wish to sieve the sauce (after step 3) prior to serving in order to remove the small pieces of grated garlic and ginger, but these two lazy cooks prefer to leave them in.

Spicy Peanut Sauce

To Make 6 Average Servings
Allow 10 minutes to prepare
*Each serving provides: 210 kcal, 2 g protein, 3 g carbohydrate,
21 g fat, 1 g fibre*

Metric		Imperial/American
1	clove garlic	1
2 tbs	freshly grated ginger (or 1 tbs dried ginger)	2 tbs
1	lemon	1
100 ml	sunflower oil	7 tbs
25 ml	soya sauce	1½ tbs
½ tsp	chilli powder	½ tsp
3 tbs	peanut butter	3 tbs
25 ml	water	1½ tbs

1 Skin and crush the garlic and put it in a blender.
2 Grate the ginger in with the garlic.
3 Squeeze the lemon and add the juice.
4 Add all the other ingredients and blend to a rich, creamy texture. If it seems too thick, add a little more water and blend again. Check the seasoning and adjust if necessary before serving.

This can be served cold, but is equally good gently heated in a small saucepan and poured hot over a mixed salad. Other suggestions are given under individual recipes.

Try also serving it as a dip – with *Plain Oatcakes* (page 216) or with sticks of raw carrot, fennel or celery.

Orange and Coconut Sauce

To Make 4–6 Average Servings
Allow 10 minutes to prepare
Each serving (of 6) provides: 139 kcal, 1 g protein, 6 g carbohydrate, 12 g fat, 3 g fibre

Metric		Imperial/American
30 g	margarine	1 oz/2 tbs
1½ tbs	wholewheat flour	1½ tbs
¼ litre	orange juice	½ pint/1¼ cups
½ tsp	salt	½ tsp
90 g	creamed coconut	3 oz/⅓ cup

1 Melt the margarine in a small saucepan over a low heat.
2 When it's completely melted but before it begins to bubble, add the flour and stir in. Continue to heat gently and stir for 2–3 minutes.
3 Add the orange juice a little at a time, stirring continuously to avoid lumps.
4 Add the salt and coconut and continue to stir until all the coconut is dissolved. Bring to a simmer and serve.

This is an unusual and fruity sauce that will liven up any steamed or blanched vegetable to give you a delicious side dish. Try it with cauliflower, broccoli or Brussels sprouts. It's also good poured over hot cooked grains such as rice or bulgur.

Toasted Almond Sauce

To Make 4–6 Average Servings
Allow 20 minutes to prepare
Each serving (of 6) provides: 136 kcal, 5 g protein, 2 g carbohydrate, 12 g fat, 4 g fibre

Metric		Imperial/American
125 g	almonds	¼ lb/1 cup
¼ litre	soya milk	½ pint/1¼ cups
25 ml	soya sauce	1½ tbs
15 ml	red wine vinegar	1 tbs
	juice of ½ lemon	
½ tsp	mustard powder	½ tsp
½ tsp	ground nutmeg	½ tsp

1 Coarsely chop the almonds, put them in a dry pan over a medium heat and stir continuously till they are lightly toasted (about 5 minutes). Remove from pan and place in a blender.
2 Add all the other ingredients and blend till smooth.
3 If the sauce is to be used in a casserole and baked, it can be used just as it is. Otherwise, transfer to a small saucepan and heat gently till warmed through.

This is good poured over steamed or blanched green vegetables just before serving or over a casserole before baking to get a crunchy topping.

For variety, use lemon juice instead of vinegar or ground cloves instead of nutmeg.

Custard

To Make 4–6 Average Servings
Allow 15 minutes to prepare
*Each serving (of 6) provides: 88 kcal, 3 g protein, 14 g carbohydrate,
1 g fat, 1 g fibre*

Metric		Imperial/American
2½ tbs	cornflour	2½ tbs
3 tbs	raw demerara sugar	3 tbs
1 tbs	vanilla essence	1 tbs
½ litre	soya milk	1 pint/2½ cups
	pinch of salt	

1 Put the cornflour in a large basin or jug, add the sugar, vanilla essence, a pinch of salt and a little of the cold soya milk and stir till smooth.
2 Put the rest of the soya milk in a saucepan and bring nearly to the boil then remove from heat and pour into the cornflour mixture, stirring continuously.
3 Return the custard to the saucepan, bring quickly back to the boil, stirring continuously, and serve.

This may be served hot, just as it is, poured over sweet flans and tarts or poured into individual serving-dishes over sliced fresh fruit and served hot or chilled. It can also be used for trifles.

Proprietary brands of custard powder are basically cornflour with artificial colouring added to imitate the traditional yellow of non-vegan custard made with egg yolks.

Hot Chocolate Sauce

To Make 3–4 Average Servings
Allow 10 minutes to prepare
Each serving (of 4) provides: 132 kcal, 4 g protein, 9 g carbohydrate, 9 g fat, 1 g fibre

Metric		Imperial/American
30 g	margarine	1 oz/2 tbs
1½ tbs	fine cornmeal	1½ tbs
3 tbs	cocoa powder	3 tbs
3 tbs	raw demerara sugar	3 tbs
400 ml	soya milk	¾ pint/2 cups

1 Melt the margarine in a small saucepan over a low heat, then add the cornmeal and cook gently for 2 minutes, stirring continuously.
2 Add the cocoa powder and sugar and continue to heat gently for a few more minutes, still stirring all the time.
3 Begin adding the soya milk a little at a time, still stirring continuously, till all the milk is in. Continue to stir and heat gently till the mixture thickens.

Serve this rich creamy sauce hot with *Apple Pie* (page 146), *Apple and Banana Crumble* (page 145), *Fruit Juice Jellies* (page 138) or *Plain Ice-Cream* (page 242), or cold with fruit or in trifles. It can also be poured into individual serving-dishes, allowed to cool and then served chilled with a topping of chopped nuts.

Brandy Sauce

To Make 3–4 Average Servings
Allow 10 minutes to prepare
Each serving (of 4) provides: 140 kcal, 2 g protein, 7 g carbohydrate, 10 g fat, 1 g fibre

Metric		Imperial/American
45 g	margarine	1½ oz/3 tbs
1½ tbs	fine cornmeal	1½ tbs
¼ litre	soya milk	½ pint/1¼ cups
25 ml	maple syrup	1½ tbs
45 ml	brandy	3 tbs
1 tsp	vanilla essence	1 tsp

1 Melt the margarine in a small saucepan over a low heat then add the cornmeal and cook gently for 2 minutes, stirring continuously.
2 Continuing to stir, add the soya milk a little at a time, then the maple syrup. Continue to heat gently and stir till the mixture thickens.
3 Remove from heat, stir in the brandy and vanilla essence and serve.

This is delicious served hot with *Plain Ice-Cream* (page 242), *Fruit Flan* (page 155), *Chocolate Tart* (page 154) or *Apple and Banana Crumble* (page 145); try it also cold with cold *Baked Apples* (page 143) or *Peach Pudding* (page 144). Any left over makes a delicious addition to trifle.

Basic French Dressing

To Make a Jarful (275 ml)
Allow 5–10 minutes to prepare
Each (2 tbs) serving provides: 252 kcal, negligible protein, negligible carbohydrate, 27 g fat, negligible fibre

Metric		Imperial/American
1	lemon	1
1	clove garlic (optional)	1
1 tsp	salt	1 tsp
1 tsp	freshly-ground black pepper	1 tsp
½ tsp	mustard powder	½ tsp
	enough olive oil to fill a jam jar	

1 Squeeze the lemon and put the juice in a suitable jar – jam jars are perfect.
2 Skin and crush the garlic and add it to the jar.
3 Add the salt, pepper and mustard powder and fill the jar nearly to the top with olive (or other suitable vegetable) oil.
4 Seal the jar and shake well till all the ingredients are thoroughly mixed.

This dressing will keep well for days if stored in the fridge. When you finish a jar, immediately prepare another and this way you'll always have a dressing ready for your green and other salads.

For variety, try white wine vinegar, or cider vinegar, instead of lemon juice – each adds its own distinct flavour.

Fruit Juice Dressing

To Make 4–6 Average Servings
Allow 5 minutes to prepare
Each serving (of 6) provides: 79 kcal, negligible protein, 1 g carbo-hydrate, 8 g fat, 0 g fibre

Metric		Imperial/American
45 ml	sunflower oil	3 tbs
75 ml	orange (or other suitable) juice	5 tbs

1 Put the ingredients in a jar and mix thoroughly by shaking.

Most fruit juices can be used to make light and unusual dressings which go particularly well with the more substantial kinds of salad produced when you include grains, rice or potatoes; they also make a welcome change from the conventional savoury varieties. Orange, apple and grapefruit are especially suitable, but why not experiment with other, more exotic kinds? Perfectionists would, of course, use freshly-squeezed juice.

Tahini Dressing

To Make a Jarful
Allow 10 minutes to prepare
Each (3 tbs) serving provides: 272 kcal, 4 g protein, 5 g carbohydrate, 27 g fat, 2 g fibre

Metric		Imperial/American
1	lemon	1
75 ml	tahini	5 tbs
75 ml	olive oil	5 tbs
75 ml	water	5 tbs
25 ml	soya sauce	1½ tbs

1 Squeeze the lemon and put the juice into a suitable jar. (Jam jars are perfect.)
2 Add all the other ingredients, seal the jar and shake till thoroughly mixed. Refrigerate till needed.

This goes well with any kind of sprout salad, but try it also with potato salad, sliced raw courgettes, cauliflower or shredded cabbage.

Tofu Dressing

To Make a Jarful
Allow 10 minutes to prepare
Each (3 tbs) serving provides: 154 kcal, 2 g protein, 1 g carbohydrate, 16 g fat, negligible fibre

Metric		Imperial/American
125 g	tofu	¼ lb/½ cup
2	cloves garlic	2
1	lemon	1
75 ml	oil	5 tbs
75 ml	water	5 tbs
15 ml	soya sauce	1 tbs
½ tsp	mustard powder	½ tsp
½ tsp	salt	½ tsp
½ tsp	freshly-ground black pepper	½ tsp

1 Crumble the tofu into a blender.
2 Skin and crush the garlic and add it to the tofu.
3 Squeeze the lemon and add the juice.
4 Add all the remaining ingredients and blend to a thick, smooth, creamy consistency.

Use this dressing to turn almost any raw, chopped or grated vegetable into a delicious starter. Try it with finely chopped cucumbers, grated carrots or sliced courgettes. Or try pouring it over a steamed or blanched green vegetable as a side dish to a rich and substantial main course.

For variety, try adding a herb you particularly like, or a pinch of cayenne pepper to give it a spicy kick.

Yoghurt Salad Dressing

To Make 4–6 Average Servings
Allow 5 minutes to prepare (if you have the yoghurt)
*Each serving (of 6) provides: 13 kcal, 1 g protein, 1 g carbohydrate,
1 g fat, negligible fibre*

Metric		Imperial/American
125 ml	*Vegan Yoghurt* (page 240)	¼ pint/½ cup
1 tsp	freshly grated ginger (or ½ tsp dried ginger)	1 tsp
	salt and pepper to taste	

1 Put all the ingredients in a salad bowl and mix thoroughly before
adding the salad itself.

This is excellent with potato salad, cucumber, sliced raw courgettes,
Asparagus Salad (page 131), cauliflower, or avocados. For variety, try
using ground cinnamon or cloves instead of ginger.

Cashew Cream Dressing

To Make a Jarful
Allow 5 minutes to prepare
*Each (3 tbs) serving provides: 82 kcal, 2 g protein, 3 g carbohydrate,
7 g fat, 2 g fibre*

Metric		Imperial/American
90 g	cashew pieces	3 oz/¾ cup
125 ml	soya milk	¼ pint/½ cup
	juice of 1 lemon	
15 ml	soya sauce	1 tbs
½ tsp	freshly-ground black pepper	½ tsp

1 Put all the ingredients in a blender and blend to a thick, smooth,
  creamy consistency.
2 Transfer to a suitable storage jar (jam jars are perfect) and
  refrigerate till needed.

This is rich, creamy and slightly sweet. Fill avocado halves to the brim
with it and sprinkle on some celery seeds to make a starter, or serve it
poured liberally over thinly-sliced tomatoes.

For variety, try white wine vinegar instead of lemon juice, or add a
pinch of mustard.

Mayonnaise

To Make a Jarful
Allow 10 minutes to prepare
*Each (3 tbs) serving provides: 140 kcal, 1 g protein, 1 g carbohydrate,
14 g fat, 1 g fibre*

Metric		**Imperial/American**
1	lemon	1
125 ml	soya milk	¼ pint/½ cup
15 ml	soya sauce (or ½ tsp salt)	1 tbs
75–90 ml	olive oil	5–6 tbs

1 Squeeze the lemon and put the juice into a blender.
2 Add the soya milk and soya sauce (or salt).
3 Blend together while very slowly adding the oil till the mixture
  thickens.
4 Transfer to a suitable storage jar (jam jars are perfect) and chill till
  needed.

The mayonnaise can be stored for several days sealed in its jar in the
refrigerator.

Serve it on salads or as directed in recipes. Try it, for example, with
potato salad, garnished with fresh chopped dill.

Avocado Dressing

To Make a Jarful
Allow 10 minutes to prepare
Each (3 tbs) serving provides: 47 kcal, 2 g protein, 1 g carbohydrate, 4 g fat, 1 g fibre

Metric		Imperial/American
1	ripe avocado	1
1	lemon	1
125 ml	soya milk	¼ pint/½ cup
½ tsp	mixed spice	½ tsp
½ tsp	salt	½ tsp
½ tsp	freshly-ground black pepper	½ tsp

1 Scoop out the flesh of the avocado and put it in a blender.
2 Squeeze the lemon and add the juice.
3 Add all the remaining ingredients and blend to a rich, smooth, thick, creamy consistency.
4 Transfer to a suitable storage jar (jam jars are perfect) and refrigerate till needed.

This sumptuous, pale-green dressing can be used exactly as you would use mayonnaise. It is at its best served immediately after making as, despite the presence of the lemon juice, it gradually darkens, though this does not affect its taste.

If you want to make it a little thinner, simply use some extra soya milk at step 3.

For variety, try adding 1 tbs freshly-grated ginger.

Spreads

Savoury Spreads

Sweet Spreads

Spreads

Spreads are useful for sandwiches and snacks or as one course of a large meal, served with breads, biscuits or celery. They're also good as travel food. Take a jar of home-made spread with you when you go abroad and all you'll need, to remain blissfully vegan in an omnivore world, is locally bought bread and fruit.

But beware of supermarket spreads. Though many look as if they might be vegan, careful study of ingredients lists often reveals the presence of dairy products such as milk powder or whey. Besides, who needs them? As we hope this section demonstrates, it's easy to make a mouth-watering array of spreads without recourse to animal remains.

We've given a range of different techniques to get you started and hope you'll soon start inventing your own – especially as jars of home-made spread make welcome presents for vegan and omnivore friends alike.

Since most of the vegan spreads in wholefood shops use the French word '*pâté*' in their names we suspect manufacturers are trying to cash in on the snob-appeal of *pâté de foie gras* – traditionally taken, along with caviar, to represent the epitome of high living. So we hope our readers will forgive us a brief digression on the subject.

Literally translated *pâté de foie gras* means '*fatty liver paste*' and it is in our view one of the most appalling products of the food industry. It is made by force-feeding geese – literally by *screwing three kilos of fat-enriched maize down their throats at a time*. This is the equivalent in human terms of force-feeding someone thirteen kilos of oily spaghetti. The birds are restrained between sessions of this torture in tiny cages to prevent any movement which might work off surplus fat. This mindless cruelty continues for weeks till their livers have swollen to four times their normal weight and they are then killed. How anyone could want to eat the diseased livers of these unfortunate creatures beggars the imagination and anyone who buys even one pot of this obscene product should understand that they are helping perpetuate a truly barbaric trade.

Tahini Spread

To Make a Jarful
Allow 10 minutes to prepare
Each (3 tbs) serving provides: 200 kcal, 7 g protein, 11 g carbo-hydrate, 15 g fat, 2 g fibre

Metric		Imperial/American
1	lemon	1
75 ml	tahini	5 tbs
75 ml	water	5 tbs
60 g	sunflower seeds	2 oz/6 tbs
1½ tbs	miso	1½ tbs

1 Squeeze the lemon and put the juice in a blender.
2 Add the remaining ingredients and blend to a smooth, thick paste.

This is strong and piquant and should be spread sparingly on plain biscuits or bread. It also makes a good sandwich filling.

Cashew and Sunflower Spread

To Make a Jarful
Allow 10–15 minutes to prepare
Each 100 g provides: 229 kcal, 6 g protein, 12 g carbohydrate, 18 g fat, 3 g fibre

Metric		Imperial/American
4	spring onions (or 3 tbs freshly-chopped chives)	4
125 g	cashew pieces	¼ lb/1 cup
125 g	sunflower seeds	¼ lb/1 cup
125 ml	water	¼ pint/½ cup
	salt and pepper to taste	

1 Wash, trim and chop the onions and put them in a blender.
2 Add all the other ingredients and blend to a thick, smooth paste.
   Transfer to a suitable storage jar and refrigerate till needed.

Particularly good in sandwiches, but try it also spread thinly on wholewheat bread, *Plain Oatcakes* (page 216) or crispbread; it also makes a good dip, served with sticks of celery, fennel or carrot.

Savoury Spread

To Make 3–4 Jarfuls
Allow ½ hour to prepare
*Each 100 g provides: 174 kcal, 2 g protein, 12 g carbohydrate,
12 g fat, 3 g fibre*

Metric		Imperial/American
½ kg	potatoes	1 lb
125 g	margarine	¼ lb/½ cup
2	medium onions	2
2	cloves garlic	2
¼ kg	mushrooms	½ lb
2 tbs	freshly ground ginger (or 1 tbs dried ground ginger)	2 tbs
2 tsp	ground cloves	2 tsp
1½ tsp	ground nutmeg	1½ tsp
3 tsp	thyme	3 tsp
45 ml	soya sauce	3 tbs
3 tbs	buckwheat flour	3 tbs
3 tbs	soya flour	3 tbs
	salt and pepper to taste	

1 Scrub the potatoes and remove any blemishes (and peel them if you wish), then slice and plunge them into a large pan of (unsalted) boiling water. Reduce heat and simmer till tender (about 8–12 minutes). Remove from heat and drain in a colander.
2 Put the margarine to melt in a large saucepan over a low heat. Meanwhile, skin and finely dice the onions and add them to the pan. Skin and crush the garlic and stir it in with the onions. Continue to sauté until the onion goes transparent.
3 Meanwhile, wash and finely dice the mushrooms and add them to the pan. Continue to cook gently, stirring often.
4 Grate the ginger directly into the pan, then stir in the cloves, nutmeg and thyme and continue heating gently and stirring for a few more minutes.
5 Remove from heat, add the soya sauce and cooked potatoes then the two flours and mash all the ingredients together till you have a smooth, creamy texture.
6 Season with salt and pepper to taste and transfer to suitable storage jars. Allow to cool before serving.

This is delicious in sandwiches, spread on *Plain Oatcakes* (page 216) or on crispbread. It also makes a good filling for pasties or individual savoury tarts.

For variety, try different combinations of herbs and spices.

Tomato Spread

To Make 3–4 Jarfuls
Allow ½ hour to prepare
Each 100 g provides: 178 kcal, 3 g protein, 13 g carbohydrate,
13 g fat, 3 g fibre

Metric		Imperial/American
½ kg	potatoes	1 lb
125 g	margarine	¼ lb/½ cup
2	medium onions	2
125 g	mushrooms	¼ lb
45 ml	sunflower oil	3 tbs
6 tbs	tomato paste	6 tbs
2 tsp	marjoram (preferably freshly chopped)	2 tsp
2 tsp	basil (preferably freshly chopped)	2 tsp
½ tsp	cayenne pepper	½ tsp
45 ml	soya sauce	3 tbs
3 tbs	buckwheat flour	3 tbs
3 tbs	soya flour	3 tbs
	salt and pepper to taste	

1 Scrub the potatoes and remove any blemishes (peel them if you wish), then slice and plunge them into a large pan of (unsalted) boiling water. Reduce heat and simmer till tender (about 8–12 minutes). Remove from heat and drain in a colander.
2 Put the margarine in a large saucepan over a low heat.
3 While it is melting, skin and finely dice the onions, add them to the pan and sauté until transparent.
4 Wash and finely dice the mushrooms, add to the pan with the sunflower oil and sauté till tender.
5 Stir in the tomato paste, marjoram, basil and cayenne and continue heating gently for a few more minutes.
6 Remove from heat, add the cooked potatoes and all the remaining ingredients and mash to a smooth, creamy texture.
7 Check the seasoning and transfer to suitable storage jars. Allow to cool before serving.

Use as a sandwich filling, or spread on plain biscuits or crispbread; or try cutting celery into bite-sized sticks and spreading it in the hollows.
   For variety, try different combinations of herbs or add 2 tsp *Garam Masala* (page 253) at step 2 and omit the cayenne pepper.

Savoury Apple Spread

To Make 3–4 Jarfuls
Allow ¾ hour to prepare
Each 100 g provides: 108 kcal, 5 g protein, 15 g carbohydrate,
4 g fat, 4 g fibre

Metric		Imperial/American
¼ kg	brown lentils	½ lb/1 ¼ cups
¾ litre	water	1 ½ pints/3 ½ cups
¾ kg	Bramley cooking apples	1 ½ lb/3 medium
1	large onion	1
25 ml	olive oil	1 ½ tbs
3 tbs	tahini	3 tbs
	salt and pepper to taste	

1 Put the lentils in a saucepan with the water and simmer, partially covered, till they soften. (Add more water from time to time, as necessary, to prevent them from sticking.)
2 Peel, core and slice the apples, put them in another saucepan with 2 tbs of water and cook to a mush.
3 Skin and finely chop the onion, place it in a frying-pan with the oil and sauté till it begins to brown.
4 Put all the ingredients together in the largest pan, add the tahini and salt and pepper to taste and mix well. The finished spread has a thick, crunchy texture.
5 Transfer the mixture to suitable storage jars (jam jars are perfect), seal and refrigerate till needed.

This makes a tasty sandwich filling or can be spread on wholewheat bread or crispbread as a light snack. Try also serving it as a dip with sticks of celery or carrot. It can also be used as a filling for pasties or individual savoury pies.

Walnut and Garlic Spread

To Serve 4–6
Allow 10 minutes to prepare
*Each serving (of 6) provides: 369 kcal, 4 g protein, 2 g carbohydrate,
38 g fat, 2 g fibre*

Metric		Imperial/American
2	cloves garlic	2
¼ kg	walnuts	½ lb/2 cups
100 ml	olive oil	7 tbs
½ tsp	salt	½ tsp

1 Skin and crush the garlic and put it in a blender.
2 Add all the other ingredients and blend until the walnuts are
   reduced to tiny pieces.

This is so rich that although the recipe makes only a little, it will go a
long way. Try spreading it thinly on *Plain Oatcakes* (page 216) or
crispbread.

   The walnuts can be ground by hand, using a pestle and mortar and
then mixed with the other ingredients – if you haven't got a blender.

   For variety, try adding 5–6 tbs water at step 1 to make a less rich,
smoother, creamier consistency that makes a good sandwich filling.

Chutney

To Make 3–4 Jarfuls
Allow 1 hour to prepare
Each 100 g provides: 45 kcal, 1 g protein, 10 g carbohydrate,
0 g fat, 2 g fibre

Metric		Imperial/American
2 tbs	pickling spice	2 tbs
¼ litre	cider vinegar	½ pint/1¼ cups
½ kg	onions	1 lb/2 large
1	large cooking apple	1
½ kg	tomatoes (preferably green)	1 lb
60 g	dried apricots	2 oz/½ cup
2 tsp	mixed spice	2 tsp
¼ tsp	chilli powder	¼ tsp
2 tsp	salt	2 tsp
90 g	raisins	3 oz/3 tbs
45 ml	apple concentrate	3 tbs

1 Put the pickling spice and vinegar into a small saucepan, bring to the boil then reduce heat, cover and simmer for 10 minutes.
2 Meanwhile, finely chop the onions and put them in a large (preferably heavy) saucepan.
3 Coarsely chop the apple and the tomatoes and add them to the pan.
4 Strain in the vinegar (the pickling spices may now be discarded) and bring quickly to the boil, then reduce heat and simmer, covered, for 20 minutes, stirring often.
5 Halve the apricots and add them to the pan together with all the remaining ingredients and simmer for a further 20 minutes, still stirring often to prevent sticking.
6 Allow to cool and transfer to suitable storage jars – jam jars are ideal.

The vinegar acts as a preservative so you can make lots of this fruity chutney if you want to.

For variety, try adding at step 2 other finely chopped vegetables such as peppers, carrots or cauliflower, or add 1 tbs freshly-ground ginger (or 2 tsp dried ground ginger) or other spices to suit your own taste.

Carob and Banana Spread

To Make a Jarful
Allow 10 minutes to prepare
Each 100 g provides: 179 kcal, 5 g protein, 15 g carbohydrate,
12 g fat, 6 g fibre

Metric		Imperial/American
½ kg	bananas	1 lb/3 large
1	lemon	1
125 g	ground almonds	¼ lb/1 cup
3 tbs	carob powder	3 tbs

1 Peel the bananas and mash them to a pulp in a bowl.
2 Squeeze the lemon and add the juice.
3 Add the ground almonds and carob powder and continue to stir and mash to form a thick, smooth paste.

This nutritious spread makes a good substitute for margarine when spread on wholewheat bread.

Store in a sealed jar in the refrigerator and it will keep for a week or two.

For variety, use cocoa instead of carob powder.

Apple Butter

To Make 3–4 Jarfuls
Allow 5 hours to prepare
Each 100 g provides: 78 kcal, negligible protein, 19 g carbohydrate, negligible fat, 3 g fibre

Metric		Imperial/American
1½ kg	apples (see note)	3 lb
400 ml	water	¾ pint/2 cups
2	lemons	2
¼ kg	raw sugar	½ lb/1 cup
2 tsp	ground cinnamon	2 tsp
½ tsp	ground cloves (or 12 whole cloves)	½ tsp
½ tsp	ground nutmeg	½ tsp
2 tsp	ground ginger	2 tsp
2 tbs	raisins or sultanas	2 tbs

(Note: the quantity of sugar specified assumes you are using Bramley cooking apples. If you use sweeter or eating apples, the amount of sugar can be reduced accordingly.)

1 Peel, core and chop the apples and put them in a large saucepan together with the water.
2 Finely grate the lemon rinds into the saucepan, then squeeze the lemons and add the juice.
3 Bring the apples to the boil and simmer, covered, till completely soft (about 20–30 minutes).
4 When the apples are done, remove them from the heat and add the sugar and spices. At this point you can either blend the mixture to make it really smooth, or stir it till any remaining lumps break down. Transfer the mixture to a large, open, casserole dish. Stir in the dried fruit and bake in a cool oven (150°C/300°F/gas mark 2) for 4 hours, stirring every half-hour or so.
5 Prepare suitable storage jars by soaking them in hot water and draining them. Spoon in the apple mixture and seal immediately. Allow to cool before serving. Once opened, the jars should be kept in the refrigerator.

We are indebted to a friendly denizen of San Francisco for this traditional American recipe, though he isn't responsible for the addition of the ground ginger.

Almond and Apricot Spread (Sugarless Marzipan)

To Make 2 Jarfuls
Allow ½ hour to prepare
Each 100 g provides: 294 kcal, 10 g protein, 8 g carbohydrate, 25 g fat, 9 g fibre

Metric		Imperial/American
60 g	dried apricots	2 oz/½ cup
¼ litre	soya milk	½ pint/1¼ cups
1 tsp	almond essence	1 tsp
¼ kg	ground almonds	½ lb/2 cups

1 Finely chop the apricots, put them in a small saucepan with the soya milk and bring to the boil, then reduce heat and simmer, uncovered, till they begin to break down (about 20 minutes). Don't worry if the soya milk separates.
2 Transfer to a blender, add the almond essence and blend to a thick, smooth consistency.
3 Transfer the blended mixture to a mixing-bowl and stir in the ground almonds a little at a time to form a firm paste.
4 Transfer to suitable storage jars (jam jars are perfect) and refrigerate till needed.

Note that it's important to use high-quality, sweet apricots for this recipe. Wholefood shops often sell a cheaper variety which have a bitter taste and these are fine for savoury dishes but are not suitable here.

It may surprise you to find our recipe for sugarless marzipan in the *Spreads* section, but it makes such a marvellous sandwich filling or extra topping for jam-tarts that it seemed to us a pity to relegate it to annual use as a topping for Christmas cake. You can also make wonderful little sweets by toasting whole almonds and wrapping them in the marzipan to form little egg shapes.

If you want to use it more traditionally to coat a celebration cake, there will be enough here to do a medium-to-large one.

Date Spread

To Make a Jarful
Allow 15 minutes to prepare
Each 100 g provides: 262 kcal, 4 g protein, 18 g carbohydrate,
18 g fat, 11 g fibre

Metric		Imperial/American
60 g	dried dates	2 oz/½ cup
30 g	dried apricots	1 oz/¼ cup
60 g	margarine	2 oz/6 tbs
7 tbs	gram flour	7 tbs
125 ml	apple juice	¼ pint/½ cup

1 Finely chop the dates and apricots and set aside.
2 Melt the margarine in a small saucepan over a low heat. Stir in the flour and cook gently for a few minutes. (It will form a firm dough-like roux.)
3 Slowly stir in the apple juice a little at a time, then add the chopped dates and apricots, still stirring continuously for another minute or two.
4 Remove from heat, transfer to a jar, or covered dish, and allow to cool completely before serving.

This sweet, sugar-free spread is excellent as a sandwich filler or simply spread on bread or toast. It can also be used as extra topping for jam-tarts.

Baking

Pastries and Breads

Biscuits and Cakes

Baking

The refined white flour that is used to make most mass-produced bread, biscuits and cakes has had nearly all of its vitamins, minerals and fibre removed and has had added to it chemicals to preserve, stretch, strengthen and bleach it, synthetic vitamins to replace some of those that were taken out during refining, and chalk to make it lighter. The tasteless, spongy, white, plastic substance that is finally baked from this appalling product and called 'bread' could not by any stretch of the imagination be called 'the staff of life'. But it is worse than worthless. There is now increasing evidence that it is positively harmful to health:

> 'It is now generally accepted by the medical profession that a generous intake of dietary fibre is one of the best measures against constipation and many other diseases of the bowel. Dr Hugh Trowell . . . suggested that fibre might also protect against diabetes . . . that a lack of fibre in the diet may be much more important as a contributory cause in diabetes than an excess of sugar as had previously been thought.' (Dr Jim Mann in the *Diabetics' Diet Book*, Martin Dunitz, 1982.)

Careful attention to diet is just as important for vegans of course. This is why we have used 100 per cent wholewheat flour throughout this section and why, where we have used sugar, we have specified raw varieties which retain much of their vitamin and mineral content. But in any case, in our view, the resulting bread, biscuits and cakes are not only better for your health but actually taste better as well.

We've also specified fresh yeast. This can be bought in many wholefood shops and in some bakers and delicatessens. Dried yeast works perfectly well but is more likely to contribute a 'yeasty' flavour. (If you do have to use it, always use half the quantity specified for fresh yeast.)

A word or two about bread-making. If you've never baked bread before, start with *Basic Wholewheat Bread* (page 205) because this recipe contains the most detailed description of the method. But we recommend *Three Seed Bread* (page 206) for daily use because of its almost perfect protein balance (see page 266).

It's a mystery to us why bread recipes always use sugar to get the yeast going. This is not only unnecessary but one recipe we've seen actually warns that the yeast will be killed if the sugar solution is too strong. Our recipes should provide you with ample proof that you don't need to use sugar at all.

Another way in which our bread recipes differ is that we start with a measured quantity of warm water and add the yeast and flour to it. This is such an easy way to arrive at a dough of perfect consistency that once you've got used to the method you'll probably wonder why you ever did it differently.

It's strange that even proficient and experienced cooks often claim (almost boast) that the one thing they cannot do successfully is make bread. This is nonsense. Bread-making is not only easy, it's also one of the most satisfying forms of cookery there is – good for the soul as well as the body. It's true that it takes a few hours (although most of the time you aren't required to do anything other than wait for the yeast to do its stuff, so that it's easy to do other things at the same time) but there's nothing to compare with it for the sensual pleasure of kneading the dough or the delightful odours that pervade your home once the bread is in the oven.

Finally, a word or two of warning. While it's certainly true that the vegan cakes and biscuits in this section have little in common with the cholesterol and starch bombs that are daily promoted on our television screens, we nevertheless view them as occasional treats to be eaten with restraint. The fact that we've given so many recipes should not be taken as an encouragement to stuff oneself with them but rather as evidence of our wish to lay to rest once and for always the prejudice that vegans are practising a form of self-denial. We refuse to be held responsible for any lack of self-discipline on the part of our readers that might result from the amazing sensual delights we have created!

Basic Shortcrust Pastry

To Make a 20–23 cm (8–9 in) Flan Shell (for a pie you'll need half as much again)
Allow ¾ hour to prepare (including 20 minutes to chill)
Each serving (of 8) provides: 213 kcal, 4 g protein, 21 g carbohydrate, 13 g fat, 3 g fibre

Metric		Imperial/American
¼ kg	100 per cent wholewheat flour	½ lb/2 cups
125 g	margarine	¼ lb/½ cup
60–75 ml	iced water	4–5 tbs

1 Put a few ice cubes in a jug with a little water.
2 Put the flour and margarine into a large mixing-bowl and, using two knives, chop it up into pea-sized pieces. Quickly use your fingers to rub them in till the mixture resembles coarse breadcrumbs. Try to do it quickly enough to prevent the warmth of your hands from melting the margarine.
3 Pour 1 tbs of the iced water evenly over the mixture and toss the granules of flour to mix it in. Add another 2 tbs in the same way and then try compressing the mixture to see if it will hold together. (If it won't you can add *a maximum of* 1–2 tbs more of water.) Now pick it up in your hands and squeeze it into a ball, then put it back in the bowl and into the fridge for 20 minutes.
4 Prepare a suitable flan case by greasing it with margarine and sprinkling it with flour.
5 Place the dough on a floured surface and, sprinkling it with more flour as necessary, roll it out to the size and thickness you need. Pick it up by rolling it gently round your rolling-pin and then unrolling it again over the prepared flan-case. Repair any small breaks or cracks and shape the edge into scallops between floured fingers and thumbs.
6 Prick the pastry-case all over with a fork and spread some dry beans over it as weights to prevent it from puffing up during baking – it's a good idea to keep a jarful just for this purpose.
7 Bake for 10–12 minutes in the centre of a hot oven (218°C/425°F/gas mark 7). Remove from oven and set aside to cool on a rack before removing the dried beans.

Any leftover pastry can be used to make jam-tarts or pasties, filled with savoury spreads, peanut butter or tahini.

Basic Sweet Pastry

To Make a 17–20 cm (7–8 in) Shell
Allow ¾ hour to prepare (including 20 minutes to chill)
*Each serving (of 8) provides: 188 kcal, 4 g protein, 19 g carbohydrate,
11 g fat, 2 g fibre*

Metric		**Imperial/American**
125 g	100 per cent wholewheat flour	¼ lb/1 cup
60 g	rolled oats	2 oz/¾ cup
30 g	sunflower seeds	1 oz/3 tbs
30 g	raw demerara sugar	1 oz/2 tbs
½ tsp	ground cinnamon	½ tsp
90 g	margarine	3 oz/⅓ cup
45 ml	iced water	3 tbs

(Note: see *Basic Shortcrust Pastry* (page 203) for a more detailed description of the method.)

1 Put the flour, oats, sunflower seeds, sugar and cinnamon in a large bowl and mix well together.
2 Cut in the margarine and continue rubbing it in till the mixture resembles coarse breadcrumbs.
3 Add the iced water a little at a time until the mixture holds together to form a fine dough. Chill in the refrigerator for at least 20 minutes.
4 Prepare a suitable flan case or dish by greasing it with margarine and dusting it with flour.
5 Flatten the dough between your hands, put it into the prepared flan case and press it into shape till the whole case is evenly lined. (Or roll it out if you prefer.)
6 Prick the base with a fork and bake in the middle of a hot oven (218°C/425°F/gas mark 7) for 10 minutes.
7 Allow to cool on a rack before attempting to remove from the case.

Leftover pastry or trimmings can be used to make jam-tarts.

Basic Wholewheat Bread

To Make 3 × ½ kg (1 lb) Loaves
Allow 3 hours to prepare (including rising times)
*Each 30 g (1 oz) slice provides: 76 kcal, 2 g protein, 12 g carbo-
hydrate, 2 g fat, 2 g fibre*

Metric		Imperial/American
650 ml	hand-warm water	1¼ pints/3 cups
30 g	fresh yeast	1 oz/2 tbs
1½ kg	100 per cent wholewheat flour	3 lb/12 cups
125 ml	sunflower oil	¼ pint/½ cup
½ tbs	salt	½ tbs

1 Put the hand-warm water in a large mixing-bowl, crumble in the yeast and stir until completely dissolved.
2 Add enough flour to make a thick batter and stir until flour and yeast are thoroughly mixed. Cover and put in a warm place for half an hour.
3 Stir in the oil and salt. Now begin adding more flour and stirring till the dough begins to hold together.
4 Turn the dough out on to a floured surface and knead, adding more flour as necessary, till it becomes smooth and elastic.
5 Sprinkle flour in the mixing-bowl, put the dough back in and sprinkle more flour on top. Cover and put in a warm place to rise. It should double in size in about an hour.
6 Turn the dough out on to the floured surface and knead again for a few minutes before cutting it into 3 equal pieces and kneading each separately for a further few minutes.
7 Shape into loaves, place in greased, floured ½ kg (1 lb) bread tins, cover and leave to rise for a further 20 minutes. Preheat an oven to very hot (232°C/450°F/gas mark 8).
8 Bake in the middle of the oven for 15 minutes, then reduce heat to moderate (177°C/350°F/gas mark 4) for a further 30 minutes. A well-baked loaf rings hollow when tapped. Depending on your oven, you may need to turn them upside down in their tins for the final 10 minutes.

This is an easy recipe but don't expect it to turn out exactly right first time – remember, practice makes perfect. Seal loaves you don't need immediately in plastic bags and store in the freezer or freezer compartment of your fridge: they'll stay fresh for weeks. Don't ever *wash* bread tins and they won't stick.

Big manufacturers of factory-made wholewheat bread use the cheapest available oils which are usually of animal origin and also put in preservatives, artificial flavouring, colouring agents and sugar. So home-made bread not only tastes better, it's better for your health too.

Three Seed Bread

To Make 3 × ½ kg (1 lb) Loaves
Allow 3 hours to prepare (including rising times)
Each 30 g (1 oz) slice provides: 89 kcal, 3 g protein, 13 g carbo-
hydrate, 3 g fat, 2 g fibre

Metric		**Imperial/American**
650 ml	hand-warm water	1¼ pints/3 cups
30 g	fresh yeast	1 oz/2 tbs
1½ kg	100 per cent wholewheat flour	3 lb/12 cups
60 g	poppy seeds	2 oz/6 tbs
60 g	sesame seeds	2 oz/6 tbs
60 g	sunflower seeds	2 oz/6 tbs
125 ml	sunflower oil	¼ pint/½ cup
½ tbs	salt	½ tbs

1 Put the hand-warm water in a large mixing-bowl, crumble in the yeast, stir until completely dissolved, then add enough flour to make a thick batter. Cover and put in a warm place for half an hour.
2 Stir in the three seeds, the oil and the salt and mix thoroughly. Now begin adding more flour and stirring. When the dough begins to hold together, turn it out on to a floured surface and knead, adding more flour as necessary, till it becomes smooth and elastic. Put it back into the bowl, cover and put in a warm place to rise. It should double in size in about an hour.
3 Turn the dough out and knead again for a few minutes before cutting it into 3 equal pieces and kneading each separately for a further few minutes.
4 Shape into loaves, place in greased, floured ½ kg (1 lb) bread tins, cover and leave to rise for a further 20 minutes. Preheat an oven to very hot (232°C/450°F/gas mark 8).
5 Bake in the middle of the oven for 15 minutes then reduce heat to moderate (177°C/350°F/gas mark 4) for a further 30 minutes.

Apart from the fact that the three seeds add a delicious crunchy texture and nutty taste, they also complement the protein content of the flour to make an almost perfect balance of the essential nutrients so this bread really could be described as *the staff of life*.

You can make it even darker, richer and tastier if you take the trouble to *roast* the three seeds between steps 1 and 2. Spread them out on an ovenproof dish and bake in a very hot oven (232°C/450°F/gas mark 8) till they brown (about 15 minutes), turning occasionally to prevent burning. This extra step also has the advantage of pre-heating your oven – and the resulting loaves are as scrumptious as cake without the calories.

Oat Bread

To Make 3 × ½ kg (1 lb) Loaves
Allow 3 hours to prepare (including rising times)
Each 30 g (1 oz) slice provides: 77 kcal, 2 g protein, 12 g carbo-hydrate, 2 g fat, 2 g fibre

Metric		Imperial/American
60 g	rolled oats	2 oz/¾ cup
¾ litre	water	1½ pints/3½ cups
30 g	fresh yeast	1 oz/2 tbs
1½ kg	100 per cent wholewheat flour	3 lb/12 cups
125 ml	sunflower oil	¼ pint/½ cup
½ tbs	salt	½ tbs

1 Put the oats in a small saucepan with just under half the water and bring quickly to the boil, then reduce heat and simmer for 5 minutes, stirring continuously.
2 Remove from heat, stir in the rest of the water and cool down to hand-warm (by partially submerging the saucepan in cold water if you like).
3 Pour the oat mixture into a large mixing-bowl, crumble the yeast into it and stir until completely dissolved. Add enough flour to make a thick batter, cover and put in a warm place for half an hour.
4 Stir in the oil and salt. Begin adding more flour and stirring. When the dough begins to hold together, turn it out on to a floured surface and knead, adding more flour as necessary, till it becomes smooth and elastic. Put it back into the bowl, cover and put in a warm place to rise. It should double in size in about an hour.
5 Turn the dough out and knead again for a few minutes before cutting it into 3 equal pieces and kneading each separately for a further few minutes.
6 Shape into loaves, place in greased, floured bread tins, cover and leave to rise for a further 20 minutes. Preheat the oven to very hot (232°C/450°F/gas mark 8).
7 Bake in the middle of the oven for 15 minutes, then reduce heat to moderate (177°C/350°F/gas mark 4) for a further 30 minutes.

If you try adding raw oats to ordinary wholewheat dough as you make it, you'll find they absorb all the water and make the resulting bread very dry. But this loaf is wonderful – light and creamy in texture and with a nutty, slightly sour-creamy flavour.

Onion Bread

To Make 3 × ½ kg (1 lb) Loaves
Allow 3 hours to prepare (including rising times)
Each 30 g (1 oz) slice provides: 77 kcal, 3 g protein, 13 g carbohydrate, 2 g fat, 2 g fibre

Metric		Imperial/American
650 ml	hand-warm water	1¼ pints/3 cups
30 g	fresh yeast	1 oz/2 tbs
1½ kg	100 per cent wholewheat flour	3 lb/12 cups
3	medium onions	3
125 ml	sunflower oil	¼ pint/½ cup
½ tbs	salt	½ tbs

1 Put the hand-warm water in a large mixing-bowl, crumble in the yeast, stir until completely dissolved, then add enough flour to make a thick batter. Cover and put in a warm place for half an hour.
2 Skin and finely chop the onions and add them to the batter. Stir in the oil and salt and mix thoroughly. Now begin adding more flour and stirring. When the dough begins to hold together, turn it out on to a floured surface and knead, adding more flour as necessary, till it becomes smooth and elastic. Put it back into the bowl, cover and put in a warm place to rise. It should double in size in about an hour.
3 Turn the dough out and knead again for a few minutes before cutting it into 3 equal pieces and kneading each separately for a further few minutes.
4 Shape into loaves, place in greased, floured bread tins, cover and leave to rise for a further 20 minutes. Preheat an oven to very hot (232°C/450°F/gas mark 8).
5 Bake in the middle of the oven for 15 minutes, then reduce heat to moderate (177°C/350°F/gas mark 4) for a further 30 minutes.

This produces a moist, tasty loaf that goes particularly well with savoury tarts and flans but is also good spread with peanut butter, tahini or one of the many savoury spreads from the *Spreads* section.

Spice Bread

To Make a Small ½ kg (1 lb) Loaf
Allow 1½ hours to prepare
Each 30 g (1 oz) slice provides: 98 kcal, 3 g protein, 17 g carbo-hydrate, negligible fat, 2 g fibre

Metric		Imperial/American
1 tsp	anise seeds	1 tsp
¼ litre	boiling water	8 fl oz/1 cup
60 g	raw demerara sugar	2 oz/3 tbs
15 g	fresh yeast	½ oz/1 tbs
350 g	100 per cent wholewheat flour	¾ lb/3 cups
3 tsp	ground cinnamon	3 tsp
1 tsp	ground nutmeg	1 tsp
1 tsp	ground cloves	1 tsp
125 ml	apple concentrate	¼ pint/½ cup

1 Put the anise seeds in a bowl, pour the boiling water over them, cover and set aside to infuse.
2 When the infusion has cooled to hand-warm (and not before!) add the sugar, stir until completely dissolved, then crumble in the yeast. Continue stirring until all the yeast has dissolved before adding about a third of the flour. Mix again thoroughly, cover and set aside for 20 minutes.
3 Now stir in the spices, the apple concentrate and the rest of the flour, and mix to a sticky, wet dough.
4 Transfer the dough to a well-greased, floured bread tin, cover and leave in a warm place to rise for about ½ hour.
5 Push the dough down to make a hollow in the middle and bake in the middle of a hot oven (218°C/425°F/gas mark 7) for 15 minutes then reduce heat to moderate (177°C/350°F/gas mark 4) for a further 25–30 minutes.
6 Turn out on to a rack and allow to cool before serving.

Serve this cut very thinly and spread with margarine. It's also good toasted.

For variety, try different combinations of spices; or try adding some cut orange peel; or forming the mixture into bun shapes at step 4 to make a sort of tea-cake.

Spiced Biscuits

To Make about Two Dozen
Allow 40 minutes to prepare
Each biscuit provides: 61 kcal, 1 g protein, 7 g carbohydrate, 3 g fat, 1 g fibre

Metric		Imperial/American
180 g	wholewheat flour	6 oz/1½ cups
60 g	any raw sugar	2 oz/3 tbs
1 tsp	baking powder	1 tsp
2 tsp	ground cinnamon	2 tsp
1 tsp	ground cloves	1 tsp
1 tsp	ground ginger	1 tsp
½ tsp	ground nutmeg	½ tsp
90 g	margarine	3 oz/⅓ cup
45 ml	water	3 tbs

1 Put the flour, sugar, baking powder and all the spices in a bowl and mix thoroughly.
2 Cut in the margarine and continue rubbing it in till the mixture resembles coarse breadcrumbs.
3 Add the water and toss the mixture around till it forms a firm dough.
4 Using liberal amounts of flour, roll the mixture out to about half the thickness of ordinary biscuits and cut into biscuit shapes with a pastry-cutter. Bake on a greased baking sheet in the middle of a moderate oven (177°C/350°F/gas mark 4) for 20 minutes.
5 Allow to cool on a rack before serving.

Lemon Biscuits

To Make about Two Dozen
Allow 50 minutes to prepare
*Each biscuit provides: 94 kcal, 1 g protein, 12 g carbohydrate, 4 g fat,
2 g fibre*

Metric		Imperial/American
125 g	wholewheat self-raising flour	¼ lb/1 cup
125 g	wholewheat semolina	¼ lb/1 cup
125 g	raw demerara sugar	¼ lb/¾ cup
2	lemons	2
125 g	margarine	¼ lb/½ cup

1 Put the flour, semolina and sugar in a bowl and mix well together.
2 Finely grate the lemon rinds into the bowl and mix again.
3 Cut in the margarine, then use your fingers to rub it well in till the mixture resembles coarse breadcrumbs.
4 Squeeze the lemons and add the juice a tablespoonful at a time (up to a maximum of 3) till the mixture holds together.
5 Roll the dough out on a floured surface to about ½ cm (¼ in) thick and cut into biscuit shapes, using a pastry-cutter.
6 Bake on a greased baking sheet in the middle of a fairly hot oven (190°C/375°F/gas mark 5) till golden brown (about 20–30 minutes).
7 Allow to cool on a rack before serving.

Carob and Walnut Cookies

To Make about Two Dozen
Allow ¾ hour to prepare
*Each cookie provides: 92 kcal, 2 g protein, 7 g carbohydrate, 6 g fat,
1 g fibre*

Metric		Imperial/American
180 g	wholewheat self-raising flour	6 oz/1½ cups
60 g	carob powder	2 oz/8 tbs
60 g	any raw sugar	2 oz/3 tbs
125 g	margarine	¼ lb/½ cup
60 g	chopped walnuts	2 oz/½ cup
100 ml	water	7 tbs

1 Put the flour, carob powder and sugar in a bowl and mix well together.
2 Cut in the margarine and continue rubbing it in till the mixture resembles coarse breadcrumbs.
3 Add the chopped nuts and toss around till thoroughly mixed.
4 Now begin adding the water a tablespoonful at a time until the mixture forms a firm dough.
5 The dough may either be rolled out on a floured surface to about ½ cm (¼ in) thick and cut into biscuit shapes with a pastry-cutter, or cut up and formed into biscuit shapes with the hands.
6 Bake on a greased baking sheet in the middle of a moderate oven (177°C/350°F/gas mark 4) for 20–25 minutes.
7 Allow to cool on a rack before serving.

Orange and Cinnamon Biscuits

To Make about Two Dozen
Allow 40 minutes to prepare
*Each biscuit provides: 99 kcal, 2 g protein, 13 g carbohydrate, 5 g fat,
2 g fibre*

Metric		Imperial/American
125 g	wholewheat self-raising flour	¼ lb/1 cup
150 g	wholewheat semolina	5 oz/1¼ cups
60 g	rolled oats	2 oz/¾ cup
60 g	raw demerara sugar	2 oz/3 tbs
1 tsp	ground cinnamon	1 tsp
1	orange	1
125 g	margarine	¼ lb/½ cup
2 tsp	lemon juice	2 tsp

1 Put the flour, semolina, oats, sugar and cinnamon in a bowl and mix thoroughly.
2 Finely grate the orange rind and add the peel to the bowl.
3 Put the margarine to melt in a small saucepan over a low heat.
4 Meanwhile, squeeze the orange and stir the juice into the melting margarine. Add the lemon juice and mix thoroughly.
5 Now stir the melted margarine and juice into the bowl of dry ingredients and combine into a smooth dough. (Add an extra tablespoonful of orange juice or water, if necessary, to get a firm consistency.)
6 Roll the dough out on a floured surface to about ½ cm (¼ in) thick and cut into biscuit shapes using a pastry-cutter or, if you prefer, take teaspoonfuls of the dough and flatten out to form biscuit shapes with your hands.
7 Bake on a greased baking sheet in the middle of a moderate oven (177°C/350°F/gas mark 4) till golden brown (about 30–35 minutes).
8 Allow to cool on a rack before serving.

Ginger Snaps

To Make about Two Dozen
Allow 50 minutes to prepare
Each biscuit provides: 94 kcal, 1 g protein, 12 g carbohydrate, 4 g fat, 1 g fibre

Metric		Imperial/American
125 g	wholewheat self-raising flour	¼ lb/1 cup
125 g	wholewheat semolina	¼ lb/1 cup
125 g	raw demerara sugar	¼ lb/¾ cup
2 tbs	freshly grated ginger	2 tbs
	(or 1 tbs ground dried ginger)	
125 g	margarine	¼ lb/½ cup
45 ml	soya milk	3 tbs

1 Put the flour, semolina, sugar and ginger in a bowl and mix thoroughly.
2 Add the margarine and, using two knives, chop it up into pea-sized pieces. Now use your fingers to rub it well into the dry ingredients.
3 Add 2 tbs of the soya milk. If the mixture doesn't bind together, add a third spoonful.
4 Roll the dough out on a floured surface to about ½ cm (¼ in) thick and cut into biscuit shapes, using a pastry-cutter.
5 Bake on a greased baking sheet in the middle of a fairly hot oven (190°C/375°F/gas mark 5) till golden brown (about 20–30 minutes).
6 Allow to cool on a rack before serving.

Although we've given a quantity for ground dried ginger, the fact is that biscuits made with freshly-grated ginger are a revelation. Taste them once and you'll never want to use dried ginger again.

Sesame Shortbread

To Make a 23 cm (9 in) Round
Allow ½ hour to prepare
Each 20 g (¾ oz) slice provides: 103 kcal, 2 g protein, 9 g carbo-hydrate, 7 g fat, 1 g fibre

Metric		**Imperial/American**
180 g	wholewheat flour	6 oz/1½ cups
30 g	raw demerara sugar	1 oz/2 tbs
125 g	margarine	¼ lb/½ cup
1 tbs	sesame seeds	1 tbs

1 Put the flour and sugar in a bowl and mix well.
2 Put in the margarine and continue rubbing it in till the mixture resembles coarse breadcrumbs.
3 Prepare a suitable flan case, dish or tin by greasing it with margarine and dusting it with flour.
4 Put the mixture into the dish and press it down with your hands until it is an even thickness all over. Prick it all over with a fork and mark it into 16 portions. Sprinkle the sesame seeds on top and press them in lightly.
5 Bake in the middle of a hot oven (218°C/425°F/gas mark 7) until it is just beginning to go golden brown (about 12–15 minutes).
6 Allow to cool on a rack before removing from tin or dish.

Plain Oatcakes

To Make about Three Dozen
Allow ¾ hour to prepare
Each oatcake provides: 51 kcal, 1 g protein, 6 g carbohydrate, 3 g fat, 1 g fibre

Metric		Imperial/American
125 g	rolled oats	¼ lb/1½ cups
90 g	oatmeal	3 oz/¾ cup
90 g	wholewheat flour	3 oz/¾ cup
½ tsp	salt	½ tsp
75 ml	oil	5 tbs
125 ml	water	¼ pint/½ cup

1 Put the oats, oatmeal, flour and salt into a large bowl and mix thoroughly.
2 Stir in the oil a little at a time until thoroughly mixed.
3 Slowly stir in just enough water, a little at a time, to form a firm, sticky dough.
4 Now roll the dough out on a floured surface to about half the thickness of ordinary biscuits and, using a pastry-cutter, cut into small discs.
5 Bake on a greased baking sheet in the middle of a moderate oven (177°C/350°F/gas mark 4) until they begin to brown (about 25 minutes).
6 Allow to cool on a rack before serving.

These are perfect for scooping up dips; or try spreading them with peanut butter, tahini or any of the home-made spread recipes as a light snack.

Coconut Oatcakes

To Make a Dozen
Allow 40 minutes to prepare
Each oatcake provides: 239 kcal, 4 g protein, 21 g carbohydrate,
16 g fat, 5 g fibre

Metric		**Imperial/American**
60 g	rolled oats	2 oz/¾ cup
90 g	oatmeal	3 oz/¾ cup
90 g	wholewheat flour	3 oz/¾ cup
125 g	desiccated coconut	¼ lb/1 cup
90 g	raisins	3 oz/½ cup
30 g	sunflower seeds	1 oz/3 tbs
30 g	sesame seeds	1 oz/3 tbs
75 ml	oil	5 tbs
125 ml	apple juice	¼ pint/½ cup

1 Put the oats, oatmeal, flour, coconut, raisins, sunflower and sesame seeds in a large bowl and mix thoroughly.
2 Stir in the oil a little at a time until thoroughly mixed.
3 Slowly stir in the apple juice till the mixture forms a firm dough.
4 Roll the dough out on a floured surface to about 1 cm (½ in) thick and cut into rounds with a pastry-cutter. (If any raisins find their way to the surface, push them back inside the dough or they may burn.)
5 Bake on a greased baking sheet in the middle of a moderate oven (177°C/350°F/gas mark 4) till they go golden brown (about 20–30 minutes).
6 Allow to cool on a rack before serving.

With their balanced mixture of cereals, seeds and fruits, these substantial cakes make perfect snacks for journeys since they provide not only carbohydrates, oils, vitamins and minerals, but also have an excellent protein balance.

Fruit Scones

To Make about a Dozen
Allow ½ hour to prepare
Each scone provides: 157 kcal, 4 g protein, 22 g carbohydrate, 7 g fat, 3 g fibre

Metric		Imperial/American
300 g	wholewheat flour	10 oz/2½ cups
1½ tsp	baking powder	1½ tsp
90 g	sultanas	3 oz/5 tbs
90 g	margarine	3 oz/⅓ cup
125 ml	soya milk	¼ pint/½ cup

1 Put the flour, baking powder and sultanas into a large mixing-bowl and mix thoroughly.
2 Add the margarine and, using two knives, chop it into pea-sized pieces. Use your fingers to rub it well into the dry ingredients.
3 Add just enough soya milk, a little at a time, to form a firm dough.
4 Roll the dough out on a floured surface to about 1 cm (½ in) thick and use a pastry-cutter to cut it into scone shapes.
5 Bake on a greased baking sheet in the middle of a hot oven (218°C/ 425°F/gas mark 7) till golden brown (about 10–20 minutes).

These are at their best served hot, straight from the oven, sliced open and spread with margarine or, if it's a special occasion, with *Cashew Cream* (page 238) and jam. In the unlikely event that your guests leave you any, store them in an airtight tin. If they start to dry out, try slicing them in half and toasting the halves separately.

Savoury Scones

To Make about a Dozen
Allow ½ hour to prepare
*Each scone provides: 165 kcal, 5 g protein, 20 g carbohydrate, 8 g fat,
2 g fibre*

Metric		Imperial/American
¼ kg	100 per cent wholewheat flour	½ lb/2 cups
60 g	buckwheat flour	2 oz/½ cup
2 tsp	baking powder	2 tsp
2 tsp	mustard powder	2 tsp
45 g	sunflower seeds	3 tbs
90 g	margarine	3 oz/⅓ cup
45 ml	soya sauce	3 tbs
	juice of 1 lemon	
100 ml	soya milk	7 tbs

1 Put the flours, powders and sunflower seeds in a large bowl and mix thoroughly.
2 Add the margarine and, using two knives, chop it up into pea-sized pieces. Use your fingers to rub it well into the dry ingredients.
3 Stir in the soya sauce and the lemon juice, then add the soya milk a little at a time and mix to form a firm dough.
4 Roll the dough out on a floured surface to about 1 cm (½ in) thick and cut into rounds using a pastry-cutter.
5 Bake on a greased baking sheet in the middle of a hot oven (218°C/425°F/gas mark 7) till just beginning to brown (about 10–20 minutes).

These are at their best hot, straight from the oven. Slice them in half and spread them with margarine or any of the spreads from the *Spreads* section – they're every bit as good as cheese scones and with none of the cholesterol.

Store them in an airtight container and toast them if they go stale.

Poppy Seed Tart

To Serve 8–12
Allow 1 hour to prepare
Each serving (of 12) provides: 343 kcal, 8 g protein, 30 g carbohydrate, 22 g fat, 5 g fibre

Metric		Imperial/American
1	*Sweet Pastry Shell* (page 204)	1
90 g	blue poppy seeds	3 oz/¾ cup
¼ litre	soya milk	½ pint/1¼ cups
125 g	ground almonds	¼ lb/1 cup
125 g	wholewheat flour	¼ lb/1 cup
90 g	raw demerara sugar	3 oz/5 tbs
45 ml	oil	3 tbs
½ tsp	almond essence (or more to taste)	½ tsp

(Note: if you haven't already made the sweet pastry shell, do step 1 below before you do.)

1 Put the poppy seeds in a small saucepan, add the soya milk, bring quickly to the boil, then remove from heat, cover and set aside for 20 minutes.
2 Put the ground almonds, flour and sugar in a bowl and mix thoroughly.
3 Now stir in the oil, the soaked poppy seeds with their soya milk and the almond essence. Mix thoroughly to form a thick paste.
4 Transfer the mixture to the pastry shell, smooth the top and bake in a moderate oven (177°C/350°F/gas mark 4) for 30 minutes.
5 Allow to cool on a rack before serving.

Poppy seed tarts and cakes like this are popular in Austria and Germany but should you find the filling a bit too substantial for your taste, try putting a layer of stewed dried apricots (or wholefruit jam) in the pastry shell and topping it with half the quantity of the poppy seed mixture.

Banana and Date Cake

To Make a Small 15 cm (6 in) Round Cake
Allow 1½ hours to prepare
Each 60 g (2 oz) slice provides: 159 kcal, 3 g protein, 22 g carbo-
hydrate, 7 g fat, 3 g fibre

Metric		**Imperial/American**
300 g	wholewheat flour	10 oz/2½ cups
1 tbs	baking powder	1 tbs
180 g	dates	6 oz/1½ cups
3	ripe bananas	3
3 tsp	vanilla essence	3 tsp
125 ml	soya milk	¼ pint/½ cup
125 g	margarine	¼ lb/½ cup
	a few whole almonds for decoration	

1 Put the flour and baking powder in a large bowl and mix thoroughly. Roughly chop the dates and mix well in.
2 Put the bananas, vanilla essence and soya milk in another bowl, mash together till thoroughly combined and set aside.
3 Melt the margarine in a small saucepan over a low heat, then stir it into the flour. Now add the mashed bananas and combine the two mixtures thoroughly by stirring and turning with a spoon.
4 Pour the cake mixture into a small, lightly greased cake tin (a 15 cm/6 in round one is ideal), decorate the top with a few whole almonds or other nuts and bake in the middle of a warm oven (163°C/325°F/gas mark 3) till a knife inserted in the centre comes out cleanly and the cake is golden brown on top (about 1 hour).
5 Allow to cool before removing from tin.

Carrot and Sultana Cake

To Make a ½ kg (1 lb) Cake
Allow 1½ hours to prepare
Each 60 g (2 oz) slice provides: 154 kcal, 2 g protein, 21 g carbo-hydrate, 7 g fat, 3 g fibre

Metric		Imperial/American
¼ kg	carrots	½ lb
¼ kg	wholewheat flour	½ lb/2 cups
1 tbs	baking powder	1 tbs
60 g	sultanas	2 oz/1 tbs
125 g	margarine	¼ lb/½ cup
125 g	raw demerara sugar	¼ lb/¾ cup
1 tbs	sesame seeds	1 tbs

1 Clean, top and tail (and if necessary peel) the carrots then coarsely grate them and set them aside.
2 Put the flour, baking powder and sultanas in a mixing-bowl and mix thoroughly.
3 Melt the margarine in a small saucepan over a low heat then add the sugar and stir until dissolved. Remove from heat and pour over the flour mixture.
4 Add the grated carrots and mix well in.
5 Transfer the cake mixture to a small, lightly greased, cake or bread tin, sprinkle the sesame seeds on top and bake for about 50 minutes in a warm oven (163°C/325°F/gas mark 3) till a knife inserted in the centre comes out cleanly.
6 Allow to cool before removing from tin.

Lemon Sponge Cake

To Make a 2-Layered 23 cm (9 in) Round Cake
Allow 40 minutes to prepare
*Each slice (of 8) provides: 270 kcal, 4 g protein, 34 g carbohydrate,
13 g fat, 5 g fibre*

Metric		Imperial/American
¼ kg	fine-milled 100 per cent wholewheat flour	½ lb/2 cups
1½ tbs	baking powder	1½ tbs
90 g	raw demerara sugar	3 oz/5 tbs
125 g	margarine	¼ lb/½ cup
75 ml	hot water	5 tbs
25 ml	malt extract	1½ tbs
3	lemons	3

1 Sift the flour and baking powder into a bowl, add the sugar and mix well by lifting and sprinkling, using a spoon.
2 Put the margarine to melt in a small saucepan over a low heat. Remove from heat as soon as it's melted.
3 Put the hot water in a jug together with the malt extract and set aside.
4 Finely grate the lemon rinds, add to the dry ingredients and mix in by lifting and sprinkling as before.
5 Squeeze the lemons, add the juice to the water and malt mixture and stir till the malt has completely dissolved.
6 Preheat an oven to fairly hot (204°C/400°F/gas mark 6) and prepare two suitable sponge tins by lightly greasing and flouring them.
7 As quickly as you can, add the melted margarine to the dry ingredients and stir well in, followed immediately by the water, malt and lemon juice mixture. Beat well for a few moments only before transferring equal amounts to each of your two prepared sponge tins and placing them in the preheated oven.
8 Bake till the top goes firm and golden brown (about 20–25 minutes). Cool on a rack before removing from the tins.
9 Fill with jam, lemon or orange marmalade or *Vegan Piping Cream,* flavoured with lemon juice (page 237).

Almond and Apricot Cake

To Make a Small 15 cm (6 in) Round Cake
Allow 1½ hours to prepare (if you have pre-soaked the apricots)
Each 60 g (2 oz) slice provides: 210 kcal, 5 g protein, 14 g carbo-
hydrate, 15 g fat, 6 g fibre

Metric		**Imperial/American**
180 g	dried apricots	6 oz/1½ cups
¼ litre	soya milk	½ pint/1¼ cups
125 g	chopped almonds	¼ lb/1 cup
125 g	wholewheat flour	¼ lb/1 cup
125 g	ground almonds	¼ lb/1 cup
1½ tbs	baking powder	1½ tbs
125 g	margarine	¼ lb/½ cup
60 g	raw sugar	2 oz/3 tbs
1 tsp	almond essence	1 tsp
	a few whole almonds for decoration (optional)	

1 Finely chop the apricots, put them in a bowl, pour the soya milk over, cover and leave to stand for several hours – preferably overnight.
2 Sprinkle the chopped almonds on an ovenproof plate and put them in the top of a hot oven (218°C/425°F/gas mark 7) till they begin to brown (about 8–12 minutes). Remove from the oven and set aside. Leave the oven door open and reduce heat to warm (163°C/325°F/ gas mark 3).
3 Put the flour, ground almonds and baking powder in a bowl and mix thoroughly.
4 Melt the margarine and sugar in a small saucepan over a low heat before adding it to the flour mixture. Mix well in and then add the soaked apricots (together with any remaining liquid), the roasted almonds and the almond essence and combine all the ingredients together thoroughly.
5 Transfer the mixture to a greased, floured cake tin, decorate with more almonds (whole ones look good, if you have them) and bake in the middle of a warm oven (163°C/325°F/gas mark 3) for about 50 minutes till a knife inserted in the centre comes out cleanly.
6 Allow to cool before removing from tin.

Carob Cake

To Make a 20 cm (8 in) Round Cake
Allow 1 hour to prepare
*Each slice (of 8) provides: 333 kcal, 7 g protein, 39 g carbohydrate,
17 g fat, 4 g fibre*

Metric		Imperial/American
¼ kg	100 per cent wholewheat flour	½ lb/2 cups
125 g	carob powder	¼ lb/1¼ cups
1½ tbs	baking powder	1½ tbs
125 g	dark raw muscovado sugar	¼ lb/7 tbs
100 ml	oil	7 tbs
25 ml	malt extract	1½ tbs
25 ml	vanilla essence	1½ tbs
¼ litre	warm water	½ pint/1¼ cups
	Topping	
60 g	margarine	2 oz/6 tbs
3 tbs	carob powder	3 tbs
30 ml	maple syrup	2 tbs

1 Sift the flour, carob powder and baking powder into a bowl, add the sugar and mix well by lifting, turning and sprinkling, using a large spoon.
2 Preheat the oven to moderate (177°C/350°F/gas mark 4) and prepare a suitable 20 cm (8 in) round cake tin by lightly greasing with margarine and dusting with flour.
3 As quickly as possible, add the oil, malt extract, vanilla essence and warm water to the bowl and beat together (using an electric mixer if you prefer) till well combined.
4 Pour the mixture into the prepared tin, smooth the top and make a slight hollow in the centre (to prevent splits forming). Bake in the middle of the oven for about 40 minutes till a knife inserted in the centre comes out cleanly.
5 Allow to cool before removing from tin.
6 Cream all the topping ingredients together (using a mixer if you prefer) till thick and smooth. Spread evenly over the cake and smooth out any imperfections using a knife dipped in cold water.

Celebration Cake

To Make a Large 23 cm (9 in) Round Cake
Allow 3½ hours to prepare (if you have pre-soaked the dried fruit)
*Each slice (of 12) provides: 321 kcal, 4 g protein, 56 g carbohydrate,
9 g fat, 6 g fibre*

Metric		Imperial/American
¼ kg	sultanas	½ lb/2 cups
¼ kg	raisins	½ lb/2 cups
125 g	currants	¼ lb/1 cup
¼ litre	sweet white wine	½ pint/1¼ cups
125 g	margarine	¼ lb/½ cup
90 g	raw demerara sugar	3 oz/5 tbs
45 ml	molasses	3 tbs
¼ kg	100 per cent wholewheat flour	½ lb/2 cups
125 ml	soya milk	¼ pint/1 cup
2 tbs	mixed spice	2 tbs

1 Put all the dried fruit in a bowl, pour the wine over and leave to soak overnight. Stir from time to time to make sure all the fruit is coated.
2 Put the margarine and sugar in a large mixing-bowl and cream well together before stirring in the molasses, flour, soya milk and mixed spice. An electric mixer may be used if you prefer.
3 Fold in the soaked dried fruit and stir till evenly distributed through the mixture.
4 Line a 23 cm (9 in) round cake tin with grease-proof paper. Pour in the mixture and bake in a cool oven (150°C/300°F/gas mark 2) for about 3 hours till a knife inserted in the centre comes out cleanly.
5 Allow to cool on a rack before removing from tin.

This is a perfect cake for really special occasions such as birthdays or Christmas. It's marvellous as it is, but you may wish to cover it with *Sugarless Marzipan* (page 197) and ice it as well – if you prefer not to use sugar icing, try dissolving creamed coconut in a little hot water, pouring it over the cake and smoothing it with a knife dipped frequently in hot water.

The Alternative Dairy

The Alternative Dairy

Soya Milk

Soya Milk as a Health Food

Soya milk has a high protein, vitamin and mineral content and is naturally low in fat (and what fat there is in it is in any case the unsaturated type). So it is easy to digest and never provokes the allergic symptoms that many people suffer from cow's milk. Cow's milk is mucus-forming and has other dangers too of course – chiefly the result of its high cholesterol level which has now been accepted by the medical profession at large as a major contributory factor in heart disease. (It is not a coincidence that countries that have a low consumption of dairy produce are virtually free from heart disease.)

Sweetened, Unsweetened or Concentrated

Soya milk is available in these and several flavoured varieties. We haven't specified sweetened or unsweetened in the ingredients lists of individual recipes because the sweetened brands are only very slightly sweet and so it doesn't really matter very much which you use. But as a rule of thumb, *use the unsweetened variety in any recipe, the sweetened only in dessert or sweet recipes.*

A couple of brands of concentrated soya milk are available. We haven't specified these anywhere but if it is all you could get, simply dilute it according to the instructions on the packet and proceed with the recipe as printed. In just a few cases you may like to use it undiluted in order to produce a richer, thicker texture in a particular dish. It can also be used as a kind of single cream and poured over fruit.

Soya Milk as a Drink

From 1995 European law requires soya milk to be labelled 'soya drink'. This is ridiculous. Few of the vegans we know drink it. Mostly we use it as an ingredient in cookery. But if you are one of the few, remember that brands vary enormously. Some are delicious, a few are dire. So keep trying till you find one you like. *Tip*: brands with a slightly beany taste can be improved with a few drops of vanilla essence.

Soya Milk in Hot Drinks

Added to tea in the normal way, soya milk produces a perfectly good ordinary cuppa. But with coffee, there can be problems. If you make a half and half mixture of hot coffee and cold soya milk, all will be well; but if you like your coffee strong with just a dash of milk, you're out of luck. The acidity and high temperature of the coffee combine to cause the milk to coagulate (actually it's a good demonstration of the first stage of making tofu!) and although this doesn't affect its taste in any way, it does seem to disturb sensitive souls. But then, it doesn't seem such a difficult thing for people who like strong coffee to go all the way and start drinking it black.

Vegan Cappuccino

Soya milk makes excellent cappuccino. Simply carry your favourite brand round in a suitable container and ask café staff to use it to make the frothy topping. (It sometimes provokes worthwhile debates on dietary ethics!) You can also make a passable cappuccino by simply shaking the bottle vigorously and pouring the frothed up milk over strong black coffee.

Margarine

From the health point of view, soft margarines made from cold-pressed oils and containing a high proportion of polyunsaturated fat are best, though they do also tend to be the most expensive. Hard margarines contain a higher proportion of hydrogenized (i.e. 'saturated') fat. We have assumed that you will only use these for biscuit and pastry recipes and that they will not form a large part of your diet. But if you really are addicted to biscuits and pastry and want to eat some every day, it would be a good idea to use soft, polyunsaturated margarine in these recipes too. It produces a friable, crumbly dough that is difficult to handle and roll out, but, once baked, has a wonderful, mouth-watering texture.

Wholefood shops are the best places to buy high-quality, guaranteed vegan margarines. Most of the margarines to be found in such abundance in large supermarkets are not vegan. (Close scrutiny of the list of ingredients usually reveals the presence of *whey*, a product of the dairy industry, dried cow's milk, and often reclaimed animal fats.) However, such stores do usually stock one or two brands of kosher margarines, which are vegan, and these may well prove the easiest to obtain. They also stock several brands of 100 per cent vegetable fats (such as *Trex*) that make acceptable substitutes for margarine in many of the baking recipes. Jewish delicatessens also sell kosher margarines, of course, and so provide another useful source of supply for vegans.

Although you may initially have to spend a certain amount of time scouting out a regular supplier, once you've found the vegan margarines you like you can simply stick to them, and stocking up will be no harder than buying any other ingredient.

Egg Substitutes

None of the recipes in this book requires eggs, but should you wish to work with other cookery books and recipes that do include them, here are a few alternatives.

For savoury recipes, try replacing each egg specified with *1 tsp soya flour blended with 1 tbs water*; or *60 g (4 tbs) peanut butter*; or *60 g (4 tbs) soft tofu blended with 1 tsp water*; or *60 g (4 tbs) mashed potatoes* (whichever seems most appropriate).

For sweet recipes, try replacing each egg with *60 g (4 tbs) of puréed mango*; or with *½ mashed banana*.

Tofu

What is Tofu?

Tofu is the Japanese word for *soya bean curd*. Originating in China, it has been made in the Far East for more than 2000 years and is the chief source of high-quality protein for more than a billion people throughout the world.

It first became widely available in this country in the early 1970s as a result of the upsurge of interest in macrobiotics and this is the probable reason for the adoption of the Japanese name for it here – even though most people's first encounter with it will probably have been in a Chinese restaurant.

It is highly nutritious yet low in calories, 100 grams of tofu providing 8 grams of protein, 4 grams of (polyunsaturated) fat, negligible carbohydrate and only 63 kilocalories.

Buying Tofu

Tofu can be bought in wholefood shops and Chinese stores and it's clear that it is daily become more popular so, as with soya milk, we don't anticipate that you'll have any trouble finding it. It comes in a number of different forms, ranging from *silken tofu*, which is the softest, to a firm, hard-pressed tofu which is a bit like cream cheese. *Smoked tofu* is another form which has recently become more widely available in wholefood shops. This is delicious to eat just as it is, or it can be used in savoury recipes where you want a stronger, smoky flavour. There is also a Japanese brand of *instant tofu* (oddly enough, we've seen it only in Chinese supermarkets). We found it horrible and wouldn't recommend it for anything.

Keeping Tofu

Completely fresh tofu is quite odourless and pure white in colour. It can be kept, floated in water in a refrigerator, for up to a week, provided the water is changed every day.

Note that if you put tofu in the freezer compartment of your refrigerator, it will keep for ages, but it will also completely change its character, becoming granular and chewy. In this state it will readily soak up marinades, opening up yet another set of cooking possibilities for this versatile ingredient.

Cooking with Tofu

Tofu is the perfect ingredient because it is bland in flavour and so can be led in any direction you choose, making it equally suitable for savoury or sweet dishes. Its texture too lends itself to a range of uses. Firm tofu is best for slicing or cubing; soft (or silken) tofu is best for blending. We haven't specified which kind to use unless it is likely to materially affect the recipe in question. However, if you are working on a recipe that requires firm tofu and you have only soft tofu to hand, you can firm it up by wrapping it in a clean tea-towel and pressing it between two wooden chopping-boards for about 20–30 minutes.

Home-made Tofu

Although it isn't difficult to make tofu in the home (by adding a coagulant such as lemon juice to soya milk, then straining and pressing it) we decided not to include a method for this because it's time-consuming and messy, and because so many brands are now so readily available.

Vegan Yoghurt

How to Get 100 per cent Vegan Yoghurt

If you keep soya milk in an open jug in your refrigerator, you will find sooner or later that a jugful 'goes thick'. *Don't throw it away!* Apart from the fact that it still tastes perfectly good and can be used as you would use single cream – on cereals or fruit – it presents a golden opportunity to make 100 per cent vegan yoghurt using either of the two methods given. Once you've made your first-ever batch in this way, you can reserve 2 tablespoonfuls as a starter for the next batch.

How to Make Vegan Yoghurt in a Hurry

If you're too impatient to await the chance arrival of the bacteria described above (which clearly have an affinity for soya milk) you can start your first-ever batch by buying a packet of dried culture (obtainable in most wholefood shops) or even an ordinary plain shop yoghurt. Note that in this case **Method 1** must be used and the resulting yoghurt won't be 100 per cent vegan, of course, because even the dried cultures contain some cow's milk products. Furthermore, the bacteria that are used to culture most cow's (and goat's) milk yoghurts (*streptococcus thermophilus* and *lactobacillus bulgaricus*) have the unfortunate effect of making soya yoghurt taste slightly 'beany'. This can be countered by stirring in a little vanilla essence; if you get the quantity exactly right, this cancels out the 'beany' taste without giving the yoghurt a vanilla flavour.

The Difference between the Two Methods

The two methods given produce quite different flavours and textures. **Method 1** produces a strong, thick yoghurt and will work with both the opportunistic and the bought cultures but it's more trouble. **Method 2** produces a mild, thin yoghurt that goes well with muesli, cereals and fresh fruit and is so trouble-free and easy to make that it's surely worth having a jar of it permanently 'ticking over' in your fridge – but it won't work with the bought cultures which like higher temperatures (*thermophilus* means 'warmth-loving').

With both methods the taste will vary from batch to batch. The very first batch will be very mild – whichever method or culture medium you use – but the taste will get stronger from batch to batch and with **Method 1** and bought culture, it may end up too strong for your taste after a number of batches – in which case you'll just have to start again from scratch.

Whatever the life history of the batch you have to hand, if it's too mild in flavour for the use you have planned for it, simply stir in lemon juice a little at a time till you get the strength you want.

Vegan Cream Cheese

Once you're good at making *Vegan Yoghurt*, why not go a stage further and make your own *Vegan Cream Cheese*? Simply strain your latest batch of *Vegan Yoghurt* through fine muslin to produce the most delicious, home-made soft cheese. The easiest way is to use a freshly laundered white handkerchief and a clothes peg and hang it over the sink. The resulting soft white cheese is great just as it comes, spread on bread or biscuits. But it's even better blended with a little salt, freshly-ground white pepper and crushed garlic. Du pain, du vin, du *Vegan*!

Vegan Ice-Cream

A Simple Method for Home-Made Vegan Ice-Cream

We began our experiments with vegan ice-cream by simply substituting vegan ingredients into the traditional home ice-cream making method involving (endless!) alternating freezings and churnings. But this didn't work well and in any case we found it such a bore that we decided to try a completely different approach instead. Luckily, with fresh fruit ice-creams, this worked the first time and is, in essence, the method given. What you do is simply peel and chop fresh fruit, freeze it into solid chunks, then put these into a blender together with the remaining ingredients listed and blend to a wonderful, instant ice-cream. (Depending on your blender, this may take a few seconds or a few minutes.)

With most fruits no sweetener is needed, but where one is, we've used *maple syrup*. If you're prepared to include honey in your vegan diet, then this can obviously be used instead.

We've given recipes for several variations on this theme, but you can use virtually any fresh fruit, so why not invent ice-creams of your own?

For plain or flavoured ice-creams, of course, another method had to be found which, in the event, proved equally simple. You deep-freeze ⅔–¾ of the recipe soya milk then blend the resulting ice cubes with the remaining ingredients as before.

These simple methods produce a light texture, half-way between conventional ice-cream and a sorbet, which we find preferable to most commercially-produced ice-creams. But if you want to get nearer the richer, fattier texture of the latter, double the quantity of sunflower oil and use *concentrated soya milk* instead of ordinary.

Vegan Cream

Many wholefood shops now stock excellent vegan single creams which are delicious poured over fresh fruit, cakes and desserts, such as *Apple and Banana Crumble* (page 145). They can also be used as an alternative to soya milk if you want to increase the texture and richness of a savoury recipe. However they are ridiculously expensive, considering their simple ingredients, so do try making your own first from the recipes which follow.

Vegan Single Cream

To Make 1–2 Jarfuls
Allow 5 minutes to prepare
*Each 100 g provides: 163 kcal, 2 g protein, 2 g carbohydrate,
16 g fat, negligible fibre*

Metric		Imperial/American
125 g	tofu	¼ lb/½ cup
75 ml	sunflower oil	5 tbs
125 ml	water	¼ pint/½ cup
125 ml	soya milk	¼ pint/½ cup
2 tsp	vanilla essence	2 tsp
25 ml	maple syrup (optional)	1½ tbs

(Note: if you're planning to use the cream for a savoury dish you should, of course, omit the maple syrup.)

1 Put all the ingredients in a blender and blend to produce a rich cream.
2 Transfer to suitable storage jars and refrigerate till needed.

This will enrich your morning cereal and is also good poured over cakes, fruit pies or puddings when you want to add extra moistness without the added calories of *Vegan Double Cream*.

Vegan Double Cream

To Make 1–2 Jarfuls
Allow 5 minutes to prepare
*Each 100 g provides: 268 kcal, 4 g protein, 5 g carbohydrate,
26 g fat, 1 g fibre*

Metric		Imperial/American
125 g	tofu	¼ lb/½ cup
75 ml	sunflower oil	5 tbs
100 ml	soya milk	7 tbs
15 ml	vanilla essence	1 tbs
25 ml	maple syrup (optional)	1½ tbs

(Note: for a thicker cream use half the amount of soya milk. If you're planning to use the cream for a savoury dish you should, of course, omit the maple syrup.)

1 Put all the ingredients in a blender and blend to produce a rich, thick cream.
2 Transfer to suitable storage jars and refrigerate till needed.

This simply made vegan cream is every bit as sumptuous as its cousin which is habitually stolen from calves but, unlike its cousin, it contains nothing that is bad for you. Tofu is high in protein, low in fats and carbohydrates and contains no cholesterol. So even if you hadn't decided to become vegan, it would make sense to eat it instead of dairy cream, wouldn't it?

Serve it with fresh fruit salads, on *Apple Pie* (page 146), on puddings, fruit tarts or flans, or simply add it to any dessert when you want to make the occasion a little bit special.

If you're on a diet, try making it with only 2 tbs sunflower oil instead of 5.

Vegan Piping Cream

To Make a Jarful
Allow 10 minutes to prepare
*Each 100 g provides: 257 kcal, 2 g protein, 6 g carbohydrate,
25 g fat, 1 g fibre*

Metric		Imperial/American
1½ tbs	fine cornmeal	1½ tbs
125 ml	soya milk	¼ pint/½ cup
1 tsp	vanilla essence	1 tsp
1 tsp	maple syrup (optional)	1 tsp
60 g	margarine (see below)	2 oz/4 tbs
45 ml	extra soya milk (optional)	3 tbs

1 Put the cornmeal in a small saucepan and add the soya milk a little at a time, blending in carefully to remove any lumps.
2 Add the vanilla essence (and the maple syrup if you want a sweetened cream) and then begin heating and stirring gently and continuously till the mixture thickens. Remove from heat and stand the saucepan in cold water to cool.
3 Put the margarine in a small bowl or jar and mash it with a fork till it begins to cream. Begin adding the cooled cornmeal mixture and continue mashing and blending till you have a rich, smooth, creamy consistency. (An electric mixer may be used if you prefer.) If it seems too thick, add some extra soya milk – but don't thin it too much or it won't hold its shape when you pipe it.
4 Transfer to a suitable storage jar and refrigerate till needed.

Note that if you use a soft margarine you'll get a texture similar to whipped double cream whereas a hard margarine will give more that of clotted cream.

The cream is ideal for decorating fruit flans, tarts or cakes as it will hold its shape perfectly when piped. Made thinner, it can be floated on coffee.

Adding cocoa or carob powder not only colours the cream but also makes it flow more smoothly for fine piping effects.

Cashew Cream

To Make a Jarful
Allow 5 minutes to prepare
*Each 100 g (made with orange juice) provides: 197 kcal, 4 g protein,
8 g carbohydrate, 18 g fat, 3 g fibre*

Metric		**Imperial/American**
180 g	broken cashew pieces	6 oz/1½ cups
125 ml	fruit juice	¼ pint/½ cup

1 Put all the ingredients in a blender and blend to produce a rich,
   thick cream. (Add a little more or less juice to get the consistency
   you prefer.)
2 Transfer to a suitable storage jar and refrigerate till needed.

Almost any fruit juice can be used to ring the changes on this rich, thick
cream, but apple juice is probably the best one to start with.

It goes particularly well with *Fruit Juice Jelly* (page 138) or fresh fruit
salad.

Although whole cashew nuts are expensive, most shops sell broken
pieces quite cheaply so this gourmet cream needn't be a rare treat.

Coconut Cream

To Make a Jarful
Allow 10 minutes to prepare
Each 100 g provides: 239 kcal, 3 g protein, 3 g carbohydrate,
24 g fat, 10 g fibre

Metric		**Imperial/American**
125 ml	water	¼ pint/½ cup
125 g	creamed coconut	¼ lb/½ cup
45 ml	soya milk	3 tbs
½	lemon	½

1 Put the water in a small saucepan over a low heat.
2 Coarsely chop the creamed coconut to make it easier to dissolve and add it to the saucepan. Stir until there are no lumps left. Remove from heat.
3 Squeeze half a lemon and put the juice into a blender.
4 Add the soya milk to the blender and then the dissolved coconut and blend till the mixture thickens.
5 Transfer to a suitable storage jar and refrigerate till needed.

You can buy creamed coconut in any wholefood shop and in some larger stores as well as oriental shops.

Coconut cream made according to this recipe will set quite firm if refrigerated and can be used as a topping for fresh fruit salads, jellies or cakes. It's very, very rich, so serve sparingly.

Vegan Yoghurt – Method 1

To Make 1½ litres (3 pints)
Allow 20 minutes to prepare, 6–8 hours to ferment
*Each 100 g provides: 52 kcal, 3 g protein, 2 g carbohydrate, 2 g fat,
1 g fibre*

Metric		**Imperial/American**
1½ litres	soya milk	3 pints/7½ cups
3–4 tbs	starter culture	3–4 tbs

(Note: if you haven't made yoghurt by this method before, read the
remarks below before beginning.)

1 Put the soya milk in a large saucepan and bring it quickly to the
  boil, stirring continuously. Remove from heat and cool down to
  hand-warm. (The quickest way is to stand the saucepan in a bowl of
  cold water while you're getting the containers ready.)
2 Put the starter culture in a jar, add a little hand-warm milk and stir
  in. Repeat until you have a jarful of thoroughly dissolved culture.
  Pour it back into the saucepan and stir until thoroughly combined.
3 Transfer to suitable storage jars (jam jars are ideal), seal, put in a
  warm place, cover and leave for at least 6 hours.
4 Refrigerate till needed.

Maintaining the right temperature is the secret of success with this
method. If the milk is too hot, you'll kill the starter culture but if it isn't
kept warm enough, the fermentation won't get started. Hand-warm is
about right. (Perfectionists may like to know that the ideal temperature
is 45°C/112°F.) Airing-cupboards are ideal places to store the jars
during fermentation but if you haven't got one, don't give up – simply
wrap them in several layers of blankets and keep them away from
draughts. (You can also use a wide-mouthed vacuum flask, though
getting the yoghurt out again can be tiresome.)

With this method you can use any of the following as a culture: a
packet of dried culture bought from a wholefood shop, some plain
yoghurt bought anywhere, some leftover yoghurt from a previous
batch, or an opportunist culture that has decided to move in with you
(see introductory remarks to this section).

Note that with this method the *proportions* of the container affect the
end result. To get an even, creamy consistency right through it should be
about 1½ times as deep as it is wide. (Shop yoghurt tubs are an example
of the ideal shape.) If you use a shallow dish you'll get separated curds
and whey.

Vegan Yoghurt – Method 2

To Make ½ litre (1 pint)
Allow 5 minutes to prepare, 1–2 days to ferment
*Each 100 g provides: 52 kcal, 3 g protein, 2 g carbohydrate, 2 g fat,
1 g fibre*

Metric		**Imperial/American**
3–4 tbs	starter culture	3–4 tbs
½ litre	soya milk	1 pint/2½ cups

(Note: if you haven't made yoghurt by this method before, read the remarks below before beginning.)

1 Divide the starter culture equally between 2 or 3 storage jars (jam jars are ideal) then fill each jar with soya milk, seal and shake vigorously.
2 Place in the refrigerator till fermented (1–2 days).

Note that this simple method will only work with the opportunistic culture that occasionally arrives to thicken an uncovered jug of soya milk that has been in use for a day or two (see page 000 for more details). Of course, once you've got some and made your first batch, you can reserve 2–3 tablespoonfuls as a starter for the next.

Also note that the very first batch you make will be little more than a thickened, mildly flavoured milk but the taste will gradually strengthen and the texture gradually thicken from batch to batch. If you want to strengthen the taste of the batch you have to hand, simply stir in a little lemon juice.

With this method there is no need to keep the jars warm during fermentation – once you've filled and shaken them you can simply put them in the fridge to ferment and forget about them for a day or two.

This yoghurt is excellent poured over breakfast cereals, fresh fruit and puddings, or stirred into soups just before serving. It's also all right for making *Lassi* (page 252) though you'll probably need to add a little lemon juice as already mentioned.

Plain Ice-Cream

To Serve 4–6
Allow 4–5 hours to prepare (including freezing time)
Each serving (of 6) provides: 216 kcal, 2 g protein, 10 g carbohydrate, 18 g fat, 1 g fibre

Metric		Imperial/American
400 ml	soya milk	¾ pint/2 cups
100 ml	sunflower oil	7 tbs
45 ml	vanilla essence	3 tbs
45 ml	maple syrup	3 tbs

1 Pour 275 ml (½ pint/1½ cups) soya milk into ice-cube trays and place in the freezer or freezer compartment of your refrigerator till frozen solid (about 4–5 hours).
2 Put the remaining 125 ml (¼ pint/½ cup) soya milk into a blender together with the sunflower oil, vanilla essence and maple syrup. Add the now-frozen soya milk cubes, blend till very smooth and creamy and serve.

We had some trouble getting this exactly right. The degree of solidity of the soya milk ice cubes seems to be critical if you want to be able to serve the ice-cream immediately after making it – too soft and you'll end up with iced milk-shakes; too hard and you may have difficulty getting it to blend completely. Either way, don't even consider giving up! If it seems too soft, simply put it back in the freezer for half an hour to thicken. If the milk cubes are too hard, simply persist with the blending till they have completely broken down. It's worth it because it makes an ice-cream that feels lighter than its dairy counterpart. But if you want to get nearer to dairy ice-cream, increase the quantity of sunflower oil and substitute *concentrated* soya milk (obtainable from most wholefood shops) in step 1.

Banana Ice-Cream

To Serve 4
Allow 4 hours to prepare (including freezing time)
*Each serving provides: 273 kcal, 3 g protein, 25 g carbohydrate,
18 g fat, 5 g fibre*

Metric		Imperial/American
½ kg	bananas	1 lb/3 large
	juice of ½ a lemon	
125 ml	soya milk	¼ pint/½ cup
75 ml	sunflower oil	5 tbs
2 tsp	vanilla essence	2 tsp

1 Peel and coarsely chop the bananas, put them into a bowl and place
   in the freezer or freezer compartment of your refrigerator for at least
   4 hours. (It's a good idea to turn the fridge to maximum if possible.)
2 Put all the remaining ingredients in a blender, add the now-frozen
   banana chunks and blend to a rich, thick, smooth consistency.

If the ice-cream is a little too soft for your taste, put it back in the freezer
for about half an hour or so before serving. In fact, it can be kept in the
freezer for as long as you like provided you remember to defrost it for at
least 2 hours, and churn it with a spoon before serving. However,
despite the lemon juice, it will discolour slightly if kept for long though
this doesn't affect the flavour.

Pineapple Ice-Cream

To Serve 3–4
Allow 4 hours to prepare (including freezing time)
Each serving (of 4) provides: 242 kcal, 2 g protein, 16 g carbohydrate, 19 g fat, 2 g fibre

Metric		Imperial/American
½ kg	pineapple	1 lb/½ large
75 ml	sunflower oil	5 tbs
125 ml	soya milk	¼ pint/½ cup

1 Peel the pineapple, carefully removing all traces of skin and scales, then coarsely chop it, put the pieces into a bowl and place in the freezer or freezer compartment of your refrigerator for at least 4 hours.
2 Put the oil and soya milk into a blender, add the now-frozen pineapple chunks and blend to a thick, smooth, creamy consistency and serve.

If the pineapple chunks are frozen so hard that they prove difficult to blend, just persist, adding a little extra soya milk if necessary. The ice-cream may be returned to the freezer and kept for as long as you like provided you remember to get it out at least 2 hours before serving.

This ice-cream doesn't need any sweetener at all. If you can't get fresh pineapple, you can make it with tinned, unsweetened pineapple chunks, but remember to drain them before putting in the freezer for step 1. If you're using tinned pineapple and would rather make a sorbet, simply use the liquid from the tin instead of the oil and soya milk at step 2.

Chocolate Ice-Cream

To Serve 4–6
Allow 4–5 hours to prepare (including freezing time)
Each serving (of 6) provides: 215 kcal, 3 g protein, 7 g carbohydrate, 19 g fat, 1 g fibre

Metric		Imperial/American
400 ml	soya milk	¾ pint/2 cups
100 ml	sunflower oil	7 tbs
3 tbs	unsweetened cocoa powder	3 tbs
25 ml	maple syrup	1½ tbs
2 tsp	vanilla essence	2 tsp

1 Pour 275 ml (½ pint/1½ cups) soya milk into ice-cube trays and place in the freezer or freezer compartment of your refrigerator till frozen solid (about 4–5 hours).
2 Put the remaining 125 ml (¼ pint/½ cup) soya milk in a blender together with the remaining ingredients. Add the now-frozen soya milk cubes, blend till completely smooth and serve.

If the ice-cream seems a little too soft to serve immediately, put it back in the freezer for half an hour or so. If the soya milk ice cubes are too hard, continue blending till they're completely soft.

This ice-cream can be stored in your freezer for as long as you like provided you remember to defrost it for at least an hour before serving.

Peach Sorbet

To Serve 4
Allow 3 hours to prepare (including freezing time)
Each serving provides: 88 kcal, 2 g protein, 19 g carbohydrate,
1 g fat, 3 g fibre

Metric		Imperial/American
½ kg	ripe peaches	1 lb/4 large
1	lemon	1
25 ml	maple syrup	1½ tbs
2 tsp	vanilla essence	2 tsp
125 ml	soya milk	¼ pint/½ cup

1 Stone and coarsely chop the peaches, put them in a bowl and place in the freezer or freezer compartment of your refrigerator for at least 3 hours.
2 Squeeze the lemon and put the juice in a blender.
3 Now add all the remaining ingredients together with the now-frozen peach chunks and blend to a thick, smooth consistency. Serve immediately.

If you don't want to serve this sorbet immediately, you can refreeze it for as long as you like; but note that you must remember to defrost it for at least 2 hours before serving.

Miscellaneous Recipes

Mushrooms on Toast

Per Serving
Allow 10 minutes to prepare
Each serving provides: 474 kcal, 8 g protein, 25 g carbohydrate, 38 g fat, 8 g fibre

Metric		Imperial/American
45 g	margarine	1½ oz/3 tbs
125 g	mushrooms	¼ lb/1 cup
2 slices	wholewheat bread	2 slices
	salt and pepper to taste	

1 Melt the margarine in a saucepan over a low heat.
2 While it is melting, wash and slice the mushrooms (or leave them whole if they're the button variety) and add them to the saucepan. Turn them every few minutes with a wooden spoon or slice.
3 Meanwhile, toast the bread and arrange on a plate.
4 As soon as the mushrooms are beginning to brown, add salt and pepper to taste, pour over the slices of toast and serve.

Mushrooms are so good done in this simple way that they really don't need any additions but, for variety, try adding ½ tsp *Garam Masala* (page 253) at step 1, or a little freshly-grated ginger. For a more substantial variation, make *Creamed Mushrooms* (page 97) and pour these over freshly-made toast.

Scrambled Tofu and Herbs on Toast

Per Serving
Allow 10 minutes to prepare
Each serving provides: 427 kcal, 15 g protein, 25 g carbohydrate, 31 g fat, 5 g fibre

Metric		Imperial/American
30 g	margarine	1 oz/2tbs
125 g	firm tofu	¼ lb/½ cup
2 slices	wholewheat bread	2 slices
½ tsp	mixed herbs	½ tsp
	salt and pepper to taste	

1 Melt the margarine in a small saucepan over a low heat.
2 Now crumble in the tofu and stir gently till it's warmed right through.
3 Meanwhile, toast the bread and arrange it on a plate.
4 Add the mixed herbs and salt and pepper to taste and stir for a few seconds before pouring over the slices of toast. Serve immediately.

This filling, protein-rich dish can be made in a few minutes when you're short of time or inclination to cook something more substantial or complicated.

For variety, try adding finely chopped onions and a little more margarine at step 2 or different herbs at step 4; or substitute *Garam Masala* (page 253) for the mixed herbs. Freshly-chopped herbs lift it into a different category altogether and only add another few moments to the preparation time.

Porridge with Fruit Juice

Per Serving
Allow 10 minutes to prepare
*Each serving (made with orange juice) provides: 283 kcal, 7 g protein,
58 g carbohydrate, 4 g fat, 4 g fibre*

Metric		Imperial/American
50 g	rolled oats	1½ oz/½ cup
¼ litre	fruit juice	½ pint/1¼ cups
	salt to taste	

1 Put all the ingredients in a small saucepan, bring to the boil, stirring
  continuously, then reduce heat and simmer, uncovered, till the
  porridge thickens. Add more juice if necessary to prevent the
  mixture from becoming too thick. Continue simmering for a few
  more minutes, still stirring continuously.
2 Remove from heat, transfer to individual bowls and serve with a jug
  of the same fruit juice, iced, to pour over and cool the porridge.

Porridge can be made with most fruit juices. Orange, apple, pineapple
and apricot are particularly good. If you have any leftovers, serve them,
chilled, as a dessert.
  For variety, try adding ¼ tsp ground cinnamon or cloves.

Lassi (Traditional Indian Sweet or Salty Yoghurt Drink)

To Serve 4–6
Allow 5 minutes to prepare
*Each serving (of 6, made with salt) provides: 22 kcal, 1 g protein,
1 g carbohydrate, 1 g fat, negligible fibre*

Metric		Imperial/American
¼ litre	*Vegan Yoghurt* (page 240)	½ pint/1¼ cups
¾ litre	iced water	1½ pints/3½ cups
1 tsp	salt (or 1 tbs any raw sugar)	1 tsp

1 Put all the ingredients in a blender and blend for a few seconds till thoroughly mixed.
2 Refrigerate till needed. Serve ice cold.

If you like your curries hot, salt lassi is the drink to serve with them. It has a cooling effect in the mouth and throat that is little short of miraculous. But either salt or sweet lassi can be served any time as a refreshing drink.

Note that it can be made several hours in advance so long as it is kept covered in a refrigerator and is well stirred before serving.

Also note that if the batch of yoghurt you're using happens to be rather bland, it's a good idea to add the juice of a lemon to the mixture.

Garam Masala
(Basic Indian Curry Spice Mixture)

To Make about 2 Tablespoonfuls
Allow 5 minutes to prepare

Metric		Imperial/American
1 tsp	cardamom seeds	1 tsp
5 cm	stick of cinnamon (or 1 tsp ground cinnamon)	2 in
2 tsp	whole cumin seeds (or 1 tsp ground cumin)	2 tsp
½	clove nutmeg (or ½ tsp ground nutmeg)	½
1 tsp	whole cloves (or ½ tsp ground cloves)	1 tsp
1 tsp	whole black peppercorns (or ½ tsp ground pepper)	1 tsp
1 tsp	ground turmeric	1 tsp

1 Use a coffee-grinder to grind all the whole seeds into a coarse
  powder.
2 Add the already-ground ingredients and seal in a jar till needed.

Most wholefood shops and good grocery stores keep a wide range of
whole seeds and spices but you can also get them in local Indian or
Chinese shops. Always use freshly-ground spices if you can – only then
will you end up with a dish that is enhanced by the intermingling of
many subtle aromas and flavours. But it isn't a good idea to make up
large quantities because they soon lose their pungency, even when
tightly sealed and kept in a cool, dark place.

For variety, try adding or substituting from the following list:
*caraway, coriander, fennel, fenugreek, mustard or poppy seeds, ground
ginger,* or *chilli.*

Basic Batter Mixture

To Make about a Dozen Pancakes or to Batter about 1 kg (2 lb) of
Fruit or Vegetables
Allow 25 minutes to prepare (including 20 minutes to stand)
Each pancake provides: 97 kcal, 4 g protein, 8 g carbohydrate,
4 g fat, 2 g fibre

Metric		**Imperial/American**
125 g	100 per cent wholewheat flour	¼ lb/1 cup
60 g	soya flour	2 oz/¾ cup
2 tsp	baking powder	2 tsp
	salt to taste	
125 ml	soya milk	¼ pint/½ cup
125 ml	water	¼ pint/½ cup
45 ml	oil	3 tbs

1 Put the flours, baking powder and salt to taste into a bowl and mix
   thoroughly.
2 Now add the milk a little at a time and then the water, stirring
   continuously until the mixture becomes smooth and creamy. For
   fritters keep the mix fairly thick; for pancakes, make it thinner: the
   thinner the mix the lighter the pancakes.
3 Beat in the oil a little at a time with a whisk, a fork or an electric
   mixer. Allow to stand for 20 minutes before use.

This can be prepared several hours in advance if you wish or, if you
have some left over, simply cover and store in the fridge for use later.

Use it to make pancakes, fruit or vegetable fritters or sweet or
savoury puddings.

Skinned Tomatoes

Allow 10 minutes to prepare ½ kg (1 lb)
(Note: many of our recipes call for skinned tomatoes so here is a simple method of skinning them.)

1 Put the tomatoes in a small mixing-bowl and pour over enough boiling water to cover them completely. Leave to stand for 1 minute.
2 Now pick up each tomato individually with a fork and using a very sharp knife to break the skin, pull it away in swathes.

Whole, tinned tomatoes can be bought relatively cheaply in super-markets and work well enough in most recipes, but always read the labels to see if any preservatives, flavouring or colouring have been added. If you have a good greengrocer or street market near by, however, or if it is simply against your philosophy of life to use tinned produce under any circumstances, then you will obviously prefer to use fresh ones, in which case this method will be useful. Shops and street markets are occasionally flooded with very cheap but absolutely taste-less, pale-pink tomatoes and when this happens your finished recipe will probably taste better if you use tinned ones.

Skinned Peppers

Allow 20 minutes to prepare ½ kg (1 lb)

Method 1
1 Cut the peppers in half lengthways, remove the seeds and then cut them in half lengthways again. Flatten them as much as possible by patting them down on a chopping-board and then place them under a hot grill till the skins have turned completely black. This will take about 10–15 minutes and you'll need to turn them from time to time to get them black all over.
2 As soon as they are, drop them in a bowl of cold water before picking them up one at a time with a fork and peeling the skin off with a sharp knife.

Method 2
1 Pick the peppers up individually by plunging a fork into the stalk end and hold in a flame while turning continuously till the skin goes completely black.
2 Plunge the whole, now black, peppers into cold water for a few moments before peeling with a sharp knife.
3 Cut in half and remove the pith and seeds before chopping or using as directed in the recipe.

This is a bit of a performance, so if you're impatient or pressed for time, it's simpler and in our view quite satisfactory to use tinned ones – but read the labels first to check that they don't contain any preservatives, flavouring or dyes.

Soaking and Cooking Pulses
(Dried Peas and Beans)

Allow several hours to prepare depending on type (see below)
1 Put the pulses in a large saucepan and pour over enough boiling
   water to cover. Leave to stand for 5 minutes.
2 Drain and repeat.
3 Drain and repeat but this time leave to stand for 1 hour.
4 (Optional) Drain and repeat and leave to stand overnight.
5 Change water, bring quickly to the boil, then reduce heat and
   simmer, partially covered, till tender.

Approximate Cooking Times
(assuming pre-soaked as above)
(Note: the time pulses need to cook varies with their age and quality.
Generally, the fresher they are, the less time they need. The times given
assume fresh pulses, recently bought from a reliable shop.)

20–30 minutes (10 minutes in a pressure-cooker)
   aduki beans, field beans, mung beans, dried peas
½–1 hour (15–20 minutes in a pressure-cooker)
   black beans, black-eyed beans, flageolet beans, lentils (only green
   need soaking), lima beans, split peas
1–2 hours (½–1 hour in a pressure-cooker)
   broad beans, butter beans, chick peas, haricot beans, red kidney
   beans (NB: see warning below!)
3–4 hours (1–1½ hours in a pressure-cooker)
   soya beans

All pulses cook quicker if pre-soaked as described above, but the chief
object of the method given is to eliminate their one drawback – their
well-known and unfortunate tendency to cause flatulence and farting.
This is because of the large quantities of potassium oxide salt they
contain. It is not harmful and the problem is easily solved by the method
given. Alternatively, the effects may be much reduced by adding anise,
fennel or caraway seeds to the recipe. We have done this in most cases. If
all else fails, make an infusion of any (or all) of these seeds in boiling
water and sip it slowly.

   If all this puts you off the whole idea of pulses, pause for a moment to
consider their virtues. They contain more protein, weight for weight,
than almost any other food (including beef steak!) as well as a wide
range of minerals and vitamins, and they have a very high fibre content.
Warning: red kidney beans should be boiled rapidly for at least 10
minutes before eating. Never slow casserole them unless they have been
boiled for 10 minutes first.

Sprouting Seeds and Pulses

Several days to prepare depending on type
(Note: if you haven't sprouted seeds or pulses before, read the remarks below before beginning.)

1 Soak 60–90 g (2–3 oz/2–3 tbs) of your chosen seed or pulse in tepid water overnight.
2 Rinse in cold water and drain. Put the rinsed seeds or pulses in a large jar and cover with muslin, gauze or blotting paper. Store in a cool, dark place.
3 Rinse in cold water daily till ready. If you want them to turn green, set them out in sunlight (or daylight) for their last few hours. This won't affect their nutritional value however.
4 Remove any loose skins (if necessary) by floating them in cold water. Drain thoroughly and serve.

Special Notes on Individual Pulses

Alfalfa Seeds: the most commonly sprouted seeds, easy and delicious.
Chick Peas: very quick; can be eaten as soon as the first shoot appears or kept for up to 4–5 days; delicious and nutty.
Lentils: must be *whole* (i.e. *brown* not *red*).
Mung Beans: easy but unpredictable; lift out sprouted ones by their shoots and leave others longer; a few will not sprout at all.
Red Kidney Beans: easy and attractive but probably not worth bothering with because *they must be boiled for at least 10 minutes or they remain poisonous even when sprouted.*
Rice: must be *wholegrain* (white rice is *dead*).
Sesame Seeds: can be eaten as soon as a shoot appears but, unlike alfalfa seeds, can't easily be induced to grow for very long.
Soya Beans: easy, rich in protein and minerals (especially calcium and iron) and delicious; need more frequent rinsing – twice daily or more, or they'll go off; eat when they're about 7 cm (3 in) long.
Sunflower Seeds: eat as soon as a shoot appears; they can't be induced to grow for long before going off.
Wheatberries: smell and taste of the countryside in summer but remain rather chewy.

It is a sobering miracle to watch a steel-hard, indigestible raw bean transform itself in a few hours into a crunchy plant-shoot. Why anyone should think it worthwhile to use time and energy to factory-process beans into the simulated mince-meat of TVP is a mystery of an altogether more prosaic kind.

Listed above are the most widely available and easy to use seeds and pulses, but it's always worth experimenting with others.

Purpose-made bean-sprouters can be bought in many wholefood shops. They consist of 2 or 3 stacking dishes to spread the pulses on, a tray to catch the rinsing water and a cover to keep off insects; but a simple jar, covered with muslin held in place with an elastic band serves just as well.

Injured or discoloured pulses won't sprout and may go mouldy and infect the whole batch, so it's better to pick them out first – spreading them on a tray will help you to find them.

Failures can be caused by *chemicals* (wholefood shops are the safest places to buy them), *injuries* (have they been chipped or stripped of their skins?) or *age* (how long have they been in stock?).

Non-Alcoholic Fruit Punch

To Serve 8–12
Allow 20 minutes to prepare

Metric		Imperial/American
1 litre	apple juice	2 pints/5 cups
2 tsp	ground cinnamon	2 tsp
12	whole cloves	12
2 tbs	freshly grated ginger (or 2 tsp ground dried ginger)	2 tbs
1	lemon	1
1	orange	1
1	lime (or another lemon)	1
1 litre	orange juice	2 pints/5 cups
1 litre	pineapple juice	2 pints/5 cups
	a few sprigs of mint	
	ice cubes	

1 Put a quarter of the apple juice in a small saucepan, add the spices, bring quickly to the boil then reduce heat and simmer, uncovered, for 15 minutes.
2 Meanwhile, peel the ginger root and grate it into the saucepan, squeeze the lemon and add the juice. Stir from time to time.
3 Thinly slice the orange and lime (another lemon will do if you couldn't get a lime) and put the slices into a suitable serving-bowl or large jug.
4 Pour all the remaining fruit juices into the bowl, add the contents of the saucepan, a few sprigs of fresh mint and the ice cubes and serve.

Virtually any fruit juice can be used to ring the changes on this fruit cocktail. Serve it on hot summer days (or nights) or as an alternative to alcohol at parties.

Wine Punch

To Serve 12–16
Allow 20 minutes to prepare

Metric		Imperial/American
¼ litre	water	½ pint/1¼ cups
2 tsp	ground cinnamon	2 tsp
12	whole cloves	12
2 tbs	freshly grated ginger (or 2 tsp dried ground ginger)	2 tbs
1 litre	orange juice	2 pints/5 cups
1 litre	apple juice	2 pints/5 cups
4 bottles	white wine	4 bottles
4 bottles	red wine	4 bottles
1	lemon	1
1	orange	1
3 bottles	tonic water (optional)	3 bottles
	ice cubes	
	a few sprigs of mint	

1 Put the water into a small saucepan, add the spices, bring quickly to
   the boil, then reduce heat and simmer, uncovered, for 15 minutes.
   Meanwhile, peel and grate the ginger into the saucepan, stirring
   from time to time.
2 Pour the juices and all the wine into a suitable serving-bowl or large
   jug.
3 Add the contents of the saucepan to the bowl as soon as it's ready.
4 Thinly slice the lemon and the orange and add the slices to the bowl.
5 Add the tonic water and ice cubes to the bowl and stir well.
   Decorate with sprigs of mint and serve.

This punch is miles better if you can afford to use *champagne* instead of
tonic water, but even if you can't, it gives a welcome lift to the sort of
cheap plonk most of us have to drink at parties. If you can't afford even
the cheap plonk and have to ask your guests to 'bring a bottle', you can
still use the recipe by preparing it beforehand without the wine and
simply add it as your guests arrive – though it's probably not a good
idea to let them see you adding the tonic water! It sweetens the punch
and adds sparkle but some people are puritanical about such things.

A Simple Table Wine

Allow 7 hours to prepare, 5–6 weeks to ferment and mature

Metric		Imperial/American
	For up to 15 litres (3 gallons)	
2 tsp	wine yeast	2 tsp
½ kg	bananas	1 lb
	Plus for each 5 litres (1 gallon)	
1 litre	grape concentrate (red, white or rosé)	2 pints/5 cups
½ kg	refined granulated sugar	1 lb/3 cups
1 tsp	yeast nutrient	1 tsp
2	vitamin B tablets	2

(Note: if you haven't made wine before, read the remarks below before beginning.)

1 Activate the yeast: i.e. half fill a small bottle with hand-warm water, add the wine yeast, shake well, stop with a cotton-wool bung and put it in a warm place. Peel and slice the bananas, put the flesh in a bowl (discard the skins), pour boiling water over, cover and set aside. Put the grape concentrate in a warm place too. Leave for 5–6 hours.

2 Put half the sugar in a suitable fermentation vessel and add enough hot water to dissolve it completely. Strain in the liquid from the bananas (discard the flesh). Add the grape concentrate. Make up the liquid to your chosen amount, using cold water till you get the ideal temperature (hand-warm, 25°C/77°F). Add the yeast solution and nutrient and stir thoroughly. Cover the fermentation vessel and leave in a warm place for 4 days.

3 After 4 days, dissolve the rest of the sugar in jugfuls of the must (the correct name for the fermenting grape juice solution), tip it back into the fermentation vessel and stir well in. Leave in a warm place for another week. Stir daily.

4 Siphon the must into 5 litre (1 gallon) demijohns, add 2 crushed vitamin B tablets to each jar and top up with cold water if necessary. Plug the jars with cotton-wool bungs and leave in a warm place for a further 7–10 days. Disturb the must by shaking the jars with a circular motion every day if you can remember.

5 Move the jars to a cool place and leave completely undisturbed till the wine clears (about 2–3 weeks).

6 Siphon into bottles. The wine will continue to improve in flavour and texture for several weeks – if you can resist drinking it!

All you really need for home wine-making is a large vessel to ferment the must in – a plastic bucket will do provided it has a cover – glass demijohns to store it in and a wine-maker's siphoning tube.

Normal kitchen standards of hygiene will suffice unless you plan to keep the wine for a year or more before drinking it, but take great care to keep the must covered at all times to keep out the dreaded vinegar bug. If you want to lay down a long-term cellar, every single implement must be sterilized before use and the yeast must be de-activated with Campden tablets before the bottling.

This simple recipe works nearly every time, but if you do have problems the rule of thumb is: *if in doubt rack it* – that is, siphon it into a fresh clean demijohn. There isn't room to go into the subject more deeply here, so, if racking does not work, consult one of the many books for beginners.

Note that the bananas don't flavour the wine at all, but do give it a rich, smooth texture – sufficient even to fool some connoisseurs!

Rum Truffles

To Make about 15
Allow about 2 hours to prepare
*Each truffle provides: 135 kcal, 3 g protein, 7 g carbohydrate, 9 g fat,
5 g fibre*

Metric		Imperial/American
60 g	raisins	2 oz/3 tbs
90 ml	dark rum	3 fl oz/⅓ cup
90 g	firm margarine	3 oz/⅓ cup
125 g	gram flour	¼ lb/1 cup
45 ml	maple syrup	3 tbs
50 g	carob powder	5 tbs/½ cup
3 tbs	desiccated coconut	3 tbs

1 Put the raisins in a small bowl, pour the rum over and set aside for at least ½ hour.
2 Melt the margarine in a small saucepan, stir in the gram flour to make a firm roux and cook gently for 2–3 minutes. Stir in the maple syrup, rum and raisins and continue stirring till thoroughly mixed. Remove from heat.
3 Set 2 tbs of the carob powder aside and add the rest to the saucepan. Mix thoroughly to a thick, slightly sticky, uniformly coloured paste. Set aside for 20 minutes.
4 Put the desiccated coconut and the remaining 2 tbs of carob powder on a plate and mix together till the coconut becomes carob-coloured.
5 Now, take teaspoonfuls of the truffle mixture, drop them on to the coconut and roll them around to make well-coated little balls of about 2 cm (1 in) diameter.
6 Refrigerate for at least an hour before serving.

These are about as decadent as we are proposing to get in this book and we advise you not to make too many of them lest your friends should overdose themselves. Serve them with freshly-brewed black coffee and brandy to round off a really special meal. They also make a delightful, thoughtful present for a vegan friend.

For variety, use brandy or liqueur instead of rum, or finely chopped dates instead of raisins.

Appendix 1

Notes on Vegan Nutrition

Food for Health

For perfect health, the human body needs carbohydrate and fat (for energy), protein (for the building and repair of tissues), fibre (for good digestion), plus tiny amounts of complex substances called vitamins, certain minerals and, of course, water. This brief summary of these individual constituents of your diet describes what they are and how we, as vegans, can make sure we eat adequate amounts of them.

Carnivores, and even some vegetarians, may forget that all living tissue on our planet is made from the sun's energy via the miracle of plant growth, but not vegans whose everyday diet is based on nothing else.

Carbohydrate

When sunlight falls on green plants, they mysteriously spin their substance from carbon dioxide and water. How they do it is still not fully understood. We take it for granted simply because it happens all the time. Sugars and starches are two forms of plant substance, known as carbohydrates, that the plant produces as a way of storing energy for use when the sun isn't shining and these form the chief source of energy in human food. And only plants can do this – although carnivorous animals such as dogs and lions seldom eat plants directly, they do eat animals that have eaten nothing else. Since these sugars and starches are present in all plants, sugars predominantly in fruit, starches in seeds and roots, there is no difficulty in getting an adequate supply in an exclusively vegan diet.

Fat

There are three main kinds of fat. Two of them, *saturated* and *monounsaturated*, can be made in the body from carbohydrate and so are not essential in the diet. They occur chiefly in animals which store them as an energy reserve (even lean meat contains a lot) and are high in cholesterol. The third kind, *polyunsaturated*, cannot be made in the body but must be taken in the form of plant food. It contains no cholesterol.

> 'The Royal College of Physicians advocate a generous intake of polyunsaturated fatty acids but a restricted intake of saturated fatty acids for the prevention of coronary heart disease.'

The conclusion seems obvious – not only are vegetable oils necessary, but a healthier way to take the fat we need.

The Health Education Council now recommends that fat should not form more than 30–35 per cent of the total energy intake. Nearly all omnivores and some vegetarians often exceed this figure by 10–20 per cent or more – and it's animal fat at that – but:

'A vegan diet composed mainly of unrefined cereals, pulses and nuts supplemented with smaller amounts of fruit and vegetables will be high in fibre and starch and provide 60–70 per cent of the total energy in the diet from carbohydrate.'

Which is just what the doctor ordered!

Protein

Proteins are enormous molecules which are broken down by the body's digestive processes into their component parts, called amino acids, and used as building blocks for tissues such as skin and muscle. There are several different kinds of these amino acids commonly found in plants and animals but although plants can synthesize all they need, there are eight kinds that humans and other animals are unable to make. These are called the essential amino acids and, as the body is unable to store them, they form a vital part of our daily food.

All these building blocks must be present together for the body to be able to use them and, as their proportions vary from one plant to another, it makes sense to combine two or more plants in a particular dish to ensure 'a good protein balance'. (For example, *Three Seed Bread*, page 206, *Tomato & Lentil Flan*, page 61, *Poppy Seed Tart*, page 220, and so on.)

But, contrary to popular belief, there is no problem at all in getting enough of these protein building blocks from plant food.

'Cereals, nuts, potatoes and oil seeds contain about 10 per cent of their available energy as protein and pulses about 30 per cent; fruit, leafy vegetables and roots and tubers (other than potatoes) generally contain very little protein.

'The Department of Health & Social Security recommend that 10 per cent of the daily energy intake should come from protein. This means an intake of 55 grams/day for women and 68 grams/day for men leading a sedentary life. *These recommended intakes can easily be satisfied by a vegan diet based mainly on cereals, potatoes, pulses, nuts and oil seeds and supplemented by smaller amounts of fruit and vegetables.*' (Our italics)

Fibre

Some of the carbohydrates synthesized by plants are used to form the basic structure of their cell walls. Called cellulose or fibre, these can only be easily digested by herbivores (such as sheep, cows and horses) by a process of fermentation that takes several days and, in the case of cows, requires five stomachs! As a result, fibre was once thought not to be an essential part of the human diet. But more recent research has shown that it is in fact vital for healthy digestion in humans because it provides roughage that helps the food pass through the gut more quickly, thereby preventing constipation and the build-up of toxins. It also helps to control blood sugar levels by slowing down the absorption of sugars and starches – particularly important for diabetics – and keeps down the blood cholesterol level, thereby reducing the risk of heart disease. There is also evidence that it reduces the risk of bowel cancer. Finally, and perhaps most importantly of all, it gives a feeling of fullness without the consumption of more food than is good for you.

Vitamins

Plants are such a rich source of nearly all the vitamins we need that only two need concern us here: B_{12} and D.

Vitamin B_{12}

'Vitamin B_{12} is unique among the vitamins being made exclusively by micro-organisms. Cereals, fruit, nuts, pulses, vegetables and other plant foods are apparently free from the vitamin unless contaminated by micro-organisms that produce the vitamin and by insects. Thus vegan diets are most likely to be lacking in vitamin B_{12}. The highest amount of vitamin B_{12} in foods is found in liver and kidney although it is present in all flesh and dairy foods. The vitamin is produced commercially from bacteria and a number of vegan foods, such as Tastex, Barmene, Plamil and Granogen, are now supplemented with the vitamin. The daily requirement for vitamin B_{12} is very small, in the region of 1–3 micro-g/day (1 micro-g is a millionth of a gram), and this makes the study of vitamin B_{12} nutrition very difficult.'

Furthermore, the human body can store up to four years' supply of the vitamin, so that although the body may use 3 micro-gs daily, we don't actually need to *eat* some every day.

It seems likely that in our original 'natural' state, eating rain-washed fruits, roots and berries in the primeval forest, human beings would have developed or absorbed the necessary intestinal flora to synthesize the tiny amounts needed and have had the capacity to absorb them directly from the gut without needing to take them in through the mouth. Even with today's sprayed and fertilized crops, many vegans claim to have remained healthy for years without supplementing their diets with B_{12}.

Luckily, there are natural sources of B_{12} other than dead animal flesh, for it is almost always found in plant products that are the result of fermentation, such as beers (particularly stout), wines, miso, yoghurt, etc.

Amounts may be small, however, and if you plan to be exclusively vegan on a permanent basis, it's probably better to be safe than sorry and take a vitamin B_{12} supplement. Even though you probably won't actually need it, it won't do you any harm! In any case, the vitamin B_{12} tablets available in wholefood shops are produced by fermentation processes similar to those occurring in the production of beer or miso, and have just as much claim to being described as 'natural'.

Vitamin D

'Plant foods do not contain vitamin D, which is associated with the absorption of calcium and bone development, but individuals can synthesise the vitamin for themselves by the action of sunlight on their skin. Vitamin D deficiency can occur in children reared on a vegan diet if they are not sufficiently exposed to sunlight or not given a dietary source of the vitamin.'

So vegans who shun the sun should make sure they're getting enough of the vitamin in their diet. This isn't difficult in practice since it is added as a supplement to all margarines and to some soya milks. Vitamin D pills are also available. These remarks apply particularly to young children, especially those of Asian families, who tend to keep them out of the sun.

Minerals

We also need a number of minerals in our diet for good health but since these are widely distributed through a whole range of plants there is generally no problem getting them.

Plant foods, especially fruit and vegetables, contain less salt than foods of animal origin. The correct quantity of salt is a matter of much dispute in the medical professon, but there is some evidence that the typical Western diet contains too much of it and that this leads to problems of high blood pressure and difficulties with the heart and kidneys. So, once again, the vegan diet may alleviate rather than cause symptoms.

Summary

If you eat from a wide range of the recipes given in this book, using the ingredients specified, you are most unlikely to suffer any nutrient, vitamin or mineral deficiency.

But if you are cautious by nature and want to be absolutely sure of your supply of vitamin B_{12}, take care to include some stout beer, yoghurt, wine and miso in your diet on a regular basis and take vitamin B_{12} pills which are themselves, as has been pointed out, produced by a process of natural fermentation.

If you wish to know more on the subject, we recommend you to read *Vegan Nutrition* by T. A. B. Sanders, published by the Vegan Society, which is the source of all the quotes in these brief notes.

Appendix 2
Seven Reasons to be Vegan

1 Health

It would be possible to follow a 100 per cent vegan regime and not be eating healthily – but you'd have to work at it. For example you could have white bread and jam for breakfast, chips and beans for lunch and baked beans on white toast for dinner. Providing you persisted, after a while, if you didn't die of boredom, you'd die of something else.

But people who become vegan generally do so only after a lot of thought and the diet they choose usually consists of high-quality wholefood cereals, grains and pulses supplemented with fresh fruit, salads and vegetables – the diet, in short, that we present in this book and this is what we mean by 'a vegan diet' in this section.

There is increasing evidence that a vegan diet like this is to be strongly recommended on health grounds:

- Factory-farmed animals are fed a dubious array of artifical food-stuffs, chemicals, hormones and antibiotics. The long-term effects of eating these toxic substances isn't known. The recent world-wide panic over BSE may be no more than a hint of horrors to come.
- The high levels of cholesterol found in all meat and dairy products are now generally thought by the medical profession to be dangerous for human health. 'Natural' meat came from animals that roamed and ran wild. They had virtually no fat on them and what they had was unsaturated. Factory-farmed animals get no exercise at all and their flesh – even the lean – contains up to 50 per cent saturated fat.
- Cow's milk produced by the dairy industry has been found to contain significant quantities of pesticides, antibiotics and teat dip disinfectants. Their effect on humans has not been investigated. Again, it cannot be beneficial.
- A surprisingly large number of people are allergic to cow's milk, especially young children. Eczema, asthma, tonsillitis and gastro-intestinal disturbances are some of the problems that can result. People may suffer from a range of distressing symptoms for years before discovering that the symptoms simply disappear as soon as they stop drinking the cow's milk that caused them.
- The typical Western diet provides about 12 grams of salt a day – about 2 teaspoonfuls – most of it coming from meat and meat products. This is certainly too much and may lead to high blood pressure and all its associated risks. Vegan diets are relatively low in salt.

• Vegan and vegetarian foods do not attract the noxious bacteria that are responsible for salmonella and other forms of food poisoning.

Further evidence was published by the Health Education Council in a leaflet in 1985:

'A hundred years ago, most people ate plenty of fibre from bread and potatoes, but lacked a fully adequate varied diet. Diseases caused by a lack of vitamins and minerals were common. Today, the problems are different. Many people now eat too much meat, dairy produce and sugar, and too little fibre for good health . . .

'Research has shown links between what we eat and many modern diseases. For example:

• Heart disease may be linked with too much fat.
• Diabetes and tooth decay may be linked with too much sugar.
• High blood pressure and strokes may be linked with too much salt.
• Bowel cancer, constipation and diverticulosis (a common bowel problem) may be linked with too little fibre.
• Obesity may be linked with too much fat and sugar, and too little fibre. Diabetes, high blood pressure, strokes and heart disease are all associated with obesity too.'

All the fats referred to in this quote are the saturated type, found chiefly in foods of animal origin. Just over a quarter of the fat eaten in the typical Western diet comes from meat; butter and margarine provide another quarter; milk and cooking fats account for another; and the remaining quarter is made up of cheese and 'hidden' fats in pastry, sweets, ice-creams and other 'convenience' foods.

The simple fact of converting to a vegan diet removes all the cholesterol and nearly all the saturated fat and reduces the total quantity of polyunsaturated fat to the 30–35 per cent of the total energy intake which is recommended by the Health Education Council for general good health and the prevention of heart disease.

If all this leaves you unmoved, consider this: Britain's longest-lived man, Harry Shoerats, died in February 1984, aged 111. He was born in Russia in 1872 and settled in Britain in 1917. He attributed his longevity primarily to his vegan diet of fruit, nuts, vegetables and cereals. He did not retire from his work as a craftsman until the age of 104 and cycled to work daily till his 100th birthday.

2 Economic

If you follow a diet based on the recipes in this book, you'll certainly find yourself spending a lot less on food on a personal basis, but the consequences of a shift to a vegan diet among the population at large would be considerably more far-reaching.

Animals reared for their meat have been calculated to use 90 per cent of the plant food given to them simply to sustain their own bodily processes. Only 10 per cent finally arrives on the plates of omnivores. It would be hard to imagine a more uneconomic or wasteful way of using the world's resources.

If there were a major shift towards veganism in the industrialized nations, the prices of plant foods would fall everywhere, especially in the Third World.

3 Ecological

More than 40 per cent of the world's tropical rain forest has been destroyed this century. The current rate of disappearance is 50 hectares a minute. Most people might think it fatuous to suggest that becoming a vegan could have the slightest effect on this. Yet it is a simple fact that most of the vast areas that are being destroyed and laid down to grass in South America are being levelled for no better reason than the raising of beef cattle for the North American steak and hamburger market. As a result, the world is losing rare species at a frightening and accelerating rate.

Similar pressures apply wherever land is farmed intensively. Britain's countryside is fast being turned into a vast, bleak, prairie-like landscape devoid of hedgerows or trees simply in order to produce yet more contributions to the EEC grain mountains, most of which are sold off as animal feed. Countless species of our wild birds, animals, butterflies and wild flowers are threatened as a result.

At sea, intensive fishing has destroyed the vast herring shoals that once roamed around Britain's shores (and the North Sea fishing industry with them) and everyone knows how near several species of whale have come to extinction.

The list, alas, goes on and on. There are hundreds of other species whose habitats are threatened by the millions of omnivores *our* species counts among its members.

> 'The average Briton now consumes up to 8 beef cattle, 36 pigs, 36 sheep and 550 poultry birds in the average lifetime.' (*The Animals Report*, Richard North, Penguin, 1983.)

Multiply this by the 56 million people in the UK and you begin to realize the scale of the problem.

Clearly, every single person who becomes vegan immediately ceases their personal contribution to this inexorable demand for the products of the intensive farming of animals. So *everyone who becomes vegan ceases to be part of the problem and becomes part of the solution* – helping to ease the intolerable pressure that humanity now exerts on every other species to the farthest reaches of the globe.

4 Altruistic

'Why do you people care more about animals than about humans?' is a challenge that is often thrown at vegans and vegetarians by irritated omnivores.

Leaving aside the fact that it is clearly an emotional response, probably stemming from their own feelings of guilt, it is simply not true:

'If Americans were to reduce their meat consumption by only 10 per cent for one year, it would free at least 12 million tons of grain for human consumption – or enough to feed 60 million people . . . Indeed, if Americans were to stop eating grain-fed beef altogether the grain thus released would be enough to feed all the 600 million people in India.' (*Animal Liberation*, Peter Singer, Thorsons, 1983.)

Not to mention the 'few' starving millions in central Africa!

For the truth is that if you wish to put the welfare of humanity first, you can hardly do better than *become vegan*!

So the next time an irritable omnivore challenges you in this way, why not throw the challenge right back by asking: 'Why are you so indifferent to the starving people in the Third World that you selfishly continue to eat more than ten times the grain you need in the form of animal protein?'

If all this sounds a bit too idealistic for you, consider this: since the case for the vegan diet as healthier is now irrefutable (and generally accepted by the medical profession) what better way can there be of showing your love and concern for those closest to you than by preparing for them not only food they will enjoy, but food that is good for their health?

5 Compassionate

'A human being is a part of a whole, called by us "Universe", a part limited in time and space. He experiences himself, his thoughts and feelings as something separated from the rest – a kind of optical delusion of his consciousness. This delusion is a kind of prison for us, restricting us to our personal desires and to affection for a few persons nearest to us.

'Our task must be to free ourselves from this prison by widening our circle of compassion to embrace all living creatures and the whole of nature in its beauty.' (Albert Einstein.)

'If true, the Pythagorean principles as to abstaining from flesh, foster innocence; if ill-founded they at least teach us frugality, and what loss have you in losing your cruelty? It merely deprives you of the food of lions and vultures . . . let us ask what is best – not what is customary. Let us love temperance – let us be just – let us refrain from bloodshed.' (Seneca.)

'I, for my part, wonder of what sort of feeling, mind or reason that man was possessed who was first to pollute his mouth with gore, and allow his lips to touch the flesh of a murdered being; who spread his table with the mangled form of dead bodies, and claimed as daily food and dainty dishes what but now were beings endowed with movement, with perception and with voice.' (Plutarch.)

What would such compassionate and thoughtful men as these have said of the catalogue of misery and suffering we now inflict on animals in the name of profit and of science? For the abuses they wrote of were trifling compared with the scale and quality of the practices of factory farming, or the wholesale abuses inherent in the routine testing on innocent and defenceless creatures of the unnecessary, trivial products of the cosmetics industry?

Most omnivores, if they were forced to spend a single day enduring the conditions of the average factory farm would renounce meat-eating for life. It is not lack of imagination that prevents them from discovering this, but a deliberate, conscious decision to remain ignorant for fear that *knowing the full consequences of their demand for cheap meat would be too painful to endure.* Such people are more guilty of the suffering inflicted on animals in their name than any German citizen was, in the Second World War, who sought to prove afterwards that he or she simply 'didn't know' what was going on in the concentration camps.

But if what is done in factory farms is appalling, it pales into insignificance compared with the horrors inflicted in laboratories in the name of science.

'In Britain, where experimenters are required to report the number of experiments performed, official government figures show that 4,443,843 experiments on animals were performed in 1981. In the United States there are no figures of comparable accuracy. Under the Animal Welfare Act [*sic*] of 1970 the US Department of Agriculture publishes a report listing the number of animals used by facilities registered with it, but this list is incomplete in many ways. It does not include rats, mice, birds, reptiles, frogs, or domestic farm animals used for experimental purposes; it does not include animals used in secondary schools, or by government agencies; and it does not include experiments performed by facilities that do not transport animals interstate or receive grants or contracts from the federal government. According to this very incomplete report, somewhere between 1.6 and 1.8 million animals are used in experimentation each year. The number of dogs is 200,000, cats 50–70,000, primates 50,000, rabbits, hamsters and guinea pigs around half a million each . . .

'Surely, one day . . . our children's children, reading about what was done in laboratories in the twentieth century, will feel the same sense of horror and incredulity at what otherwise civilised people can do that we now feel when we read about the atrocities of the Roman gladiatorial arenas or the eighteenth-century slave trade.' (*Animal Liberation*, Peter Singer.)

Ask yourself what possible response can any sane and compassionate person have to this unforgivable lapse on the part of humanity, other than determinedly and single-mindedly to boycott any or all of the products of such practices?

6 Ethical

'If man's aspirations towards right living are serious . . . he will first abstain from animal food because . . . its use is simply immoral, as it requires the performance of an act which is contrary to moral feeling – killing.' (*The Ethics of Diet*, Tolstoy.)

But are humanity's aspirations serious? We often claim to have attained the highest level of consciousness of any living creature on earth. Whether this is true or not – and it must be open to doubt in view of the mindless, institutionalized cruelty of our factory farms, vivisection laboratories and the torture of our own kind in prisons around the world, it is certainly true that we have become the guardians of this planet and of all its life forms. So, with all our faults, we must try to behave as responsibly as we can.

Is factory farming a responsible way to behave? Even the most recalcitrant meat-eater can hardly deny that cruelty and suffering are inherent in it. In an attempt to divert attention away from their own doubts, which often stem from the fear of having to change, such people launch into debates about *how much* pain animals can suffer compared with humans. But this is irrelevant. If we agree that suffering is bad, and that animals do suffer as a consequence of our actions, then it doesn't matter how much they suffer but that they suffer at all. So we must change our action or stand condemned of callousness.

Nor is it good enough to support the theory but fail to support the practice: 'They pity, and they eat the objects of their compassion.' (*The Citizen of the World*, Oliver Goldsmith, in *Collected Works*, Clarendon Press, Oxford, 1966.)

> 'If a boycott is the only way to stop cruelty, then we must encourage as many people as possible to join the boycott. We can only be effective in this if we ourselves set the example.' (*Animal Liberation*, Peter Singer.)

> 'A vegetarian diet is the acid test of humanitarianism.' (Tolstoy.)

7 Spiritual

Orthodox Buddhists and Hindus have always been vegetarian and often vegan for their religions are founded on the belief that life is sacred – not just *human life*, as in Christianity, but *all* life. But, just as importantly, both these great religions also teach that not only is a vegan diet correct in ethical terms, but that it is also more conducive to spiritual peace of mind and the acquisition of the virtues of humility and compassion. Christians have, of course, always admired just these two virtues above all else in their own founder and leader, so it is odd how little heed is paid to his own words on the subject:

> 'Not by shedding innocent blood, but by living a righteous life shall ye find the peace of God . . . Blessed are they who keep this law; for God is manifested in all creatures. All creatures live in God, and God is hid in them . . .
>
> 'The fruit of the trees and the seeds and of the herbs alone do I partake, and these are changed by the spirit into my flesh and blood. Of these alone and their like shall ye eat who believe in me and are my disciples; for of these, in the spirit, come life and health and healing unto man . . .'
> (From *The Gospel of the Holy Twelve*, trans. by G. J. Ouseley.)

It would seem that the Jesus in this apocryphal gospel is advocating veganism. In another early gospel, translated into English directly from the Aramaic tongue Jesus is thought to have spoken, there is a specific warning of the dire consequence of the killing and eating of animals:

> 'And the flesh of slain beasts in his own body will become his own tomb. For I tell you truly, he who kills, kills himself, and

whoso eats the flesh of slain beasts, eats the body of death.'
(From *The Gospel of Peace of Jesus Christ by the Disciple John*,
Trans. by E. B. Szekely, C. W. Daniel, London 1937.)

But isn't it enough to be vegetarian? Why do I have to become *vegan*?

The problem is that the industrial production of milk, butter, eggs and
cheese is totally dependent on the existence of the rest of the factory
farming industry with all its odious practices. Repeated frustrated
pregnancies are required to keep dairy cows lactating and in any case
they are slaughtered for meat as soon as their milk yield drops, and it is
the fate of their unfortunate calves to be removed from their mothers at
birth and sent either straight to the slaughterhouse or to veal production
units. Most eggs come from battery systems of course (including those
with names like 'Farm Fresh') but even free-range egg production entails
the killing of the unproductive – the cocks (only half of a batch of fertile
eggs will hatch into hens) and even the productive hens are sent for
slaughter as soon as their laying days are over.

So we see that even buying a carton of milk in a supermarket or half a
dozen free-range eggs in a wholefood shop makes a tiny, but significant,
contribution to industrial slaughter.

Well, if these seven reasons haven't convinced you, let us add an eighth!
Neither of the authors of this book found their food even half as
enjoyable before becoming vegan as we have since. So, if you can't bring
yourself to change your diet for health, economic, ecological, altruistic,
compassionate, ethical or spiritual reasons, then *change it for the sheer
pleasure of eating the wonderful vegan dishes we have invented for you!*

Appendix 3
Useful Addresses

Australia
Organization for Farm Animal Liberation, PO Box E65, East Parramatta, NSW 2150. Tel: (02) 683 5991
Vegan Australasian Network, PO Box 429, Twantin, QLD 4565.
Vegan Society of Australia, PO Box 85, Seaford, VIC 3198. Tel: (03) 786-6192
Vegan Society of Brisbane, PO Box 400, South Brisbane, QLD 4101. Tel: (07) 857-5589
Vegan Society of New South Wales, 12 Eastview, Greenwich, NSW 2007. Tel: (02) 436-1373
Vegan Society of Queensland, 36 Hargreaves Road, West End, QLD 4101.

Belgium
Belgian Vegan Society, Kapeliestraat 66, B 9220 Hamme.

Canada
Canadian Vegans for Animal Rights, c/o General Delivery, Port Berry, Ontario LOB 1NO. Tel: (416) 985-3308
Canada EarthSave Society, Suite 103-1093 West Broadway, Vancouver, BC V6H 1E2. Tel: (604) 731-5885.

Denmark
Vegana, Kirsten Jungsberg, Radmund Steinsalle 45, DK-200, Copenhagen. Tel: (31) 743-404

Finland
Vegaaniliitta Ry, PO Box 320, FIN-00151, Helsinki. Tel: (0) 296-3025

France
Société Véganiste de France, Stéphane Hennion, 12 Allée Jacques Becker, 93300 Aubervilliers. Tel: (1) 4833-6341

Germany
Vegane Offensive Ruhrgebeit, c/o Langer August ev, Braunschweigerstrasse 22, 44145 Dortmund. Tel: (231) 208-385159

Ireland
Vegan Information Centre for Ireland, c/o Mrs C. Gunn-King, 'Braidujle', 120 Knockan Road, Ballydoghan Td, nr Broughshane, Ballymena, N. Ireland BT43 7LE

Italy
Movimento Vegano Italiano, Via F. Ili de Dio 375, 20099 Sesto San Giovanni, Milano.

Netherlands
Vegans International/Dutch Vegan Society, PO Box 1087, 6801 BB Arnhem. Tel: (85) 420746

New Zealand
New Zealand Vegan Society, PO Box 26/356, Epsom, Auckland.
Save Animals from Experimentation, PO Box 647, Auckland 1.

Portugal
Frenta Vegana, Apdo 75, Torre de Marinha, 2840 Seixal.

South Africa
Vegans in South Africa, Box 36242, Glosderry 7702. Tel: (021) 797-9026

Spain
Asociación Vegana Española, Apartado Postal 38.127, 28080 Madrid.

Sweden
Swedish Vegan Society, Klövervägen 6, S-64700, Mariefred. Tel: (159) 12467

United Kingdom
Animal Aid, 7 Castle Street, Tonbridge, Kent TN9 1BH. Tel: (01732) 365-446
Animal Concern, Scotland, 121 West Regent Street, Glasgow G2 2SD.
Animal Liberation Front, BCM Box 1160, London WC1 3XX.
British Union for the Abolition of Vivisection, 16a Crane Grove, London N7 8LB. Tel: (0171) 700-4888
Compassion in World Farming, 5a Charles Street, Petersfield, Hampshire GU32 3EW. Tel: (01730) 264-208
Friends of the Earth, 26 Underwood Street, London N1 7JQ. Tel: (0171) 490-1555
National Anti-Vivisection Society, 261 Goldhawk Road, London W12 8EU. Tel: (0181) 846-9777

PETA (People for the Ethical Treatment of Animals), PO Box 3169, London NW1 2JF. Tel: (0171) 388-4922
Vegan Business Connection, 180 Mansfield Road, Nottingham NG1 3HW. Tel: (0115) 958-5666
The Vegan Society, 7 Battle Road, St Leonards-on-Sea, East Sussex TN37 7AA. Tel: (01424) 427-393
The Vegetarian Society, Parkdale, Dunham Road, Altrincham, Cheshire WA14 4QG. Tel: (0161) 928-0793
Vegfam, The Sanctuary, near Lydford, Devon.
World Society for the Protection of Animals, 2 Langley Lane, London SW8 1TH. Tel: (0171) 793-0540

United States of America
American Anti-Vivisection Society, 801 Old York Rd #204, Jenkintown, PA 19046-1685
American Vegan Society, 501 Old Harding Highway, Malaga, NJ 08328. Tel: (609) 694-2887
Animal Liberation Inc., 319 West 74th Street, New York, NY 10023
Animal Rights Network, PO Box 5234, Westport, CT 06880
Beauty Without Cruelty (American branch of British group), 175 West 12th Street, New York, NY 10011
Friends of Animals Inc., 11 West 60th Street, New York, NY 10023
Mobilization for Animals, PO Box 337, Jonesboro, TN 37659
PETA (People for the Ethical Treatment of Animals), PO Box 42516, Washington DC 20015
Society for Animal Rights, 421 South Gate Street, Clarks Summit, PA 18411
United Action for Animals, 205 East 42nd Street, New York, NY 10017
Vegan Action, PO Box 4353, Berkeley, CA 94704
Vegan Association of Connecticut, 1696 Whitney Avenue, Hamden, CT 06517. Tel: (203) 288-9181
Vegan Network, 319 Nickuson Street, Suite 102, Seattle, WA 98109
Vegetarian Activist Collective, 616 6th Street, Brooklyn, NY 11215
Vegetarian Resource Group, PO Box 1463, Baltimore, MD 21203. Tel: (410) 366-8343
World Society for the Protection of Animals, 29 Perkins Street, PO Box 190, Boston, MA 02130

Appendix 4

Selected Bibliography

Animal Factories, Jim Mason and Peter Singer (Crown, New York, 1980)

Animal Liberation, Peter Singer (Thorsons, Wellingborough, 1983)

Animal Liberation: A Graphic Guide, Lori Gruen, Peter Singer and David Hine (Camden Press, 1987)

Animal Rights and Human Obligations, Tom Regan and Peter Singer (Prentice Hall, New Jersey, 1976)

Animal Rights – A Symposium, David Paterson and Richard Ryder (eds) (Centaur Press, 1979)

Animal Suffering, Marian Stamp Dawkins (Chapman & Hall, London, 1980)

Animal Welfare in Poultry, Pig & Veal Calf Production (HMSO, London, 1981)

Animals, Men and Morals: An Enquiry into the Mal-Treatment of Non-Humans, Stanley and Roslind Godlovitch and John Harrison (eds) (Gollancz, London and Taplinger, New York, 1972)

Animals, Politics and Morality, Robert Garner (MUP, 1993)

The Animals Report, Richard North (Penguin, London, 1983)

Animals' Rights, Henry Salt (Centaur Press, 1980)

A Bibliography on Animal Rights and Related Matters, Charles Magel (University Press of America, Washington, DC, 1981)

The Civilised Alternative, Jon Wynne-Tyson (Centaur Press, 1972)

McCance and Widdowson's The Composition of Foods, A. A. Paul and D. A. T. Southgate, fourth revised ed (HMSO, London, 1978)

Diabetes, Coronary Thrombosis and The Saccharine Disease, Cleave, Campbell and Painter (John Wright & Sons Ltd, Bristol)

The Extended Circle, Jon Wynne-Tyson (ed.) (Centaur Press, 1986)

Food Fit for Humans, Frank Wilson (Daniel, 1975)

Food for a Future, Jon Wynne-Tyson (Centaur Press, 1979)

Food Science – A Chemical Approach, Brian A. Fox and Allan G. Cameron, third ed (Hodder & Stoughton, London, 1977)

History of the Humane Movement, Charles D. Niven (Johnson, 1967)

In Defence of Living Things, Christine Townend (Wentworth, Sydney, 1980)

Medical Nemesis, Ivan Illich (Calder & Boyars, London, 1975)

The Moral Status of Animals, Stephen R. L. Clark (OUP, 1977)

The Philosophy of Compassion, Esmé Wynne-Tyson (Centaur Press, 1970)

The Question of Animal Awareness, Donald Griffin (Rockefeller University Press, New York, 1976)

The Rights of Animals, Brigid Brophy (*Sunday Times*/Vegetarian Society, 1965)

The Savour of Salt – A Henry Salt Anthology, George Hendrick and Willene Hendrick (eds) (Centaur Press, 1989)

The Scientific Conscience, Catherine Roberts (Centaur Press, 1974)

Vegan Nutrition, Gill Langley (The Vegan Society, 1995)

Vegan Nutrition, T. A. B. Sanders and Frey R. Ellis (The Vegan Society, 1985)

Vegan Nutrition: Pure and Simple, Michael Klaper MD, (Gentle World, 1988)

Veganism – Scientific Aspects, T. A. B. Sanders (The Vegan Society, 1983)

A Vegetarian Sourcebook, Keith Akers (G. P. Putnam & Sons, New York, 1983)

Victims of Science, Richard D. Ryder (Davis-Poynter, 1975)

Why Vegan, Kath Clements (GMP, 1995)

Appendix 5

Abbreviations and Measures

Metric
g = gram(s)
kg = kilogram(s)
ml = millilitre(s)
C = Celsius

Imperial
oz = ounce(s)
lb = pound(s)
fl oz = fluid ounce(s)
F = Fahrenheit

Nutritional Analysis
kcal = kilocalorie(s)

Table of Approximate Conversions Used in the Recipes

Metric	Imperial	American
15 g	½ oz	NB:
30 g	1 oz	the number of
60 g	2 oz	tablespoonfuls
90 g	3 oz	or cups varies
125 g	¼ lb	according to
150 g	5 oz	the ingredients
180 g	6 oz	
225 g	7 oz	
¼ kg	½ lb	
300 g	10 oz	
350 g	¾ lb	
½ kg	1 lb	
575 g	1¼ lb	
¾ kg	1½ lb	
1 kg	2 lb	
5 ml	1 tsp	1 tsp
15 ml	1 tbs	1 tbs
125 ml	¼ pint	½ cup
200 ml	8 fl oz	1 cup
¼ litre	½ pint	1¼ cups
400 ml	¾ pint	2 cups
½ litre	1 pint	2½ cups
650 ml	1¼ pints	3 cups
¾ litre	1½ pints	3½ cups
1 litre	2 pints	5 cups

Note: The standard measure for a tablespoon is 15 ml and we recommend that you use measuring spoons, as ordinary spoons vary in size from 15 ml to 25 ml

Exact Conversions

100 g = 3.53 oz   1 kg = 2 lb 3 oz   1 litre = 1.76 pints
1 oz = 28.35 g   1 lb = 453.6 g   1 pint = 568 ml

Oven Settings and Temperatures

Description	Celsius	Fahrenheit	Gas Mark
very cool to cool	107–149	225–300	¼, ½, 1, 2
warm	163	325	3
moderate	177	350	4
fairly hot	190–204	375–400	5, 6
hot	218	425	7
very hot	232–246	450–475	8, 9

Appendix 6

Glossary of Unusual Ingredients

Including US equivalents of common English terms

(*Note:* all the items listed are readily available in wholefood shops, some in Chinese or Asian shops and a few in the larger supermarkets, delicatessens and good grocery stores.)

Agar Flakes   A setting and thickening agent derived from seaweed. It is rich in iron and other minerals and has no taste, making it suitable for sweet and savoury dishes. It is also found in more concentrated powder form. (See **Gelozone**.)

Apple Concentrate   Concentrated apple juice. Used instead of sugar as a sweetener and for its flavouring qualities.

Arrowroot Powder   Used to make thin or transparent sauces and glazes. In Victorian times it was commonly given as a bland food to convalescents because it is so easy to digest. It is derived from the root of a plant of the same name and sometimes sold in wholefood shops labelled with its Japanese name 'kuzu'.

Aubergine   = Eggplant (US).

Bean Sprouts   The sprouted shoots of seeds and pulses. Used in salads and in Chinese stir-fried dishes. (See *Sprouting Seeds and Pulses*, page 000.)

Buckwheat   A variety of wheat with an unusual, triangular-shaped seed. It originated in Russia and was once called beechwheat. It is nearly always sold ready roasted.

Bulgur   Kernels of wheat that have been cooked, dried and cracked. Fine grades require no cooking if soaked. Coarser grades cook much like rice but need less water. It has a pleasant, nutty taste.

Carob Powder (or flour)   Flour made from the roasted, ground seed-pods of the locust tree. It is nutritious, naturally sweet and has a similar taste to chocolate.

Chick Peas   A pulse in the form of rock-hard, cream-coloured peas that are ubiquitous in the Middle East. They can be sprouted for use in salads, ground to make gram flour, or cooked and mashed to make hummus.

Chick Pea Flour   = Gram Flour.

Cornmeal (fine)   = Cornstarch (US). Finely-milled, wholegrain cornmeal can be found in most wholefood shops. Used as a thickening agent.

Courgettes   = Zucchini (US).

Creamed Coconut   Solidified extract of coconut. It can be used as a thickening in stews, melted and blended to produce an alternative thick cream, or thinned right down and poured over cakes to set into an alternative, sugar-free icing.

Demerara Sugar = Dark brown sugar (US). See also **Raw Sugar.**

Fennel Similar in texture and crispness to celery, this delightful, fresh vegetable has a pleasant liquorice flavour. The variety most often found in street markets in the UK and USA originates in Italy and is called 'Florence'.

Fennel Seeds Similar to anise seeds, but milder in flavour. Said to be an antidote to flatulence.

Garam Masala Basic ground curry spice mixture (page ooo). Ten times better than commercial ready-made curry powder!

Gelozone Vegan proprietary setting agent which is easier to use and cheaper than **Agar Flakes** and is now available in most wholefood shops and some supermarkets.

Ginger We recommend you to use the fresh root if you can get it because it loses a lot of its delicate, pungent aroma when dried. Fresh ginger root can be bought in Chinese and other ethnic stores, many street markets and in some wholefood shops and large supermarkets. To prepare the root, cut off a single branch, peel it (potato peelers are fine) and grate it for immediate use. The ginger plant originates in the West Indies and looks a little like lily-of-the-valley. It has been used for centuries for its medicinal qualities as it is said to be good for the digestion, soothing to sore throats and settling for upset stomachs and diarrhoea.

Gram Flour Made from ground chick peas and used for its nutritional value and as a binding agent. Also sold as chick pea flour.

Grilled = Broiled (US).

Healthfood Many shops with this name over their door sell cakes, biscuits and sweets that are crammed with sugar, eggs, butter and cream. Such food cannot by any stretch of the imagination be described as 'healthy'. We have preferred to avoid such misconceptions by using the term 'wholefood' throughout.

Juniper Berries The dark, bluish-black fruits of the juniper tree. Pungent and sweet if eaten raw, they are used for seasoning and to impart aroma (particularly in gin). They have been used as a herbal remedy for centuries and are considered to be beneficial for a range of medical conditions.

Miso A paste traditionally made in Japan from fermented soya beans. It is extremely rich in vitamins and minerals and is used to flavour soups and stews. The bacteria which made it are still alive when you buy it and are said to be good for you, so it's best to add it to a dish just before serving and thereby avoid cooking and killing them.

Poppy Seeds Used since ancient times as a condiment and medicine. Extremely nutritious and a valuable source of protein.

Raw Sugar Generally speaking we have avoided using sugar, or used it sparingly and have always specified 'raw' sugar because in this less-refined state it still contains much of its original fibre, vitamins and minerals.

Sugar is a plant's way of storing energy and is a component of all vegetation. But the white, granulated form commonly found in most grocery stores is so chemically pure that it is no longer possible to tell which was its plant of origin.

Although it is now generally acknowledged by the medical profession that the large-scale consumption of refined white sugar is responsible for many of the illnesses that are symptomatic of our civilized society, it is worth reminding ourselves that we may eat as much as we want of the original, unrefined plants. Your jaws will ache and your stomach be full long before you can eat the equivalent, in raw sugar-cane or sugar-beet, of even 2 or 3 spoonfuls of the white granulated stuff!

Soya Flour Made from ground soya beans. It has a high protein content and makes a useful contribution to the protein balance of wholewheat bread. We've also used it as a thickening and binding agent.

Soya Milk Milk made from soya beans by a process of grinding, soaking and filtering. See introductory notes in *The Alternative Dairy* (page 000).

Soya Sauce Made from fermented soya beans and used to season and flavour soups, stews, stir-fries and so on. Every part of the Far East has its own variation. We always buy Japanese soya sauce – called 'shoyu' or 'tamari' – from wholefood shops because it is made by a painstaking, traditional process that does not involve the use of any chemical additives or sugar. The brands available in large stores and Chinese shops contain preservatives, dyes, sugar and the ubiquitous monosodium glutamate.

Spring Onions = Scallions (US).

Tahini Ground sesame seed paste. Available in pale and dark forms. We always buy the dark type because it is made from the whole, unhulled seeds and has more flavour as well as a high fibre content. Used as a spread and to thicken sauces and dressings.

Tofu Soya bean curd. See introductory notes in *The Alternative Dairy* (page 000).

Wholefood Grains, pulses, seeds etc. which have not been chemically adulterated or refined.

Wholewheat Berries Live, unhulled kernels of wheat containing the bran, germ and gluten as well as the starch which is all that is left after refining into white flour. They can be sprouted and eaten as a salad, or cooked like rice.

Wholewheat Semolina Ground particles of durum wheat. We've used it in biscuit recipes to make them crispy. Don't buy the refined varieties found in large supermarkets.

Index

294

"Tony Hall's life is a unique combination of heroic public service and deep spirituality. *Changing the Face of Hunger* is his personal invitation for us to serve, as well as guide on how we may all learn to unite the will of the spirit with the work of the flesh!"

— MARTIN SHEEN
Actor, Social Activist

"Tony Hall both understands and lives the application of faith to public life better than any other Member of Congress that I've known. From Ethiopia to Appalachia, he has demonstrated his deep commitment to changing the face of hunger. I highly commend this book to all who hunger for a new and more compassionate politics."

— JIM WALLIS
Author of *God's Politics* and
editor of *Sojourners*

"Tony Hall is a rarity in public life: an honest politician who cares more about others than himself. He knows and cares about hunger more than most. After reading this book, you will, too."

— CAL THOMAS
Syndicated Columnist/Fox News
Contributor

"Tony Hall is a clear, inspiring voice of conscience against hunger, with a remarkable gift for storytelling and gentle persuasion. He shows us that hunger can be eradicated and reminds each of us of our own responsibility toward that end, both in America and around the world. By writing *Changing the Face of Hunger*, Tony Hall has done us a service by telling his own story—but even more importantly—by encouraging us to make his story our own."

— TOM HARKIN
(D-Iowa),
U.S. Senate Committee on
Agriculture, Nutrition and Forestry

"I've frequently referred to Tony Hall—jokingly—as my favorite Democrat. He has had the courage all these years to stand virtually alone in his party in defense of life. He has been one of the most principled and effective congressman, focusing particularly on issues of world hunger and human rights. As I've come to know Tony personally my respect for him has grown. He is the real thing—a political figure who puts his Christian faith to work. If you want to put your faith to work, this book will inspire and move you. Tony Hall makes a clear and powerful witness of the transforming power of Christ in a man's life."

— CHARLES W. COLSON
Founder and Chairman,
Prison Fellowship

"A wonderful book by a wonderful man! It takes us with him as he visits the poor of the world, and tells what we must do to respond to their needs if we are to be faithful Christians."

— TONY CAMPOLO
Professor of Psychology,
Eastern University
Author of *Speaking My Mind*

"Whether serving in Congress or as Ambassador to the U.N. food and agriculture agencies, Tony Hall has been a great friend and advocate for humanitarian organizations dedicated to fighting poverty and hunger around the world. This memoir is a testament to his commitment to action in alleviating poverty, as well as a primer on how all Americans can get involved. He challenges each of us to follow the simple wisdom of Mother Teresa: To do the thing that's in front of you."

— KEN HACKETT
President,
Catholic Relief Services

"This is the only book I've recommended in common with Cal Thomas and Chuck Colson, except for the G. Gordon Liddy workout book. Tony Hall is a hero to the widest spectrum of Americans and citizens of the world, because of who he is and what he's done for the poor. I urge everyone to read this fascinating and inspiring book."

— AL FRANKEN
Comedian, talk show host,
Author of *The Truth (with jokes)* and
other best-selling books

"*Changing the Face of Hunger* will hopefully do just that. Tony Hall has been an inspiration for years to me and others committed to doing what they can to bring justice to the hungry. His stories and experiences prove that one person can make a difference. His witness and leadership in Congress were a true example for others of using a position of power to help the powerless. Hopefully this great book will contribute to building the public will necessary to end hunger and poverty in our country and around the world."

— DAVID BECKMANN
President, Bread for the World;
Alliance to End Hunger

"Ending Hunger requires us to put aside our differences and work together. Tony is a great example of someone who has done this successfully."

— JEFF BRIDGES
Actor

"Hunger knows no language, no race, no class, no gender. It is the deprivation of the body and starvation of the soul. Tony Hall discovered that when one of us is hungry, we all are in need. When we deny people food, we are robbing them of the most basic of human rights. This is the story of one man, one human being who urges the whole human family to take a stand, to reach out to our brothers and sisters who are suffering all around us and begin the rise of a compassionate world community."

— JOHN LEWIS
U.S. Representative (D-Georgia),
Civil Rights Leader

"A person of conscience, Tony Hall's life reflects his faith, and his witness to suffering has only deepened his commitment to doing something about it. He has used his public service, in the United States Congress, and at the United Nations, to address the needs of the poorest and most hungry people in the world, and he now calls on us to do the same. *Changing the Face of Hunger* chronicles Tony's noble efforts to call all of those with much to serve those who have little."

— NANCY PELOSI, U.S.
Representative (D-California),
House Minority Leader

"Hunger is one of the five inexusable 'global giants' that still plague our planet in the 21st century. For years, Tony Hall has been on the front lines of the battle against hunger. He's committed to engaging every person possible in the fight and has traveled the globe toward that end. *Changing the Face of Hunger* is a gripping account of how the battle is being fought around the world. Using both the voice of reason and the voice of passion, this collection of amazing stories will compel you to think about what we must do together to end poverty and hunger."

—RICK WARREN,
Author of *The Purpose Driven Life*

CHANGING
THE FACE
OF HUNGER

CHANGING THE FACE OF HUNGER

TONY HALL

with **Tom Price**

Published by
THOMAS NELSON
Since 1798

www.thomasnelson.com

CHANGING THE FACE OF HUNGER

Published by W Publishing Group, a Division of Thomas Nelson, Inc., P.O. Box 141000, Nashville, Tennessee 37214.

W Publishing Group books may be purchased in bulk for educational, business, fund-raising, or sales promotional use. For information, please e-mail SpecialMarkets@ThomasNelson.com.

All Scripture quotations are taken from the New Revised Standard Version Bible, © 1989 by the Division of Christian Education of the National Council of the Churches of Christ in the USA. Used by permission. All rights reserved.

Page Design: Walter Petrie

Library of Congress Cataloging-in-Publication Data

Hall, Tony, 1951–
   The changing face of hunger / by Tony Hall.
      p. cm.
   ISBN-10: 0-8499-1869-3 (tradepaper)
   ISBN-13: 978-0-8499-1869-8 (tradepaper)
   ISBN 978-0-8499-0050-1 (hardcover)
      1. Hunger—Religious aspects—Christianity. 2. Food supply—Religious aspects—Christianity. 3. Church and social problems. I. Title.
BR115.H86H35 2006
261.8'325—dc22   2005031465

Printed in the United States of America

07 08 09 10 11 RRD 9 8 7 6 5 4 3 2 1

DEDICATION

Mostly, I dedicate this book to a wonderful "gift of God," the meaning of the name Matthew, our son, who God chose to go before us. He is a constant source of inspiration, and his bravery in his losing battle with cancer showed us how to live and how to die.

Also, I would like to dedicate this book to my wife Janet, who has walked through the valleys and mountains with me, and to our daughter, Jyl, who always inspires me and is a source of refreshment and renewal.

I heard the voice of the Lord saying,
"Whom shall I send, and who will go for us?"
And I said, "Here am I; send me!"

—Isaiah 6:8

CONTENTS

ACKNOWLEDGMENTS

O n the pages of my life, there have been many people who were always there for me and who helped make me look good.

I want first to thank my wife Janet and daughter Jyl for their constant love and encouragement; Dad, my two brothers Mike and Sam, and especially my mom, who always says "I love you." I also want to thank Janet's family; you couldn't ask for better in-laws.

Congressman Frank Wolf plays an important role in the pages of this book. For more than 20 years he and I fought the good fight together in Congress and had a darn good time at it. Thank you, Frank and Carolyn.

My buddies, Nick and Jody Sabatino, let me be me and provided a place over the years for me to do just that.

John Nakamura has been my prayer partner these past few years and has traveled the world with me. Thanks, John and Janice. And thanks to Marvin Marcus, who introduced me to my wife.

To my staff in Congress and at the U.S. Mission to the U.N. Food and Agricultural Agencies in Rome: I want to thank each one of you for your loyalty and, for some of you, a great length of service. To single out just a few: Rick Carne, who started with me; Michael Gessel, a great press secretary; Ernie Loevinsohn, who taught me most of what I know about hunger; Bonnie Ruestow, who served me so many years; Marty Rendon, Max Finberg, Deborah DeYoung, David Goldberg, George Lowrey, David Austin, Tom Studevant, Jim Vangrov, Bobby Turner, Gary Froelich, Bob Zachritz, Madeline Iseli, Ruth Snyder, Donna Riddlebarger, and Carol Prewitt. I also want to acknowledge the wonderful people who have carried on the vision of the Congressional Hunger Center, Ed Cooney and Margaret Zeigler.

Farley Chase, our agent, worked tirelessly to help us transform our ideas

into a clear plan for writing this book. His colleague, Scott Waxman, contributed important advice. We are grateful that our publisher, David Moberg, saw the value in what we wanted to write. We thank the *Dayton Daily News*, for giving us access to its library, and the Kettering Foundation, for supporting Tom's research into the Community Council for the Homeless.

I especially want to thank the many people who have mentored me over the years and taught me the importance of trying to live the words of Jesus of Nazareth, including Jerry Regier, Roy Cook, Doug Coe, Margie and Chuck Wright, Barbara Priddy, Sam Hines, John Staggers, Tom Skinner, Jim Hutchins, Sam Owen, and Fred Heyn.

There have been so many other people along life's way who contributed a great deal to my life. Even though there is not space to mention all of you, I want you to know that I remember and I am grateful to you.

ETHIOPIA

Opening My Eyes,
Filling My Heart

V iewed from the twin-engine prop plane making its way north from the capital of Addis Ababa to the village of Alamata in the rebel-controlled countryside, Ethiopia showed off a rugged, oddly beautiful landscape.

As Addis disappeared behind us, plains and plateaus gave way to ridges and peaks that thrust their sharp edges into the cloudless blue sky. Rifts in the mountains suggested miniature versions of America's Grand Canyon. The bright sun and clear sky heightened the stark beauty of the scene.

Here and there a patch of green stood out. But the overriding color scheme was made up of browns and grays. Dirt and dust dominated the land. The riverbeds were dry. Crops would not grow. Forests had been sacrificed for firewood. Tree roots had been dug up for food.

Ethiopia had suffered grievously from drought in the early 1970s. In the early 1980s, famine returned. Now, in November 1984, as I made my first trip to the country, I was told that even cacti could not survive in the dry earth.

I had heard reports that two hundred thousand Ethiopians had died already, nearly a million likely would die by the end of the year, and millions more were at risk. International relief groups were issuing alarming calls for help. Television news organizations were beaming disturbing pictures of hunger into homes in the United States and other Western countries. But none of this prepared me for what I was about to experience. I have often told people that as a public official, in order to understand a situation, I have to see

it, walk around in it, walk in the shoes of the people who are there. To deal successfully with an issue, I have to develop a passion for it. Passion is what enables someone to become an effective advocate, to touch other people's hearts, to move other public officials, to get the public mobilized to want to do something. That is why I felt I needed to go to Ethiopia in 1984 and why I have gone to many other such places in the years since.

The plane on which I was traveling was ferrying supplies to a camp run by the World Vision Christian relief organization. Ernie Loevinsohn and I had hitched a ride from Addis, as had two members of Mother Teresa's Missionaries of Charity, who had a mission at World Vision's compound. We landed on Alamata's dirt airstrip, which, we were told, had to be swept for land mines each morning because of the civil war that was exacerbating Ethiopia's tragedy.

The relief compound was surrounded by barbed-wire fence, which seemed in stark contrast to the World Vision workers' dedication to serving the poor and the missionaries' commitment to living among the neediest. The barrier was necessitated, however, by the fact that relief workers were able to help only a fraction of the overwhelming number of desperate Ethiopians standing outside the fence and needing assistance.

Thousands of severely malnourished Ethiopians had made their way to Alamata and surrounded the compound, hoping for food and medical treatment. In addition to malnutrition, many also suffered from dehydration, dysentery, malaria, cholera, and tuberculosis. We were told that dozens had died of starvation or related illnesses outside the compound overnight. Inside, three children had died just before we arrived that morning. A doctor—a Brit or an Australian, I judged by his accent—was about to make his morning rounds. He invited me to join him.

As we walked through the crowd outside the compound, hundreds of hungry people grabbed at our hands and tugged at our pant legs, begging for help. Many of the adults held up their children, trying to thrust them into our arms. They understood what the doctor was doing. Because supplies were severely limited, he explained to me, he could provide treatment for starvation to only a half dozen children each day.

"I have to pick six or seven kids that we can save," he said. The ones who

4

seemed most likely to recover if treated would be nurtured through the several stages of recovery from starvation, receiving the food and medicine they needed. Most of the rest of the starving would die within days.

As I watched the doctor choose his next handful of patients and pass over the many, I thought of my own children, Jyl and Matt, who were eight and four at the time, the same ages as many of the starving youngsters who surrounded me. I fished my sunglasses out of my shirt pocket and put them on, as I would many times over the next few days—not to protect my eyes from the tropical sun, but to hide my tears. I would soon discover that things were even worse elsewhere.

World Vision had found a Jeep and a driver to take Ernie and me to our next destination, Korem, a village that was a one- to two-hour drive north of Alamata. NBC correspondent Peter Dent joined us.

Our Jeep was the only motor vehicle on the dirt road that wound its way up the hills to the plateau on which Korem sits. We passed some walkers and an occasional well-off person on a donkey, but mostly we were alone. The view on the ground confirmed my impressions from the air. The landscape was rugged, rocky, and brown. Everything was dry. Nothing grew.

Ethiopia had been in a state of perpetual civil war for years. The overthrow of Emperor Haile Selassie in 1974 had led to the establishment of an oppressive Communist dictatorship that was opposed by regional armies, especially in the north where we were traveling. The warfare compounded the effects of the famine as the government diverted relief supplies to its troops, and the fighting disrupted attempts by relief organizations to deliver supplies to the starving. These facts were at the forefront of our minds when we crested a hill and heard loud automatic-weapons fire nearby.

Our driver jammed on the brakes, turned off the ignition, and bolted from the Jeep. Nearby pedestrians dived into the roadside ditches, so Peter, Ernie, and I did the same. After lying in the dust for a few moments, I stuck my head up to look for our driver. People nearby screamed at me. Although I didn't understand their language, I knew immediately that they were telling me to keep my head down.

The gunfire continued sporadically for a while. We had no reason to believe it was aimed at us, but it was unnerving nevertheless. Lying there in the dust,

we were filthy and we were scared. Finally, after about ten minutes of silence, we decided to move.

We ran for the Jeep. With our driver nowhere in sight, I jumped behind the steering wheel and took off, speeding as fast as I could, leaving a cloud of sand and dust and rocks behind us. Nobody told me to slow down. When we approached Korem, however, our apparent brush with Ethiopia's civil war lost all sense of significance. In a day of repeated shocks, this was beyond anything imaginable.

I had seen poverty as a Peace Corps volunteer in Thailand. As a member of Congress, I had made hunger one of my top concerns. I had helped to establish the House Select Committee on Hunger and had become chairman of the committee's International Task Force. I had sought to understand the extent of poverty and hunger in my congressional district in Dayton, Ohio. And this was not my first congressional fact-finding trip to the third world. But I had never seen anything like this. And neither had Ernie, the Staff Director of the hunger committee, who had worked for years in international relief organizations.

Tens of thousands of starving people had walked—some up to 150 miles—to get to this high, bleak plateau, having heard that food, water, clothing, and blankets would be distributed here. But their demand for help had so quickly exceeded the available relief supplies that there was essentially nothing for most of them. So they just waited, hoping for assistance that would not arrive until days after our visit. Because this was a large, flat expanse of land, it was possible to take in the entire scene at once, and it was overwhelming.

The sky was pure blue, the sun piercing. The temperature was 75 or 80 degrees—a perfect California afternoon. Except that here all the land was brown and dusty. And forty thousand to fifty thousand people were encamped here—some in makeshift tents, some in grass huts, some in wooden sheds that relief organizations had erected for the most severely ill, but most in the open. All were malnourished, some closer to death than others. They wore dusty, rough robes. Some appeared nearly naked, their clothing was so worn. Flies lit on their bodies, and they were too feeble to brush them away. They were docile, weak to the point of exhaustion because they

had no food and because the cold nights further drained their nearly nonexistent energy. While Ethiopia is a tropical country, nighttime temperatures can drop to near freezing on this high plateau.

Perhaps what struck me most from the distance was the sound. Children cried. Women wailed. The sick coughed. But mostly the air was filled with an eerie, low moan. Thousands of people had simply come to the end. They just lay there, and they suffered, and they moaned, and they died.

We were told that fifty-six people had died the day before we arrived, and sixty-one the day before that. A week earlier, the death toll averaged more than one hundred people a day. The bodies would be carried to the edge of the encampment and laid out. I had never seen anyone die before. That day at Korem, I witnessed twenty-five children's deaths in the few hours we were there.

As I walked among the people, I was drawn to the children. Teenagers, weighing fifty pounds or less, were so wrinkled they could be mistaken for the elderly. I saw an eight-year-old child who weighed twenty-three pounds. These children had the distended bellies that are the telltale sign of extreme hunger. Every bone could be counted. When they died, they just stopped breathing. If a child was with his or her mother, you'd then see the mother react, sometimes with nothing but resignation, sometimes with deep grief. Some mothers hugged their dead children tightly; some lay down beside their children and sobbed. As I walked, I saw this happen again and again. Perhaps worst of all, I saw children die alone, saw adults die alone.

Our runaway driver sheepishly showed up at Korem, head down, appearing embarrassed that he had deserted us on the road. He took us back to Alamata, where Ernie and I climbed into the same World Vision plane to fly back to Addis. I sat by myself at a window, staring at the countryside below and struggling to comprehend the horror I had seen.

That night Ernie and I were invited to dinner at the home of the U.S. chargé d'affaires. Because the U.S. government disapproved of Ethiopia's Communist government, we did not have an ambassador in Addis at the time.

The chargé was away, so Ernie and I had the elegant mansion to ourselves. We had showered, scrubbed the day's dirt and dust from our bodies, and put on clean clothes. Now we were being led into a large dining room with a long

banquet table that was set with beautiful silver and china and decorated with fresh-cut flowers.

Ethiopian waiters in white jackets and white gloves served us a lavish meal. I can't recall the exact menu, but the meal included salad, meat, potatoes, vegetables, bread, butter, wine, and a selection of desserts. I know we could have had seconds if we'd asked.

Ernie and I sat there, looking at each other, looking at all this food, and thinking about what we had seen just a few hours earlier. This meal, prepared for the two of us, would have fed one hundred or more of the hungry at Alamata or Korem.

Neither of us could eat. We didn't feel like talking. So we pushed back from the table and went to our rooms for the rest of the night.

I called Janet, my wife, and tried to explain what I had seen that day. But it was too hard. I couldn't talk. I tried to read, which is what I normally do at the end of the day, but I couldn't do that either. So I just sat on my bed and thought.

The next day I encountered stark evidence of the way that Alamata and Korem had changed my perspective on the world. We flew south this time, to visit a relief center serving the seminomadic Bume people near Ethiopia's border with Sudan.

Once again we flew over a brown, arid land. When we were on the ground, we again were told how there had been little rain, the river had dried up, the harvest had failed, and the Bume's primary food source at this time was the roots of trees. We saw naked children with swollen bellies. One mother told us how each family would give one or two children the responsibility of keeping the family supplied with water. They would have to walk long distances with buckets to a source of drinkable water. Sometimes a child would walk most of the day to obtain the water and take it back home.

But there was little sickness. The children had not yet descended into a severe state of malnutrition. The nakedness was normal: the Bume, children and adults, wore little or no clothing all the time. World Vision had built a warehouse, and people said food would be on the way.

I thought to myself, *This isn't as bad as I expected it would be.*

But, of course, it would be very bad if the food didn't arrive soon. And I

worried about the people we couldn't visit because they lived in the extreme backcountry, beyond airstrips and roads and international relief organizations.

It was not until we were on the airplane during the long flight home that I could begin to sort out and make sense of what we had seen.

This was, of course, a natural disaster. Drought had caused a famine that was causing millions of people to go hungry. And this was not an unprecedented occurrence. The region is susceptible to frequent droughts. Earthquakes, volcanic eruptions, and locust swarms are also recurring parts of the environment. When the current drought began to take its toll in the early 1980s, the nation was still suffering the effects of a great drought-caused famine from the early 1970s. The sequence of drought, famine, hunger, and starvation had been repeated in Ethiopia for centuries.

But there was more to it than that. Desperation and ignorance led to poor farming practices that exacerbated water shortages and caused deforestation, soil erosion, and desertification. The repressive Communist government did not want the world to learn of its troubles and had tried to hide the extent of the disaster, which was compounded by the regime's ideological economic policies. The civil war was killing tens of thousands of people outright, disrupting aid efforts, and creating hundreds of thousands of refugees. As part of its military campaign against the rebels, the government was blocking relief shipments to rebel-controlled areas as well as stealing food in order to feed its army. The wealthy world was taking too long to understand the need and too long to respond.

In addition to making visits to the Ethiopian backcountry, Ernie and I were able to meet with relief workers in Addis.

One man, named Solomon, described and illustrated the human-caused aspects of the disaster. He had spent a year and a half in jail because he refused to pledge allegiance to the Marxist doctrine of the government. He also was persecuted, he said, because of his Christian faith, and some three hundred Christian leaders were still in jail. He believed that Ethiopia was suffering because the government had turned its back on God, but that the suffering would make the people strong.

Others confirmed some of the gruesome stories we had heard about Ethiopian dictator Mengistu Haile Mariam. It's true, they said, that he kept lions

in the basement of his palace—visitors could hear them roar. He used them to frighten prisoners during interrogations and to frighten the Ethiopian people into staying in line.

One of the most astounding things we learned from our conversations in Addis was that the residents of Ethiopia's capital did not know the extent to which malnutrition, hunger, and death existed in their country. Their ability to travel was restricted, and their news media were controlled by the government, so they were kept in the dark.

Another thing we learned was that Ethiopia's needs were broad. While food was required immediately, we were told, it had to be the right food. And food alone would not solve this nation's enormous problems.

Two kinds of nutrition aid were needed. Now, and for a long time even after the famine finally passed, many Ethiopians would lack basic rations, such as grain, to feed their families. The malnourished and starving urgently needed special feeding regimens and medical treatment to nurture them back to health. There was great demand for medicines to treat the sick, as well as vaccinations and inoculations to protect all Ethiopians from diseases that had been conquered in the developed world. Many also needed blankets and tents. And the relief organizations required trucks to carry the supplies to the far-flung suffering communities. To prevent the endless recurrence of drought, famine, and death, relief efforts would have to include the drilling of water wells, the construction of irrigation projects, and the education of primitive farmers in effective and sustainable agricultural practices.

I spent my time on the flight home just as I had on that flight from Alamata to Addis Ababa within Ethiopia—in a window seat, staring outside. The protective shock was wearing off, and I was having difficulty coping with what I had seen over the last several days. It wasn't just the human suffering that I found so disturbing, but also the human cruelty that had helped to cause the suffering and was delaying relief. It's something I've never been able to completely come to grips with—how humans can treat one another with such inhumanity. Here we were, in the closing years of the supposedly civilized, supposedly modern twentieth century, and we were in the process of killing more people in that one modern, civilized century than in the entire previous history of humankind.

In retrospect, I can see that many of the problems I would deal with over

the coming two decades were thrown at me during that one trip to Ethiopia: drought, famine, hunger, starvation, illness, lack of shelter, lack of clothing, political oppression, religious persecution, war, hatred. I encountered the seeds of solutions as well: the dedicated workers in private aid agencies, religious relief organizations, and government assistance programs; the advocates for human rights and humanitarian assistance; and the enormous power of the news media to call the world's attention to a problem and inspire action to solve it. If it hadn't been for the BBC's pioneering reporting in Ethiopia, the response from the developed world would have come even later. If other media hadn't followed with their reporting, the food, medical, and developmental assistance would not have been as robust or as effective.

It was to those signs of hope that my thoughts turned as the large commercial airliner carried me toward home.

I recalled the World Vision workers and Missionaries of Charity at Alamata. Every day, they were able to save maybe a half dozen children out of thousands of people who were gathered around them and pleading for help. It would be easy to look at that effort and wonder, *What's the point? That's such an insignificant number when so many are suffering.* But if the relief workers weren't there at all, no one would have been saved. And if they were saving six a day, that's more than forty a week. And as the weeks rolled on, you'd be talking about hundreds.

While I was at Alamata, one of the sisters asked me if I'd like to see their generator room. I wondered why, in this scene of suffering and death, she'd want to show me a generator. I followed her into a hut with a twig roof and a dirt floor and discovered that the "generator room" was their chapel. It was here they came to pray, renewing themselves for their difficult tasks every day. They called it their generator room because it was where they restored their power to go on with their work.

That led me to think about a discussion I'd had shortly before I began my trip to Ethiopia.

I had, for a few years, been meeting weekly in Washington with a small group of men to pray and discuss the Scriptures. One day, one of the men in the group said to me, "Tony, don't you think it's time you brought God into your workplace?"

It was a question that troubled me a great deal. I was becoming a strong believer, and my faith was becoming the central driving force in my life, including being the prime motivator of my involvement in humanitarian issues such as hunger. But this faith was relatively new to me, and I was highly uneasy about flaunting it in public.

My workplace was Congress and the broader field of politics and public affairs. Although I made no secret of the growing importance of faith in my life—including my public life—I told reporters who covered me that I did not want to wear it on my sleeve and I had no intention of shoving it down other people's throats. I had seen too many public people profess their faith and then not live up to their words. I had seen people talk about God to advance their own purposes, then cause faith to be diminished in others' eyes when their hypocrisy was exposed.

I wanted to do what my friend suggested it was time for me to do. But I didn't know how. On this flight out of Ethiopia, I found the answer.

I thought about how, in a political career, you can flit from campaign to campaign, from issue to issue, and really accomplish nothing. I thought about how we do so many things in our lives—so many things in Congress—that amount to nothing, how a good portion of our time is wasted. Because I often talked about the importance of passion, I asked myself what I was passionate about and realized that many of those passions didn't amount to much.

I thought about what I had witnessed in Ethiopia and how that compared with what most of us experience in the United States. We've never seen anything like it—we're so sheltered; our lives are so easy. If we're thirsty, we turn on a faucet and drink clean water. Our food is plentiful and good and healthful. We're well protected from danger. We have freedoms galore. So we don't understand disasters such as I witnessed in Ethiopia. We don't know of the need for our help. We don't know what to do.

In the past, when I returned from a trip to the third world and told friends what I had seen, they couldn't believe my stories, even though what I had seen during those trips had been nothing like the devastation I had witnessed this week. *How protected we are in America,* I thought. *How well-off we are.*

Contemplating my friend's question, I remembered learning that there are at least two thousand verses in the Bible that deal with the hungry, the sick,

the poor, and the oppressed. No biblical instruction is clearer or repeated more often than our responsibility to "the least of these," as Jesus said (see Matthew 25:34–40).

I realized that helping people in need was how I was to bring God into my workplace, in a way that was right and clear and pure and not self-aggrandizing or hypocritical. This was how my life in Congress was to matter. I would travel among "the least of these," witnessing their needs, bringing those needs to the attention of my colleagues in Congress, my constituents in Dayton, and as many other people as I could—and work to have those needs addressed.

The relief workers at Alamata had taught me that I didn't have to solve every problem in the world. I just had to try to solve those I could.

Some years later, I had the great privilege of meeting Mother Teresa herself. I asked her how we could hope to solve the problems of the hungry, the sick, the poor, and the oppressed since there is such an overwhelming number of them. She replied, "You do the thing that's in front of you."

The lesson I took from her answer is this: If all of us did what was in front of us, think of how many problems we would solve. If each of us would take care of a neighbor, sit and talk with someone who is lonely, or feed someone who is hungry, think of what a better world this would be.

That, of course, is what Mother Teresa's missionaries were doing in Alamata in 1984. That's what I have been trying to do since I witnessed their example. In these two decades, I've seen many horrible things in front of me. I've also seen many good people working to make these horrible things better.

I'm writing this book to put these things in front of you.

CHAPTER 2

BROTHERS BEYOND POLITICS

Succeeding by Finding Common Ground

★ ★ ★

When I returned from Ethiopia, I asked my good friend Frank Wolf to travel there too. "You must see what's going on there," I told him. "I won't be able to help them unless I have a partner, and I need you to be my partner."

So Frank quickly hopped a plane to Africa. He came back and joined my campaign to assist the starving Ethiopians. It was one of countless efforts we have made together on behalf of the hungry, the oppressed, and the poor— "the least of these"—over the last two decades.

At a quick glance, Frank and I would appear to be unlikely partners. He's a Republican U.S. representative from the South (Virginia). I'm a Democrat from the Midwest. When we cast our votes on the floor of the House, we disagreed almost all of the time. But we agree on some issues, and we've chosen to focus on those agreements. We have learned that if you concentrate on what unites you instead of what divides you, there's nearly no limit to what you can accomplish.

Our journey to personal friendship and political partnership began when a mutual friend asked me to join a prayer and Bible study group with Frank and two other House members, Dan Coats of Indiana and Bob McEwen, whose Ohio congressional district adjoined mine. We met once a week in one of our congressional offices, read Scripture, discussed it, and prayed. All that was fine. But we also talked about politics—a great deal of the time. As the only

Democrat in a group with three conservative Republicans, I didn't find that part so fine at all. After a couple of months, I finally told them I was going to stop attending the meetings for a while.

"I came to these meetings because I wanted spiritual growth," I explained. "I wanted to understand God better. I didn't want to sit around and talk about politics. We're in Congress. We talk about politics all day long. What makes this meeting any different from anything else going on up here? Guys, I need to take a break."

I didn't say, "I quit." But in my mind I was cutting it off, because it wasn't working for me. We weren't focused enough on God, the Bible, and prayer. We weren't really getting to know one another. So I drifted away. Bob and Dan remained my friends throughout our congressional careers, but this particular prayer group just didn't work.

Awhile later, our mutual friend came back to me and said, "Why don't just you and Frank get together? Take it easy. Try to get to know each other. Maybe take a trip somewhere together."

We both were leery of trying this again. Growing up in America, you're taught by society that to be successful, to be a leader, you have to be an island. You can't be vulnerable to others. You can't let people really get to know you, because they'll discover your weaknesses. And if they know your weaknesses, they'll take advantage of you.

This is an especially natural tendency for politicians. If I'm a Democrat, I can't be vulnerable to Republicans, because if they get to know me, they'll take advantage of me, and they might beat me in the next campaign. And I'll be really careful around Democrats who might run against me sometime in the future.

As a young politician, I learned to be partisan, to support my party no matter what, to be rough, to be sharp with my words, to be leery of developing personal relationships with people on the other side. But over time, I also observed that extreme partisanship often fails, leaving legislation unapproved, problems unsolved. Deep inside, I didn't feel good about my extremely partisan conduct, and I knew the American people didn't like it at all. (And the atmosphere in Washington was a lot milder back then than it is now.) Frank was having similar thoughts. He and I knew we shared faith. So we decided to make another attempt at fellowship.

I told Frank why I had left the original prayer group, so we agreed we wouldn't discuss politics. Instead, we prayed and discussed Scripture. We talked about our families, how we met our wives, what we did before we entered Congress. As the months passed, we began to let ourselves be vulnerable to each other, and I began to like him very much. When you each become vulnerable, you start to trust, your friendship can grow, and you can begin to do some really important things.

We took our first trip together in 1985 to Romania, which was ruled by Communist dictator Nicolae Ceaşescu. We were asked to make the trip by Christian Solidarity International, a Switzerland-based human rights organization concerned about the suppression of religion in Romania. It became a profound experience for Frank and me because it combined several matters of great importance to both of us—faith, human rights, and public policy. Frank's daughter Virginia; my wife, Janet; and Republican Representative Chris Smith of New Jersey traveled with us. We saw horrendous religious persecution and inspiring faith (which I describe in detail in chapter 5).

Traveling together, praying together, and witnessing dark oppression as well as bright faith deepened our relationship. We didn't talk about the partisan politics that divided us. We talked about the common challenge in front of us—how to promote religious freedom in Romania. When we returned to Washington, we launched a campaign to end the oppression in Romania and to provide encouragement to the Romanian activists who were fighting for freedom. I'm convinced our efforts made a modest contribution to the eventual fall of the Ceauşescu regime and the development of democracy there.

Traveling together, working together on important issues like human rights, creates a bond. You begin to trust each other. Then all the partisan baloney starts to fall away. Differences that seemed so consequential lose their significance. Frank and I disagreed on the vast majority of issues that came to Congress—taxes, appropriations, gun control, military spending, labor policy, various foreign policy matters, even the details of subjects about which we shared an overall agreement. We simply put them aside in our personal relationship and worked together on the issues on which we did agree, such as hunger, human rights, abortion, and family issues.

Over the years, we took half a dozen trips together to places such as Sierra

Leone, Benin, Afghanistan, Pakistan, the Balkans, and other regions in Europe and the United States. We worked to prevent international trade in diamonds that financed wars in Africa, to expose and prohibit slavery that was still being practiced in parts of the third world, to combat genocide in Sudan, to immunize children, to feed the hungry, to minimize abortion, and to teach others what we had learned about the value of fellowship and cooperation across divides.

During this time, Frank became my best friend in Congress. Our relationship has become my model for dealing with others. Focusing on issues of common concern has enabled me to work with and develop rewarding friendships with people who are both more conservative and more liberal than I am on many issues, but who share my passion for serving "the least of these" in some way. It also has empowered me to seek cooperation on specific projects from some highly unlikely partners, including even some people who are notorious for truly evil conduct.

A sort of mirror image of my relationship with Frank is my friendship with Al Franken, the comedian and liberal political advocate. Al and I don't share the same faith. (He's Jewish.) We don't see eye to eye on some social issues, such as same-sex marriage and abortion. You won't find me mimicking his fondness for telling off-color jokes and salting his public speaking and writing with vulgar language. But Al is firmly committed to assisting the disadvantaged, he's a strong supporter of efforts to end hunger, and he provided deep comfort to my family during our darkest personal hours.

In August 1992, our eleven-year-old son, Matt, was diagnosed with leukemia. After chemotherapy and radiation treatments failed to cure him, he spent months at New York's Memorial Sloan-Kettering Cancer Center being prepared for a bone-marrow transplant, which he received in November 1994. While Matt was there, a good friend of mine met Al, told him about my family, and said he should befriend us.

One day, Al telephoned, introduced himself, and asked if he could come visit us at the hospital. I said sure, and he came to meet us. I thought, *This is an amazing thing. Here's this guy from* Saturday Night Live, *a real celebrity, and he just came over to cheer up my son.* Then he asked if he could come back the next weekend and bring a friend. I said, "Sure. Who is it?" And he said, "Chris Farley."

So the next weekend, Al Franken and Chris Farley—two *Saturday Night Live* TV stars—came to the hospital to entertain Matt. Other people in the ward wanted to meet them, too, so Al and Chris went around entertaining everybody. They were hilarious. They were wonderful. Matt loved it. And that's how our relationship started.

Later, Al and I got to talking about hunger. I described what I had seen at some of the places I'd visited and also told him a bit about what I was doing to try to make things better. He seemed quite interested, so I suggested he take a look at the Bowery Mission Transitional Center in New York.

The center is remarkably successful at helping homeless men with drug or alcohol problems get back on their feet. It's also a great example of a faith-based organization operating with government support, in this case from New York City's Department of Homeless Services. It was run at the time by Bobby Polito, who later headed the second President Bush's Center for Faith-Based and Community Initiatives. Men live at the center for six to nine months while making the transition to a healthy life. While there, they receive counseling, job training, and other assistance. The center says that fewer than 10 percent of its graduates fall back into addiction.

After he visited the center, Al told me he was impressed by its effectiveness. I then asked him if he'd like to help in my work by joining the board of the Congressional Hunger Center, which I had founded in 1993 as an organization related to but independent of Congress. He agreed, and he's been active in the center ever since.

I've learned not only that people can work together across differences but also that everyone has special talents they can contribute to a cause. Not only can our differences be overcome, but our diversity gives us strength. In this case, Al is a celebrity and a marvelous comedian. He entertains at Hunger Center fund-raising events. In 2004, as a contestant on the "Celebrity *Jeopardy*" television program, he announced that the center was his favorite charity and told the national TV audience a bit about our work. He then went on to win $50,000 for us. On the political side, he came to Dayton and campaigned for Al Gore during the 2000 presidential campaign because I asked him to.

Even more important to my family, Al has become an exceptionally supportive friend. Throughout Matt's difficult illness and then after his death in

1996, Al would call to cheer and comfort us. He also made moving remarks at Matt's funeral. Nothing can be more devastating to a parent than the death of a child, and nothing can take away the pain totally. But Janet and I will always be grateful for the solace Al offered to us.

Another celebrity who has worked with me over many years is Martin Sheen, who is most famous recently for portraying President Josiah Bartlet in *The West Wing* television series. Like me, he was born and reared in Dayton (as Ramón Estévez; Martin Sheen is a stage name). Unlike me, Martin is a Roman Catholic. But his faith is real and deep and of great consequence to him, as mine is to me, and we have an identical understanding of God's admonition that we are to serve the poor.

Martin has been involved in many demonstrations on behalf of the hungry, the homeless, and the poor. In 2001 he helped Frank's and my diamonds campaign by cutting a television ad that was broadcast on NBC at the end of a *West Wing* episode. He came back to our common hometown—which he regularly visits, quietly, to see family—to campaign for my reelection to Congress.

Cal Thomas, the conservative media commentator, and his wife, Ray, fasted and prayed for Matt during his illness and have become close friends. Another conservative, John Nakamura, a retired farmer and former agriculture adviser to Republican governors in California, became my constant traveling companion.

I met John through a prayer breakfast I led in Washington for about fifteen years. Those who attended were a wonderfully eclectic collection of folks from around the Washington area—black, white, Asian, rich, poor, ministers, local politicians, some members of Congress, even some homeless people. Participation in the group made John and me friends, though not close friends. We developed a stronger friendship as a result of a chance encounter in South Korea in the mid-1990s.

I had just come out of North Korea, had met with some people in South Korea, and was feeling frustrated and depressed. As I explain in detail in a later chapter, enormous numbers of North Koreans were dying in a famine. Because of the North Korean government's repression of its people, threats to peace, and isolation from the free world, I couldn't drum up support for significant aid from the United States or from our allies in Asia. I believed that God had commanded us to feed the hungry, no matter where they lived. I had

just spent time with innocent people, including children, who were severely hungry and at risk of death. But even my friends and some religious leaders questioned why I wanted to help this enemy. John happened to be in South Korea with a friend, and I ran into them. And I poured out my heart.

"John," I said, "I can't do this work anymore. I try to work with these ministers, who supposedly are men of God, and they won't help me feed the hungry. My own government thinks I'm crazy. I want to feed these people, but it seems nobody wants to help. I can't do this alone. I've got to have somebody with me. Frank has been with me on some trips, but he can't go everywhere with me."

John thought about what I said. Then he replied, "I want to be your partner. I will go on these trips with you, and I will support you, and I will pray with you."

Since then, John has traveled all over the world with me. He even moved to Rome and continued to travel with me during my term as ambassador. His agricultural background made him a perfect partner for addressing hunger. His fellowship strengthened me and enabled me to continue my work, even through difficult times such as those I experienced while trying to help people in North Korea. The Bible says that as iron sharpens iron, one person sharpens another (Proverbs 27:17). And Jesus said he would be present whenever two or more are gathered in his name (Matthew 18:20). I have found both to be true.

Another thing I have found to be true is that if you ask, you often will receive. Perhaps more remarkable than the relationships I've just described are the times I've received cooperation from some of the most feared and reviled individuals on the planet.

In November 2004, for example, I found myself standing in the desert in Libya, as Libyan trucks, piled high with bags labeled "USA," disappeared into the sandy distance on their way to Chad, to feed hungry refugees from the civil war in Sudan. The desert scene caused me to imagine I was playing a part in *Lawrence of Arabia*. The political reality that Libya had joined the United States in a humanitarian mission was nearly impossible to believe.

Libya had been our enemy. Our State Department had declared it a state sponsor of terrorism, and that designation remains in effect as I write this. Libyans had been implicated in the 1988 terrorist bombing of Pan Am Flight 103 over Lockerbie, Scotland, which killed 259 passengers and crew

members—including 189 Americans—and 11 Scots on the ground. The United Nations had imposed sanctions.

In recent years, however, Libyan leader Mu'ammar al-Gadhafi had begun to take steps to join the civilized world. In 1999 he gave up two Libyans charged in the Pan Am bombing, and they were tried by a Scottish court. In 2003 the Libyan government accepted responsibility for the actions of the bombers, agreed to pay compensation to the victims' families, and renounced terrorism. The government paid compensation to victims of other terrorist acts that Libyans had perpetrated. Libya promised to dispose of its weapons of mass destruction and to end certain missile programs, and it began to cooperate with international agencies to implement those pledges. As a result, UN sanctions were lifted in September 2003, and the United States government was pondering whether to alter its view of this North African nation. I had been following these developments, and I began to wonder if we could use al-Gadhafi's image-enhancement campaign to solve a difficult problem we faced in the Darfur region of neighboring Sudan.

I had visited Sudan several times, both as a congressman and since I had become the United States ambassador to the United Nations food and agricultural agencies in Rome in 2002. Sudan—especially Darfur—is the site of some of the most horrific atrocities I've ever seen.

As a man of faith, I'm especially troubled by atrocities committed in the name of religion. Sudan's civil war, which has raged for most of the last fifty years, is, to a great extent—though not entirely—a product of religious conflict between the Muslim north and a south peopled by Christians and believers of several indigenous faiths. This is a place where great evil is done in God's name. The never-ending warfare has taken a tremendous toll, especially in the south. The fighting has created more than four million refugees and killed more than two million.

The conflict complicates relief efforts, and so does the weather. Supplies for Darfur—a landlocked area in Sudan's west—must be trucked twelve hundred to fifteen hundred miles from Port Sudan on the Red Sea or from the port of Douala in Cameroon on the Atlantic Ocean. During the rainy season—April through October throughout most of Sudan and longer in the south—the roads (where there are roads) can become impassable, and relief agencies routinely lose vehicles in flash floods.

During a briefing at World Food Program headquarters in Rome, I learned that a superior route could be taken through Libya, a route through an area with better roads and less rain. I broached the idea with State Department officials in Washington. Then I phoned Libya's ambassador to Italy and asked to talk with him.

Meeting in the ambassador's office, I explained the problem. "If we can ship food through your country," I said, "we can take it into Chad, which has refugees from Darfur, and we can take it into Darfur when the other routes are closed. It can be a third route to keep the food flowing."

He seemed open to the idea. Negotiations began. And in July 2004 the United States, the European Commission, the World Food Program, and Libya concluded an agreement that allows such shipments to occur into 2014. The first convoy of trucks left the Libyan port of Benghazi on the Mediterranean Sea in mid-August and arrived at the Oure Cassoni refugee camp in eastern Chad three weeks later. It carried food donated by Switzerland to feed 165,000 Sudanese refugees in Chad. The first U.S. food arrived at Benghazi in early November, three weeks after shipping out of New Orleans. I was able to meet that shipment when it arrived at Al Kufrah, an ancient trading post on the edge of the Sahara Desert. It was an awesome sight.

At Al Kufrah, Libya's asphalt roads end in sand, and the convoy drove off into the stark desert. The 350 trucks hauled 6,500 metric tons of sorghum, cornmeal, lentils, vegetable oil, and a corn-soy blend—enough to feed two hundred thousand refugees for more than two months, all in containers stamped plainly with the initials "USA." Each truck carried a driver, a mechanic, and a goat, in addition to the relief supplies. From the Mediterranean to the refugee camps in Chad, the convoy would drive seventeen hundred miles, mostly through desert. At the dinner break during each grueling day of desert travel, the travelers would slaughter goats to provide the meat for their meals. The trucks were Libyan. The drivers and mechanics were from Chad and Sudan. The food came from the United States. The whole process was coordinated by the World Food Program.

I flew to Al Kufrah on a Libyan airplane to represent the United States at this landmark occasion and to meet with Libyan and World Food Program officials who also came to witness the event. For lunch, we sat around eating dates and other fruits and chatting. The Libyans said they had never

met an American before. And that underscored how remarkable this situation was.

It had started simply, in a phone call to a former—possibly current—enemy, with a request for help in a humanitarian cause. This cause was nonpartisan, nonpolitical, nonideological, and important to humankind. *If we can help hundreds of thousands of people by getting the OK from somebody who was an enemy and still may be an enemy, and we don't have to compromise anything,* I thought, *why wouldn't we do it?*

I had learned that such an approach could succeed a decade and a half earlier when Frank Wolf and I coaxed U.S. and Soviet leaders to cooperate in fending off starvation in Ethiopia. It was considered a significant event at the time, coming as it did at the end of the Cold War.

Ethiopia was still suffering from drought, famine, and civil war. Rebels in the northern regions of Tigray and Eritrea were making significant military progress against the troops of the central Communist government, which was still headed by Mengistu Haile Mariam. Because of the war, relief supplies could not be delivered into areas where some five million people were at immediate risk of death. The Eritrean People's Liberation Front, which was seeking independence from the central government, had targeted the port of Massawa, the main entry point for food and other emergency supplies. Food unloaded there had been destroyed. The fighting threatened to keep the port closed for months.

In a carryover from the Cold War, the Soviet Union provided weapons to the Mengistu government. The United States and other countries had sent food to Ethiopia and had more in the pipeline that was being blocked by the war. Both publicly and privately, Frank and I asked the first President Bush and Soviet president Mikhail Gorbachev to join forces in pressuring all parties in the war to observe a "food truce." We wrote newspaper opinion pieces, appealed to representatives of the Ethiopian factions, and met with U.S. and USSR officials.

"Now is the time for an eleventh-hour humanitarian offensive, led by President Bush, joined by President Gorbachev and working through the U.N. Security Council," we wrote on the *Washington Post*'s op-ed page on February 21, 1990, for instance. Our article continued:

Nothing less than a full-scale international assault against hunger in Ethiopia, led by the superpowers and the United Nations, has a chance of success.

A "food truce," through which white-flagged relief convoys would cross battle lines to reach civilians, could be arranged.

Most of the results of the thaw in the Cold War have thus far been political: new governments in Czechoslovakia and Poland, steps toward German reunification and an end to one-party rule in the Soviet Union. Here is the chance—indeed the duty—to use the warming of relations for humanitarian ends.

President Bush and President Gorbachev answered our pleas. The result was a cease-fire that permitted delivery of food and other relief supplies to those Ethiopians who were facing starvation in the absence of aid.

This hopeful approach to enemies, whether past or present, led me to request a simple humanitarian act by a man who at this writing remains a fugitive from the United Nations war crimes tribunal at The Hague.

In July 1995 I traveled to the Balkans, where ethnic groups were fighting to control pieces of what once had been Yugoslavia. In Croatia I marveled at the beauty of the Adriatic coast and its role as a low-cost Riviera during peacetime. In Sarajevo, which had so successfully hosted the 1984 Winter Olympics, I encountered some of the worst horrors of this civil war.

Yugoslavia, a multiethnic state that Communist dictator Josip Tito held together for decades after World War II, slowly deteriorated following his death in 1980, then crumbled along both ethnic and religious fault lines in the 1990s. When I arrived, Bosnians, mostly Muslims, were under siege in Sarajevo, surrounded by Bosnian Serbs, mostly Christians, who were led by Radovan Karadzic, the president of the Serbian Democratic Party. Sarajevo desperately needed food, but UN relief caravans were blocked by Serb military forces. The people were desperate, emotional, and in shock. I saw many women, children, and older people but no men, young or old. They were either fighting or hiding in the forest.

Karadzic, who already stood accused of war crimes, had representatives in Washington. So before I left the United States, I told them I'd like to meet him during my trip. Our State Department asked me not to do so. "I'm not going over there to make policy," I replied. "We have a humanitarian crisis, and I

want to ask him to lift his snipers to at least let some food into Sarajevo." The Serb representatives said Karadzic would see me.

Even though Karadzic's headquarters were just a few miles from Sarajevo in the mountain town of Pale, we couldn't travel safely between Muslim- and Serb-controlled territory in Bosnia. So I and three aides who were traveling with me had to fly from Sarajevo to Rome, then to Frankfort and on to Belgrade, the capital of Serbia. From there we drove six hours to Pale.

We arrived in the evening, exhausted from having slept only about an hour each of the previous four days. Karadzic immediately summoned us into his headquarters for talks. He knew about my faith, said he was a believer, and suggested that we pray. He offered us dinner. We talked from about seven or eight o'clock that night to two or three o'clock the next morning.

I stressed the humanitarian purpose of my trip. "The whole world looks on you as a monster," I told him, "and I can see you're worried about that." He said he wasn't the monster the world thought he was and that he wanted to change his image. "If that's the case," I replied, "do something. Don't just talk." Pointing out the convoy of food trucks that couldn't pass his military lines, I continued, "Allow this convoy to get into Sarajevo."

"Yeah," he said finally, "I'll take care of it."

This conversation occurred during the time that Bosnian Serbs were committing perhaps the worst atrocities seen in Europe since World War II. Mimicking the Nazi attacks on Jews, Bosnian Serb troops seized the small spa town of Srebrenica, rounded up the men and boys, and slaughtered more than seven thousand of them. Yet here was their leader, calmly sitting and talking with me, promising to do good.

Two years later Frank and I traveled to Bled, Slovenia, a beautiful little town by a lake at the foothills of the Alps, where people from across the Balkans were meeting as part of a long-term effort to learn to live in peace. Frank and I told them how we reached across our political differences to work together. I also told them about my strange encounter with Karadzic.

Afterward, a man came up to tell me he had been in Sarajevo at that time. "All of a sudden," he said, "Karadzic let this big food convoy come in, and we never understood what happened."

These kinds of experiences make me particularly frustrated about the lack

of civility and cooperation within our own politics and government. Frank and I weren't the only members of Congress to build a close working relationship across partisan lines. There are other small clusters of members who meet in regular prayer groups. The House hunger committee was a bipartisan enterprise from the moment Mickey Leland, an African-American Catholic Democrat from Texas; Benjamin Gilman, a white Jewish Republican from New York; and I led the effort to create it in 1983. After the committee was abolished a decade later (which I write about in detail in chapter 6), Frank, Missouri Republican Bill Emerson, and I created the Congressional Hunger Center to keep working on the issue. The center's board is cochaired by one member of Congress from each party.

Bipartisanship also defines the House and Senate hunger caucuses, less-formal successors to the House Select Committee on Hunger. Nebraska Republican Tom Osborne and Massachusetts Democrat Jim McGovern—who represent quintessential "red" and "blue" states—cochair the House caucus. The Senate caucus has four cochairs—Democrats Blanche Lincoln of Arkansas and Richard Durbin of Illinois, along with Republicans Gordon Smith of Oregon and Elizabeth Dole of North Carolina.

Osborne and McGovern are the prime House sponsors of the Hunger-Free Communities Act, a legislative proposal that has long been one of my goals. It would set the objective of cutting hunger in the United States in half by 2010 and ending it by 2015. Lincoln, Durbin, and Smith joined Indiana Republican Richard Lugar to introduce the bill in the Senate. Many legislators also work across party lines to represent the special interests of the communities or states that they share.

It's hard—almost impossible—to build close, personal friendships with people and then publicly attack them. I can't tell you how many times Frank and my other conservative Republican friends have leaped to my defense when I've been attacked unfairly from the right.

It is possible to disagree about issues; Frank and I disagree about most political matters. But you can have debate—civil debate—on the many issues you disagree about while still working together to achieve the few goals you share. It's difficult to work together on the few common goals, however, if your many debates turn vicious, bitter, personal, and blindly partisan. Unfortunately, in

recent years, this kind of debating has become common practice in Washington. And that's one major reason I'm happy that I decided to leave Congress after almost twenty-four years.

It's nearly unfathomable to me why our politicians are incapable of understanding the value of civility, friendship, and cooperation. If, to achieve a specific humanitarian goal, I can find common ground—however briefly—with the likes of Karadzic and al-Gadhafi, why in the world can't Republican and Democratic politicians in the United States find the common ground where they could solve our nation's very real problems? Why can't we all come together to answer our common summons to help the poor?

There are Republicans who refuse to work with Democrats and Democrats who refuse to work with Republicans. There are people of faith who refuse to work with people who don't have faith, Christians who refuse to work with non-Christians, even members of one Christian denomination who refuse to work with members of another Christian denomination.

I'll work with anyone who shares a common goal with me. As a follower of Jesus, I would like my friends to believe, and I hope that they will come to do so someday. But I'm not going to refuse to work with them because they don't share my beliefs. And I'm not going to try to push my faith down their throats. It's really up to them, not me, to figure out their relationship with God.

What I can do is follow Jesus's command to serve the poor. My friends and others who work with me see what I do and come to understand why. Often people ask me why I work to help people in need. It's remarkable how many people have become believers after getting involved in humanitarian work.

The poet Edgar Guest once wrote, "I'd rather see a sermon than hear one." I've carried that sentiment with me ever since I first heard it. It follows Jesus's instruction to "let your light shine before others, so that they may see your good works and give glory to your Father in heaven" (Matthew 5:16).

WALKING WITH MOTHER TERESA

Doing What's in Front of Her

The first time I met Mother Teresa, she took my left hand in hers and said, "I want you to always remember something." Then she used her other hand to deliberately fold each of my five outstretched fingers, one by one, into my palm. With each fold, she said a word: "For . . . the . . . least . . . of . . . these. I want you to always think of this. For the least of these." She also said, "Pray and keep a pure heart and be humble." Then she took me with her on her rounds through Calcutta and taught me a great deal more about how one should go about serving the poor.

The overarching lessons I have learned from my travels are that there is need in the world far beyond most affluent Westerners' comprehension and also that there is hope. No place did I find that hope shining more brightly than in the dark slums of this great Indian city. The world has heard of Mother Teresa's accomplishments, but you cannot fully understand the power of her faith and love unless you were able to accompany her in her work. And were you, like me, able to do that, your life was forever changed.

I was with a small group of believers from the United States. We began our day at the Missionaries of Charity compound in Calcutta, which was made up of plain wood-and-concrete structures where the missionaries lived and carried out some of their work, and where Mother Teresa kept a modest office. Everything there was clean and simple—drab, even. Mother Teresa's office had off-white walls, as I recall, and a simple table with simple wooden chairs. The

compound included a small hospital, facilities for caring for quite a few orphans, and a little chapel. The plainness of Mother Teresa's living and working conditions struck me, because it contrasted so dramatically with the grandeur of her mission and the enormity of her accomplishments.

We accompanied Mother Teresa first to a hospice. It was a single large room in which sixty to seventy poor Indians who were very sick lay on simple iron beds and waited to die. It was primitive, but it was clean and peaceful and comfortable. The missionaries washed the patients, fed them, talked with them, touched them. Normally, dying brings great sadness. But with Mother Teresa and her missionaries, death was peaceful and pure because of all the love that filled the room.

We next went to a home for severely retarded children. The facility resembled the hospice—another big room, spartan, devoid of color, and housing maybe sixty children, most of them lying or sitting on iron beds. These places would not meet U.S. standards for health-care, educational, or service facilities.

No one wanted these kids. They were so mentally disabled that it appeared they were unaware of their surroundings. Many were physically disabled as well. The room was filled with incoherent babbling. Yet when Mother Teresa walked in, these kids lit up as if the sun had suddenly come indoors. They all started to yell and expressed excitement in wonderful ways. She walked through the room, hugging each child. When she touched them, they glowed. It was amazing to see how much she loved them and how much they loved her in return.

She had the same effect at an orphanage we visited, although there the children were healthy and energetic. When we walked in, the kids—fifty to sixty of them, ages three to about nine—jumped on us as if they were playful puppies. They hopped up and down, hung on us, touched us, wanted to play with us. So we sat on the bare floor in this large playroom, which contained only a few toys, all of them fairly simple, and played with these kids, joked with them, touched them. They craved attention, craved physical contact, and they responded to Mother Teresa's love.

I noticed throughout the day that wherever we went, she touched everyone she was working with. She made everybody feel her love. And the poorest, the sickest, the most physically and mentally disabled responded with joy and love. Touching the poorest and the sickest is not an easy thing to do. They often don't look good. They don't smell good. They may not be clean. They

may be slobbering or defecating in their beds or throwing up. Sometimes flies swarm around them. You wonder what germs are swarming as well, what illnesses they have that they might pass on to you. Yet none of that seemed to bother Mother Teresa. And the touching, the hugging, the demonstration of love seemed to be perhaps the most important thing she did.

I thought of this later, far away in Kinshasa, the capital of the Democratic Republic of the Congo, where my friend John Nakamura and I noticed the streets seemed to be filled with children who appeared to be homeless. They were not, it turned out, orphans of war or of AIDS. Rather, they had been declared "witches" by self-proclaimed religious doctors and had been banished by their families, left to fend for themselves despite their young age.

We were able to visit a Catholic organization that was taking care of some of these kids. The children told us how they had been kicked out of their homes, had to scratch for subsistence on the streets, had no family to love them. As we prepared to leave, we hugged them, and these outcast children responded powerfully. They hugged us back tightly. They cried and cried. They kept holding on to us. They didn't want to let us go. Their reaction drove into my soul just how important love and touch are to people who are deprived of both.

Another time I thought back to Mother Teresa's example was when I met Sister Surupa at a clean but primitive hospital run by the Missionaries of Charity in Port-au-Prince, Haiti. The hospital, which cared for AIDS and tuberculosis patients, had few of the modern medical tools we take for granted, and five patients had died just the day before.

"What care can you hope to give in this place?" I asked her.

"Loving care is what we give," she replied.

With Mother Teresa in Calcutta, we visited orphans, lepers, polio victims, the handicapped, the mentally ill, the mentally disabled, and the dying. Every time she entered a room, everyone in the room came alive. If you just looked at her, you would hardly call her a beautiful woman. Physically, she was not an imposing figure. She probably was less than five feet tall. But she had a beauty and an aura about her that I have never seen in anyone else.

The facilities we visited that day were scattered around the city. Sometimes we drove from one site to another. Sometimes we walked. At one point while we were walking, I became overwhelmed by the vastness of the sickness and

poverty that surrounded us. There were masses and masses of people living practically on top of one another in the crowded slums. It was swelteringly hot. Open sewage flowed along the street. Cattle and other livestock wandered everywhere. People were lying on the streets, living on the streets. It didn't smell good. I thought not only of the squalor that surrounded me at that moment but of the horrors I had seen in my earlier travels. At that kind of moment, you wonder if there's really any way you can make a difference that truly matters.

Someone asked Mother Teresa, "Don't you think what you do is kind of a drop in the bucket?"

And she answered, "No, it's a drop in the ocean. But if I didn't do it, it would be one less drop."

"But," I said, "the problems of the world are so vast. How can you possibly hope to solve them?"

"You do the thing that's in front of you," she replied. And that was the most important lesson she taught me.

"A man asked me that question many years ago when I first started my ministry on the streets," she told me. "There was a woman very sick in front of me, like that man you're looking at right there," she continued, pointing to a man lying on the ground in front of us. "Her face was bitten by ants and rats. I took care of her and loved her, and that's how I started my ministry on the streets."

We can't all go to Calcutta to help these people. But if we each do the thing on our street—do the thing that's in front of us—we will make the world a much better place.

Mother Teresa's story is a personal example of both doing what's in front of you and reaching across many boundaries. She was born in 1910 in Macedonia, of Albanian descent. At age eighteen she joined the Loreto Sisters in Ireland. They sent her to teach high school in Calcutta.

What she saw in front of her there were the poor, the sick, the homeless, and the orphans, living on the streets of the slums with no one to help them. So in 1948 she left the school to work with the poorest of the poor. In 1950 she founded the Missionaries of Charity to love and care for people whom no one else would help in a country that is 80 percent Hindu, 13 percent Muslim, and 2 percent Christian. She learned Bengali, the major local language, and became a citizen of India. She said her goal was to "make a Hindu a better

Hindu, a Muslim a better Muslim, and a Christian a better Christian." In its early years, the order opened a hospice, then an orphanage, then a home for lepers, then other facilities to care for the neediest.

Originally a small band of nuns, the Missionaries later added brothers as well. Today Mother Teresa's movement has grown to encompass forty-five hundred sisters, five hundred brothers, and countless thousands of volunteers who serve "the least of these" in more than one hundred countries. To the original homes for the dying, orphans, and lepers have been added numerous facilities for unwed pregnant women, AIDS patients, the mentally and physically disabled, the destitute, and others. In the words of Pope John Paul II, "A great host of people—of all beliefs and none—have become involved in this work of love which has spread throughout the world."[1] Beyond even that, Mother Teresa has inspired countless others to do their own good works, even if they don't have the all-consuming commitment that she demonstrated and that her missionaries still exhibit.

She had no power, as power is traditionally measured. She didn't hold a government office. She didn't own a gigantic business. In fact, this humble woman owned nothing except a few changes of the plain Indian clothing she wore everywhere. She lived among the poor. She spent most of her time with the poor. Yet she influenced the entire planet.

The importance of her work was recognized when she was awarded the 1979 Nobel Peace Prize, which she accepted with the request that the usual gala banquet be canceled and the money saved be donated to the poor. In her acceptance speech—and wearing her simple Indian sari—she asked her audience to "find the poor here, right in your own home, first, and begin love there, and find out about your next-door neighbor—do you know who they are?"

Her profound impact on the world was dramatically demonstrated at her death in 1997. President Clinton summed up her life perfectly by describing her "ministry of action—of passion and compassion." He said, "She led by serving and showed us the stunning power of simple humility."[2] The president asked First Lady Hillary Clinton to lead the United States delegation to the funeral, and she invited me to attend. It was an extraordinary sight.

The government of this overwhelmingly Hindu country declared national days of mourning and honored the diminutive Roman Catholic nun with a

state funeral, a tribute reserved for high government officials with only one previous exception—Mahatma Gandhi in 1948. In the days leading up to the funeral, tens of thousands of ordinary Indians made their way to St. Thomas Catholic Church, where her body was laid out. The body was carried from the church to the funeral site—an indoor sports arena that could accommodate thirteen thousand people—by the same military gun carriage used in the funeral processions for Gandhi and Jawaharlal Nehru, India's first prime minister. In Mother Teresa's case, the procession featured nuns from her order and representatives of the poor, the disabled, the sick, the orphaned, and the homeless. Dignitaries from several dozen countries attended the funeral mass, including presidents, prime ministers, first ladies, and three queens.

Cardinal Angelo Sodano, the Vatican secretary of state and the pope's personal representative, presided. The choir sang hymns in several languages. The prayers and eulogies were both multilingual and multifaith, including contributions from Catholics and Protestants as well as a Hindu, a Muslim, a Buddhist, a Sikh, and a Zoroastrian.

The media revealed her broad appeal when obtaining comments from both dignitaries and people on the streets.

"At a time when humankind is being increasingly driven by selfish motive, she gave selflessly to those whom society has forsaken and forgotten," said Atal Bihari Vajpayee, head of India's leading Hindu nationalist political party.

Manik Chatterjee, caretaker of a Hindu temple, said, "It is not possible in one hundred thousand people to replace her. What she did, no one else can do."

"When someone is so good," said a Muslim named Mohammad Qasim Ali, "their religion does not matter. She was a foreigner, not even an Indian. But people thought she was one of us."

"Crossing the frontiers of religious and ethnic differences," said Cardinal Sodano during the funeral mass, "she has taught the world this lesson: it is more blessed to give than to receive."

It's amazing how many extremely effective humanitarian organizations sprang to life when one person or one small group of people did what was in front of them. The Grameen Bank—along with the global microcredit movement it has inspired—can trace its origin to economics professor Muhammad Yunus's visit to a poor village in Bangladesh in 1976, for example.

"I became involved in the poverty issue not as a policymaker or a researcher," Yunus recalled three decades later. "I became involved because poverty was all around me."[3]

As an economist, Yunus said, he dealt with theories about international trade and billions of dollars in business transactions. But while confronting the poverty in front of him, he "wanted to find something specific to do to help another human being just to get by another day with a little more ease than the previous day."[4]

In the village of Jobra, near Chittagong University, where he headed the Economics Department, Yunus met Sufiya Begum, a twenty-one-year-old mother of three who made bamboo stools. Raw materials for each stool cost just twenty-two cents. But she had no capital. So she had to borrow, either from moneylenders who charged interest as high as 10 percent a week, or from a middleman who would buy each completed stool for just two cents more than she paid for the raw materials. If she could borrow at a reasonable rate—as established businesses and middle-class individuals can—she could earn enough to save and improve her economic standing, Yunus reasoned.

Yunus and a student surveyed the village and identified forty-one other craftspeople who were in the same straits as Begum. The professor then reached into his pocket and loaned the forty-two people a grand total of $27. All of the borrowers repaid their loans. And Yunus thought he had discovered the secret to helping the underprivileged lift themselves out of poverty.

With a great deal of difficulty, he convinced a bank to devote $300 to such loans. But the bank required him to guarantee each loan, and the lending procedures were extremely cumbersome. In late 1977 another bank, the Agriculture Bank, put $30,000 into starting an experimental Grameen Branch in the village. In mid-1979 a consortium of national banks enabled Yunus to open another two dozen branches, and he took a leave of absence from the university to oversee the enterprise. With support from the national banks and the Ford Foundation, expansion continued into the early 1980s. In 1983 Grameen became an independent bank. In 1998 it stopped relying on grants from donors to pay some of its expenses.

Grameen, which means "village" in the Bangla language, breaks many established rules of banking. In addition to lending to the poorest of the poor, it

demands no collateral and does not require borrowers to sign legal instruments. The bank doesn't threaten borrowers with court action if they fail to repay—and it doesn't have to. Its default rate is a remarkably low 1 percent.[5]

Because traditional Bangladesh banks seldom loan to women, Yunus set a goal of giving women half of Grameen's loans. Later he determined that a loan to a woman tended to bring more benefit to the family than a loan to a man. Now women comprise 96 percent of the bank's borrowers.[6]

The bank also counts about forty-five thousand beggars among its borrowers. Their loans are interest-free and long-term, so the installment repayments can be small. They often finance something as basic as a blanket or mosquito netting. Beggar borrowers aren't required to stop begging but are encouraged to seek other ways to generate income. Grameen has loaned beggars close to $1 million, and half of those loans have been repaid.[7]

Today Grameen fields a staff of about 14,000 to operate more than 1,500 branches. Since its inception, it has loaned nearly $5 billion, including a projected $550 million in 2005 alone.

From its beginning of loaning tiny sums to village craftspeople, Grameen now offers a wide range of loans, such as loans for housing, education, and even high technology. More than 600,000 houses have been built with Grameen loans that average just $210. More than 6,000 students have received higher-education loans, including about 100 who attend medical school and nearly 200 who are studying to become engineers. About 140,000 have borrowed to purchase mobile telephones, which they use to bring phone service to villages that have never had it before. These so-called telephone ladies sell the use of their phones to villagers one call at a time. Some earn $300 to $400 a month in a country with an annual per capita income of about $450. The bank has placed a special emphasis on putting phones in the hands of beggars to provide an alternative source of income. A majority of Grameen's borrowers have lifted their families above Bangladesh's poverty line. Borrowers own 94 percent of the bank's equity. The bank pays 8.5 to 12 percent interest on deposits that total about $400 million.[8]

Yunus has been a tireless campaigner for microcredit, spreading the concept far beyond Bangladesh. He was not the first person to consider the value of tiny loans, nor the only person to try to put the idea into effect, writes David Bornstein in his book *How to Change the World*. But Yunus "worked

without pause to institutionalize and market his idea," Bornstein says. And "it is unlikely that micro credit would have grown into a major global movement without Yunus' vision, single-mindedness, persuasiveness and energy."[9]

Yunus certainly influenced me.

Just as I believe we have the capability to banish hunger from the world, Yunus believes we can eradicate poverty, "if we want to."[10] And he makes a powerful argument that his approach—acknowledging a responsibility to the poor but helping them to become entrepreneurs rather than simply giving them relief—can bring people together across ideological gaps.

"You may be a revolutionary, a liberal or a conservative—you may be young, or you may be old—but we can all work together on this one issue," Yunus writes in his autobiography, *Banker to the Poor.*[11] "It's amazing," he said later. "Whether I'm talking to Republicans or Democrats, Labor parties or Conservative parties or Christian Democrats, they all agree on supporting this idea."[12]

I travel around the third world to learn about poor people's needs and ways that I and my wealthy country can help. But in Bangladesh, from Yunus, I learned how his knowledge could help the poor in America.

Yunus talks of the need to "reverse the age-old vicious circle of low income, low saving and low investment," replacing it with a "virtuous circle of low income, credit, investment, more income, more savings, more investment, more income."[13] There's no reason that approach can't work in the United States, home to the most entrepreneurial people in the world.

There are plenty of poor Americans who have the ability to run a small business, who are willing to work hard, but who never get a chance. In fact, many are already doing it; we just don't recognize it and don't give them the small support they would need to grow. I'm talking about women who operate informal day-care centers by taking neighbors' children into their homes, men who push a mower along sidewalks while carrying a can of gasoline and looking for lawns to cut, others with buckets and sponges who offer to wash neighbors' cars.

After learning from Yunus, I introduced or cosponsored several pieces of legislation that provided government support for microlending and changed welfare rules that penalized poor people who earned and saved while trying to improve their families' economic state. Ironically, we supported microenterprise abroad through our foreign aid programs before we encouraged it at home. And it works.

I met a woman in a small town in southeastern Ohio who used a microenterprise loan to start a car-wash business—not with large, expensive machinery but with a few people who wash autos with their hands. Stories like hers have been replicated across the country. A woman in Arkansas borrowed $475 to buy the used equipment she needed to open a beauty shop. A $650 loan enabled a woman in Nebraska to start a greenhouse and landscaping business.[14]

Yunus views "every single human being as a potential entrepreneur. I am totally convinced from my experience of working with poor people," he says, "that they can get themselves out of poverty if we give them the same or similar opportunities as we give to others. These millions of small people with their millions of small pursuits can add up to create the biggest development wonder."[15]

I have met many people like Muhammad Yunus during my travels—people who did what was in front of them. Many have eased one person's misery through a simple act of kindness. Some, such as Yunus and Mother Teresa herself, began by reaching out to a few people, then went on to change a large chunk of the world.

I try to pass their lessons on whenever and wherever I can. While I was ambassador in Rome, I often was asked to speak to Italian audiences about my travels. Once, at a high school in the southern region of Molise, the students asked me what they could do to make the world better.

"We can't all go to Calcutta," I replied. "Look around you. Your next-door neighbor maybe just lost her mother, or maybe her father just lost his job, or maybe there's somebody sick in their family. They need your attention. They need you to love them. They need you to talk to them. They need a friend.

"Maybe there's an outcast here in the school whom everybody looks down upon or makes fun of. First, don't do that. Then be his friend.

"Somebody around here needs a helping hand, and you can provide it, and oftentimes it's a very simple thing. Just look around you, and you'll see it. If you don't see it, then ask. If you just scratch the surface a little bit, you'll find something that you can do. And after a while, if you see problems that are bigger, and you're a leader, and you have the passion, you'll figure out a way to bring in other people and raise money and do whatever needs to be done to address whatever problems you want to address."

ALL IN THE FAMILY

Doing What's in Front of Us

★ ★ ★

One of the most heart-wrenching and heartwarming scenes I've ever witnessed during my travels took place at an orphanage in Uganda, where my wife, Janet, and I had taken our kids to volunteer. An enormous proportion of the orphans were HIV-positive or had AIDS. Some were visibly sick. The orphanage was so poor that the babies didn't wear diapers. Our daughter, Jyl, then fifteen years old, was holding, hugging, and playing with a baby who had both thrown up and urinated on her. Yet Jyl was acting as if nothing was wrong. "They just need somebody to love them," she told us.

Because I have been a congressman and an ambassador, my humanitarian activities have received a lot of public attention. Not so well known is the fact that Janet and Jyl are dedicated humanitarian workers as well, as was our son, Matt, until he died of leukemia at age fifteen in 1996. Jyl, in fact, earned a master's degree at Asbury Seminary in Kentucky and is setting out on a career of service to the poor.

Janet has been involved in these activities as long as I have. They've always been discussed at the family dinner table. From the time Jyl and Matt were old enough to understand, we made a concerted effort to expose them to the needy and to teach them the importance of helping those who are less well-off than we are.

Because of Janet's and my activities, we were able to take our kids to some pretty exotic places and to help them experience firsthand the extremes of

privilege and deprivation. At home and abroad, they met high-ranking government officials and people with great wealth, including some who use their government positions or their affluence to help the poor. They also met people who had nothing. We took them to work at soup kitchens and in church service projects near our home in Washington, something any parent can—and, I think, should—do. From time to time, I took them with me in my work around Dayton.

If you introduce children to these things, let them see hunger and poverty in the flesh, let them share in helping, then serving the poor becomes part of their lives. After a few of these experiences, Matt and Jyl never questioned why I would leave home to travel overseas or help in a homeless program or work for the hungry. In fact, they would ask to come along.

Jyl says her first memories of being exposed to these issues flow from conversations around the family dinner table or in front of the television. Just as I had been involved in humanitarian activities before my trip to Ethiopia, she had begun responding to family discussions of hunger and poverty when she was about six years old, before she had any direct experiences with severe poverty. She did so by donating some of her allowance to good causes. Also, as it had on me, my trip to Ethiopia had a profound effect on her.

Jyl didn't accompany me to Ethiopia then, of course. She was just eight years old. But I talked a lot about my experiences there after I returned. I can become quite emotional, and I guess I often teared up when discussing what I saw. Jyl noticed my emotion and grasped the fact that doing something to help was important to me. When appeals for aid to Ethiopia would come on the television while we were watching some show together, they moved her too. Later she said that my reactions to these things showed her clearly that God was working in my life.

One of the first times we involved our children in a hunger project was in 1985, when Jyl was nine and Matt was four. I organized a forty-hour fast in Dayton to raise funds for antihunger programs there and overseas (an event I write about in detail in chapter 7). Although the kids didn't fast, Janet and I took them to Dayton with us so they could experience the occasion. I also took Matt with me to visit a Dayton homeless shelter.

In Washington, where my family and I spent most of our time, we all

worked in local soup kitchens. I helped start a gleaning program, through which a Maryland farmer let us collect unharvested produce from his fields for delivery to Washington food programs. Matt and Jyl often would go with me to pick fruit there. They also helped in our church's project to deliver food to the poor, many of whom were refugees of civil war in El Salvador. One year, we spent Christmas in Florida and agreed we each would give the family a present that couldn't be purchased. Janet's gift was to take us all to work in a soup kitchen on Christmas Day. As we did these things, the children would ask questions, mostly about why people had to be so poor, why they couldn't find a place to live, why they were so poorly dressed, why some acted strangely.

We also just tried to be good friends and neighbors. We'd take food to neighbors who were sick, visit with friends who were lonely or troubled. We tried to show Matt and Jyl that they just had to look around themselves to find good deeds that needed doing. And they did.

Once, while visiting a home for the elderly, Jyl noticed that many residents seemed lonely and didn't receive many visitors. So she started to regularly visit two women who shared a room. She'd sit with them on weekends. They'd tell her stories about their lives and ask her what she was up to.

Janet wanted to expose our children to the widest possible array of experiences, so she arranged in 1987 for Jyl to spend some time with an extraordinary Ethiopian couple who then were living in Fort Wayne, Indiana. Marta Gabre-Tsadick had been the first woman appointed to the Ethiopian Senate during the reign of Emperor Haile Selassie, and she had served as the hostess at his palace. When Communist rebels overthrew Selassie in 1974 and began executing members of Selassie's family and government, Marta fled with her husband, Demeke Tekle-Wold. They ended up as refugees in Indiana, where, with the Reverend Charles Dickinson and his wife, they founded Project Mercy in 1977.

Initially, Project Mercy provided emergency relief and relocation assistance to African refugees. Following the collapse of Ethiopia's Communist dictatorship in the early 1990s, Marta and Demeke returned to their homeland and have built at the village of Yetebon one of the most effective private relief and development projects I've seen anywhere in the world.

Jyl considers meeting Marta and Demeke to be one of the formative

experiences of her life. Our families remain close to this day. We visit them from time to time when we are in Africa, and they have visited us in Washington and Rome. Jyl has described Marta and Demeke as being like grandparents to her.

At age eleven, Jyl learned something of hunger, poverty, and oppression by talking with Marta, Demeke, and other Ethiopians who had found refuge in Indiana at that time. Perhaps more important, she learned about and became comfortable in an alien culture, even though it had been transplanted temporarily to the American Midwest. Understanding the society of the people who need help is essential for anyone trying to succeed in humanitarian ventures.

The trip to Uganda, however, was what really set Jyl on the path to a lifetime of service to the poor. Again, the idea was Janet's—another part of her plan to expose our children to the very best and the very worst aspects of life on earth. "We have only a limited amount of time to teach our children," Janet said. Knowing and helping the poor had become a regular part of their lives at home. Living with Marta and Demeke had enlightened Jyl. But Janet believed it was important for both Jyl and Matt to witness firsthand the severe deprivation that exists in the third world.

Janet and the kids spent a month in Uganda, the first two weeks without me because Congress was in session. Jyl noted the staggering contrasts she experienced that month. We stayed in a diplomatic residence in the capital of Kampala. We were driven to the orphanage in a car provided by President Yoweri Museveni. At the orphanage, we worked with children who had nothing—not even, Janet pointed out, parents.

The orphanage was poor. The children slept on the floor. There wasn't enough money to put the babies in diapers. They had few toys to play with. Matt, who was ten at the time, played soccer and other games with the older children. It was wonderful to see the orphans' faces light up with smiles when they saw him coming. Jyl, who was fifteen, devoted herself to the babies. When she sat on the floor, they would crawl all over her. One by one, she'd hold them, hug them—love them. We had other activities planned for our stay in Kampala, but Jyl returned to the orphanage nearly every day.

The experience was "a shock," she recalled many years later. "I was just completely overwhelmed that there were people who lived like this. I don't

know if I'd even met an orphan up to that point. It just broke my heart, and it changed my life forever."

About the babies with AIDS, she said, "I'd just hug them and hold them, because I thought, *How many people are here to hold these children? And who knows how many days they have till they die?* I thought, *I don't want to do anything else with my life but to do this kind of thing.* I think that's when I really started to believe this is what life is about. It's about caring for one another, reaching out to those who are hurting, and giving from my own surplus."

Because Matt was younger, this trip didn't have such a profound effect on him. But as he got older, he developed a tremendous heart for people who were hurting. And these people sensed it when he was around them. I'll never forget one time, after he got sick, when I visited a homeless shelter in Dayton. His illness had been reported in the Dayton media, and even the homeless were aware of it. Several homeless men came up to me and asked, "How's your son? How's he doing? We think about him all the time." And I thought to myself, *These guys slept out in the cold weather on the street last night. They don't know where their next meal is coming from. And here they are worrying about me and my son.* When you care for the hungry, care for the poor, they return it to you in the way they can.

Jyl recently decided to earn a master's degree in theology to help her prepare for a career in ministering to "the least of these." As part of her studies, she wrote a paper titled "A Biblical Theology of Mission to the Poor." To write it, she searched for all of the biblical references to the poor and struggled to understand their meaning.

"It is interesting," she writes, "that Jesus did not solve the problems of poverty everywhere he went. Jesus often repeated that this burden was on us all." Later in the paper, she concludes that "giving to and caring for the poor should bring joy and purpose into people's lives. The fruit of God's love in our lives, and our response to it, is love. The response to forgiveness is forgiveness. The response to mercy is mercy. I hope to continue to educate people on the need for mission and care for the poor. I believe that holistic mission is caring for both the material and spiritual needs of others."

In addition to studying, Jyl is helping her fellow students get involved in humanitarian action. She's compiling a list of activities students could undertake

in the local community. She counsels students about finding the activities that would be best for them. She helped to found a local chapter of Amnesty International to join the fight for human rights around the world. She participates in letter-writing campaigns to public officials in the United States and abroad. She volunteers in political campaigns.

Janet and I, of course, are thrilled by the path she is taking—by the fact that she wants her life to count and that she wants to serve the poor. I'm sure this desire is rooted in what she experienced in Dayton and Washington and Africa. It's no coincidence that Frank Wolf's children have chosen similar paths.

When Frank and I traveled through Romania during the dark days of the Nicolae Ceauşescu regime, Frank brought his daughter Virginia along. It was a horrifying and inspiring trip, as I describe in chapter 5. Virginia, then a college student, experienced everything we did. She even joined us in speaking to congregations in Romanian churches that the Communist government was trying to destroy. Shortly after returning from Romania, Frank took his entire family on a trip through Europe, including behind the then-still-hanging Iron Curtain in East Germany. He called it a true eye-opener.

Frank's children worked in their church's mission projects. As in our house, Frank's humanitarian activities—and the reasons for them—were topics of conversation around the family dinner table. When you follow the message of the Bible, Frank says, you feed the hungry, clothe the naked, free the oppressed, and serve the poor.

Frank both talked the talk and walked the walk, as they say, and his children have too. Among them, they have worked with the poor and homeless in Washington, taught in Romania and Honduras, worked with the needy in Bolivia, and helped to start Christian schools in Washington, D.C., and Princeton, New Jersey.

Janet and I are well aware that Jyl did not have a typical childhood—and neither did Frank's children, for that matter. Jyl has seen great luxury and abject poverty up close. And she experienced the horrible personal tragedy of losing her younger brother to cancer when he was just fifteen years old.

We're not rich. Despite what many voters think, most members of Congress aren't rich. We are better off than most Americans, however, as are most federal legislators. And many rich people participate in politics. So Jyl has been

in the homes of some very wealthy families and ridden in their limousines. She has attended functions at the White House and met presidents. She has accompanied me to national political conventions. She has traveled in two dozen countries. She has visited Janet and me in our diplomatic residence just inside the ancient wall in Rome.

She also has worked in grassroots politics, especially in my campaigns—riding in parades, knocking on doors. She attended public schools where she was in the racial minority. She has done humanitarian work in places of extreme poverty, as I've already told.

Jyl's desire to serve grew from these diverse experiences. But any parent can inspire a child to want to do good in any community—you don't have to go to Africa. Your kids learn by your example.

You don't force your kids to participate in a humanitarian project. You talk about serving others. You live it. You do it. You take them along with you when you do it. They need to see it with their own eyes. They need to feel it. They need to try to understand the shoes the other person is walking around in.

You can take them with you to work in a homeless shelter or food bank in any American city. They can serve by visiting shut-ins down the street. If they feel this service is genuine in your life, it will stay with them throughout their lives. They'll never forget.

As Jyl said recently, "My parents could have talked to me till they turned blue, and I wouldn't have really been that interested in their preaching about helping people. I had to see it in their lives—I had to see them really having a heart for what they're doing—or I would have thought they were just talking."

I have known and learned about many families that have made a difference in people's lives in small but important ways. Sometimes people's initially modest efforts end up accomplishing great things beyond their wildest imaginations.

Often I discover the parents in these families have been doing good works since their own childhoods. Their parents encouraged them to serve, and they pass this ethic on to their own children. When this happens, it's likely to continue for generations.

Geri Critchley remembers how she and her eight siblings were reared in Forestville, Connecticut, by devout Roman Catholic parents who "gave their lives to the community and to the church." The family put on "fairs for the

missions" every year, selling popcorn, setting up games in their yard, and hosting a dance in the garage. When she was little, Geri didn't understand exactly what the funds they raised were used for. She just knew they gave the money to their priest and he did something good with it.

Her father was a wonderful singer, she recalls, and he organized his large family into a singing group. Each Christmas Eve, they would carol for shut-ins.

As a young adult, Geri joined the Peace Corps and served in Somalia. Later, when she began rearing her own children, it was natural for her to introduce them to service at an early age.

"It was a conscious decision on my part to make sure they understand that it's in the giving that you receive," Geri explains. "But I didn't really 'teach' them. It just sort of permeated our lives."

Geri and her children held lawn sales to raise funds for Special Olympics. They delivered food to a soup kitchen. She took them along on her various service projects. She sent them to Catholic schools that emphasize service as an integral part of education. As they got older, they took on projects of their own.

When he was about fourteen, her son, Otis Plioplys, spent a summer building and upgrading houses on an Indian reservation. Later, as an avid golfer, he became inspired by Tiger Woods's efforts to bring golf to inner-city children. So Otis began teaching golf to kids on an urban course in Washington. His high school—Georgetown Prep, in a Washington suburb—has its own golf course, and he arranged for his inner-city golfers to spend a day playing there. He recruited fellow Georgetown Prep golf team members to be golf tutors for the day. He convinced some restaurants to donate food for the event. He did what was in front of him. Or as Geri puts it, "he used what he knew to do something good."

As juniors at Stone Ridge School, not far from Georgetown Prep, Geri's daughter, Hiliary Plioplys, and her best friend, Elizabeth Schroth, organized a group they called People for Peace. The purpose, Hiliary said, was to increase their fellow students' awareness of world affairs and "to do something ourselves to make a difference."

During school meetings, they made announcements about current events. They staged a volunteer fair to alert students to opportunities for public service in their community. They held bake sales and a grilled-cheese-sandwich

sale to raise money for various causes. They ran a "shoe drive," collecting used but good shoes to donate to an organization in Kenya. Then they met Tom Ehr, executive director of War Child USA, an international relief and development organization that focuses its work on children affected by war.

He told the girls his organization had raised funds to purchase relief supplies for children in refugee camps in Kosovo, a war-torn section of the Balkans. War Child didn't have enough money to hire trucks to deliver the supplies, however.

"He told us," Hiliary recalls, "'If you want to make a difference, it's about $5,500 per truck, and we need about four. Any effort you guys make to raise money for that would be great.'

"I thought, *This is crazy! $5,500—that's insane!*"

But Hiliary and Elizabeth took on the challenge. They made announcements at school, posted signs, and encouraged students to donate and to solicit contributions from their families and friends. They convinced school administrators to set aside a day when students wouldn't have to wear Stone Ridge uniforms if they brought in a contribution for the Kosovo drive. They received donations from alumni. They got their message through to even the youngest students.

"One little girl at the school had a bake sale to raise money and donated something like $23.75, and she was so happy to be able to donate it," Hiliary says. Another child, a kindergartner says raised funds with a lemonade stand.

One of Hiliary's mother's friends told Hiliary about putting her young granddaughter to sleep the night before dress-down day. "We were praying for everyone in the family," her mother's friend related, "and my granddaughter added 'those little children in Kosovo.' I asked her, 'How did you know about that?' And she said, 'Oh, at my school everybody knows that. We learned about it, and we're dressing down tomorrow, and I'm going to bring in my fifty cents.'"

When dress-down day arrived and People for Peace finished adding up the contributions from the school's eight hundred students, "everybody completely flipped," Hiliary says. More than $16,000 was collected that day. When all the contributions came in, they totaled $17,500. War Child used the money to hire three trucks and purchase additional supplies.

The project's spectacular success focused attention on Hiliary's little group. People for Peace received grants to stage a rally promoting service on Youth Service Day. The event, held at Washington's John F. Kennedy Center for the Performing Arts, drew students from around the Washington area and featured a performance by famed folksinger and social activist Peter Yarrow. The kids designed T-shirts displaying a statement attributed to Mahatma Gandhi: "You must be the change you wish to see in the world."

Hiliary was asked to speak at a conference of the National Society of Fundraising Executives (now called the Association of Fundraising Professionals). There she met Doris Buffett, investor Warren Buffett's sister, whose Sunshine Lady Foundation underwrites charitable giving by young philanthropists. Each year, Hiliary can donate up to $10,000 of the foundation's assets to nonprofit organizations that meet the foundation's funding criteria.

Now a college graduate, Hiliary plans to attend medical school in preparation for a career in international public health. In doing so, she follows both parents' leads. Her father, A. V. Plioplys, is a physician. Her mother is her inspiration to serve the less fortunate.

"I think, in my innate character, because of my upbringing, is the belief that you should, through your career and your everyday actions, leave the world a better place than when you came into it," Hiliary explained. "I'm not happy unless I'm helping other people in some way. It's part of who I am. My mom's that way, and I'm that way."

Not far from Hiliary's home, Maureen and Greg Gannon have instilled their commitment to service in their four daughters. Maureen (known as Mo) and Greg actually met while doing good. After graduating from the University of Notre Dame, Greg reinvigorated a tutoring program for disadvantaged children in Washington. A recent graduate of Villanova University, Mo was a volunteer tutor in the program, called Higher Achievement.

The program runs after-school tutoring and summer classes for middle school students in poor neighborhoods who have the motivation to succeed. The goal is to get them admitted to the Washington area's best public and private high schools and then into college. More than three-quarters of the participants have been admitted to what Higher Achievement defines as "quality high

schools." Nearly all of the participants—not just those attending the best high schools—have gone on to higher education.

Now the development director of the Catholic archdiocese of Washington, Greg remains on the Higher Achievement board. He, Mo, and their children have been active in various volunteer programs.

When oldest daughter, Katie, was about nine years old and youngest daughter, Margy, was about three, Greg organized a gleaning project at the family's church, Blessed Sacrament. Over the years, he expanded the effort by recruiting students and families from nearby Catholic schools. Participants would attend Sunday morning Mass, then travel to a farm. They'd glean for about two hours, break for a potluck picnic, then glean for a few more hours. Even Margy participated from the beginning.

Later Greg started a canned-food drive, again beginning at Blessed Sacrament, then expanding. Each year, he recruited volunteers, divided the Blessed Sacrament parish into sections, and assigned responsibility for canvassing each area. The Gannon family stapled flyers promoting the drive to grocery bags and distributed the bags to the volunteers. The flyers asked the neighbors to fill each bag with canned food and to leave it on the doorstep. The volunteers delivered the bags to homes in their neighborhood. A week from the date of the grocery bag distribution, drivers accompanied by children returned to collect the bags. The volunteers then gathered at the church for a snack and to count the cans.

After the drive became established within the Blessed Sacrament parish, Greg started recruiting families who lived outside the parish but whose children were enrolled in the Blessed Sacrament School. He asked them to solicit contributions in their neighborhoods. The drive became so popular that neighbors started looking forward to it. Many would make a special shopping trip and leave several full bags at the door. Greg has relinquished leadership of the drive to others, but it has become an institution in the community, now collecting more than forty thousand cans of food a year.

"I think as human beings we have the obligation to sort of look after the people who are less fortunate than we are, that we have a responsibility to give back," Mo said. "If you're lucky enough to have more than you need, you should share some of that.

"I think you can really instill that in your kids. I think our kids are pretty aware of how much they have and how much a lot of other people don't have."

The Gannon girls' actions prove Mo's point. All four participated in additional volunteer programs while living at home and continued to do so after they left for college. Katie worked in soup kitchens while a student at Villanova University in Philadelphia and tutored Mexican immigrants in English when she lived in San Diego for three years after graduation. Margy, a freshman at McDaniel College in Maryland, worked with Special Olympics while in high school. Megan is active in her sorority's service programs at Miami University of Ohio. Colleen volunteered in tutoring and mentoring programs while an undergraduate at Notre Dame. She's now teaching in a rural Catholic school in Louisiana while working toward a master's degree in education at Notre Dame during the summer.

Katie, who now teaches at Saint John's College High School in Washington, says the girls' volunteer work today can be traced to those childhood experiences collecting cans and gleaning food that otherwise would go to waste.

"When we would go through those fields to glean, it seemed there was enough to feed thousands of people and it was all going to spoil," she says. "It gave you some insight into how wasteful our country is in general, and that there are people who have so much and people who have so little.

"It motivates you more than parents just saying, 'Eat your dinner, because there are kids who don't have enough to eat.'"

CHAPTER 5

ROMANIA

Faith Deposes Might

★ ★ ★

Romania in 1985 was one of the most oppressed places on earth, yet its government enjoyed relatively friendly relations with ours. This was one of the great contradictions of the Cold War years, when the United States government—proclaiming the cause of freedom—would prop up dictators simply because they weren't Communists. In Romania, our position was even more convoluted, because dictator Nicolae Ceaușescu *was* a Communist. By distancing himself from the Soviet Union, he had been able to convince successive U.S. administrations that it was somehow in our best interest for him to remain in power.

The illegitimacy of that position was apparent from the moment my traveling party landed in Bucharest, the Romanian capital, at the end of June 1985. Despite the supposed amity between the U.S. and Romanian governments, U.S. diplomats immediately hustled us from the airport to a so-called bubble room in the American embassy.

A bubble room is equipped with all sorts of antispying technology to prevent eavesdropping on meetings that take place there. Once safely inside, we were warned of Romania's robust intelligence apparatus. We were cautioned to assume that everything we did, wherever we were, including in our bedrooms, would be *observed*, not just listened to. The Romanian government had one of the worst human rights records in the world, the embassy personnel informed

us. The secret police terrified the people. Romanians also had to endure the lowest standard of living in Europe outside Albania.

I had traveled through desperately poor places before—places much poorer than Romania, in fact—so seeing the poverty of the Romanian people would not be a unique experience for me. But this was my first trip among people subject to such severe political repression. And the fact that I had brought Janet along on this trip made the situation that much more disturbing.

Christian Solidarity International, a Switzerland-based human rights organization, had asked me—along with Frank Wolf and Republican Representative Chris Smith of New Jersey—to investigate reports of religious persecution in Romania. Frank's daughter Virginia and Janet accompanied us. Very quickly we all observed the truth of the briefing at the embassy. The oppression was so heavy, you could actually feel it. We were stopped and questioned wherever we went. We constantly spotted signs that we were being followed. We had numerous meetings with people who we thought would help us to understand the real state of affairs there but who played down or denied the extent of repression—because they were afraid. We sat in meetings—sometimes at meal tables—with government officials who baldly lied to us when we had incontrovertible evidence of the contrary truth. We also witnessed great bravery and inspiring faith among Romanians who held fast to their convictions and refused to stop worshiping in the manner they believed they should, despite the fierce government pressure.

We had been told that the government's campaign against religion included deploying bulldozers to destroy churches, so we visited one. It looked like the ancient ruins around Rome. Half of the church had been reduced to rubble. Some walls still stood in the other half, and they supported a partial roof. Members of the church had spread tarps across what was left of that roof so they could continue to worship there. It resembled the damage found in the aftermath of war. This damage had been done not by some enemy nation's bombs, however, but by this country's own government-directed heavy machinery.

This congregation demonstrated great faith, resiliency, and defiance by resuming services in their church. I have never seen spirit more beautiful and powerful than I witnessed there. It showed me that spirit often is strongest

among the oppressed, because it's the only place they can turn for support. I saw it in all four churches we visited during this trip.

On the way to the town of Aradia, for instance, we were delayed. Government officials went to the church we were supposed to visit and told the people waiting for us that we weren't coming. They then ordered the people to disperse. But the people stayed. And when we arrived, the pews were filled, the aisles were packed, and many other people stood outside. They were singing hymns in hearty voices when we walked in. The love and faith in that building were so strong they seemed to have a physical presence.

The government tried to block all of our church visits. Secret Service officers went to places we planned to explore and warned the people not to meet with us. We knew the people at all four churches faced imprisonment, beatings, and torture for displaying their faith in public. Many of them had relatives or friends who had been imprisoned or killed or who had simply disappeared. Yet each church overflowed with worshipers, many of them wearing tattered gray clothing. We were told people had stood for as long as three hours awaiting our arrival. When we finally did show up, they hung on to every word when we spoke to them. And we listened intently to their tales of oppression.

They told us of priests and pastors who had become informants for the secret police and of the way that people in all walks of life spied on one another. They showed us toilet paper that had been manufactured from Bibles confiscated by the government. Ceauşescu, it seemed, viewed the Bible as an extremely dangerous instrument in the hands of the faithful, so he made Bibles hard to come by.

Janet carried a beautiful new Bible into the churches we visited. At one church, the people expressed great admiration for it. Because Bibles were denied them, they had an enormous hunger for the written Word of God. Janet responded to their desire by giving the Bible to them. I later thought about what a wonderful act of kindness she had performed and regretted that I hadn't done the same.

At each church, people would touch us and hug us to express love as well as gratitude for the fact that we had come to be with them. Some kissed us on both cheeks in the European way. Many wept. Some stuffed pieces of paper into our hands or pockets. When I got to my hotel room that night, I counted

a dozen of those notes, and so did Frank and Chris. They were pleas for us to help specific individuals—a husband who had been in jail for ten years, for instance, or a neighbor who was missing. The universal message was this: "Let the outside world know what is happening here."

As we traveled from city to city, we stopped once at a farm that had been described as one of the more prosperous in the region. The farm family served us a very simple meal outside. They and their neighbors were warm, emotional, and generous. I noticed that the farm had no indoor plumbing and that the house and tools seemed quite primitive. It looked much like I imagine farms in the United States looked around the end of the nineteenth century.

I got the impression the family had gone to a great deal of trouble—and what for them would have been great expense—to obtain the ingredients needed to prepare the meal. You could tell this was the best they could offer and they were proud of what they had prepared. We did everything we could to show gratitude and pleasure. But to our American tastes, the food was terrible. It seemed they had thrown everything they had into a soup, including things most Americans would never eat. I remember specifically noticing chicken feet floating in the broth.

Some of us became sick and had to run to the outhouse, which consisted only of a shelter around a hole in the ground. There was no seat. There was no toilet paper.

I didn't expect the common people in a repressive Communist country would possess many luxuries, but I was surprised to find this extent of poverty anywhere in Europe. We were told Romania had run so short of power the previous winter that gas was turned off across the country in late January. The elite's offices and houses remained heated, but I wondered how many of the poor had died from the cold.

Our visits brought great hope and encouragement to the people we met. They lived in a closed society that tried to shut them off from the rest of the world. They couldn't know whether people outside cared about them and were trying to help. They drew strength from us, because we showed that others were thinking about them and endeavoring to set them free. At the same time, we drew strength—and a mandate—from them. Seeing their plight made us realize that they were depending on us to assist and that we had to

come to their aid. Witnessing their courage and faith inspired us. I felt honored to meet them, share their vision, and be asked to help.

We also drew inspiration from stories about people we didn't get to meet, especially Father Gheorghe Calciu, who spent more than two decades in Romanian prisons for opposing Communist oppression. Ceauşescu released Father Calciu from jail before our trip to Romania but kept him under house arrest, so we weren't able to visit him. We finally met him later, after he was allowed to leave Romania. He visited us on Capitol Hill to thank us for our efforts to free him and for our work on behalf of the Romanian people, and to urge us to press on.

Calciu first was arrested for protesting Communist rule in Romania after World War II. He was released sixteen years later, in 1964, and was ordained as a Romanian Orthodox priest in 1972. He was imprisoned again in 1979 after delivering a series of sermons the preceding year that denounced religious persecution.

Calciu vexed the government during his second imprisonment because he had become well known not only in Romania but around the world. His very imprisonment called attention to Ceauşescu's repression. The government was afraid to let him go free, because he probably would resume his public protests. It feared that killing him might upset Romania's relations with the United States and other Western nations. U.S. and European citizens were conducting letter-writing campaigns to Western government officials, asking them to pressure the Romanian government to free Calciu. They also wrote to Ceauşescu himself to plead for Calciu's freedom.

When Calciu came to see us in Washington, he described what had happened inside the prison during his second incarceration. First, he said, he was tortured—beaten, deprived of food and drink, stripped of all but tattered clothes, and confined to a windowless, unheated cell. He was allowed to sleep six hours a night on a wooden board. Then the board would be removed, and he was left with only the concrete floor to stand, sit, or lie on. The jailers subjected him to psychological pressures that were designed to break his will. They insulted him, his family, and his faith. They even urinated on him. He was given a pot to relieve himself in, and twice a day he was required to empty it in a restroom. While walking there, he would be hit and pushed. If he spilled

anything, he had to clean it up with his bare hands. Always deprived of wine, often deprived of bread, he couldn't fully celebrate his church's Divine Liturgy (or Mass) on most Sundays.

When all this failed to cause Calciu to accept the legitimacy of Ceauşescu's policies, prison officials concocted a scheme to have the priest killed while deflecting the blame away from the government. They promised leniency to two hardened criminals in the prison if they would murder him. They then made the prisoners his cellmates.

The two criminals informed Calciu they planned to kill him. They forced him to stand for long periods, beat him, and required that he obtain their permission before eating, drinking, or using the chamber pot. Then, after about a month, they told him they had decided not to kill him. He asked for their permission to celebrate the Divine Liturgy with the bread and water they had in the cell. They agreed, and he was stunned when they knelt with him to pray. His faith was so strong that it turned these would-be killers away from murder and toward prayer.

Amazingly, after all his ordeals, Calciu had no bitterness toward those who had so mistreated him. He was not a large man, less than five and a half feet tall, relatively slight of build. When he came to visit us, he was wearing an orthodox priest's black cassock. His hair and beard were a mixture of white and gray. His face was warm, gentle, and joyful. His countenance was alive, hopeful, and at peace. I recognized the great faith that had sustained him for all those decades of persecution.

Before we left Romania, we met with several government officials and were stunned by their audacious lies. They were openly hostile, treating us as if we were enemies. They told us that Romanians enjoyed great religious freedom. They denied that some of the bulldozed churches ever existed, even though a number of them had stood for centuries. They asserted that other churches had been demolished because they violated building codes. They said those who alleged persecution were liars, that imprisoned Christians were murderers and thieves. Father Calciu, they charged, had been a Nazi. When we asked about reports that nearly twenty thousand Bibles had been turned into toilet paper—some of which we held in our hands—a foreign ministry official called it "a story manufactured by a Hungarian in Connecticut"!

We knew these words were false. And though these Romanian officials spoke with great firmness, you could see the dishonesty in their faces—especially in their eyes. The foreign minister, in particular, looked like a violent mobster. He was a burly man with a stern demeanor, and I thought he probably chewed nails for breakfast. The closed nature of these men's society was demonstrated when the trade minister mentioned he had "heard that" a Romanian ambassador had resigned—something we had learned two weeks earlier in the United States.

Romania's Ministry of Culture and Cults exercised substantial control over the Romanian Orthodox Church hierarchy and cowed leaders of other faiths through the force of fear. Before Father Calciu's imprisonment in 1978, for example, the Romanian Orthodox patriarch expelled him from the church because of his antigovernment sermons. A Romanian Orthodox archbishop told us that "there are no martyrs in the Romanian Orthodox Church." A Roman Catholic bishop admitted that "we're not living in a bed of roses." But, he added, "we are not being persecuted, or we would not be allowed to meet." We met a priest who had access to a printing press and asked if he would allow it to be used to print Bibles. He said no.

We felt both sadness and anger when we left the meetings with these church leaders. We understood that they had reason to be afraid. Still, we wished they had exhibited more courage, as had many rank-and-file clergy and believers.

In our meetings with government officials, we demanded more freedom for the Romanian people and the release of prisoners like Father Calciu. We gave them a paper, signed by all three of us, that put them on notice that we planned to take action in Congress if their human rights record didn't improve. If we didn't detect an increase in freedom, we would work to do away with Romania's Most Favored Nation status—a designation that eased the country's ability to sell its products in the United States, a benefit that every nation wanted. Romania's independence from the Soviet Union had won the designation. We believed Ceaușescu's clear record of oppression provided a reason to rescind it, an action that would cost Romanian exporters about $1 billion a year.

While we were inspired by the courageous demonstrations of faith we had witnessed in the churches we visited and in the stories we heard about brave dissidents like Father Calciu, Romania's repression beat down on us like a

deadweight. When we returned to the United States, Frank, Chris, and I immediately sought news media coverage of the repression in Romania, and we got involved in letter-writing campaigns. We delivered one letter to Nicolae Gavrilescu, Romania's ambassador to the United States, demanding action on a dozen specific abuses of religion, including the detention of Father Calciu. Sixty-six of our House colleagues sent a letter to the Romanian government. Senate Majority Leader Bob Dole and our State Department also called for Ceauşescu to change his ways.

Calciu was freed shortly after our trip, and he took refuge in the United States. Ceauşescu did not respond directly to our demands, however, so in September we sent a follow-up telegram, which he also ignored. In October we introduced legislation to suspend Romania's Most Favored Nation status for six months, with reinstatement contingent on an increase in religious freedom and an improvement in the country's overall human rights record. Republicans Paul Trible of Virginia and William Armstrong of Colorado offered similar legislation in the Senate.

The road to passage of the legislation was hard. The Reagan administration and leaders of both parties in Congress opposed us. First, we were warned that attacking Romania would make it more difficult for the people living there. Frank and I took this argument seriously and contacted Romanians who had been imprisoned or tortured or had relatives killed. "It can't get any worse than it already is," they told us.

We testified before congressional committees in support of our resolution, and the committee members sympathized in public with our goals, praised our statements, and thanked us for our good work. In private, they repeated the arguments that successive administrations had made about Romania's importance to U.S. foreign policy.

"It's not as bad as you think it is," they said. "They're kind of distancing themselves from the Soviets. We have a chance to change them by cooperating with them. Sure, these are bad guys, but they aren't as bad as the really bad guys. This is an opportunity to put a crack in the Soviet Bloc. This is the wise, realistic approach, as opposed to your impractical idealism."

Some of these committee members thought they really understood Romania because they had visited there. But they had met with the government officials

in Bucharest, been wined and dined and treated as the visiting dignitaries they were. They didn't travel to the places we did. They didn't visit bulldozed churches or poverty-stricken farms. They didn't hear common people tell their horror stories. Their "realistic" argument worked on the surface. But they never scratched below the surface to see what was really going on.

The fact is that I am a realist. I look at the world and see that the future belongs to freedom and democracy. I know it's not going to happen overnight, that it takes time to break the chains of oppression like those that were locked in Romania. But our policy in Romania—as in too many other parts of the world today—was penny-wise and pound-foolish. It focused on the short term and ignored the long run. "Don't rock the boat now," the leaders told us. "Don't worry about it now."

But the Romanian government was just as bad as, if not worse than, the Soviet Union when it came to oppressing its own people. By treating Ceauşescu as the rightful leader of Romania—by treating him even as a friend!—we were legitimizing him in the eyes of those who did his bidding, and we were dashing the hopes of those who longed for freedom.

Father Calciu noted after his release that while he was in prison in the 1980s, Ceauşescu "was traveling all over Europe, attending merry banquets offered him by presidents, kings, and queens. The triumphant reception of their president convinced the guards that Ceauşescu was esteemed in the free world and precious to Romania, and therefore, anyone who didn't accept his decisions had to be killed. And I was one of those people."[1]

I knew the people of Romania would seize control of their government in the long run—and, in fact, they did. And when that happens—in Romania and elsewhere—the people remember if we stood with their oppressors or if we worked for freedom.

I believe we should try our best to build peaceful relationships with all governments, regardless of whether we find them personally attractive. But we also can exert peaceful pressure for change. At the very least, we shouldn't reward countries for bad behavior. And we were rewarding Ceauşescu's Romania for very bad conduct.

Frank, Chris, and I—along with other representatives and senators who worked with us—grabbed some attention in the news media. But for a couple

of years, the administration and leaders in Congress blocked our proposals at various stages of the legislative process. Nonetheless, we were winning the long-term battle for public and congressional opinion. By 1988 it became clear that we were going to succeed. Both the House and the Senate approved the six-month suspension of Romania's Most Favored Nation status. Before the legislation could take effect, Ceauşescu renounced the status on his own, complaining that the United States was meddling in Romania's internal affairs.

By then, those internal affairs weren't going so well for Ceauşescu. It seemed very appropriate that his government's religious persecution was what sparked the protests that led to the toppling of his regime.

In mid-December 1989, word got around the city of Timisoara that Ceauşescu's secret police were about to arrest and deport a Hungarian Reformed Church pastor named Laszlo Tokes. Like Father Calciu, Rev. Tokes had been an outspoken critic of the Communist regime, complaining about the suppression of religion and denouncing Ceauşescu from the pulpit. Also like Calciu, Tokes was disowned by church leaders who feared the government. They ordered him out of his church, and the police were sent to remove him when he refused to comply.

When police arrived, they encountered a growing crowd of Tokes supporters who had surrounded the church to protect him. At first, the demonstrators prayed and lit candles. Later, the confrontation between police and protesters turned violent. Word of the clashes spread quickly across the country, and soon anti- Ceauşescu crowds formed in Bucharest and other cities. As the number of demonstrators in the capital grew by the tens of thousands, soldiers joined the protesters in confronting the secret police. Within ten days, the government fell and Ceauşescu was executed. Our State Department estimated that fifteen hundred people died in this fast-moving revolution.

Later, both Tokes and Calciu explained how their faith supplied the guidance and strength they needed to confront their oppressors and how faith played an essential role in overthrowing the Ceauşescu regime.

"I think that 'protest' is the most important part of the word *Protestant,*" Tokes said in an interview with the *Boston Globe.* "To protest against something and to protest for something, this is my tradition."[2]

In a speech to the Hungarian Reformed World Conference, Tokes said Ceauşescu "wanted to deprive us of God and alienate us from other people. It was like taking an ax and chopping at the roots of our communities." But, the pastor added, "as Reformists we can answer this with a truly Reformist saying: 'If God is with us, who can be against us?' Those who love God will come to no harm. That is the answer of the Word, an answer based on faith."[3]

Father Calciu related his experience in nearly the same way. Speaking to a conference of the Christian Relief Effort for the Emancipation of Dissidents, he described how he expected to be murdered by Ceauşescu's agents in prison:

> There were many of them. I was alone and defenseless. There was no law to prevent them from committing such a crime. There were no moral principles to stop them.
>
> I had faith. They had force. Then again, they had nothing, because they did not have God. I had the love and spiritual help of my fellow man, praying for me throughout the world. They had nothing but their hate. And because this conflict was a spiritual one, they were defeated, in spite of all the material power on their side.[4]

Our experiences while traveling in Romania and later working against the Ceauşescu regime solidified my relationship with Frank and confirmed the course of my human rights activism.

Frank, Chris, and I all learned that if you focus on an issue, join forces across partisan lines, and stay together, your effectiveness soars. We also learned that people in places like Romania in the 1980s depend on us to help them. It's a very lonely battle for them. And it can be a lonely battle for a member of Congress who takes on an issue like this. Constituents and other legislators will ask, "Why are you messing around with Romania? Nobody cares. How many Romanians live in your district?" But I believe a government is measured—a country is measured—by how we reach out to the poor, how we help the hurting, how we fight for the oppressed.

The other thing these experiences underscored is that what we did mattered. The oppressed of Romania took strength from knowing that people

outside were working on their behalf. It was hard work, but we convinced our fellow legislators that the United States should not reward Ceauşescu for his evil deeds. And we discovered that even Ceauşescu knew what we were doing, and it angered him.

THE FAST

Follow God, Lead by Example, and the People Will Respond

* * *

I n March 1993 I found myself burning with anger.

I had helped to create, and later chaired, the House Select Committee on Hunger. It had been the vehicle that empowered me to call public attention to the problems of hunger, poverty, and oppression at home and overseas. It enabled me to summon witnesses to hearings that caused Washington-based media to report about tragedies—such as famine in Africa, oppression in Haiti, and hunger on U.S. Indian reservations—they otherwise might have ignored. It financed my trips to trouble spots around the world, entitled me to useful support from the State Department, and increased the likelihood that foreign governments would cooperate with me. It provided me with a dedicated, expert staff who made me so much more effective in my work. It helped me convince other committees to consider legislation that the hunger committee devised but did not have the authority to bring before the full House for passage.

The *New York Times* had termed the hunger committee "the conscience of the Congress." We were widely credited with causing or contributing to a significant number of important accomplishments—establishing the office of the United Nations undersecretary for humanitarian affairs; convening a humanitarian summit among conflict- and poverty-stricken nations in the Horn of Africa; preserving threatened U.S. nutrition programs for poor women, infants, and children; expanding disaster-relief programs; funding

child-survival activities; establishing programs to help welfare recipients start small businesses; and heightening public and government awareness of child-hood immunization shortcomings, famines in various nations, hunger in poor U.S. communities, and other humanitarian challenges around the world. And this wonderful committee was about to be taken away from me.

Even though Democrats comprised the House majority, a group of relatively young, conservative Republicans was growing in influence. Many citizens were responding favorably to these legislators' attacks on Congress itself as a bloated, wasteful, ineffective institution. Many Democratic lawmakers were running scared, fearful that we would lose the powers of the majority we had enjoyed for nearly forty consecutive years. (And, in fact, Republicans did take control of the House and the Senate in the elections of 1994.)

These Republicans had seized on the idea of making Congress more efficient by reducing the number of committees, and they started by taking aim at four "select" committees, including my hunger committee. The select committees were created to investigate and make recommendations about a specific topic. Unlike "standing" committees, the select committees did not have the authority to take legislation to the House floor. They did not oversee the budgets of any government agencies. They had relatively small staffs and relatively small budgets. (The hunger committee's budget was the smallest in the House.) And they didn't have rich and powerful constituencies that cared about their work, the way the agriculture industry cares about the Agriculture Committee or the defense industry cares about the Armed Services Committee.

My anger was compounded by the knowledge that the poor and the hungry don't speak with a loud voice on Capitol Hill or in political campaigns. They don't have a political action committee that makes big campaign contributions to influential legislators. They don't hire well-connected and well-paid lobbyists to advance their interests in Congress and the administration. House members would not pay a significant political price for killing off the hunger committee, and they could pretend they were striking a blow for efficiency and common sense by whittling down the size of the federal government.

I worked hard to convince my colleagues to save the hunger committee, but by March it was clear that I would lose. If the House did not vote to keep the select committees functioning by March 31, they would cease to exist. While I

was able to gather support from 180 House members, I needed 218 for a majority. The leaders of my party—the majority party—could have kept the hunger committee in business to serve the poor. They could have helped me round up the votes. But Speaker Tom Foley said he would not even schedule a vote if I could not prove I would win. The Republicans had the Democratic leaders running scared, and the select committees were sacrificed so that Democrats could appear to be cutting wasteful spending.

I was heartbroken and irate. I no longer would be a chairman. I no longer would have this vehicle for doing the work that made my political life worthwhile. Since my first trip to Ethiopia nearly a decade before, I had used the committee to be a loud voice for the disadvantaged and the downtrodden. It was how I brought God into my workplace, obeying the many biblical admonitions to care for those in need. I grasped for a way to respond.

My first inclination was to search for a way to strike back, to get revenge, to find a means for releasing my anger. I considered quitting Congress. I conjured up hateful images of the institution that had been my home for fourteen years. I now saw it as a viper pit, filled with hypocrites who cared about nothing but their own reelections. I tried everything I had learned in many years in politics—about how to work the system, how to get people to do what I wanted, how to get back at them when they wouldn't. And none of that had worked. There seemed to be no fruitful avenue I could take. The committee was condemned to death. I could not will it into a longer life.

Sensing my frustration and anger, my wife, Janet, said to me one evening, "Tony, have you thought about going on a fast?"

It was a startling question, because I actually had considered fasting a couple of weeks earlier. I had set the thought aside because our twelve-year-old son, Matt, was battling cancer, and I didn't think it would be good for the family if I intentionally put myself through an ordeal. Matt had now finished a round of chemotherapy and was back in school, however. And a fast had enormous appeal.

For one thing, it was a way I could do *something*. More important, fasting has long played a powerful role in faith. A real fast would be an act of self-denial, focusing not on myself but on God. (In my anger, I had been focusing passionately on myself.) I thought it would be especially appropriate to fast

because of hunger. Then Janet and I read chapter 58 of Isaiah, and the appropriateness became brilliantly clear:

> *Is not this the fast that I choose [God says through the prophet]:*
>   *to loose the bonds of injustice,*
>   *to undo the thongs of the yoke,*
> *to let the oppressed go free,*
>   *and to break every yoke?*
> *Is it not to share your bread with the hungry,*
>   *and bring the homeless poor into your house;*
> *when you see the naked, to cover them,*
>   *and not to hide yourself from your own kin? . . .*
> *If you remove the yoke from among you,*
>   *the pointing of the finger, the speaking of evil,*
> *if you offer your food to the hungry*
>   *and satisfy the needs of the afflicted,*
> *then your light shall rise in the darkness*
>   *and your gloom be like the noonday.*
> *The* LORD *will guide you continually,*
>   *and satisfy your needs in parched places,*
>   *and make your bones strong.*
>
>   (verses 6–7, 9–11)

This fast would be a new way for me to bring God into my workplace. While it would be a great spiritual journey for me, a way to ease the pain I was suffering because of the death of my committee, it also would provide a new vehicle for me to reach out to the people (and maybe my colleagues in Congress), to call their attention to hunger, and to ask them to do something about it.

It was not easy for me to decide to take this step, however. I wondered, *How will my colleagues react? My constituents in Dayton, Ohio?* Would they understand that I was fasting, not as a protest, but as a personal act of witness, a way to ask God to help me through this difficult time, and an attempt to show others that hunger is not a problem that we should ignore? Would they understand that it was not a hunger strike—which is a threat to starve oneself, even

to death, unless some demand is met? Would I be committing political suicide? Would I be perceived as a flake? Would I become a laughingstock?

A public fast would be completely out of character for Tony Hall the congressman. I had never sought bright spotlights. I had never tried to call attention to myself, other than as it was necessary to win elections and continue to do the work I loved. I had always been a team player, an insider. My other committee assignment was Rules, the ultimate insiders' committee. The Rules Committee had just thirteen members—nine Democrats and four Republicans, when Democrats held the majority. Committee members work under the guidance of their party's leaders to set the rules by which almost every piece of legislation is considered by the full House. It is an enormously powerful committee that gets almost no attention from the mass media but avid attention from every member of the House.

Rules Committee members enjoy enormous influence over the other representatives, because every representative from time to time has to make a case at Rules. As an elected politician, I had been able to devote substantial effort to the issues of hunger, poverty, and oppression because I always took good care of my constituents back home as well. I used my Rules Committee membership as a lever in both of those efforts—to pass legislation that helped my district and to advance the interests of the hungry, the poor, and the oppressed. Would I be able to continue doing that if I alienated my colleagues—especially the leaders—by acting in what they might perceive an outrageous fashion?

As I struggled with what to do, I sought advice from people who regularly counseled me in matters of faith and from others who regularly advised me about Congress and politics—and from a few who did both. I was surprised when all of the people of faith believed the fast was absolutely the right path to take. I was not surprised that my congressional staff cautioned me against it. As far as we knew, no member of Congress had ever done anything like this before. My staff worried—as did I—that a fast would be seen as too radical, the people would not understand, and my political career could be destroyed.

I suffered serious bouts of self-doubt, asking myself, *Who do I think I am, to be calling Congress—and the nation—to task?* But I also believed that we in Congress worried far too much about our own reelections and that we did far

too little to really lead. And I was concerned enough and angry enough to take a bold stand.

I prayed long and hard over this decision. I prayed especially that I would not look foolish and embarrass myself. I did not want to be seen as a showboater or a clown. Every morning after I woke up but before I climbed out of bed, I would toss and turn and worry. I wondered if I was crazy. I knew that I was scared. But when I prayed, I felt comfort and peace. I felt God was very close. I knew he would have to be close if I were to do this.

Finally, I plunged forward in a true leap of faith. I cast the worldly advice aside and said, "Here I am, God. Lead me. Guide me. I'm at your mercy." From that point forward, as we planned for announcing the fast, I felt a great deal of excitement, intensity, and energy. I continued to pray and to consult with my brothers and sisters in faith. I planned some details with my staff. I consulted doctors and Dick Gregory, who had fasted many times to promote social justice and had become an expert at it. But the trepidation never left me. I kept wondering if I really was capable of the task I had set before myself.

On March 31, 1993, the day the committee died, I held a press conference on a lawn outside the Capitol, announcing that I would begin to fast on April 5, eating nothing and drinking only water. Reporters wrote that I was angry, which I was. The House, I said, "has lost its conscience. Congress is afflicted with famine. We are hungry for heart—heart for the needy, the powerless, and the forgotten. We have shown that we place our own comfort and political security ahead of the well-being of our most vulnerable people. If we're not going to address this issue—the most basic of rights—what do we stand for in Congress?"

But what I really wanted to focus the public's attention on was what we could do together to continue the fight against hunger without the committee's leadership. I recalled that I had led a forty-hour fast in Dayton in 1985 to raise awareness of hunger and to raise money for relief. It had succeeded far beyond my expectations, attracting more than four thousand participants, raising more than $300,000 (which was split between activities in southwestern Ohio and Africa), and inspiring people to get involved in antihunger programs.

This fast would be different, much more of a spiritual experience. I wasn't seeking to raise money. I was asking God to help me through a difficult time.

But I also was, as I said at the press conference, "issuing a call to summon a broad and creative response from all those who share my concern."

First, I explained, "this is a call to the nation to reflect upon what is going on around us in America and in the world concerning hunger. Second, this is a call to the leadership and to the members of Congress to address this situation. Third, this is a call to the nation and members of Congress to fast with me, to share in the physical suffering of the hungry, and to consider how all of us can be moved to make a difference in our communities and in the world."

I acknowledged that the hunger committee would not be reconstituted, but I requested that Congress create some kind of permanent organization to address the issue. I asked for a national conference on food security. And I said I was looking for some new or increased effort to fight hunger overseas.

To the inevitable question of how long I would fast, I said I didn't know. I explained that I would not injure my health but that I was determined to continue until I was assured in my heart that the awareness of hunger—and America's conscience—had been raised to a higher level.

If people fast and meditate and discover what it's like to go hungry for a while, I thought, *maybe they'll become committed to helping us solve this problem.* But I really didn't have a plan. I didn't have a list of demands to be met. I didn't have a private checklist of responses that would cause me to decide the fast was a success. I just placed myself in God's hands and embarked on an adventure with an unknown destination.

Several of my House colleagues attended the press conference and said they would join me for part of the fast, as did some antihunger activists. Elsewhere in the country, other activists announced that they, too, would fast in solidarity. But I wondered how many others would understand. And the signs were not auspicious the next morning, when I went to a regularly scheduled congressional prayer breakfast and my colleagues avoided talking with me.

On April 4 I had my last pre-fast meal—a great American feast of fried chicken, mashed potatoes, gravy, Caesar salad, shoofly pie, and white wine. On April 6 I boarded a plane for some meetings in Dayton during Congress's Easter/Passover recess. While in flight, I again stewed in anxiety. *My constituents won't understand, and they'll stop supporting me,* I thought. *My colleagues will shun me.*

I also worried about the physical aspects of not eating for an extended time. Dick Gregory had described to me the various stages of hunger and said the desire to eat eventually would subside. He advised that I fill myself with water in the early days as a way of easing the hunger pangs. Doctors in the Capitol Physician's Office didn't want me to do this, and they asked me to let them examine me every week. Other doctors reminded me that the human body is a remarkably resilient machine. A healthy person can fast from one to two months without suffering irreversible harm. The body survives by drawing protein from fat and muscle. Because I was five foot nine and weighed 180 pounds, one doctor noted wryly, I would have "reserves to draw on." Janet also commented that it would do me good to lose some weight. These assurances did not stop me from worrying about how bad I would feel when I became hungry, however. Other than those forty hours in 1985, my only experience with fasting was in connection with a Wednesday morning prayer group. And I always felt famished by eleven o'clock in the morning!

On the other hand, I was so angry with Congress that I wasn't sure I really cared what my colleagues would think or really cared if I might lose my next election. I had now crossed a bridge, I realized, and had blown it up behind me. I felt at peace in God's care. And the next three weeks turned out to be a triumph beyond my wildest imagination.

After my plane touched down in Dayton, I went to Courthouse Square, a plaza in the center of the city, where about three hundred people had gathered to demonstrate solidarity with my fast. Principal Theodore Wallace of Chaminade-Julienne, a Roman Catholic high school in Dayton, announced that he would fast with me for three days that week. About 340 C-J students, along with 60 parents and staff, pledged to forgo at least one meal and to donate the value of the meal to the Dayton Area Emergency Food Bank. Noting that this was the week before Easter, Mr. Wallace said fasting would be particularly timely as we would reflect on Christ's suffering on Good Friday. About forty students at the University of Dayton, another Roman Catholic school, also joined the fast. A CBS News crew traveled with me from Washington and spent three days in Dayton preparing a report. I was thrilled at the support and the attention from the media, but I also felt terribly hungry, and I was losing energy very quickly.

The media presented a truly pleasant surprise. I had no idea how they'd

react, and it turned out they reacted quite positively. Numerous reporters became interested in the story, and they covered it fairly, accurately (for the most part), and frequently. I also received favorable commentary from editorial writers and columnists on the right as well as the left. My hometown newspaper, the *Dayton Daily News*, covered the fast thoroughly and supported me repeatedly in editorials and columns. My sincerity must have appeared evident, because I received compliments even from commentators who approved the death of the select committees. *Roll Call*, Capitol Hill's local newspaper, for instance, called the select committees "redundant" and said they "had to go." But in the same editorial, the paper said, "At a time when politicians are so calculating and 'responsive' that they often can't remember what they really believe, it's refreshing to see a congressman who cares so much about a cause. We admire Hall for his courage and for setting an offbeat but inspirational example to colleagues who, from time to time, need to be shaken up."[1]

Physically and psychologically, the first week of the fast was the hardest. I was horribly hungry—I could say "in agony"—and getting weaker by the day. I thought constantly about what I would like to eat—that last meal of fried chicken, mashed potatoes, and Caesar salad; some future meals with some of my favorite foods, such as steak, roast beef, and key lime pie. But I also thought about all the people who have no realistic hope for a future meal of any kind, and I found the strength to continue.

Family mealtimes were the worst. I couldn't go to the table because the food would be too tempting, and not being able to eat it would be agonizing. Janet, Matt, and Jyl would try to hide from me when they snacked between meals. So I spent these times alone, praying, reading, thinking about what I was doing, and contemplating the importance of the family meal. Normally, we probably don't think about how much mealtime means to the family. But it's one of the few times when we all sit down together and talk about the day, the week—about anything.

I followed Dick Gregory's advice to fill up on water. I really poured it down. Since it was the only thing I was consuming, I paid a great deal more attention to it than I ever had before. I really noticed the difference in taste when I drank from the tap at home, the office, or someplace else. My sense of smell also

heightened throughout the fast. I could tell what people had eaten because their bodies gave off aromas that I had never noticed before.

The hardest day of the fast came on Easter, which was my seventh day without eating. Janet and I had gone on a retreat in Maryland with some friends, and our friends prepared a typical big American holiday dinner—turkey, potatoes, dressing, pie, cake. It drove me nuts. I had to leave them, go outside and take a walk, to get away from those wonderful aromas. I decided that if I could get through this day, I would be over the hump. I did, and I was.

Just as Dick Gregory said, the sensation of hunger faded in about a week. It's as if the body gives up on getting food and stops demanding it. From then on, I could join my family at mealtimes and not be bothered a bit. It was a revelation about the poor and the hungry, to whom I came to feel exceptionally close as the fast went on. I now fully understood, in a way I never had before, a strange phenomenon I had witnessed during famines: starving children who refused to eat when food was finally offered to them.

The absence of hunger pangs did not mean I wasn't feeling the physical effects of the fast, however. I'd wake up in the morning feeling fine. My head would be clear. I would think I had lots of energy. But after noon, I would fade. The energy would desert me and weakness would take over. I'd need to nap. Then, when I woke from the nap, I'd feel like I couldn't get up because I was so tired. Lacking the fuel of food, my body temperature apparently dropped, and I felt cold all the time. It also seemed my brain slowed down in the afternoon; I felt "dull." I thought of poor children who don't do well in school, who fall asleep in the afternoon, who become poor students because of poor nutrition. Remarkably, some of my vital signs—blood pressure, the results of blood tests—actually improved.

Oddly, I also sometimes felt lonely, even though I knew I was getting a great deal of support. Part of that feeling stemmed from my inability to shake my worries about what people really thought of what I was doing.

Because of the recess, I couldn't judge the reaction of Congress during the first two weeks of the fast. Throughout the country, however, the outpouring of support was overwhelming. I appeared on numerous television and radio programs, and the fast was written about in newspapers everywhere. Humanitarian organizations put the word out to their supporters.

Groups organized supportive events. Individuals from every state wrote me incredibly moving letters.

The people of Dayton were particularly supportive, organizing rallies, prayer vigils, and even a parade! Thousands of people wrote messages on paper plates—protesting the death of the hunger committee and calling for a replacement—and mailed them to Congress. More than fifteen thousand high school and college students from thirty-four states participated in antihunger activities organized by the National Student Campaign against Hunger and Homelessness. Students in two thousand high schools and two hundred colleges joined the fast. Religious groups took actions in support. Seventeen presidents and CEOs of major humanitarian organizations bought a full-page ad in *Roll Call* to publicly request that President Clinton hold a national summit on hunger. Actors Jeff Bridges and Valerie Harper organized a celebrity fast to call attention to the issue. Among the eclectic group of celebrities who stopped eating for a day were Susan Sarandon, Graham Nash, Phyllis Diller, the late Steve Allen, Edward James Olmos, Cassandra "Elvira" Peterson, former astronaut Buzz Aldrin, and basketball star Olden Polynice.

The House got back to business after the recess on April 19, and it quickly became clear that the representatives hadn't missed the public response to my call for action against hunger. They had read about it in their hometown newspapers, perhaps seen a report on a network television program. In many of their districts, schools, religious institutions, or local chapters of humanitarian organizations had taken action. For the members of Congress, this really was bringing it all back home—the place most of them look for their directions. A *Washington Post* writer observed "at least a puzzled acknowledgment from his Hill colleagues that something unusual is going on here."[2]

On April 20, I went to the House floor for the first time since beginning the fast and attended my first Rules Committee meeting. I was so weak, I had to ask an aide to drive me from my office building to the Capitol because I could walk only short distances without becoming exhausted. The other representatives treated me quite a bit differently from the way they had three weeks before. They wanted to talk with me. They were warm. They commented on my loss of weight. They inquired about my health. They were curious about what was happening to my body.

As that third week of my fast rolled on, people from around the country continued to rally at my side. As the days added up to weeks, people realized how committed I really was to this cause, and their support grew deeper. Now, with Washington full of government officials once again, the big and powerful institutions began to respond—with the "leaders" following the people, as they almost always do.

I knew the time to end the fast was nearing when I received a phone call from my friend Bill Stanton, a former Republican representative from Ohio who now was an executive at the World Bank, the planet's richest financier of development in the third world. "Tony," he said, "we're really moved by your fast, and we are prepared to have a world conference on hunger and put money behind it." Because of the fast, he said, colleagues at the bank had approached him, asking if he knew me and if he understood what I was up to. Their inquiry, Bill explained, led to discussions about what the bank could do to elevate awareness of hunger and how it might be able to direct more of its resources to attacking the problem.

When the conference was held in Washington that November, participants included former U.S. president Jimmy Carter, who has devoted his postpresidential life to promoting peace and bettering the lot of the poor; United Nations secretary general Boutros Boutros-Ghali; World Bank president Lewis Preston; President Ketumile Masire of Botswana; the World Bank's senior managers; and representatives of many humanitarian organizations that do the real work of bringing relief and education directly to the poor and hungry. The bank announced that as a symbolic gesture designed to inspire others to take similar action, it would make a $2 million grant to the Grameen Trust, an affiliate of the Grameen Bank, one of the most effective antipoverty organizations in the world, which makes small loans to help poor people start small businesses. World Bank officials also said they would ask the bank's sponsoring governments for permission to expand its direct work with the poor.

Muhammad Yunus, Grameen's founder, later told me that my fast, the conference, and the World Bank's actions gave a significant boost to Grameen specifically and to microenterprise in general. The fast and the conference drew attention to hunger and poverty, he said. Many more people and institutions became aware of the value of Grameen and microfinance. Financial

support for the microenterprise movement jumped around the world. Since the fast, the World Bank alone has increased its microfinance portfolio to more than $1 billion.

Other signs that the fast had raised awareness included a letter from President Clinton—who, with Vice President Gore, had joined the fast briefly—acknowledging my "moral leadership on this vital issue." A special House-Senate committee on congressional reform invited me to testify about my call for a permanent committee to focus on human needs. The House Democratic Caucus—which includes all Democratic representatives—invited me to speak about what they could do to respond to the hunger committee's death. And the Agriculture Department announced that—complementing the World Bank's plans—it would conduct a national conference on domestic hunger and a series of regional conferences. The national conference was held in Washington in June and was followed by regional gatherings in Vermont, Texas, Missouri, and, finally, Dayton.

With the Agriculture Department announcement on Monday, April 26, 1993—made by Secretary Mike Espy, a former Mississippi congressman who had chaired the hunger committee's Domestic Task Force—I concluded it was time to end the fast. Because the fast had been a very public endeavor, I thought the breaking of it should be as well. I invited some reporters to my office, and in keeping with an advertising slogan at the time, I had a V-8.

I hadn't eaten for twenty-two days, and that thick, salty vegetable juice tasted exceptionally good. I thought I could pick out the taste of each of the vegetables that had been liquefied and mixed into this marvelous elixir—tomatoes, beets, celery, carrots, lettuce, spinach, parsley, and watercress. Well, maybe not the parsley and watercress. Unfortunately, I could only sip a little bit. Because my stomach had essentially been shut down for three weeks, I would have to coax it gradually back to use, maybe not being able to enjoy a full meal until the end of the week. I had lost twenty-three pounds—dropping from a robust 180 to a gaunt 157—and I joked that I would enjoy putting every single pound back on. A reporter asked what I would have for that first full meal, and I joked again, rattling off a long list: "Fried chicken, maybe a nice steak, maybe some blackberry pie, mashed potatoes and gravy, shoofly pie, some pasta, ice cream ...

"The wonderful thing," I added, "is I knew I could end my fast, and I was going to end it, and I had hope of someday looking forward to good food. There are so many people in the world who don't have that hope—who don't have any idea where the next meal is going to come from—and that was what the fast was all about."

The following few days were a whirlwind of activity, and I overdid it a bit—especially the return to eating. I was told to go slow, starting with small amounts of juice, fruit, and yogurt, and to stay away from meat for at least seven days. After three days, I felt so good that I ate veal and spaghetti with meat sauce. The reward for this boldness consisted of severe stomach cramps and the realization that I should pay attention to people who know what they're talking about.

The most emotional moment of the week came at the Democratic caucus on Wednesday, in the ornate, historic House Chamber, closed to all but Democratic representatives. When I walked in, these legislators—who had let my committee die and who had been put off by my decision to fast—gave me a standing ovation. Now, not only did they approve of what I had done, but they were excited about it. I chuckled to myself as I noted this adjustment in attitude, but I admonished myself to keep this change in perspective. My emotions were mixed. I was honored, but I also realized just how fickle the political system can be.

I talked to the caucus for half an hour, from notes and from my heart. I reviewed the history of the committee—why it was created in 1984 (because the issue was not being adequately addressed); how Mickey Leland, the first committee chairman, was killed in a plane crash in Ethiopia while on a committee mission in 1989; why I fasted; and why I believed the committee's work wasn't finished.

"There are many great individuals in this body, full of character and dignity and integrity," I said as I concluded my remarks. "But as a body, we lack intensity for issues like these. We used to have it. We used to speak and advocate for the hungry. We used to be a force to be reckoned with. Now it seems we spend all our time worrying about the rich. Somewhere along the line, we lost our voice for the voiceless, the have-nots, the children, the widows, the orphans, the people who stink and don't look so good.

"Let's get it back. We still have time."

When I stopped talking, they gave me another standing ovation. After the

meeting, they made me feel even better by what they said to reporters when I wasn't around.

Dick Gephardt, the majority leader, said I had delivered one of the most memorable speeches he had heard during sixteen years in Congress. "He made us feel uncomfortable," Dick said, "because we hadn't better understood what he was trying to do and the depth of his feeling about it."[3] Steny Hoyer, the caucus chair, said there was now "very broad support" for focusing on the issue. "Congressman Hall has done a great service to the country," he said.[4] Ted Strickland, a newly elected representative from Ohio and a committee supporter, said that "a lot of the members felt chagrined."[5] Many freshman legislators didn't understand the importance of the committee until the fast caught their attention, Ted explained. The next day, I attended the same prayer breakfast gathering at which my colleagues had avoided me at the outset of the fast. This time they, too, stood and applauded.

More important, these lawmakers promised to follow through on the issue. And they did. The bipartisan Congressional Hunger Caucus was created to carry on the hunger committee's work. A caucus, unfortunately, is not entitled to the same resources as a committee; caucus members fund the caucus's work with contributions from their personal office budgets (mostly mine), for instance. But we did have an office, a small staff, and a vehicle for investigating and publicizing the problems of hunger and for advocating solutions. Also with bipartisan cooperation, we created the Congressional Hunger Center, which is led by members of the House and Senate who care about the issue but is an independent organization that does not rely on congressional fickleness for its survival. The center encourages antihunger activities, provides a forum for sharing hunger information, and trains young people for careers in organizations that are working to end hunger.

A year later I fasted again—for three days during Holy Week—to remember that hunger still remained an enormous problem and that we could solve it. "A desperate situation requires something out of the ordinary," I said in talking publicly about this 1994 fast and inviting others to join me. "With a fast, you deny yourself something in order to focus on something bigger." This time President Clinton, Vice President Gore, and more than a score of my congressional colleagues participated in at least part of my fast.

To me, the value of the fast extended far beyond those specific accomplishments, because I learned—or perhaps I should say relearned—two important lessons.

The first is that if you let him, God will use you. No matter how small the work or how large the work, if you want to be used, you will be. That's how God works. He works through people. When I looked back on the fast, I realized that the things I planned didn't turn out nearly as well as the things I didn't plan. And actually, I didn't plan very much. There was no way I could imagine in advance the public reaction to what I did. And the most important thing I did was to announce the fast and ask God to guide me through it. Then good things happened. And they weren't all in the realm of public action.

As I was trying to decide whether to begin the fast, I knew I would need God to be near me. I asked him to be, and I discovered throughout the fast that he was. He fed me, not with food, but with his purpose. It was as Jesus said in Matthew 4:4: "One does not live by bread alone, but by every word that comes from the mouth of God." It didn't matter how the rest of the world reacted to my efforts, because God does not call us to be successful. He calls us to be faithful. And I was trying to be faithful to his clear admonition that we help those in need. Janet said to me afterward that she saw a spirit on me during the fast that she had never seen before and hadn't seen since. I was at peace and filled with joy, and it showed.

I also found myself feeling much closer to the hungry, poor, and oppressed people I had been trying to help for so long. Because I knew my fast would end, not to mention that it would end at the time of my choosing, I could not really have the same experience as those starving people who may never have another meal. But I did learn what it feels like to be without food for a substantial time, and God did make me feel closer to those whom Jesus called "the least of these" as he informed us of our duty to help them.

I noticed that some of these blessings extended to my family. Because of Matt's illness, we had experienced a lot of stress. During the fast, the stress was lifted. We all were comforted and had peace. Janet, Jyl, and Matt were totally supportive. Jyl fasted a bit herself. One of the great untold stories about this experience is that my minister, Jim Hutchens, fasted with me for the full three weeks.

The second lesson is that if you show the American people a need, and a

way to address that need, they will respond. Americans aren't indifferent to the needs of the poor; they're just too often unaware. And their "leaders" in government are too often afraid to challenge the people to act.

People are crying out for leaders. They want their leaders to be out in front of them, not looking back or unsure of which direction to go. They want to be guided. They want to see examples.

If you touch Americans—touch their hearts—they become emotional, they become excited, they become passionate. If you educate them and then lead them, they will help. And they will figure out how to further the cause in even better ways.

CHAPTER 7

BRINGING IT ALL BACK HOME

Doing What's in Front of Dayton

★ ★ ★

After I returned from Ethiopia and began devoting more time to the global hunger problem, I started hearing disturbing comments from some of my constituents. Even before I went to Ethiopia, I had begun learning about human rights abuses around the world because of my membership in the Foreign Relations Committee, and I had started to take some action against them. I criticized U.S. support for Ferdinand Marcos's repressive regime in the Philippines, for instance, and I protested Indonesia's occupation of the tiny independent nation of East Timor.

Not many Daytonians were aware of the appalling policies of Marcos, who justified his assaults on Filipinos' freedoms on the grounds that he was fighting a Communist insurgency. Needless to say, almost no one in Dayton had even heard of East Timor. When news media reports about my efforts on behalf of Ethiopia were added to earlier reports about my involvement with the Philippines, East Timor, and other far-off places, I started receiving letters that advanced this common theme: You care more about people on the other side of the world than you care about us; so what good are you to Dayton?

People were stopping me on the street to deliver the same message. Even my friends, trying to seem understanding and supportive, were saying things such as, "You know, Tony, we appreciate your work in the Philippines, and it's really special, and you seem to be the only guy who really cares about it. But we've got problems here in Dayton, too, and you need to do something about them."

With even friends and supporters raising these concerns, I knew I was in trouble. If I wanted to use Congress's bully pulpit to promote humanitarian causes, I would have to be reelected. But I wouldn't win many more elections if Dayton voters didn't see a connection between my work and my district. I had to convince my constituents that my humanitarian work was worthwhile. I had to bring the issue home—not just by revealing the hunger and poverty that existed in my Third Congressional District but also by involving the people of Dayton in my work.

I gathered my staff together and told them, "You and I know I care about my district, but the perception is I care more about what happens outside the district than about what happens here. We've got to bring this issue home— we've got to educate our constituents about this issue—or I won't be able to do this anymore, because they're going to vote me out."

We brainstormed and came up with an idea that was based on the popular fund-raising scheme in which people walk or run or ride bikes or do any number of other activities to attract donations to some charitable cause. What better way to raise money and call attention to hunger, we thought, than with a fast? It would be symbolic. And participants would gain some understanding of what hungry people go through when they can't find enough to eat. We asked people to stop eating for forty hours, from Friday evening until Sunday afternoon, and to solicit pledges from friends and relatives based on the amount of time they fasted. My good friend Nick Sabatino came up with a slogan—"Stop Hunger Fast"—with more than one meaning. It connoted ending hunger quickly, but it also implied that you could help end hunger by fasting.

This was in May 1985, long before the twenty-two-day fast I undertook when Congress abolished the Select Committee on Hunger in 1993. It was of far shorter duration. And it was conceived in much different circumstances. But it had the same purpose of making people think about—and, we hoped, begin to act on—this often-overlooked problem. Like my lengthy fast, it also turned out to be far more successful than I could have imagined.

We wanted to draw connections between Dayton and hungry people in other countries, both by teaching Daytonians that there is hunger in our community and by getting them involved in fighting hunger at home and abroad.

Five African diplomats—including the ambassadors of Sierra Leone and

Uganda—came to Dayton to talk about the needs in their countries. Sinclair Community College gave us space on its downtown Dayton campus, where we set up exhibits and sold African wares, as well as items to commemorate the fast, such as T-shirts, posters, and buttons. Africans who were living in the Dayton area taught about life and culture in their homelands. Events also were held at Wright State University, just outside the city. The whole thing turned into a kind of festival.

Janet joined me in the fast, and we brought Jyl and Matt along to witness the events. People in high schools, colleges, churches, and synagogues got together to participate. Young people got their parents to make pledges. I recruited some businesses to join my friends in making contributions.

By the time we broke the fast with Sunday brunch at Sinclair, some four thousand people had participated, raising more than $300,000 in the process. We donated half to relief activities in Africa and half to organizations that helped the hungry in southwestern Ohio.

More important, four thousand people of many ages, religions, and political persuasions had taken action against hunger, learned something about its presence in Dayton as well as overseas, felt a little bit of what it's like to be hungry, and begun to understand why I had become devoted to working on this issue. We had started to build a constituency for fighting hunger among the people of my congressional district. Daytonians over time not only would come to accept the idea of their congressman devoting a portion of his efforts to the hungry but would become involved themselves in creative and effective ways. They volunteered to work with existing organizations, and they created new projects of their own.

The previous winter, I had helped to organize a hot-lunch program for senior citizens on weekends. The federal government funded a meals-for-seniors program, but it provided meals only Monday through Friday. Particularly in the winter, when older folks have more difficulty getting around, not having weekend meals created a hardship.

We sought support for resuming the program in the winter of 1985, and the community's response was wonderful. The Ponderosa Steakhouse chain, then headquartered in Dayton, had acquired a prizewinning steer. The company had the steer butchered and donated the meat to the program. Local

restaurants pledged either food or money. The Miami Valley Restaurant Association made a financial contribution. Other businesses recruited volunteers. The program became so popular that more people volunteered than we could put to work.

Dayton residents also leaped at the opportunity to collect unharvested fruits and vegetables from farmers' fields and donate them to food programs. A lot of people told me the plan was ingenious, but I had to confess that I didn't think it up. Gleaning appears in the earliest books of the Bible, where God instructs farmers to leave some of their crops for the poor (see Leviticus 19:10; Deuteronomy 24:21).

Americans waste food in unbelievable quantities. Some of the waste occurs simply because harvesting is inherently inefficient. Mechanical harvesters always leave food behind. Even hand pickers fail to harvest everything. They have to move pretty quickly, and some pieces are just too hard to get. We Americans also are quite fussy about our food. It not only has to be safe and tasty; it has to look good. Perfectly healthy food is discarded simply because of its appearance.

Since food is so plentiful here, we don't worry about waste. Restaurants cook more than they will sell and throw away the leftovers at the end of the day. In almost every family, a regular chore is searching through the refrigerator to find food that has gone bad and must be pitched. I've been told that more than one hundred million tons of food go to waste in our country every year. I saw the truth of all this firsthand when one Dayton-area farmer took me to a cornfield after I asked if we could glean on his land.

"You might as well take this entire field," the farmer said, gesturing at the growing corn, which looked perfectly fine to my untrained eyes.

"Can't you sell it?" I asked.

"It's kind of imperfect," he replied, showing me some ears with missing kernels. "Americans are particular. Most Americans shopping in a grocery store aren't going to buy this corn. If you don't take it, the crows will get it, or we'll just plow it under."

Another farmer showed me a field of strawberries that farmworkers already had harvested by hand. Many berries were left for our gleaners to collect.

The Stop Hunger Fast had produced a roster of people and organizations

who wanted to help, so it was easy for us to recruit gleaners. The only tricky part was pulling enough volunteers together on short notice. Sometimes a farmer would inform us that a field had just been harvested and we needed to glean right away.

Just as the fast turned into a festival, the days of gleaning became times of great fun. Adults, kids, people of many religions, middle-class people, rich people, and some of the poor themselves joined the gleaning crews. And they came back when we needed them again.

That first year, 1986, nine farmers let us into their fields, where our gleaners salvaged more than twenty tons of fresh produce that went to feed the poor. Just as I have said so often about my humanitarian projects, this gleaning project "surpassed all our expectations," in the words of Kipra Holley, who ran our local Red Cross Emergency Resource Bank's food center. Kipra made that comment to an Associated Press reporter whose story about gleaning helped me to understand the need for leadership and the fact that Americans will respond when leaders call them to do good things.

The story reported that an attempt to glean in the Cincinnati area had not gone well. The director of a local service organization said the problem was that no public official had gotten out front to urge people to get involved, the way I had. All I had to do was get the ball rolling, and the people of Dayton created a success. The next year, I started promoting gleaning around Ohio, and over the following years, hundreds of tons of food were salvaged in our state.

Gleaning has been around a lot longer than I have, and people were gleaning elsewhere in America before we started our program in Dayton. But we did a particularly effective job of it. I used my bully pulpit to promote it around the country. People came to study our program. So we had an effect beyond simply feeding hungry people in our own community.

As we carried out projects and received publicity for them, we inspired more people to get involved. As Daytonians learned about our antihunger efforts and saw that they worked, our volunteers begat more volunteers. Some of them invented new projects that I never would have dreamed of.

We were building a constituency for the hungry. Daytonians were, as Mother Teresa had advised, doing what was in front of them. As the point man on the issue, I received many calls from people who wanted to help. Not

surprisingly, a lot of the calls came from people in the food business. Owners and managers of hotels, restaurants, catering services, country clubs, hospitals—anyplace that served meals—phoned with the same message: "We always prepare more food than we serve," they said. "We always end up just throwing it away. We hate the waste, but we don't know what to do about it."

In 1989, working with the Emergency Resource Bank, I arranged for a refrigerated truck to collect surplus food from these establishments and deliver it to food pantries and soup kitchens. Unfortunately, after this project had been in operation for a while, I came to realize that it cost about as much to rent the truck and pay the driver as it would to simply buy an equivalent amount of food in the first place. While giving otherwise-wasted food to the hungry seemed to be a great idea, our project didn't make practical sense.

I discussed my frustration with this dilemma one day while participating in a talk show on Dayton's WHIO radio station. Among the listeners was Bruce Feldman, president of Economy Linen and Towel Service, who had tuned in to WHIO while driving home from work. Since 1931 his family's company has supplied institutions in the Dayton area and elsewhere with uniforms, tablecloths, napkins, towels, and other such products. His clients were the institutions that wanted to donate their surplus food to the poor. He phoned me with an idea. Every day, his trucks visited his clients, delivered clean linens, and picked up soiled linens to be laundered. Why couldn't they pick up food too?

It took a lot of planning on Bruce's part, but he was able to launch Operation Food Share in May 1990. Economy Linen trucks started picking up food from seventeen institutions with food-service operations—seven restaurants, two caterers, four country clubs, three private clubs, and the University of Dayton. Other companies and civic organizations donated equipment or money.

The food service organizations froze their leftovers and placed them in insulated containers. During their regular rounds, Economy Linen drivers picked up those containers and dropped off empty sanitized containers for use the next day. The drivers took the food to Economy Linen's plant, where it was stored in a freezer. It then was transferred to the Emergency Resource Bank. Soup kitchens, food pantries, and homeless shelters in three counties could draw on this new source of food.

In the first year, Economy Linen's trucks salvaged more than twenty-five thousand pounds of food that otherwise would have been thrown away. They collected another fifteen thousand pounds in the next six months. By the mid-1990s, they were providing more than one hundred thousand pounds of good food each year to the poor.

But Bruce didn't stop there. Working through the Textile Rental Services Association of America, his industry's trade organization, Bruce urged other companies to adopt Operation Food Share in their communities. The first started operating in Washington in 1992, and companies in other cities followed suit.

I never would have known how to create Operation Food Share on my own. But as I have found repeatedly, if you bring a need to the attention of the American people, they will respond. And by responding, as Bruce Feldman showed, one person can make a huge difference. Later I got to thinking that my political party could make a difference, too, beyond simply electing people to office.

The Montgomery County Democratic Party owns a two-story building in downtown Dayton, most of which was going unused most of the time. Our small staff works in its offices daily, but the offices occupy just a fraction of the building. The rest of the space—a large meeting room on the first floor and smaller rooms on the second—was being underutilized.

About a block away, the Society of St. Vincent de Paul operated a homeless shelter, which they named the St. Vincent Hotel. Unfortunately, demand for beds—especially in cold weather—far exceeded the facility's capacity. *Why don't we open a shelter in our building to pick up the emergency overflow?* I thought to myself.

Dennis Lieberman, the party chairman, embraced the idea. Support wasn't unanimous, however. Some people simply believed that a political party really does have just one function—winning elections. Moving beyond that, they argued, would be inappropriate. Others, like many Americans, feared getting too close to the homeless. The headquarters served as a bit of a social center for some people who would come in, play cards, and chat with friends. They worried that the people who needed shelter would damage the property and leave the place dirty.

I argued back that it was more than appropriate for us to open an overflow shelter in our building—that we should consider it an obligation. "We like to call ourselves the party of the people," I said, "the party that represents the middle class, the workers, and the poor. If that's true, we should feel ashamed if all we do is talk about it. This building is a great asset. How can we justify not using it to help the people we claim to represent? If we really care for the poor, let's prove it by extending our hands to the homeless people who are, literally, right outside our front door."

With the party chairman and the congressman leading the way, that argument carried the day. We put beds, clean linens, and a little bit of food in two rooms upstairs, and we started taking in women and children when the St. Vincent shelter overflowed. It was a clean, warm, comfortable, and safe place for them to stay, and it became an essential part of St. Vincent's mission. The success of the shelter inspired us to open a food pantry at our headquarters. Then we opened our big first-floor meeting room to serve hot meals to the poor and homeless on Saturday afternoons.

When Dennis and I held a press conference to unveil our shelter during the winter of 1995, we were able to demonstrate that our Democratic Party really does care for the poor. We put our money—our assets—where our mouths were. And we became one more example of the good works that built the constituency for the hungry and the poor in my hometown.

By the mid-1990s, it seemed that everyone in the Dayton area had joined that constituency. When help was needed, a call went out and someone responded. And it didn't have to be a need in Dayton. Once, for instance, while I was investigating hunger and poverty in Appalachian Ohio, I asked Rev. Mel Franklin what one thing he would wish for to improve life in his little town of McArthur.

Rev. Franklin, whose United Methodist church ran a food pantry, replied, "Transportation from where we are in southeastern Ohio to where the jobs are. We don't have many jobs here. The unemployment rate is high. We've got a video store here that advertised a job for a clerk, and 250 people applied. If we had transportation, we could take people to where the jobs are around Columbus in the morning and bring them back home at night."

When I went back to Dayton, I told this minister's story to leaders of several

unions that had many members with relatives in Appalachia. The Miami Valley Regional Transit Authority donated a retired bus.

Volunteer mechanics put new tires on the bus and fixed up the engine. Working with a group called Our Common Heritage—an organization of Dayton-area residents with Appalachian roots—the union members raised money for the project. Then a bunch of the people who had been involved hopped on that bus and took it to McArthur—along with a $2,500 donation to Rev. Franklin's food pantry. When we pulled into town, we discovered that the people there had posted signs along the road to welcome and thank us.

Because of these Daytonians' Appalachian heritage, they were especially proud and excited about what they'd done, and the project was exceptionally meaningful to them. That trip from the flatland of Dayton to the hills of Appalachia was festive and full of joy—more fun, I think, for the people who were giving than for the people who received.

Rev. Franklin took that bus and did exactly what he said he'd do—drove workers to newfound jobs in the Columbus area in the morning and returned them home at night.

All of these projects produced the twin benefits of helping the poor and the hungry and teaching the people of Dayton about problems and ways that individuals can help. In addition, they also served as models for other communities to emulate, and they educated me about how to make good things happen.

Helping those in need takes leadership and commitment. But it doesn't require a large number of leaders or a heroic investment of time and effort. And *anyone* can take the lead. All you need are two or three people who acquire a vision, catch fire to fulfill it, and remain dedicated to the task. People will follow if they sense you're sincere and want to do good. When you lead by example, others will take up the cause, and some of them will become leaders too.

All of these projects demonstrated what private individuals and organizations can accomplish with little or no government assistance and a relatively small amount of money. Individual programs don't necessarily last forever. Some die, and others are born. What's important is that many people in Dayton are committed to helping the less fortunate. They've learned that doing good can be both personally fulfilling and a great deal of fun.

As a congressman who had to run for reelection every other year, I commissioned a lot of public opinion surveys. Early in my congressional career, poverty and foreign affairs were at the bottom of the issues Daytonians said they cared about. Over the years, those issues rose to second and third in my polls.

In my later years in Congress, we also asked people what they would want to talk about if they had a chance to talk with me. Almost 80 percent said they'd like to talk about hunger.

Right up through my last campaign, I faced opponents who charged that I cared more about Africa than I cared about Dayton, that I cared too much about the poor and not enough about the middle class, that I didn't take care of my district's parochial interests. After I won my first few reelections, I stopped worrying about those attacks. People would ask me how I was going to answer the attacks, and I'd say, "I'm not going to answer them. I don't have to answer them." I *did* look after my district's parochial interests, and my constituents knew that. More significant, my polls showed that the vast majority of Daytonians loved my work on hunger, poverty, and human rights. They believed it was important. Best of all, they embraced it as their own.

THE UNITED STATES

*Finding and Fighting
Hunger and Poverty
Around the Corner and
Over the Hill*

★ ★ ★

M any of my constituents, including a lot of my Dayton friends, have roots sunk deep into Appalachia. They—or their parents or grandparents—left the rural hills and hollows of southeastern Ohio, Kentucky, West Virginia, and other parts of that region to take good-paying jobs in Dayton's factories when America's heavy industries were booming. Unlike those who complained I wasn't paying enough attention to my district's parochial concerns, these constituents urged me to expand my horizons to this poor, rural section of our country they so loved.

"We know there are poor and hungry people down there," these constituents told me. "But we don't know exactly how big the problem is or what might be done about it. Is there a way we can find out what's going on in Appalachia and help the people there?"

Thrilled to have constituents who wanted to do more about hunger, I began to look into the situation. I took trips through southeastern Ohio and nearby states, both to learn and to shine a light on what I discovered. What I found bore no resemblance to the horrors I'd encountered in Ethiopia and other third world trouble spots. But I did meet desperate people and saw sad scenes that have stuck in my memory and fortified my commitment to work for poor and hungry Americans as well as people overseas.

In southeastern Ohio, for instance, I met Darryl and Martha Wagner, an

elderly couple who cried as they told me that it was impossible for them to pay all their bills. Once, Martha said, she repeatedly added water to a large can of tomato juice, continually thinning it over a two-week period during which it was their only source of food. She also described preparing an economical "chicken" soup. With an egg and flour, she made noodles for the soup. Then she told Darryl to "just pretend there's chicken in there."

Another elderly couple told me a similar story about a can of soup they watered down at each meal for three days. It was near the end of the month, and they couldn't make their Social Security benefits stretch the full four weeks.

It's a story about hungry children that remains most vivid in my memory, however, and that I return to often when I contemplate our obligation to help the needy. During a trip through southeastern Ohio, I met a single mother who lived with two children in a trailer off a country road. She and the children were among more than three hundred people, old and young, who were standing in line to get free groceries at a food bank that I was visiting in a small town not far from her home. I asked about her needs, and she described how difficult it was to keep her children well fed and how much she depended on the food bank. She did not relate what I later found to be the most compelling part of her story. I would hear that only from a food bank volunteer.

Sometimes, the volunteer told me, he would deliver groceries to this woman's trailer because it was hard for her to get into town. If the children were home when he delivered the food, the volunteer said, they would jump up and down with great excitement and joy. Good food was so scarce in this household that the children celebrated when it arrived.

Whenever I recall that story, I think, *Children should get excited about toys, about candy, about games, about holidays. Children should not get excited about food.* But if food for your family is scarce—if food from the food bank tastes better than the food your mother stretches most other times—then a visit from the food bank volunteer can be reason for joy.

That's the face of hunger and poverty in America today. It's not starvation. It's not cowering in refugee camps. It's these kids getting excited about food. It's old people diluting soup between Social Security checks. It's even families who have long enjoyed the middle-class lifestyle who suddenly fall on hard times and turn to a food bank for assistance. And I worry the problem may

get worse as companies abandon pension and health insurance programs for their workers and retirees.

American hunger often hits elderly couples who have worked hard all their lives, have never even thought about needing welfare benefits, and who depend primarily or entirely on Social Security for their income. One of them gets sick, and they discover their health insurance doesn't cover prescription drugs—or they don't have health insurance at all. Their utility bills rise faster than their income. Something breaks at home and requires a costly repair. And they find themselves visiting a food bank or a soup kitchen near the end of every month.

Many of the working poor find themselves in similar situations because their low-paying jobs carry no fringe benefits. If someone gets sick or the car breaks down, there isn't enough money to pay all the bills. They stretch their food, aren't able to buy enough healthful food, and head for the soup kitchen or food bank once a month or so.

Despite the common tendency to equate poverty with urban ghettos, Americans go hungry in the city and the countryside alike, as my trips through Appalachia demonstrated, and as Mike Espy showed me in the South.

When he was chairman of the House hunger committee's Domestic Task Force, Mike asked me to go with him to some of the poorest rural areas in one of the poorest and most rural states in the country, his native Mississippi. Most of the homes we visited there were rickety wooden houses sitting on cinder blocks with no basements. A woodstove was the standard means of heating and cooking. Few of the houses had running water or indoor bathrooms. Some didn't even have outhouses; the family just used a hole dug into the ground out in the woods. Several houses had just one room, which was sparsely furnished; a few houses had only one bed, so the children slept on the floor. In some houses, cloth was tied across the window openings in lieu of glass.

The people living in these houses owned maybe one change of clothes. The clothes they were wearing were tattered and in some cases dirty. The children for the most part didn't wear shoes. The area supported few jobs, so the adults barely scratched out a living, much of it through subsistence farming. They couldn't grow enough, however, so they were hungry.

According to Bread for the World, a respected Christian organization that has been advocating for the hungry for more than thirty years, a larger

proportion of Americans go hungry in rural places than in metropolitan areas. Not surprisingly, rural hunger is most prevalent among the poorest rural residents—white Appalachians, blacks in the Deep South, Hispanics in the U.S.-Mexico border region, and Plains Indians. But hunger can be found throughout our rich country.

Some 9.6 million Americans, including 3 million children, live in homes that experience hunger, according to Bread for the World's 2005 report on domestic hunger.[1] That means at least one person in the home frequently skips meals or eats too little at a meal. Sometimes the children go hungry. Many times parents skimp on eating so their children can eat more. Bread for the World says another 26.7 million Americans live in homes that are at risk of hunger. That means they eat a low-quality diet or have to go to food banks or soup kitchens to keep from going hungry.

Although we made great strides against hunger in America throughout the twentieth century, we've been backsliding in the last few years, information collected by Bread for the World shows. The number of Americans in those hungry or at-risk families increased by 1.4 million from 2002 to 2003, the Agriculture Department reported.[2] A U.S. Conference of Mayors survey found that requests for emergency food assistance increased an average of 13 percent from 2003 to 2004.[3] America's Second Harvest, the national food bank network, said the number of people seeking food from its members rose to 23.3 million in 2001, up from about 21 million in 1997.[4]

A majority of the city governments surveyed by the mayors couldn't meet all the requests for food they received. To avoid running out of supplies, two-thirds of the cities reduced the amount of food they made available to individual families, either by cutting the size of each distribution or limiting the number of times people could get help—or both. As a result, the cities left an average 20 percent of need unmet in 2004, up from 14 percent the year before.[5]

Illustrating the diverse face of American hunger, the mayors reported that a majority of people seeking assistance lived in families with children, and a third of adults requesting aid were employed. America's Second Harvest said 40 percent of requests to food banks came from working families.[6] The mayors reported that high housing costs, low-paying jobs, and unemployment, not surprisingly, were the leading causes of the need for assistance.[7]

Although Americans aren't starving, hunger in the United States does injure those who don't get enough of the right food to eat. Hungry children are more likely than well-fed children to be sick, anxious, or depressed. They have a harder time concentrating at school, and they're also more likely to misbehave. Looking closely, we find that some children do poorly in school and get in trouble with the law in part because they don't eat well.

Hungry people and poor people often become hopeless people. That thought occurred to me in Mississippi when Mike Espy told me about one possession nearly all of his impoverished constituents seemed to own—an insurance policy to pay for their burial. From their tiny sources of income, they managed to set aside enough to keep these policies in effect. They wanted to be buried properly, and they didn't want to burden their children with this final expense. They weren't saving for the future so they could live better lives; at a fairly young age, they had begun to save for death.

This seemed to be powerful evidence of their lack of hope. They could scratch together enough money to pay for that burial insurance even while they didn't have enough money to pay for quality food, to improve the sanitary conditions around their houses, or to dress their children in decent clothing. They weren't preparing to live; they were preparing to die.

Yet I also saw here powerful evidence that gave me hope. These poor people were capable of saving. The Grameen Bank's programs to encourage the poor to start savings accounts and to grant them small loans can work in the United States as well as in South Asia, I thought. Here in the poorest parts of Mississippi, I had found more proof for my arguments in favor of American microenterprise. Many people think that tiny loans to the poor or small savings accounts can't put a dent in poverty. But I have seen poor people turn small loans into going businesses that lifted their families to a higher economic status. Over and over again, I have seen tiny steps to help the poor grow into marvelous attacks on hunger and poverty. It's the result, as Mother Teresa said, of doing what's in front of you.

In Washington, for example, I participated in a Wednesday morning prayer group that was formed to follow the biblical instruction to pray for leaders. We prayed not only for national leaders such as the president and members of Congress but also for Washington's mayor and city council

members and business leaders and for the benefit of all of Washington. We felt the capital was a special place. It was every American's second city. If you're from Dayton, Washington is your capital. If you're from Sacramento, you may live in the capital city of California, but Washington is your capital too. We all should pray for the leaders of America and the city in which they do their work.

We didn't advertise the group, but it was open to anyone who wanted to attend, and our regular membership was quite diverse. Frequent participants included members of Congress, city officials, business executives, ministers, and local residents of various economic levels, including the poor. For a long time, we met downtown in the city's main public library, which was named for Martin Luther King Jr., a minister whose great civil rights leadership sprang from his faith and from his understanding of God's admonition to serve the poor, the hungry, and the oppressed.

I usually opened the meeting by reading from the Bible. We'd pray. Then a spiritual leader would talk about the lesson in the Scripture. Until his death in 1995, Rev. Sam Hines of the Third Street Church of God usually filled that role. Sam's church took seriously its obligation to serve the poor people who lived all around it, and he could effectively explain how the day's reading related to us and how it related to the city.

Our prayers and discussions inevitably turned to what we should and could do to serve the poor of Washington. Local agencies offered many services, but the people who needed help often didn't know how to get it. So we decided to set up a telephone hotline.

We raised funds to acquire the phone line, and we recruited volunteers to answer the calls. The sick, the homeless, the hungry, people in trouble with the law—anyone who needed help—could call. One of our volunteers would connect the caller with the appropriate agency and stay on the line until it was clear that the caller was getting the assistance needed. We called it the People's House Hotline, and it now has built a database with information about more than thirty-five hundred agencies in the Washington metropolitan area. Today it is operated by the Southeast White House—sometimes called the Little White House—a marvelous institution in Washington's poorest community, which also grew out of our prayer group, as explained below.

In addition to meeting the physical needs of Washington's poor, we prayed about reconciliation in a city very much divided by race, economic status, and partisan politics. We wanted to bring people together, perhaps in a place where they could meet, talk, share meals, and have fellowship. Eventually we raised enough money to purchase a house in Southeast Washington. It's called the Southeast or Little White House because it's on Pennsylvania Avenue (just like the president's house), it's white, and it has columns and other architectural features that suggest the more famous mansion. It's also a name of pointed irony, because the neighborhood around the Southeast White House, at 2901 Pennsylvania Avenue SE, is a world away from the president's digs at 1600 Pennsylvania Avenue NW.

For purposes of assigning addresses, Washington is divided into four sections—Northwest, Northeast, Southwest, and Southeast. The people who run the Southeast White House sometimes refer to Southeast Washington as the "forgotten quadrant," because it is the poorest section of the city, and its residents often feel neglected by better-off Washingtonians. Nearly a quarter of Southeast D.C. residents live in public housing, for example; more than a third qualify for public assistance; and more than three-quarters of the quadrant's children live in single-parent households. Because of its location in this neighborhood, the Southeast White House became not only a place of reconciliation but also a place to serve the poor.

I tell people the Southeast White House was prayed into existence. Not only did the concept spring from our prayer group, but much of the building's renovation was accomplished by volunteers from churches both nearby and far away. I remember one church recruiting a large number of volunteers—including skilled craftsmen—who put in a kitchen, new wiring, new plumbing, and new bathrooms. Other churches donated supplies or money. Several churches have created ongoing relationships with the Southeast White House. Out-of-town churches send youth groups to spend a week or so at the Southeast White House. The young people do volunteer work in inner-city Washington and visit some of D.C.'s tourist attractions. Living and working among Washington's poor, the visiting youngsters learn about the inner city and develop relationships with people they otherwise never would have met. For some of the visitors, this is their first real contact with the poor.

This White House is run by two remarkable men who themselves embody the relationships across superficial boundaries for which we prayed. Sam Morrison is a former Washington policeman. Scott Dimock retired from a private nongovernmental organization. Sam is African-American. Scott is caucasion. They walk together in serving "the least of these." And they have maintained relationship building at the core of what the Southeast White House does.

The short-term visits from out-of-town volunteers, which Sam and Scott call "urban plunges," provide great examples of that principle. So do the many meals this White House hosts. Their "Reconciliation Luncheons" bring together people who would not normally sit around the same meal table— members of Congress, affluent professionals and business executives, poor residents of the neighborhood, suburbanites, people of all races. At weekly breakfasts, men from around the metropolitan area gather for fellowship, prayer, and discussion of how to follow Jesus in the workplace and how to serve as role models for young people, especially for the youths who live in the poor community this White House serves.

The organization's Friends Mentoring Program requires a profound commitment from volunteers and demonstrates that relationships are key to Southeast White House service programs. The program matches first graders with volunteers who each commit to spending at least four hours with their assigned child every week until the child finishes high school. As I write this, more than fifty children have been matched with mentors, and the first mentor has been working with several girls for more than eight years. The similar Sibling Mentoring Program—modeled after Big Brothers Big Sisters—requires volunteers to spend ten hours a month with a child. As with the Friends Mentoring Program, sibling mentors have been paired with about fifty children, and another fifty children are on a waiting list. When mothers saw the effect the mentors were having on their children's friends, they knocked on the door of this White House and begged to have mentors for their kids as well.

Under the direction of a professional tutor, volunteers work one-on-one with students who need help with their schoolwork. The Southeast White House sponsors sports teams and classes in dance as well as in sewing, cooking, and other life skills. Washington artists teach courses in drama,

music, drawing, painting, and ceramics. "Mom's Night Out" regularly scheduled events help young mothers learn parenting and other needed skills.

The Southeast White House's value to the community can be seen in a message a Fraternal Order of Police leader sent to his fellow police officers. "I urge every member of the Metropolitan Police Department to consider lending a hand and a heart to the wonderful programs under way at the Southeast White House," wrote G. I. Greene, chairman of the D.C. Metropolitan Police Department Labor Committee. "I believe we can be excellent mentors to young men and women who are in real need of responsible adult role models. Isn't it much better to meet them at the White House instead of the Station House?"[8]

In a very different corner of Washington—the affluent Upper Northwest—another successful act of reconciliation is symbolized by another renovated house, this one known as Friendship Place. You can't exactly say this house was prayed into existence, although neighborhood religious institutions played a very important role in its creation. It actually grew out of a bitter confrontation—between affluent and poor, black and white, government and citizen—that was reconciled by many neighbors through goodwill.

The conflict began when the D.C. government announced it was going to open a fifty-bed overnight shelter for homeless men in an abandoned police station, which was located on a corner shared with a church, a nursery school, an elementary school, and the edge of a quiet, affluent, white-collar neighborhood of single-family homes. Because there weren't fifty homeless men hanging out in the vicinity of the site, they were to be bused in from other parts of the city each night and shooed out the door each morning—about the same time the little children would be arriving at school.

Neighborhood response was frenzied. Nearly one thousand people jammed a hastily called community meeting at the school, Janney Elementary, overflowing the gymnasium into the halls and onto the lawn and sidewalks outside. Lawyers were mobilized. Legal actions were filed. City officials were besieged. And the government retreated—about twenty blocks south along Wisconsin Avenue, to Guy Mason Recreation Center, on the edge of another upscale residential area at the upper end of Washington's famed Georgetown neighborhood.

The local response to the Guy Mason proposal was identical, but this time Mayor Sharon Pratt Dixon would not retreat. The battle was on—in court,

before the zoning board, and even in the National Park Service, which had participated in the recreation center's development. The mayor, a black woman, was demonized as an amoral politician who was out to boost her standing among poor and minority voters by forcing an unneeded shelter into the city's whitest and most affluent ward. The white and affluent residents of Ward 3 were demonized as racists and elitists who might talk about compassion but wouldn't tolerate social services for the needy near their backyards. The shelter's intended residents were alternately depicted as the innocent victims of a cruel economic system and of heartless rich folk, and as drug- and alcohol-crazed predators who would molest the neighborhood's children, rape the women, and mug the men. A few neighborhood residents spoke out in favor of the shelter proposal, but most expressed a mixture of outrage and fear.

The battle raged for two years. Shelter opponents spent some $100,000 in legal fees. Advocates for the homeless staged a takeover of the recreation center. They even disrupted Easter services at a neighboring church whose congregation opposed the shelter. In the end, once again, the affluent neighbors prevailed, and the mayor let the concept of the Guy Mason shelter fade away.

The issue of helping the homeless in that Northwest Washington community did not end there, however. While nearly all the residents in the area opposed placing a fifty-bed overnight shelter near an elementary school or in a recreation center, some were unsettled by the fury they witnessed among their neighbors. They did have, they believed, some obligation to help the homeless. As early as the immediate aftermath of the raucous meeting at Janney Elementary School, friends began discussing their concerns. Soon—in living rooms, coffee shops, and churches—small clusters of neighbors were independently creating a new movement.

Among those who attended the Janney meeting was Kathleen Partridge, an octogenarian who had reared four children in the house where she still lived about ten blocks away. She found her neighbors' conduct "shameful."

"It wasn't a good location" for a shelter, she agreed, "but people overreacted. They were so angry. When we came out of the meeting, we were so shocked, a few of us. We talked on the phone. We said we ought to do something. We had one small meeting at someone's house. We had another

meeting and another and another, and the ranks sort of swelled. I think it was just people calling their friends."

When the conflict shifted to the Guy Mason Center, Jean Duff experienced a similar reaction to the activities of her neighbors. Jean was rearing three- and five-year-old children within two blocks of Guy Mason, and she led a neighborhood organization that was renovating the center's playground. She didn't like the idea of an overnight shelter opening there. She also believed an overnight shelter would do nothing to solve the underlying problems that cause homelessness.

As she became acquainted with a growing number of neighbors who felt strongly on both sides of the dispute (including Mrs. Partridge and her friends), Jean searched for a common ground that didn't involve the Guy Mason shelter. She circulated a proposal to "organize as neighbors to help our homeless neighbors." To try to bridge the neighborhood fissures, she asked Lois Williams, a supporter of the shelter plans, to join in convening a commu- nity meeting. Lois, a lawyer who lived near Janney, had represented the home- less in class-action lawsuits that resulted in court orders for shelters to be opened throughout the city. She was active in a committee that advocated the creation of shelter and services for the homeless in Ward 3.

About forty neighbors attended the meeting, which was held at St. Alban's Episcopal Church, about four blocks from Guy Mason. They had represented various sides in the debates over the proposed overnight shelters. Now, Jean told them, they had to put those disputes behind them and find agreement. In the process, she redefined the issue they faced. Throughout the battles over the pro- posed city shelters, most residents of the nearby neighborhoods saw the ques- tion as, how do we stop the government from dumping fifty bums on our doorsteps? Now it was to be, how do we help our homeless neighbors? Although there weren't large numbers of homeless people wandering the streets in this affluent corner of Washington, there were some. And a few of them were quite well known in the community. The neighbors at the meeting decided to create an organization, which they called the Community Council for the Homeless.

This development brought great relief to the area's clergy, who had been deeply troubled by the conflict. They regularly preached God's admonition to serve the poor. Yet most of the members of their congregations were

adamantly opposed to the city's shelter plans. Shelter opponents held meetings at St. Columba's Episcopal Church, located across the street from the abandoned police station, and at St. Luke's Methodist Church, located across the street from Guy Mason. Clergy who commuted from the suburbs were attacked as outsiders who had no personal stake in the battle.

Especially concerned because of his church's location, St. Luke's pastor Andrew Gunn invited his fellow Ward 3 clergy to a meeting to discuss the matter. About two dozen attended. A few started thinking about offering shelter in their churches. And that thought meshed with the first plan of the Community Council, which had decided to ask local congregations to consider hosting small shelters.

St. Luke's opened the first shelter, with six beds available year-round. St. Columba's, St. Alban's, Metropolitan United Methodist, and St. Paul's Lutheran followed with shelters that would be open only during the winter months. The Roman Catholic Church of the Annunciation decided to maintain two transitional apartments for the homeless in neighborhood apartment buildings. St. Columba's started what church members called their "water ministry"—washers, dryers, and shower facilities in a corner of the church where the homeless could clean themselves and their clothing.

The churches supplied the facilities, some financial support, and a base of volunteers. But the shelters really were broad community projects, with the Community Council raising additional funds and helping to organize a larger volunteer corps to support the congregations' activities.

Providing more than a bed and a roof, the church-based shelters endeavored to help their residents move toward self-sufficiency. They offered access to counseling and training. The volunteers helped to reconnect the homeless with the broader community by sharing meals at the shelters and developing friendships with the residents.

The majority of those housed at the St. Luke's shelter "have been able to put their lives back together," Gunn says. "When they left us, they had jobs and money in the bank, were self-sufficient, and were able to move back out into the community and become productive citizens."

Thomas Omholt, the pastor at St. Paul's, tells of a shelter resident who became a Sunday school teacher at the church after gaining control over the

alcoholism and depression that had driven him into homelessness in the first place. "He's a bright guy who became gainfully employed" in the Washington area's booming high-tech industry, Omholt says.

Despite the success, the council soon concluded that the church-based shelters weren't enough. Council members raised funds to hire a social worker to research the extent of homelessness in the area, listen to what the homeless said they needed, and attempt to link them with help. Then the council decided it needed a facility from which it could coordinate the volunteers and offer such daytime services as counseling and medical care.

Primarily by soliciting religious congregations and obtaining a federal grant, the council was able to purchase a house on Wisconsin Avenue, only about three blocks from Janney School. Randy Denchfield, owner of a suburban roofing company who grew up in the neighborhood, knew that the building trades magazine *Roofing/Siding/Insulation* coordinates a charitable rehabilitation project every year. He brought the Community Council's house to the magazine's attention, and it became that year's project. A local architect did the design for free. About twenty manufacturers donated the construction supplies. About a dozen Washington-area contractors volunteered to perform the work. As a result, the house became the best-looking property along that strip of the avenue. The council christened the facility Friendship Place—to honor the name of the immediate neighborhood, Friendship Heights, and to impart an amiable message to affluent and homeless neighbors alike.

The project was not without conflict. When plans for the facility became public, nearby residents expressed concern, and about eighty-five nearby merchants signed a petition of protest. Council members listened to the complaints and promised to run the facility in a manner that would not disrupt the neighborhood. The building would house the offices of the council's staff and provide social services to the homeless during the day, but it would not become a gathering place for large numbers of the homeless. It would not house an overnight shelter or feeding center. The homeless it served would be told the importance of not creating a neighborhood nuisance.

Today a paid staff of twenty-two runs the council's day-to-day operations, which include a wide range of services for the homeless. Five formerly homeless men or women live with a resident manager in each of three houses, two

owned by the council and one by St. Columba's. A dozen formerly homeless people live in apartments managed by the council, some of which the council leases and some of which are leased by area congregations. Four congregations continue to operate small shelters in their churches. St. Columba's still offers its water ministry. A total of twenty-two congregations contribute to the council's work in various fashions. A medical doctor, a nurse, and a psychiatrist see homeless patients at Friendship Place eight hours a week. A social worker, sometimes accompanied by a volunteer, travels the streets at least five days a week and sometimes on weekends, meeting homeless people, building relationships with them, and encouraging them to use the council's services. The organization's newsletter routinely publishes the stories of formerly homeless men and women who turned their lives around with the council's help. Often the stories are written by the formerly homeless themselves.

Over the years, the council has won respect and support from many neighbors and much of the business community. The computer store next door maintained the council's computers for free in the organization's early days and now works on the more complicated computer system at a discounted price. A condominium complex, next door on the other side, provides parking for staff and volunteers. A nearby shop frames the organization's artwork and certificates. A nearby Starbucks keeps the office supplied with coffee. The neighborhood Whole Foods grocery store donates food. The council counts about 250 volunteers, about 30 of whom work every week. Three-quarters of the organization's income is donated by neighbors, and the rest comes from government programs.

And Jack Bubis—who owns a beauty shop a few doors away and was one of the early opponents of Friendship Place—now regularly cuts the hair of one of the neighborhood's longtime homeless men.

"It makes him feel good," Jack says. "It makes me feel good."

He's doing what's in front of him.

CHAPTER 9

RIPPING OUT THE ROOTS OF TERROR

Our Good Works Will Make Us Safer

* * *

Driving through southern Sudan in 2003, I came upon the remnants of a battle that had taken place ten days earlier. About one hundred vultures were picking over human bones. Some of the skeletons still wore beads and other jewelry around their necks. In what sounded like a tale from some distant past, we were told that horsemen had ridden through the village, cutting everybody down with long swords. The next morning, having contemplated the scene overnight, my traveling companion, Fred Heyn, said, "I felt like we were walking through the valley of the shadow of death."

Sudan's civil war, which has raged for most of the last fifty years, has produced some of the most gruesome scenes I have ever witnessed. In much of southern Sudan, there is little functional modern infrastructure. The people cannot raise enough food to feed themselves or earn money to purchase what they need. Malnutrition is common, and some people starve. There are few educational opportunities and little access to medical care. The fighting has driven more than 4 million refugees from their homes and killed more than 2 million. During just the two years ending in mid-2005, an estimated 180,000 people died, many from hunger and disease; about 2 million were driven from their homes, and 2.3 million needed food aid.

By the time I visited Sudan again in the latter part of 2004, its Darfur region had become infamous around the world as the site of the planet's worst current humanitarian crisis. Accompanying a convoy that was delivering relief

supplies, I came to a camp that I was told held more than 115,000 refugees. They had fled their homes to escape the violence of the war. They were terrified to go into their fields for fear of being attacked, murdered, or, in the case of the women, raped. Because of that, they weren't able to plant, so the food shortages continually became worse.

The camp was a desolate place. Under a bright blue sky, reddish-brown sand spread out in all directions, broken only by occasional clumps of weeds and lone trees with no leaves. Men and women wandered about in flowing robes.

But here there also was hope. Under international pressure, led in great measure by the United States, the warring parties had cut back the fighting, and a peace process of sorts seems to be moving forward as I write this about a year later. Tall mounds of food bags, stamped "USA," testified to the United States' leadership in providing humanitarian aid as well as in pushing peace. Nearby, someone was leading a group of children in a chant.

"USA, OK!" they shouted, bright smiles illuminating their dark faces. "USA, OK! USA, OK! USA, OK!"

I firmly believe that these children, and their parents, will remember who came to their aid in their hours of desperate need. Jesus teaches us to feed hungry people—even our enemies. I believe that's also good foreign policy.

The United States boasts not only the world's greatest military but also the world's greatest food basket. That food could be the most important arsenal for our war against terrorism, but we don't use it as effectively as we might. We distribute more food and other humanitarian assistance—by far—than any other nation. Yet in my travels, I have discovered time and again that many of the people who receive our aid don't know where it's coming from. Similarly, Americans have been at the forefront of campaigns to free political prisoners, to stop violence against the weak, and to abolish oppressive systems such as apartheid. Yet in much of the poor and unfree world, our efforts are little known, and we are viewed in a negative light.

We must provide more aid, and we must campaign more frequently and assertively on behalf of freedom. But we also must do a better job of informing those we help about what we're doing for them.

Americans' lack of knowledge about the importance of efforts to fight hunger, poverty, and oppression causes us to do too little—and to take too little

credit for what we are able to do. I was intensely frustrated for years because I couldn't convince our foreign-aid agencies to slap our name on the billions of dollars of relief supplies we shipped to the hungry and the poor. I'd see thousands of unlabeled sacks of food stacked in refugee camps or bouncing along in the beds of relief agencies' trucks. I knew they came from the United States, but nothing proclaimed that fact to the recipients. Many international agencies and nongovernmental organizations opposed identifying the supplies with a particular country, and U.S. officials went along.

Finally, our government wised up to the value of a brand, and now "USA" and the American flag proudly announce where those sacks of lifesaving supplies come from. Many bags also declare, in the local language, "Donated by the people of the United States." And this is not short-term advertising of the generosity of the American people. These bags are sturdy and durable. People in these poor countries turn the bags into luggage and use them to carry food. Now when I travel in these places, I see people carrying our flag down their streets, a constant reminder of who helped them in their time of need. I've seen this even in North Korea, where there now are six million U.S. food bags being used for these purposes all over the country.

When we feed hungry people—and help them solve other problems—we create goodwill that can last for generations, cement alliances, and make us safer in an often dangerous world. When it comes to our enemies, if we feed them, we confuse them, soften them, change them. In the long run, it's powerful foreign policy to help people in need, even if we don't get along with them, even if they don't thank us for it right away. Because they will remember.

Proof of this fact can be discovered readily in Europe. More than sixty years after the end of World War II, it's easy today to find Europeans who remember and are grateful for what the United States did then—not just in helping to win the war, but in helping to rebuild the European economies afterward, including those of our enemies.

I'll never forget how Italian prime minister Silvio Berlusconi explained his decision to support the U.S.-led war in Iraq. He said one of the reasons he loves America is our implementation of the Marshall Plan after World War II. He went on television and told his constituents that he wanted Italians never

to forget it was the United States that helped rebuild Italy, our World War II enemy, after the war.

I've heard similar statements in many other places over the years, because what the United States did after World War II was so different from what victors traditionally do. We didn't plunder the conquered countryside. We didn't enslave our defeated enemies. We fed the hungry, clothed the naked, healed the sick, and freed the oppressed. We helped them build democracies and rebuild their economies. These actions turned our former enemies into our closest friends. Not one of our current enemies has done to us anything approaching what the Japanese, Germans, and Italians did to us in World War II. Our enemies in World War II tried to conquer the world, and they killed four hundred thousand of our troops in the attempt. Now they are among our most reliable allies.

When we think about enemies, it's also important to remember that we're talking about a relative handful of leaders. Al-Qaeda may claim to represent all of Islam in its campaign of terror against the United States and other nations on its list of enemies. But most Muslims don't want to kill Americans. North Korean dictator Kim Jong Il may rattle nuclear warheads and get himself named by the U.S. government as a member of the international "axis of evil." But most North Koreans don't want conflict with Americans. I know this because I've traveled through so many countries, talked with so many people, seen how they live, and observed many opportunities for America to build goodwill by doing good works.

Even in the "Hermit Kingdom" of North Korea—which I've visited six times—I've seen signs that aid and engagement can win the hearts of the people and command the attention of rulers. Even there, I believe, it's possible to wear down barricades and move toward peace.

Korea's reluctance to deal with Western powers in the mid–nineteenth century first earned it the Hermit Kingdom title. The title has been applied to North Korea for the last half century because of its closed-door policy to most of the rest of the world.

Hearing stories of tremendous deprivation behind North Korea's tall walls of privacy in 1996, I wanted to see for myself. I told North Korea's mission to the United Nations in New York of my desire to visit. I assured them my motive was purely humanitarian, not political. I guess my years of humanitarian

travels and advocacy earned me credibility on that point, because the North Koreans surprised me greatly by saying I was welcome to go.

My trip wasn't welcomed by the U.S. government, some of my colleagues in Congress, and some of our allies in Asia, however. Even friends questioned why I would undertake such a mission. They called North Korea an enemy, pointing out that we've never formally concluded a peace treaty to end the Korean War. "Why," they asked, "would you want to help them?"

I told them I wasn't interested in the well-being of the North Korean government; rather, I was interested in the well-being of the North Korean people. There were reports that a million of those people had died already and that most of the victims were children. To those who understood my faith, I pointed out that Jesus told us to feed the hungry. He didn't say he wanted to feed the hungry except in North Korea. To that, a prominent South Korean pastor simply shrugged his shoulders and said, "You Americans are so naive."

What I discovered during my travels through North Korea is that it probably is the most poorly governed country on earth. South Korea, which evolved slowly into a true democracy during years of prodding by human rights activists—including me—boasts one of the world's most vibrant economies. North Korean dictator Kim Jong Il, who styles himself "Dear Leader," lives in luxury in the capital of Pyongyang, as does his governing elite. They scrape together enough resources to support the fourth-largest army in the world and to mount a serious nuclear weapons program. But ordinary North Koreans are horribly poor, because that totalitarian regime oppresses them, squanders what they have of wealth and income, enforces a dysfunctional Communist economic system that nearly the entire planet has rejected, and prevents them from learning anything from the rest of the world.

Former ruler Kim Il Sung (who called himself "Great Leader") set himself up as god, and his son Kim Jong Il is portrayed as the son of god. No matter where you drive throughout North Korea, you see Dear Ruler's face on billboards. The people are told that he is all-knowing. Because of that, North Korean officials find it next to impossible to admit that they have problems and need help from outside.

Away from the capital, where most of North Korea's few visitors are confined, you feel you've stepped back into a much earlier century. I never saw

direct evidence of this myself, but Chinese Buddhists on the Korea-China border told me that North Korean refugees related rumors of cannibalism. Families were said to fear leaving dead bodies unguarded because they might be snatched to be eaten! What I did see was hunger, abject poverty, and a near-complete absence of economic activity. I met people who wore hats, coats, and gloves inside their houses because there was no heat. I saw children eat grass because there was no food. A 1998 study found that 16 percent of North Korea's children were severely malnourished. Among one- to two-year-olds, the figure exceeded 30 percent.[1] I was told that two-thirds of North Korea's children were stunted in growth, that kids who looked at first glance to be eight or nine years old were actually eighteen or nineteen. The malnourishment stunted their mental development as well. The Red Cross tested water at 840 hospitals and found every sample to be contaminated. I saw people washing food and clothing in ditches of clearly contaminated water.

On my first visit, I was astonished at how quiet the countryside was, and how dark at night. There was almost no source of energy, so people couldn't drive vehicles, light buildings, or operate factories. We had to wear heavy coats indoors because of the lack of heat. We traveled for miles without encountering another vehicle on the road because of the lack of gasoline. When we did come upon a car or a truck, it usually was broken down. There was no sound of industry. At night, it was pitch black. Driving through municipalities was like passing through ghost towns. Occasionally I'd see a candle burning in somebody's window, but even that was rare.

More than three-quarters of North Korea is mountainous. The climate is marked by long, cold, dry winters and short, hot, humid summers. Farming here would be a challenge in the best of circumstances. Under the current economic system, it is disastrous. And massive floods made things even worse in 1995.

As I traveled, I noticed that much of the countryside was treeless because the people cut wood to heat their homes and cook their meager food. Because they were hungry, they harvested their crops too early and thereby made their food shortage worse. Because of their isolation, North Korean farmers were kept ignorant of the latest agricultural techniques, so they practiced archaic farming methods. They didn't know how to care for their soil. I once walked into a cornfield where each stalk had produced just a single ear. North Korean

officials have admitted that more than a million people died from the famine, but I believe the true number is much higher.

I was amazed initially by the government's willingness to let me visit. My ability to travel around the country compounded the amazement. My handlers—though clearly nervous about my activities—even let me stop the car and walk into villages where I would engage ordinary North Koreans in unscripted conversations. I always take my own interpreter with me on trips like this so that I can be sure I'm communicating clearly. That's how I get the most accurate picture of what's going on.

In one village, I met a woman who didn't have any food in her house and had eaten just one meal in the previous two days. I asked her what she had at that meal. She said a small bowl of gruel.

I saw a girl picking weeds in a park and asked her why. She said, "For food." She was small, emaciated. She looked to be seven years old but told me she was fourteen. I asked her if there was a church nearby I could visit. She said, "There are no churches in North Korea." On another occasion, my handlers tried to prevent me from seeing a little girl who was trying to eat a kernelless corncob. But I noticed her before they ran up to her, slapped the corncob out of her hand, and pushed her away.

In a town on the east coast, I visited a hospital that had no antibiotics, no anesthetics, not even any aspirin. Cotton balls and cloths were drying on the windowsills. They had been washed to be used over and over in the surgery ward. Patients were strapped to operating tables so they could be held still while being operated on without anesthesia. The hospital pharmacy stocked nothing but herbs. I had to wear a heavy coat because there was no heat. There also was no food. Patients could eat only if their families brought food to them. I visited about thirty hospitals during my six trips to North Korea and saw these conditions repeated throughout the country.

I visited many orphanages as well. People told me families took their children to orphanages because they couldn't feed them. Unfortunately, food—along with heat, light, and medicine—was scarce in the orphanages too.

People in authority often didn't tell me the truth, but I frequently was able to check the facts for myself. I had heard that many of the children who lived in orphanages were sick, primarily because of malnutrition. When visiting an

orphanage, I'd inevitably be taken to rooms filled with healthy children. But I could always hear kids crying in discomfort in other rooms. At one orphanage I visited, I asked how many sick children were there, and the woman in charge told me thirty. Later I was able to wander about the building on my own, and I counted many more sick kids in rooms I wasn't supposed to see.

I frequently encountered people with stomach problems—some who simply complained of discomfort, others who were doubled over in pain. I discovered that these problems resulted from the government's most desperate attempt to cope with famine—the production of so-called "alternative" or "substitute" food.

Workers gathered weeds, stems, bark, leaves, flowers, and other plant forms and took them to little factories, one of which I was able to visit. In America, this is yard waste that we mulch or compost or put out for the trash trucks to haul away. In these North Korean factories the government had scattered across the country, it was mixed with some grain or soybeans, ground into flour, formed into noodles, and distributed as food. This substance may sate immediate hunger pangs, but the body can't digest it properly; discomfort, diarrhea, and internal bleeding are the frequent result.

I encountered great antagonism to the United States during my first visit. In this closed society, people knew only what their government told them through the state-controlled television, radio, and newspapers. They were told that America is the evil empire. And they were told this from the earliest age. I walked into a school during my first trip and saw a poster that portrayed an American soldier bayoneting North Korean children. The message clearly was "Beware of Americans."

North Korean officials treated me a bit better during my second visit. By my third and fourth trips, they realized I really was there only to help. They thanked me repeatedly for America's food donations. They saw that I hadn't used the trips for any personal political advantage. When I left their country and talked to the media, I never maligned the North Korean government. I wanted to, but I felt there was no purpose in publicly proclaiming how terrible this government was. Plenty of other people were doing that. And biting my tongue allowed me to continue to enter the country to try to help the innocent people there.

After each trip, I reported my findings to my government, to friendly Asian

governments, and to the people through the news media. While I didn't malign North Korea's government, I did describe the hunger and poverty I witnessed. I called on our government and our affluent friends to send aid to the North Korean people. I also carried my message to churches in South Korea and to Korean churches in the United States.

At the beginning, this was a very lonely labor. There was so much hatred on all sides. Japan's hatred of North Korea was intense. North Korea hated Japan for atrocities committed during World War II. North Korea's huge military posed an immediate lethal threat to South Korea and to the nearly forty thousand U.S. troops stationed there.

The United States and some of our allies did increase aid to North Koreans. At one point we supplied 80 percent of all food aid sent there. The Japanese remained adamant about not helping, however. By 1999 I had become so frustrated with their position that I conducted a news conference in Tokyo and berated their inaction, something I felt uncomfortable doing.

"Once again I heard the many reasons why the [Japanese] government will do nothing to help, while North Korea's people starve," I said after what I called a "chilling" meeting with government officials. "All of the reasons make political sense. But they are heartless and not at all like the great nation I know Japan to be. I have visited more than one hundred countries and have seen Japan's generosity in extending aid many times. When it comes to North Korea, though, I am convinced that history will not be a kind judge. Japan's stockpile of three to five million tons of rice is slowly rotting, and storing it costs Japan more than the entire UN annual appeal. Meanwhile, two million North Koreans have starved in the worst famine since colonial times."

Someday, I said, when North Korea recovered, North Koreans would remember who didn't help them—especially those countries that were sitting on surpluses they could have given so easily.

Japanese officials didn't like a United States congressman criticizing them in public, but they did send aid.

I didn't envision this as a one-way exchange—our giving to the North Korean people and getting nothing in return. I saw it as a road to peace. The North Korean government's willingness to tolerate my activities helped to convince me that officials there wanted to improve their relationship with the

West and relieve the plight of their people, if only they—and we—could figure out how to do so.

On my last visit, North Korea's leaders made clear that they were desperate for help. Officials—right up to Foreign Minister Paek Nam Sun—begged me to ask President Clinton to visit the country before he left office. They told me, and they told other people, that they were ready to make a deal. They were ready to sign an agreement that would have led to dismantling their nuclear weapons program. It was shortly after our 2000 presidential election, and they didn't know whether they could do business with President-Elect Bush. So they wanted to cut a deal with Clinton.

I stopped in South Korea on my way home, and South Korean president Kim Dae-jung repeated the same message over and over, not letting me leave his office for two and a half hours until he was sure I was convinced. If President Clinton would talk with the North Koreans, he would obtain agreement to reduce the threat from their nuclear weapons, ease tensions along the North-South border, and supply more effective humanitarian aid to the North Korean people, Kim said.

Back in Washington, I requested a meeting with President Clinton and delivered that message to him in the Oval Office. "If you want to win the Nobel Peace Price," I told him, "this is your opportunity." He replied that he had time for just one major initiative in the few remaining weeks of his presidency, and he was focused on trying to bring peace to the Middle East.

Determined to keep pushing, I went to Erskine Bowles, the president's chief of staff, and made my case again. "Forging a lasting peace agreement between Israel and the Palestinians is a noble goal," I told him, "but one unlikely to be achieved in the time left for this administration. You'll get a deal with North Korea. I guarantee they'll lay out the red carpet, and President Clinton will be a hero."

In his memoirs, Clinton wrote that Secretary of State Madeleine Albright made the same argument. She had visited North Korea—a significant sign in itself—and told Clinton the North Koreans were ready to sign an arms agreement. But he stuck with the Middle East and reached no agreement there.

In 2002 Kim Jong Il himself attempted to engage President Bush by sending a written personal message through two well-regarded U.S. foreign policy experts—Donald Gregg, former ambassador to South Korea; and Don

Oberdorfer, former diplomatic correspondent for the *Washington Post*. Gregg and Oberdorfer revealed in mid-2005 that they were given the message while visiting Pyongyang three years earlier. Writing in the *Post*, they said Kim's message was this: "We should be able to find a way to resolve the nuclear issue. If the United States makes a bold decision, we will respond accordingly."[2]

Gregg and Oberdorfer delivered the message. But like Clinton, Bush did not initially respond. Shortly thereafter, North Korea expelled UN weapons inspectors, withdrew from the Nuclear Nonproliferation Treaty, and reopened plutonium production facilities that had been closed as the result of negotiations during the Clinton presidency.

As I write this, North Korea remains hostile, isolated, and heavily armed—and, I am convinced, still desperate for a partner to relieve its isolation. The opportunity still sits there for any American president who chooses to seize it. And glimmers of hope have emerged from the more than two years of negotiations involving the United States, China, Japan, Russia, and both Koreas. I can only hope that by the time you read this book, real progress will have been made toward disarming the Korean peninsula and easing the deprivation of ordinary North Koreans.

I believe opportunities also exist in other unstable corners of the world, where terrorists recruit their irregular armies and plot to kill Americans. In my travels, I've seen that hunger, poverty, and oppression prepare the soil for terrorism. I've seen terrorists recruit new followers by feeding, clothing, and educating them. I've also seen how we can feed and clothe children at schools that teach freedom and love, instead of letting terrorists feed them at schools that teach hate. Such efforts are sowing the seeds of peace and freedom in many conflict-ravaged places. People won't attack you if they view you as their friend. They aren't likely to blow themselves up in suicide attacks if their hearts are filled with hope rather than hatred.

Because of the tremendous difficulty of conducting diplomacy in the Middle East—and the danger posed to people who try to do good there—I have to be circumspect in naming individuals and even identifying places I've visited. When Frank Wolf and I wanted to tour some Palestinian refugee camps, for instance, friends who lived in the region suggested we not let it be known we were American congressmen. If word spread that U.S. government

officials were walking around, they said, it might trigger a riot. Our friends arranged for us to be shown around some camps by Palestine Liberation Organization representatives who were told only that we were influential Americans.

At one camp, we found something like forty-five thousand people stuffed into an area of one or two square miles—a population density resembling New York City without anything resembling New York's modern infrastructure. People lived on top of one another in very unappealing conditions. The camp's residents couldn't work outside the camp, and there was no real paying work inside the camp either. The children had few educational opportunities. Open sewers ran along the streets. There was little electricity. The people's lives were unsatisfying, they couldn't strive for anything better, and they came to the understandable conclusion that nobody cared about them.

Articulate preachers of hate thrive in places like this. It's easy to stir up animosity toward scapegoats and then recruit new terrorists.

Frank and I went to the region not only to learn about conditions there but also to talk about reconciliation, using as examples our own relationship and the relationships of others who cooperate across political, religious, and ethnic lines. We spoke to large audiences—mostly of Muslims, but also of Christians and Jews.

One time I met with about thirty young people, both Muslims and Christians, who lived near a Palestinian refugee camp. They asked me, "What are you going to do about the Palestinian question?"

I thought to myself, *What's up with these people, who live inside the Palestinian question, asking me, an American who lives far away, what I'm going to do about it?* So I asked how many of them had visited a Palestinian camp. Not a single hand went up.

I asked them, "Why would you ask me what I'm going to do about the Palestinian question when not one of you has even been in a Palestinian camp? I was in one yesterday."

This incident underscored just how isolated the Palestinian refugees are. Even people who claimed to be their brothers cared so little about them that they had never even bothered to visit a camp. Even next door to the camps, people didn't know what was going on inside the camps and didn't bother to

find out. They laid responsibility on others, but the responsibility is theirs too. They should be doing something.

Here's another example: Frank and I became friends with a wealthy fellow who lives in the region and who believes in the need for reconciliation among Muslims, Christians, and Jews. He expressed concern about the plight of the refugees, but he also had never been in a camp. Frank and I took him to one!

He's now involved with a very interesting group of Muslims and Christians who meet for fellowship in the name of Jesus, whom Muslims respect as a great prophet. These people also really care about the refugees and actually are helping. Some of them have great wealth, and some are well connected with political leaders in the region. They feed people, provide athletic equipment, build parks, support education programs, and help train refugees for various occupations. Perhaps most important, they offer some hope to people who don't possess much of that precious commodity.

The United States needs to do more for poor Palestinians and do it more publicly. It's the right thing to do, and it's the kind of thing we must do in our campaign against terror. Hatemongers throughout much of the Muslim world have done an effective job of blaming all problems on Israel, the United States, and other Western countries.

In fact, we do provide aid through the World Food Program, and that helps a lot of Palestinians. But they don't know that it's coming from America, and I think they should know. I also think we should be going inside the camps ourselves, working with the refugees who live there.

I realize the politics of the Middle East makes that difficult. But we need to find ways to let the Palestinians know that we want to be their friends and that we already are helping them. Perhaps we could give more support to non-governmental organizations that aren't clearly identified with the United States and gradually move more Americans in to work there.

There's no doubt in my mind that humanitarian aid is the most effective weapon we can deploy against terrorism—not only because it can make us look good but also because it can alleviate the poverty and despair that breed terrorists. Terrorist organizations such as al-Qaeda use food and education—or rather miseducation—to recruit new terrorists. In their madrassas (religious schools), they use a perverted version of Islam to teach hatred of

non-Muslims, justify the indiscriminate murder of innocents, and sanctify suicide bombings. We can use food and education for diametrically opposite purposes.

I met a farmer in Pakistan whose children attended one of those schools. "Why," I asked him, "do you send your children there?"

"First off," he replied, "it's free. Second, they feed my children. I can't afford to send my children to school, because I need them here to work. But if they're fed at the madrassa, I don't have to feed them, so I can afford to send them."

"But they teach hate," I said.

"I know," he said, "but where else am I supposed to send them?"

We need to expand the number of school feeding programs that we support. Governments in poor countries love school feeding because it gets kids back into the public schools. Farmers love it because they save the cost of feeding their children and their kids get educated. Good education fights hunger and poverty by preparing students for better jobs. And these schools can teach peace and respect instead of hate and violence.

To fight terrorists who label us the enemy of the poor and the oppressed, we must make clear that we are the poor and oppressed's best friend.

EVERYONE IS CALLED TO SERVE THE POOR

Learning One Universal Truth

I've traveled throughout the world many times to investigate hunger, poverty, oppression, and other matters of humanitarian concern. Many times I seek public attention during my missions, because my goals often include summoning public action to solve the problems I encounter.

I've also traveled around the world, quietly, for faith. Sometimes these faith-based missions generate more consternation within the American diplomatic corps than the humanitarian missions during which I criticize U.S. policy or seek action by our government when our government doesn't want to act. This is because in a world of many faiths, religion is a sensitive topic from which diplomats flee.

My travels of faith often are made on behalf of the National Prayer Breakfast, which invites people of all faiths from all over the world to pray together in Washington.

During one trip to a predominantly Muslim country—which I can't name because of those sensitivities—my traveling party was briefed upon our arrival by the U.S. ambassador. He seemed extraordinarily nervous about our mission. I surmised he was worried that this group of Americans, headed by an Ohio congressman he didn't know, was going to try to convert Muslim government officials to Christianity and set back the relationship between our countries for a generation. "Be careful when you talk to leaders here about

religion," he begged. I told him not to worry. We weren't about to touch off a diplomatic incident.

Accompanied by the uneasy ambassador—who I presume hoped to diffuse disaster should we offend our Muslim hosts—we went off to see the leader of one of the nation's legislative bodies. He turned out to be a gregarious man, full of life. After we had engaged in small talk for a few minutes, he asked me the purpose of our visit to his country. "Our mission is personal, not connected to government diplomacy," I told him. "We're here because of our faith. We want to invite you to our National Prayer Breakfast." In the course of explaining our purpose, I mentioned Jesus in an offhanded fashion. As our ambassador had feared, this had a dramatic effect on the legislator's demeanor—but not in the way our ambassador expected.

This Muslim government leader slapped his leg and exclaimed, "This is amazing! My mother used to talk to me about Jesus. This is one of the most refreshing talks I've had in a long time. To think that you've come all the way around the world from America to talk about something this important. It thrills me to know this. I always thought that Americans were naive and materialistic. None of them talk to me about faith, let alone Jesus. This is wonderful." Then he turned to our ambassador and said, "Why don't you come and talk to me about Jesus?"

I've told this story many times since, and it always gets a great laugh. But it also helps to illustrate two lessons I've learned during my travels.

One is that people of many faiths admire Jesus. His message transcends formal religious boundaries. The Muslim lawmaker's mother would have talked to him about Jesus, for instance, because Islam considers Jesus to be a great prophet. Many Hindus and Buddhists respect his teaching.

Another lesson is that the world's largest faiths all admonish their faithful to feed the hungry, clothe the naked, house the homeless, serve the poor, and make peace. That this admonition often is honored in the breach does not make it less true. This common ground is a place where we can end the horrible religious conflicts that kill so many in the name of God. It's also where we can join together to rid the world of hunger, poverty, and oppression, as God clearly wants us to. Thankfully, millions of Jews, Christians, Muslims, Hindus, Buddhists, and others are doing just that.

The Judeo-Christian Scriptures—both the Old and New Testaments—are jam-packed with references to the poor. And there's no mistaking what God commands us to do—not only through his words but through the very way Jesus lived his life. One of Jesus's first great miracles was to feed the multitude in the desert. He helped strangers. He touched lepers. He loved everybody. Asked once which is the greatest commandment, Jesus replied that it is to love God. And the second, he added, is to "'love your neighbor as yourself.' There is no other commandment greater than these" (Mark 12:31).

One of Jesus's most memorable prophecies is about how he will reward the righteous on Judgment Day for having fed him when he was hungry, given him drink when he was thirsty, welcomed him when he was a stranger, clothed him when he was naked, and visited him while he was in prison. When the righteous express puzzlement, not remembering having done those things for him, Jesus will explain that when they did kindness to "the least of these," they also "did it to me" (Matthew 25:40). "When you give a banquet," he taught at another time, "invite the poor, the crippled, the lame, and the blind. And you will be blessed, because they cannot repay you" (Luke 14:13–14). And Paul told the Corinthians that "God loves a cheerful giver" (2 Corinthians 9:7).

God was delivering this message long before Jesus's birth. In Proverbs, Solomon declares, "Whoever is kind to the poor lends to the LORD, and will be repaid in full" (19:17). It is the only way we are told we can lend to God, who usually is giving to us. Solomon also warns, "Whoever gives to the poor will lack nothing, but one who turns a blind eye will get many a curse" (Proverbs 28:27). In Deuteronomy, God commands his people, "Open your hand to the poor and needy neighbor in your land" (15:11). Isaiah admonishes us to "learn to do good; seek justice, rescue the oppressed, defend the orphan, plead for the widow" (1:17).

More than two thousand verses in the Bible deal with the poor. In my travels, I've seen thousands of Christians and Jews serving the poor in some of the world's most difficult places. I've also learned of Muslims, Hindus, Buddhists, and people of other faiths who help the least of their brethren.

When I paid my first visit to Ethiopia during the catastrophic 1984 famine, I found World Vision and the Missionaries of Charity laboring heroically to supply food and medical treatment to an overwhelming mass of starving people.

One of the largest Christian relief and development organizations, World Vision has been providing emergency aid, education, health care, and economic development assistance since 1950. Mother Teresa founded the Missionaries of Charity in India that same year to love and care for the poorest of the poor and the sickest of the sick, whom no one else was helping. Like World Vision, Mother Teresa's missionaries now work on every populated continent.

You've probably heard of other prominent Christian organizations that follow Jesus's instruction to serve the poor—Catholic Relief Services, the Salvation Army, Habitat for Humanity, and Bread for the World, to name just a few. There are many such groups, large and small. And thousands of individual congregations do their part—perhaps by operating their own soup kitchen or homeless shelter, or by volunteering to help in community organizations, or by donating money that can be put to use anywhere in the world.

A national survey coordinated by the Hartford Seminary in Connecticut in 1999 and 2000 found that the vast majority of American congregations did such service. About 85 percent supported a food pantry or soup kitchen. The same proportion gave cash assistance to needy families or individuals. More than half supported thrift stores. A third supported housing programs.[1] A similar survey found that more than nine in ten American mosques gave cash to the needy, and about two-thirds supported soup kitchens and collection drives for the poor.[2]

Two-thirds of America's emergency food providers are faith-based organizations.[3] And faith-based groups were prominent in the efforts to help victims of Hurricane Katrina in the American Southeast in 2005.

The Union for Reform Judaism activated its disaster relief fund, as it always does in such times, and quickly raised $2 million. In conjunction with the town of Utica, Mississippi, where the union has a camp, it opened a distribution center for relief supplies. Reform Jews across North America collected food and other supplies and shipped them to the camp. Volunteers lived at the camp and helped to staff the distribution center.

For two decades, American Jewish World Service has operated relief and development projects throughout the third world. MAZON: A Jewish Response to Hunger supports antihunger efforts around the world with $3 million in annual contributions from American Jews.[4]

One of the most effective humanitarian organizations in history, the Grameen Bank, which I write about in detail in chapter 3, was founded by a Muslim, Muhammad Yunus. It makes tiny loans to the poorest of the poor so they can create or expand their own tiny businesses. This remarkable enterprise was born in the mid-1970s when Yunus, an economics professor at Chittagong University in Bangladesh, loaned $27 to forty-two craftspeople and saw them begin to pull themselves out of poverty.[5]

In Bangladesh today, the Grameen Bank has more than fifteen hundred branches, fourteen thousand employees, and 4.75 million borrowers in thirty-seven thousand villages. The borrowers repay their loans 99 percent of the time.[6] I became so impressed with Grameen's accomplishments that I worked to bring microlending to the U.S. government's overseas aid efforts and to programs that help the poor within the United States itself. Now, lenders that are affiliated with Grameen, or simply copy Grameen's methods, operate in about sixty countries, including prosperous nations with a minority of poor citizens, such as the United States, Canada, France, the Netherlands, and Norway.

"If I could be useful to another human being, even for a day, that would be a great thing," Yunus has said. "It would be greater than all the big thoughts I could have at the university."[7]

Buddhist monk Sukho Choi, also known as Venerable Pomnyun Sunim, has been laboring for years in a cause dear to my heart—providing aid to the hungry, poor, and oppressed people of North Korea. (I tell you about my six visits to the so-called Hermit Kingdom in chapter 9.) This is particularly noteworthy because Choi is South Korean, and North Korea is his country's mortal enemy.

Informing his fellow South Koreans that more North Koreans have died from famine than perished in the Korean War, Choi has raised millions of dollars and thousands of articles of clothing to feed and clothe the needy north of the 38th parallel. Choi and his followers pressure the South Korean government to offer humanitarian aid to people in the north, and they urge other nations and international relief groups to do so as well. Choi founded several organizations that do humanitarian work in North Korea and India, help North Korean refugees in South Korea and China, and provide emergency relief when it's needed in various parts of the world. His actions demonstrate

that you don't have to be a Christian to act in accordance with Jesus's instruction to feed your enemy.

People of different faiths also are joining together in humanitarian efforts, sometimes in very difficult circumstances. In 2004 the Ramon Magsaysay Award for Peace and International Understanding—which often is referred to as the Asian Nobel Peace Prize—was given to a Muslim and a Hindu who have reached across the India-Pakistan border, working to ease long-standing animosities between their two populous and nuclear-armed nations.

Ibn Abdur Rehman, a Muslim born in the Indian state of Punjab in 1930, was forced to move to Pakistan with his family after Britain partitioned its Indian colony into the independent countries of predominantly Hindu India and predominantly Muslim Pakistan in 1947. In adulthood he became a prominent journalist, eventually rising to edit the *Pakistan Times*. Laxminarayan Ramdas, the Hindu, became a military officer and capped his distinguished career as the Indian navy's chief of staff.

In 1994, having retired from their journalistic and military careers, Rehman and Ramdas helped to create the Pakistan-India Peoples' Forum for Peace and Democracy. The group fosters dialogue between Indians and Pakistanis from all walks of life, to build understanding among residents of nations that have fought several wars and are engaged in a perpetually smoldering, religion-fueled conflict over who rules Kashmir, a predominantly Muslim state on the Indian side of the Pakistan-India border. In addition to organizing meetings on both sides of the border, the forum has lobbied both governments to ease travel restrictions between the two countries and to remove the demonizing of the other side that appears in both countries' schoolbooks.

In accepting their award, Rehman and Ramdas both discussed a fact of human relationships that I discovered in Congress and during my travels in various parts of the world: it is easier to resolve differences—and harder to demonize others—if you really get to know the guys on the other side.

Rehman said that even when the Indian and Pakistani governments conclude formal peace agreements, "the bitterness and prejudice of centuries cannot be washed away by state protocols only." Needed, he said, are many experiences like one described by an Indian teacher who led students on a visit across the

border. There the students "discovered a Pakistan that was quite different from what they had read about in their history books." Ramdas agreed that "getting the youth of both countries together has been a great achievement." The face-to-face discussions that occur during such visits are "chiseling away some of the prejudices" and helping to "lift some of the myths that had earlier been treated as gospel," he said. A decade into the forum's work, Ramdas said, "I am happy to say that we are a healthy and vibrant lot."[8]

In the Balkans, a corner of Europe riven with bloody ethnic and religious conflicts, a Christian mission brings together young adults of differing faiths to lay the groundwork for long-term reconciliation. Since 1999 the Renewing Our Minds conference has been conducted by Life Center International in Fuzine, Croatia, a beautiful town near mountains and lakes that is popular with tourists. Young people ages eighteen to thirty—primarily from the Balkans but also from other places plagued by conflict—spend three weeks in this peaceful setting, just a half hour from the Adriatic coast, getting to know one another and finding the common ground beneath their differences.

Stevo Dereta, a Baptist minister who helped to found the conference, came to the conclusion that reconciliation in the Balkans had to begin with the young. The participants arrive bearing the identities that have divided the Balkans for centuries—Albanian, Bosnian, Croat, Serb, Montenegrin, Macedonian, Slovene, Roman Catholic, Orthodox, Muslim, Protestant. Conference leaders do not ask non-Christians to convert, but the program is based on the teachings of Jesus. Participants first study Jesus and the Gospels, then examine their communities' conflicts, and finally learn about reconciliation. Follow-up programs and reunions support the participants after they return home.

The project intends to grow "a new generation of leaders eager to work towards building peace and reconciliation," in the words of Tihomir Kukolja, director of Renewing Our Minds and Life Center International.[9] He has collected testimony from participants who offer evidence that the effort may succeed. The conference "made me realize that God is one and the same for all of us," a Macedonian woman said. An Armenian man predicted that "the results of the friendships built at [the conference] will bring great changes, from forgiveness to conflict resolution."

Many people are reaching across religious boundaries within the United States as well. Often this occurs as Christians realize they have much in common with members of other denominations, despite disagreements that result in some of us calling ourselves Baptists, Presbyterians, and so forth. The Hartford Seminary study found that 7 percent of U.S. congregations were engaged in service projects with people of different faiths. A third of the congregations were working with members of different denominations.[10]

Among the most-talked-about recent events has been the decision of the National Association of Evangelicals to issue a statement titled "For the Health of the Nation: An Evangelical Call to Civic Responsibility." While evangelical churches have long carried out projects to help the disadvantaged, the association has tended to take conservative positions on public policy and to focus its political efforts primarily on issues of personal morality, such as abortion or same-sex marriage, as its fifty-two member denominations and related organizations also tend to do. By unanimously adopting this call in October 2004, however, the association's board endorsed government action to aid the poor, both at home and abroad, and to protect the environment.

"We call all Christians to a renewed political engagement that aims to protect the vulnerable and poor, to guard the sanctity of human life, to further racial reconciliation and justice, to renew the family, to care for creation, and to promote justice, freedom, and peace for all," the association declared. This includes "advocating for effective government programs and structural changes." While evangelicals will disagree about some political issues, the association acknowledged, "We have many callings and commitments in common: commitments to the protection and well-being of families and children, of the poor, the sick, the disabled, and the unborn, of the persecuted and oppressed, and of the rest of the created order."[11]

Though the Bible does not require economic equality, the association affirmed that the Bible, "condemns gross disparities in opportunity and outcome that cause suffering and perpetuate poverty, and it calls us to work toward equality of opportunity. God wants every person and family to have access to productive resources so that if they act responsibly they can care for their economic needs and be dignified members of their community."[12]

The association called on Christian politicians to "shape wise laws pertaining to the creation of wealth, wages, education, taxation, immigration, health care, and social welfare that will protect those trapped in poverty and empower the poor to improve their circumstances." It advocated making reduction of global poverty "a central concern of American foreign policy." And it proclaimed that "government has an obligation to protect its citizens from the effects of environmental degradation."[13]

God gave humans "a sacred responsibility to steward the earth and not a license to abuse the creation of which we are a part," the association declared. "Our uses of the earth must be designed to conserve and renew the earth rather than to deplete or destroy it. We urge Christians to shape their personal lives in creation-friendly ways: practicing effective recycling, conserving resources, and experiencing the joy of contact with nature. We urge government to encourage fuel efficiency, reduce pollution, encourage sustainable use of natural resources, and provide for the proper care of wildlife and their natural habitats."[14]

With few exceptions, this is a platform that could be embraced by the liberal activists who traditionally view evangelical Christians as natural political enemies—and by people of all faiths. "On issues like poverty, the cold war among religious groups is over," Rev. Richard Cizik, the association's vice president for public policy, told the *Washington Post*.[15] "I think this rallying cry for the poor may be one of the issues that can let evangelicals, Roman Catholics and mainline Protestants work together," he said in another interview with the *Christian Post*.[16]

No wonder, then, that Cizik was among scores of religious leaders and hundreds of rank-and-file believers who showed up for an interfaith convocation on hunger at Washington's National Cathedral in June 2005. Muslims, Buddhists, Sikhs, Jews, and all manner of Christians convened in the Episcopal cathedral to call for an end to hunger.

Addressing the gathering, Rev. Njongonkulu W. H. Ndungane, Anglican archbishop of Cape Town, South Africa, suggested that the event spoke to more than hunger.

"Perhaps we should learn the lesson that when we talk about doctrine and the abstract concepts of faith, we find far too many reasons to disagree," he

said. "But when we put our faith into practice, look what we can achieve together."[17]

There's no doubt about it. Jesus, after all, did not establish the Anglican Church, the Baptist Church, the Roman Catholic Church, or the Greek Orthodox Church. Jesus simply said, "Follow me."

CHAPTER 11

THE DEMOCRATIC PARTY

Finding Common Ground within Our Political Family

★ ★ ★

I didn't pay much attention to politics while I was growing up. My parents were registered Republicans, but really they were inherently nonpartisan—or bipartisan. They had as many Democratic friends as Republican friends. When the discussion around our family dinner table turned to public affairs, my parents never spoke with a partisan slant.

My dad didn't graduate from high school, but he was a smart man and a hard worker. He started a laundry business and made it successful. After I left home to attend Denison University near Columbus, Dad won a seat on the City Commission in Dayton, a predominantly Democratic city, then became mayor. His party affiliation didn't matter much because Dayton had a nonpartisan government and party labels didn't appear on the ballot.

Throughout high school and college, my big interest was sports, and I was good enough at football to become a Little All-American running back at Denison. Like so many people of my generation, however, I did get caught up a bit in the Kennedy mystique.

John and Bobby Kennedy and their extended families were young and vibrant and had ideas and great vision and were making things happen. They weren't afraid to take chances. They created things, such as the Peace Corps. They called on young Americans to serve, and many responded—including me. I have to confess, though, that my motivations for joining the Peace Corps weren't entirely altruistic. I did want to do good, but I also was looking for

adventure. And I thought it would be fun to see close-up a part of the world I didn't know anything about.

I was sent to teach English in Thailand, and that became a real wake-up call. I'd never been around poverty before. Now I was living in the midst of it, in a strange country, halfway around the world from where I had spent my entire life up to that point. It was mind-boggling just to discover that the little things we take for granted in the United States were beyond the reach of the Thais among whom I lived. All my life, if I became thirsty, all I had to do was turn on a faucet, fill a glass, and take a drink. When I was dirty, I stepped into a shower, turned on a faucet, and washed myself thoroughly under a stream of warm water. If you drank tap water in Thailand in the 1960s—where you could find it—you'd likely get very sick. Where I lived, you bathed outside by the well, contorting inside a kind of loose robe for privacy.

I returned to Dayton after about two years as a much more mature young man. The experience taught me not only about poverty but also about taking care of myself in a situation that was foreign to me. I was motivated to continue to do good, but I didn't have any clear path in mind. I started to settle into the real estate business. Then the Montgomery County Democratic Party asked me to run for the state legislature.

The Democrats thought I could be an attractive candidate. At the time, Dad was very popular as the Republican mayor of Dayton. Democratic Party leaders figured he could help me raise campaign contributions and reassure Republicans that it would be OK to vote for me. Both of my brothers were popular too. Mike had played football for Fairmont High School. Sam had won the silver medal for diving at the 1960 Olympics and had served one term as a state representative. I was fairly well known around Dayton in my own right because of my high school and college football career. I had roots in both Dayton, because of Dad's public office, and the adjacent suburb of Kettering, where my family lived until I went off to college.

The question was, was I really a Democrat? And the answer was yes. My parents' lack of strong partisanship was one factor. More important was the pull of the Kennedys, which my experience in the Peace Corps strengthened. It's hard for today's young people to understand, but politics was viewed as an honorable and exhilarating endeavor in the 1960s.

It's amazing how little I knew about public policy when I entered that first campaign in 1968. Even though the Vietnam War was tearing apart the country—and especially the Democratic Party—I focused on a few state and local issues in my race for the Ohio House of Representatives. I won, as the party leaders had anticipated, but initially I didn't make much of an impact in Columbus, the state capital. For my first two years in office, I pretty much kept my mouth shut and tried to figure out how the system worked.

People who know me today would find it hard to believe, but I was quite shy then. I was very nervous when speaking in front of groups. That natural inclination to remain silent was reinforced by the best political advice my dad ever gave me.

When I was recruited to run, I asked Dad about it.

"I'm young, I don't have any political experience, and there are so many things I don't know," I told him. "What am I going to do when somebody asks me about something I don't know anything about?"

"Tell them you don't know," he replied, "then go find the answer."

After I won election to my second term in 1970, I decided I was ready to start spreading my wings, speaking out on issues and taking stands. I became deeply involved in mental health, mental retardation, and environmental protection, which were really big issues at the time. An estimated twenty million Americans turned out for the first Earth Day in 1970. Ohio had become notorious for warehousing the mentally ill—and too often people who were misdiagnosed as mentally ill—in huge institutions. Reformers were trying to move those who weren't mentally ill into more appropriate living situations and to place those who were sick in treatment programs that really worked. Although Richard Nixon had won the White House for Republicans the year I won my first election, Democrats were on the rise in Ohio, capturing the governor's mansion and most other elected executive offices in 1970, the Ohio House in 1972, and both legislative chambers in 1974. Even though Republican Jim Rhodes took back the governor's seat in 1974, it remained an exciting time to be an Ohio Democrat.

I moved up to the Ohio Senate in 1973. Then Charles Whalen, the beloved moderate Republican who had been Dayton's congressman for six terms, announced he would not seek reelection in 1978, and I ran for his seat.

That congressional race was the only time I can honestly say I really enjoyed a campaign. The Republicans nominated a classy, smart, strong candidate—Dudley Kircher, president of the Dayton Area Chamber of Commerce. He ran as a classic urban Republican, and I was pretty much a textbook urban Midwestern Democrat. We held numerous debates, and we focused our campaigns for the most part on real issues. I think the main reason I won was that I addressed the major concerns of what then was the traditional core of the Democratic Party—blue-collar workers, Catholics, African-Americans, the poor, and the middle class. They comprised a majority of the Third Congressional District, so I won the election.

At the time, I was pro-choice. I had always felt uncomfortable with my position, but I also had always bought into the notion that a woman has the right to make up her own mind. Initially, this caused trouble for me with some longtime Democratic voters in my district, especially some Catholics. They constantly pushed me, and they became angry with me when I would not change my position. The harder they tried to push their issue—their faith—down my throat, the more stubborn I became. Later, after I changed my position, I remembered that experience as a lesson about the fact that you can't force your faith onto someone else.

A few years after I arrived in Congress, I began to come to and grow in faith. After much study and prayer, I decided that I had to oppose abortion because of my new conviction that the fetus is a child who matters to God. The media, of course, noticed—and reported—when I started to cast pro-life votes. Many pro-choice Democrats felt betrayed, and my name became mud in their circles. I noticed that some people who had been supporters and friends, when they saw me walking down the street toward them, actually would turn and walk the other way.

By this time I had held elected office for about fifteen years and had built a strong, positive personal relationship with my constituents. Most either didn't care very much about abortion, already were pro-life themselves, or were willing to accept my change on that issue because they agreed with me on so much else. Local Democratic Party leaders accepted my new position because they knew me, understood me, agreed with me on most things, and knew that on the core values of our party, I was going to keep winning.

Those leaders were right. I had no problem winning reelection in my congressional district. When I finally left Congress in 2002, I had been elected to twelve terms, more than anyone else in the history of the Third District. I knew I had to give up any thought of running for higher office, however. It was extremely unlikely that a pro-life candidate could win the Democratic Party nomination for governor or senator in Ohio, and it was unthinkable that a pro-life candidate could find a place on the national ticket. As time went on, I experienced another phenomenon—people who shared my faith but couldn't understand my politics.

Politicians of all stripes learn to shrug off disparagement of our occupation. Otherwise, we would risk becoming perpetually furious about the jokes told at our expense. Making fun of politics and government has been America's national pastime for much of our history. I doubt that Mark Twain was the first commentator to sink his barbs into public officeholders. But he was quite adept at it, writing back in the nineteenth century that "it probably could be shown by facts and figures that there is no distinctly native American criminal class except Congress."

I discovered, however, that as a man of faith, I'm subject to a special form of this traditional harassment. On more than one occasion, I was introduced to an audience as "a Christian and a congressman," then had to smile through gritted teeth as people giggled at this improbability. Once, in a church, an old fellow sitting near the front shouted, "Make up your mind, buddy! You can't be both."

The fact that I'm a Democrat elicits yet another variety of incredulity, this time often quite serious. I've stopped counting the number of times I've been asked how I can be a Democrat and a Christian. Usually I try to deflect the question with humor. "A lot of Republicans," I say, "are going to be surprised when they get to heaven—*if* they get to heaven—by all the Democrats they see walking around up there." Or I point out that when Jesus entered Jerusalem, he wasn't riding on an elephant!

Humor aside, these attitudes illustrate a serious problem for the Democratic Party. Democrats—particularly at the national level—have allowed themselves to become viewed not only as a secular party but as a party that is hostile to faith. A 2005 survey by the Pew Forum and the Pew Research Center found that a majority of Americans view the Republican Party as friendly toward religion, while less than a third feel that way about Democrats, for example. Interestingly,

nearly half of Americans say nonreligious liberals have too much control over the Democratic Party, and the same proportion say religious conservatives have too much influence on Republicans.[1]

The poll also showed why this is so significant. Eighty-one percent of Americans believe in God. Religion is very important to 60 percent and somewhat important to an additional 25 percent.[2]

Our party is not antifaith. But complaining won't do us any good. We've allowed ourselves to slip into this current hole. Now we have to find a way to climb out.

This has happened in part because of how cleverly the Republicans have been able to exploit our weaknesses. They have very publicly embraced people of faith, especially more conservative people of faith, while the Democrats at times have shunned opportunities to embrace people of faith. Republicans have set Democrats up to appear to be the antifaith party by engineering votes and running campaigns about symbols of faith—such as organized prayer in school or displays of the Ten Commandments in government buildings—which Democrats, who tend to be strong supporters of the separation of church and state, are apt to oppose. They have even managed to contrive campaigns that make Democrats appear to be proponents of same-sex marriage, although as far as I can tell, most Democrats aren't.

But Democrats have contributed to their own problems. Many Democratic public officials and candidates are uncomfortable talking about faith. This is not a moral failing. Like me, they believe it is better to show a sermon than to speak one. They worry about being labeled hypocrites, because so many politicians have misused faith for their own partisan purposes. They believe faith is a private thing. But Republicans have stepped into this vacuum and convinced many believers that they are the party of faith and we aren't.

Democrats also have let themselves be defined as the party of abortion. Absolute support for the right to abortion in all circumstances has become so important to party activists that many people perceive that it is our most important issue. It is a litmus test for national office, and that's true in many states as well.

There was a time when Republicans let themselves appear to be the narrow, intolerant party. That perception helped send GOP nominee Barry Goldwater

to a landslide loss in the 1964 presidential election. Because of the rising importance of abortion, however, Democrats became the narrow, intolerant party in much of the 1980s and 1990s. This unfortunate development became particularly obvious when Bob Casey, the pro-life Democratic governor of Pennsylvania, was prevented from speaking at the Democratic National Convention in 1992. Except for abortion, he was a solid traditional Democrat who focused on the needs of the poor, the blue-collar workers, and the middle class. Former Democrats who are pro-life still cite that as a reason for switching allegiances.

After Bill Clinton won the 1992 presidential election—in part because Republicans let intolerant extremists steal much thunder at their convention—I began working to insert a "conscience clause" in the next Democratic Party platform. The idea was to acknowledge that pro-life Democrats have a place in the party, even if the majority of party leaders are pro-choice. About forty pro-life Democrats in the House campaigned for this clause. President Clinton—a smart politician—understood the value of the big tent and supported our proposal.

In August 1996, during my first visit to North Korea, I was wakened by a phone call in the middle of the night from George Stephanopoulos, then a top Clinton aide. I was sleepy and befuddled and asked "George who?" when he introduced himself. "Tony," he said, "the president wants you to speak at the national convention in Chicago about the conscience clause you put into the platform." The North Koreans were tapping all of my phone conversations, of course. They must have thought I was somebody pretty special to get a call from the White House. I wondered if they had any idea what a conscience clause is!

I had quite the journey from famine-plagued, oppressed North Korea to the podium at the convention of the world's oldest democratic (small *d*) political party in just a few days. When I climbed onto the high stage and surveyed the large hall, I felt an important change was beginning to take place in my party.

"I'm a pro-life Democrat," I declared. "I'm one of about forty pro-life Democrats in the Congress, and many of us have felt left out by our party's position on abortion for many years. But this year is different. For the first time, the Democratic Party has included in our platform a conscience clause on this divisive issue."

I told these mostly pro-choice Democrats about the issues that were closest to my heart: "the needs of the vulnerable in our nation—the poor, the sick, the elderly, the children, and the unborn." I reminded them of Hubert Humphrey's proclamation that "the moral test of government is how that government treats those that are in the dawn of life, the children; those who are in the twilight of life, the elderly; and those who are in the shadows of life, the sick."

I talked about my experiences working among the poor and the hungry. I expressed my pride as a Democrat that our party supports government programs to aid the neediest and volunteers to work in private humanitarian organizations. I told how the Democratic Party in Dayton had opened its headquarters to shelter and feed homeless and hungry families.

"By doing this," I said, "we are showing that Democrats stand for more than just winning elections. We stand for helping people. We Democrats believe that our government, and our whole society, will be judged on how we treat the least of these among us." By adopting the conscience clause, I said, our party had reclaimed its status as "the party where every American can feel welcome and at home."

The clause declared that "the Democratic Party is a party of inclusion. We respect the individual conscience of each American on this difficult issue, and we welcome all our members to participate at every level of our party."

The clause was an important step, but only a step. Party leaders were so worried about pro-choice delegates' reactions to my speech that they went throughout the hall shortly beforehand, telling everyone to treat me with respect and not to boo. When I was introduced, I was greeted by polite applause. When I finished, I heard no more than a few isolated hands clapping.

I spoke again at the 2000 convention in Los Angeles, as did Bob Casey's sons. (He had died earlier in 2000.) That year's platform recognized that Democrats "have deeply held and sometimes differing views on issues of personal conscience like abortion and capital punishment" and described this diversity "as a source of strength, not as a sign of weakness."

As an ambassador, I couldn't take part in partisan politics in 2004, so I couldn't speak at the convention. But the Democratic platform again contained a conscience clause, this time noting that "members of our party have deeply held and differing views on some matters of conscience and faith. We

view diversity of views as a source of strength, and we welcome into our ranks all Americans who seek to build a stronger America. We are committed to resolving our differences in a spirit of civility, hope, and mutual respect." In another important step, Senate Democrats chose pro-life Harry Reid of Nevada to be their leader. As I write this, Bob Casey Jr. is the leading candidate for the 2006 Democratic U.S. Senate nomination in Pennsylvania, having been recruited into the race by the very pro-choice Senator Charles Schumer of New York, the chairman of the Democratic Senatorial Campaign Committee.

Democrats lost the 2000 and 2004 presidential elections, and Republicans currently control both chambers of Congress as well as the White House. Following the 2004 election, political analysts focused a great deal of attention on so-called values voters. The assumption was that these were people of faith and that they were conservative. Exit polls showed that one of the clearest predictors of voting preference is how often a voter attends religious services. Frequent worshipers voted for President Bush. Infrequent worshipers supported John Kerry, the Democratic presidential nominee.

These findings should give Democratic leaders pause. But they should not lead us to believe that people of faith won't vote for Democrats. We need to do several things, in my opinion. We need to engage people of faith and treat them with a level of respect that many Democratic activists have disdained in recent years. We also need to remind people of faith that there is more to being faithful in religion than opposing abortion and same-sex marriage. We must not concede the values voters to our opponents. Instead, we need to demonstrate how the Democratic Party advances the values that these voters should support. This is not a hard sell. A 2005 survey by the *National Catholic Reporter* found, for instance, that 84 percent of U.S. Catholics believe helping the poor is a very important Catholic teaching. The only other Catholic belief called very important by the same percentage was Jesus's resurrection.[3]

If you read the Bible, you'll learn that you can't be faithful to the teachings of Jesus without feeding the hungry, clothing the naked, housing the homeless, comforting the afflicted, healing the sick, befriending the stranger, and serving the poor. I've looked hard, but I've never found any passage of Scripture commanding tax cuts for the rich. I differ with most national leaders of my party

on abortion and some of the other so-called social issues. But we agree on much more. And I believe in focusing on agreement.

The trouble is that many Democratic activists haven't paid attention to their agreements with me—and with the many other people like me. They have publicly focused on what separates us, and the squeaky wheel has gotten most of the attention from the party leadership. I've felt marginalized by my party, as have many former Democratic voters who could become Democratic voters again if their concerns are listened to and they are treated with respect. It's time for party leaders to embrace these other common values with as much will and enthusiasm as they have shown for choice in regard to abortion. It's time to stop abandoning those who agree on so many important issues other than abortion. It's time pro-choice Democrats reach out to pro-life Democrats and say, "Let's work together on those issues. Let's elect candidates who will serve the poor and make peace—who will focus on the middle class instead of the rich."

Jim Wallis, evangelical activist and author, tells a wonderful story about meeting at Notre Dame University with Catholic activists who complained that the Democratic Party didn't respect them. One young woman said, "Four thousand unborn lives were lost today [to abortion]. How can I vote on anything else?" Then a young man said, "Well, nine thousand died today because of HIV/AIDS." Then another activist remarked, "Thirty thousand children died today because of utterly curable diseases, lack of food, and clean drinking water."[4]

There is plenty we can work on together, and we don't have to abandon important principles in order to do that. I can continue to work to end abortion, and they can continue to promote choice. We can work together on everything else—including reducing the demand for abortion—as long as we respect one another. *Compromise* is not a dirty word in politics. In fact, this kind of compromise is absolutely essential.

One way we can work together to reduce abortion is to reduce the number of unwanted pregnancies. I've learned from my work in the third world that education is the most effective form of birth control. In poor countries with no reliable social security system, people want to have many children who will take care of them in their old age. If the child mortality rate is high, parents want to have even more children so enough will be likely to survive. If we educate

mothers about breast-feeding, water purification, proper nutrition, and ways to keep their children healthy, more children will survive and parents won't feel the need to produce so many to begin with. If we also teach reading, writing, ways to earn money, and the wise management of finances, parents won't have to rely on their children so much for old-age security. Population growth will go down, the national economy will go up, and the people will live healthier, happier, and more prosperous lives.

Education works in the United States too. We need to teach girls and young women that having children out of wedlock and before they're capable of caring for them is a ticket to a life of poverty. We need to teach them about birth control and make it available to the poor. We need to teach them the kinds of skills that will enable them to grow up, get good jobs, and become parents when they're truly prepared for parenthood. In addition, we can work together to make adoption easier and to help young mothers cope with pregnancy and early parenthood.

It's also essential to seize those things we agree upon and exert real leadership again. Before Ronald Reagan won the White House in 1980, conservatives frequently complained that Republican politicians were just lightweight Democrats. If Democrats proposed spending a certain amount of money on a government program, Republicans would respond by proposing to spend just a little bit less. Democrats drove the public debate. Republicans always played defense.

Now Democratic officeholders and candidates look too much like lightweight Republicans. Republicans propose massive tax cuts for the rich, and Democrats say, "Let's not cut them quite so much." Democrats are neither yes nor no. They're kind of a definite maybe. And the people in the country who would vote Democratic are not quite sure what we stand for. Now it's the Democratic Party that plays defense.

I blame a lot of this on the enormous cost of campaigns and the enormous influence of rich individuals and special-interest groups that pay the cost. Democratic candidates have come to rely on the same kind of wealthy campaign contributors that Republicans do, so they feel pressure to support Republican-like policies. They've become timid about standing up for traditional Democratic policies that benefit the poor and the middle class. As a

result, poor and middle-class Americans feel that they have no real influence on the government—that it doesn't matter which party wins the elections—so many of them don't even bother to vote.

If Democrats are ever to take control of the government again, we have to prove that we deserve to govern by putting forth bold, visionary proposals that will be true to our heritage as Democrats and will enable us to show the values voters that we represent the values they should support. We need innovative ideas that will capture people's imaginations and address their real concerns.

I've observed over the years that the rich do a pretty good job of taking care of themselves. What we need is a lot of people who are committed to taking care of the poor, the middle class, and the blue-collar workers. That's what the Democratic Party traditionally has stood for, and we need to make clear that we continue to do so.

So let's just say flat out that the rich don't need any more tax cuts. Let's proudly advocate policies that will end hunger in America, put the unemployed to work, protect the good jobs of the middle class, preserve the environment, diversify our sources of energy, and make sure all Americans get the health care they need. Let's accept the responsibility of paying for the government services we want and not pass along a big debt for our children, our grandchildren, and their grandchildren to pay. And let's push for real campaign finance reform so that a rich business executive or a special-interest group can't buy a stronger voice in government than a factory worker or a custodian.

The Democratic Party has been playing defense for too long and has lost much of the opportunity to define the debate for mainstream Americans. I remember some good political advice I picked up in football: always have a good offense. In politics, when you play offense you leave the other guy only two choices. Either he agrees with you, and you win; or he disagrees, but you're still defining the debate. Let's tell people who we are and what we believe in. When our opponents contend that government is always the problem and never the solution, let's not hesitate to point out all the great things Democratic governments have accomplished, such as Social Security, Medicare, civil rights, women's rights, workers' rights, minimum wage, and environmental protection.

To start winning again, we need candidates and party leaders who lead.

Americans are looking for leaders, not politicians who wait to see which way the wind blows and which way the polls go. I speak frequently to groups of young people, and I know this is particularly true of them. They are primed for a leader to call them to a good cause, and they will respond. Democrats did well among young voters in the 2004 election, and we can do even better in the future.

It may seem odd that as a Democrat, I accepted the invitation to work as an ambassador for a conservative Republican president. But my acceptance of the position just stemmed naturally from my belief in focusing on agreement. While I disagree with many of President Bush's policies, I have found him to be a strong supporter of important humanitarian work I care deeply about.

He has done a very good job helping the poorest and the most vulnerable people in the third world. He proposed tripling the budget for fighting HIV/AIDS in Africa. He more than doubled humanitarian aid to the poorest countries and helped cancel the debt of fifty of the poorest. During the Bush administration, the United States has become by far the largest donor to developing nations.

When President Bush commissioned me as ambassador, he said, "Tony, I want you to put into action America's commitment to alleviate hunger and build hope in the world." That's the biggest job assignment I've ever had, and I believe the president has put his money where his mouth is in helping me carry out that assignment. That accomplishment surpasses partisan politics.

One of the keys to the president's success in elections has been the public's perception that he speaks plainly about what he believes. Even people who disagree with his policies respect that trait. If Democrats are going to start winning presidential elections again, our candidates have to learn to do the same.

They have to speak clearly and boldly about things that matter. They need to tell the truth, be sincere, and be comfortable in their own skin. I don't think you have to profess a specific kind of faith to win over the values voters. But I think you have to be comfortable in whatever you do say. I don't think it's a coincidence that the only Democrats to win presidential elections in the last fifty years are Jimmy Carter, perhaps the most devout president in our history, and Bill Clinton, who, despite personal sins that became so very public, was always at ease in discussing his faith. We all are sinners, after all.

I would never be the first to inject faith into a political campaign. But we

must not cede faith to the other side. If someone says people of faith can't vote for a Democratic candidate because he's pro-choice, that candidate must be ready to insist that all of the other issues be examined too. He has to be able to say that his faith commands him to feed the hungry, serve the poor, protect the environment that God created, and nurture children after they're born. These are moral issues. These are values. This is what government must do to serve "the least of these."

CHAPTER 12

WHERE WE ARE TODAY

Noteworthy Progress but Still a Long Way to Go

* * *

One evening in the fall of 2003, after a very difficult day traveling through the Democratic Republic of the Congo, I sat down for dinner at a restaurant in Kinshasa, the capital. I was tired. I was disturbed by the hardships I'd seen and the stories of atrocities I'd heard that day. I was trying to relax and restore myself for the equally disturbing work I would have to do the next morning.

A young American woman walked up and introduced herself. When she started talking, I was not the least bit unhappy that she had interrupted my meal.

"You're the congressman who sponsored the legislation on conflict diamonds, aren't you?" she asked. I nodded yes. "I want you to know that I'm here as a result of that," she continued. "I've been assigned to the Congo to help implement the Kimberley Process."

What a gratifying moment this was. For several years, Frank Wolf and I had campaigned to end the trade in so-called conflict or blood diamonds, which financed much of the warfare that ravaged the Congo and other African nations—and even helped to bankroll al-Qaeda. The Kimberley Process was the scheme that had finally been adopted to bring this insidious trade under control. And this young woman was flesh-and-blood evidence of our ultimate success.

When you do what I do, you really feed off instances like this. The problems of hunger, poverty, and oppression are so enormous and so resistant to solution that you're always in danger of feeling overwhelmed. To meet this young

woman, who was able to help solve a problem because of something Frank and I were a part of, was a powerful antidote to any temptation to give up. Fortunately, even amid the enormous troubles of Africa, there are enough such moments to keep me enthused about this work.

When people ask me if I find this work depressing, I tell them of times I've gone home in the evening, knowing I'd helped to feed thousands of people that day. I sleep well on nights like that. To those who worry these problems can't be solved, I point out that when I returned from Ethiopia in 1984, forty thousand people around the world were dying from hunger every day. Now it's twenty-five thousand. That's still an enormous number. But it would be many thousands more if people weren't out there working hard to ease the suffering.

Two activist groups told Frank and me about blood diamonds in 1999. Especially in Angola, Sierra Leone, and the Congo, warring factions were seizing control of mines and selling the diamonds to finance their armies. For a time, al-Qaeda purchased illicit African diamonds because their high value and small size made them easy to smuggle to various parts of the world where they could then be resold to finance terrorist operations.

The trade in blood diamonds was insidious because as those diamonds worked their way through the marketplace, they blended invisibly with the diamonds that had been produced by legitimate businesses. When diamonds showed up in jewelry stores, customers couldn't tell the difference. An American who purchased an engagement ring as a symbol of love had no way of knowing that the purchase was helping to finance cruelty, death, and destruction.

Al-Qaeda's involvement made blood diamonds a direct threat to the people of the United States and others who were terrorists' targets. In Africa, blood diamonds financed unspeakable atrocities on a daily basis. So Frank and I joined the international campaign to bring this trade to an end.

In Congress, we introduced legislation to require that all diamonds imported into the United States be tracked from the mine. Only diamonds certified as coming from legitimate sources could be sold here. We considered this a modest, reasonable requirement. Many other products sold in America carry labels that tell where they come from. If you can find out where wine or cheese or clothing is produced, why shouldn't you be able to learn where diamonds originate?

We also met with diamond dealers and jewelers, asking them to determine where their gems came from and to refuse to deal in blood diamonds. We added our voices to demands that international organizations forge agreements to stop the global blood-diamond traffic. As I mentioned earlier, we got Martin Sheen to cut an ad about the issue, which aired on the NBC television network after an episode of *The West Wing*. We staged protests in front of Tiffany and Cartier stores in New York. We even ended up being interviewed for a comprehensive, well-written story about blood diamonds that was published in an unexpected place—the *National Enquirer*.

This project took us to the absolute economic extremes of the earth. In London, I visited the headquarters of De Beers, the largest diamond dealer in the world, which once controlled 90 percent of the entire planet's diamond supply. De Beers officials led me on an incredible tour. We passed through rooms full of long tables that were covered with piles of raw diamonds. I saw millions of raw diamonds, tons of diamonds. They were like pebbles on a beach. A De Beers executive put four rough diamonds in the palm of my hand and said they probably were worth about $16 million.

In Africa, we saw what the blood diamonds financed. Warlords, who had launched their evil careers by commanding ragtag guerrilla bands of a few hundred fighters, used profits from the diamond trade to build armies with thousands of uniformed, heavily armed troops. These were not well-disciplined soldiers but amoral sadists who employed unspeakable cruelty to terrorize the people. Their strategy was to rule through fear.

Warfare in Sierra Leone killed tens of thousands, a third of them younger than five years old, and drove more than two million from their homes, many of whom left the country entirely. The rebels spread terror by slicing hands and arms off civilians and hacking others to death. Thousands of girls and young women were abducted, raped, and turned into sex slaves for the soldiers. As farmers fled their lands, they lost their ability to grow food, so malnutrition soared.

Frank and I visited refugee camps where we met children as well as adults whose hands and ears had been cut off. They told us stories of rebels capturing civilians and instructing the captives to choose which extremity they would lose. Others described being forced to reach into a bag and draw out a

piece of paper containing a picture of a body part, which immediately would be hacked off. One man told us rebels gave him the choice of losing both of his hands or having his two children killed. He chose, of course, to lose his hands. And after the rebels sliced them off, they killed his children anyway.

In Sierra Leone and Angola, rebels fought government soldiers for control of the country and its mineral resources. In the Congo, a half dozen other nations sent in troops to seize control of diamond mines and loot the Congo's resources. Blood diamonds were both motivating and financing the warfare.

The United States had enormous power to disrupt this trade because Americans purchase about two-thirds of all diamonds sold in the world each year. We could strike a major blow simply by stopping our own purchases. Because of our importance to the diamond market, we could apply effective pressure on other countries and on the diamond industry itself.

Diamond industry executives initially told us it would be impossible to track raw diamonds, and they opposed our calls for action. We introduced legislation anyway. And representatives of diamond-producing countries and the industry, prodded by humanitarian activist groups, met in Kimberley, South Africa, to discuss what they could do. By 2001 we were able to introduce a bill, the Clean Diamonds Act, that was supported by humanitarian groups and the industry.

Congress finally approved legislation in 2003, after I had left the House. Also that year, the talks in Kimberley produced what came to be known as the Kimberley Process Certification Scheme, a mechanism for keeping blood diamonds out of international trade. The United Nations began imposing sanctions on diamond-producing countries that didn't keep blood diamonds off the market.

The blood diamonds story provides a good example of how you have to go about trying to measure progress in the world's poorest places. (Measuring with statistics is tricky, although we must use them. It's hard to gather statistical information in such spots, so different researchers can come up with different numbers. And, of course, they change over time.) Small gains should be celebrated. Comprehensive solutions take a long time. Efforts by so many individuals, organizations, and governments reduced the

traffic in blood diamonds and thus cut the flow of funds to warlords and terrorists. But the problem is not solved.

In mid-2005, Global Witness and Partnership Africa Canada, the two activist groups that brought blood diamonds to Frank's and my attention, released a report saying that "considerable progress has been made" but "the Kimberley Process still has a long way to go."[1]

Diamonds continue to finance some fighting in the Democratic Republic of the Congo and the Ivory Coast, the groups said, even though both countries signed the Kimberley agreement. The organizations said the United States needed to publish better data about its diamond trade.

If I were to set foot in the Congo for the first time today, I'd think it was a horrible mess. And it is. But you can detect some signs of progress even there.

From the mid-1960s to the mid-1990s, Mobutu Sese Seko ruled the Congo—which he renamed Zaire—with increasing brutality, and he stole everything he could grab. With support from Rwanda and Uganda, the Congo rebels overthrew Mobutu in 1997. Fighting, which included participation by armies from a half dozen neighboring countries, continued until the last of the foreign soldiers officially withdrew from the Congo in 2003. An estimated 3.5 million died during that time from war, famine, and disease. At least two million more were driven from their homes.[2] Despite the official end to the war, conflict continues in the eastern Congo, with the purported continuing participation of foreign troops. And the entire country will suffer for many years from the effects of lengthy warfare, theft, and the disruption of all aspects of the economy.

The country's transportation system lies in ruins. Travel is further disrupted by countless land mines left over from the warfare. Per capita income is only about $100 a year. Life expectancy is forty-nine years.[3] Bandits roam the countryside, and people are afraid to return to their homes. Many Congolese lost much more than a place to live.

Traveling around the Congo, I met hundreds of girls and women who had been raped—many violently by multiple assailants. The crimes were so brutal that they required corrective surgery as well as psychological counseling.

The Congo's warlords also distinguished themselves by forcing some thirty thousand children—more than a third of them girls—to take up arms. I met

child soldiers who were eight years old, wore camouflage uniforms, and had carried assault rifles into battle. They looked lost and scared and mean. They appeared as if their very lives—certainly their childhoods—had been snuffed out of them.

They had been plucked from their homes, given guns, and immediately ordered to kill someone—perhaps a neighbor or a friend. If they didn't kill, they were told, their entire family would be killed instead. So they immediately became killers and assumed the status of both victims and victimizers.

Now these child soldiers and rape victims suffer the additional pain of being rejected by their families and communities. Many parents associate rape with shame and refuse to let raped daughters return home. Many communities fear child soldiers and want them to stay away.

The signs of hope in this unfortunate place are small but significant.

The CIA categorizes the Congo's current government as a dictatorship that is "presumably undergoing a transition to representative government."[4] Our State Department credits Congo president Joseph Kabila with making significant progress toward freedom. The government is working with the World Bank and the International Monetary Fund to repair its broken economy. And the Congo has vast natural resources—both minerals and fertile land—that could support a booming economy if the country acquires effective leadership. Inflation fell from more than 500 percent in 2000 to about 7 percent in 2003. Exports jumped by two-thirds from 2002 to 2004, according to estimates by the International Monetary Fund.[5]

The United States, the World Food Program, and other agencies and countries are helping humanitarian organizations address the difficult problems of individual victims. They offer food, lodging, and counseling to the former child soldiers to help them reclaim lives as normal children. They provide medical care and counseling to the raped girls and women.

As I have throughout the world, I encountered some remarkable individuals doing what's in front of them in the Congo. One example, I have to confess with chagrin, I almost passed up the opportunity to see.

Jay Nash, of the U.S. Agency for International Development, helped to guide me during one of my visits to the Congo. He kept asking me to visit a project he was running during his time off, using his own money. I was busy

and tired and distracted and really didn't want to add one more task to my schedule. But he was so persistent that finally I agreed. And I'm so glad I did.

Children still contract polio in the Congo. When they do, it's almost always a sentence to a lifetime of abject poverty and begging. Their parents can't afford to buy them prostheses or wheelchairs. They can't find employment. They get around by crawling or slithering on the ground like serpents. They sit or lie on the ground, and they beg.

Jay bought two houses in a compound in Kinshasa. He went to a junkyard and bought some scrap metal. He created a little workshop in his compound. He recruited a couple of kids with polio and taught them how to build simple leg braces from the scrap metal. When he brought me to see his compound, there must have been one hundred children and young adults in the yard, almost all of them wearing leg braces, a bunch of them playing soccer, others singing and dancing. It was incredible. I thought, *He has literally put these kids on their feet!*

Some of these kids were homeless. He gave them a safe, loving place to live. He taught them a valuable skill. They make braces for themselves and for others. Because they're mobile, they can get out into the community and get jobs. Some of the young adults now work full-time in Jay's shop.

I'm not the only person who has been impressed by Jay's work. I came across a story in the *Philadelphia Inquirer* about NBA star Dikembe Mutombo, a Congo native, visiting the compound and immediately pledging to donate $1,000 a month to the project.

I can tell stories like that about most of the countries I've visited. In many places, such as in the Congo, the stories are part of a bigger picture of a country slowly getting better.

Sierra Leone, for instance, has now become a functioning democracy. More than five hundred thousand people have returned to their homes there. Because the farmers are getting back on their land, rice production has risen to 86 percent of the prewar level.[6] Children are going back to school.

The country remains desperately poor even though, like the Congo, it contains great wealth in natural resources. The resources, tragically, have not been developed for the advantage of the people. One result of the Kimberley Process is to move the diamond trade away from the hands of

smugglers and toward legitimate markets that can benefit the country as a whole. Sierra Leone currently has a per capita income of just $150 a year, a life expectancy of thirty-four years, and the highest infant mortality rate in the world, 16.6 percent.[7] It once was known for education, trade, arts, crafts, and well-managed businesses. If violence and corruption can be kept at bay, there's no reason this country can't reclaim that legacy. But it won't happen tomorrow.

Angola, the third country so horribly terrorized by blood diamonds, has been at peace since 2002, except in the Cabinda province to the northeast. Our State Department describes the government there as nominally democratic. President Jose Eduardo dos Santos promised that elections would be held sometime in 2006. Primarily because of its oil deposits, Angola's economy has been growing recently.

A quarter century of civil war levied a horrendous toll, however. Up to 1.5 million Angolans died, and more than 5 million were driven from their homes. Once, Angola exported agricultural products. Now two-thirds of its people survive on subsistence farming, and the country imports about half its food. Life expectancy is less than forty-seven years.[8] Hospitals lack medicine. Schools lack books.

When I search for good news in these places, I seize on two things. One is the big picture—whether fewer people are poor, hungry, and oppressed; whether the government is moving toward democracy; whether there is evidence of growing economic activity. The other is whether I come across people who are doing what's in front of them, making life better in some particular place. People like Jay Nash.

If I focused only on the big picture and not on the individual rays of hope, it would be hard to remain optimistic. There are so many ups and downs, so many steps back to erase the steps forward.

The number of people dying from hunger each day has dropped by more than a third over the last two decades, and that's an unmistakable sign of progress. Between 1970 and 1997, the number of malnourished people throughout the world fell to 791 million from 959 million. That was more good news. However, since then, the world's hungry population has climbed back to more than 850 million, in large part because of the many troubles in Africa.[9]

Nearly 19 percent of the planet's population—1.2 billion people—earn less than a dollar a day. In West Africa, 60 percent of the people live at that income level, and throughout Africa it's about 46 percent. One in five Africans earns less than fifty cents a day. Of the thirty-seven nations with the lowest life expectancy on earth, thirty-six are in Africa. (The other is Afghanistan.) In southern Africa, 40 percent of the population—35.7 million people—undernourished. Africa is the only continent that has become poorer over the last twenty-five years.[10] Drought has damaged crops in various African regions in recent years. Swarms of locusts made things even worse in West Africa. But people—particularly cruel, greedy, or incompetent leaders—often cause the worst tragedies. Africans have a saying: When elephants fight, the grass dies. They see the truth of that aphorism every time warlords field their armies and civilians suffer worse than the soldiers. But bad leaders can destroy a country even without taking it to war, and that's what's happening in Zimbabwe.

Zimbabwe used to be the breadbasket of southern Africa. Now it's a basket case. Once an exporter of agricultural products, it now has to import food and accept donations of food that it can't afford to buy. What once was one of Africa's wealthiest and most productive economies has contracted by a third since 2000. Unemployment is around 70 percent. Inflation ranged between 300 and 600 percent in 2004. In 1998 it took twenty-four Zimbabwean dollars to buy one U.S. dollar. In late 2005 it took twenty-five thousand. In 1980 the average Zimbabwean could expect to live more than sixty-five years. Now life expectancy is less than forty years. A quarter of Zimbabwe's adult population has AIDS at a time when the country's health-care system is collapsing.[11]

Drought and flooding contributed to Zimbabwe's agricultural and economic decline, but it's largely man-made and avoidable. The man is Robert Mugabe, Zimbabwe's president, who has been guilty of corruption, human rights violations, and the implementation of policies that just don't make sense. The country's food shortage stems in large part from Mugabe's decision in 2000 to seize land from competent white farmers and give it to cronies and supporters who knew nothing about farming. In mid-2005, under the guise of "urban renewal" or "cleanup," he turned his wrath on poor black Africans, destroying shantytowns and leaving the former residents with no place to live or to work. Some seven hundred thousand people lost their homes or their

jobs.[12] All this is happening in a country with valuable mineral deposits, fertile soil, and a deteriorating infrastructure that is still better than what is found in most of Africa.

I visited Zimbabwe in August 2005 in connection with a shipment of U.S. food relief. As I traveled around to observe some of the country's problems, I met a large number of families shortly after they had been driven off their land. They told me they had documents that proved their ownership. But policemen took the documents, tore them up, and chased away the rightful property owners.

I visited a feeding center operated by Africare Zimbabwe, a nongovernmental relief organization that the U.S. government funds. I tried to visit Hopely Farm, near the capital of Harare, a military-run camp where several thousand people have been living since their homes were destroyed in the "cleanup" campaign. The authorities wouldn't let me in. I was told in a hushed tone that the government didn't want me to see the place because old people were dying there.

We're feeding the people of Zimbabwe under our policy of not letting politics interfere with humanitarian work. But Mugabe makes that work difficult. The World Food Program estimated that 4.3 million Zimbabweans needed food aid in 2005.[13] Government red tape delays delivery of food to the country and its distribution to those who need it. And Mugabe is anything but grateful for this assistance.

Two months after my Zimbabwe trip, Mugabe came to Rome to attend the celebration of the UN Food and Agriculture Organization's sixtieth anniversary. I sat in the audience. Mugabe was allowed to speak.

Instead of thanking us for the aid, he labeled President Bush and British Prime Minister Tony Blair "international terrorists" and likened them to Adolf Hitler. He called me an "agent of imperialism." It was an outrageous performance at an event that was supposed to draw attention to hunger and encourage all nations to do more to help the poor. But that's what we've come to expect from Mugabe.

Thankfully, I've observed progress in places that have suffered even worse than Zimbabwe has.

I felt as if I had arrived at the gates of hell when I traveled to the Tanzania-Rwanda border while genocide was being perpetrated in Rwanda in 1994. The

mountains above the Kagera River, which separates the two countries, were breathtaking in their beauty. The scene along the river was as ugly as anything I had ever encountered. Bloated corpses swirled in the river current. Bodies got hung up on rocks and moved in an eerie fashion with the flow of the water. *How is it possible that this could be done by human beings to other human beings?* I wondered.

I struggled to describe the scene adequately to people back in the United States. "Can you imagine visiting something as beautiful as Niagara Falls, only to realize with horror that you're seeing rotting corpses floating in the water below?" I asked. "This is not a modern war. It's a feudal war. People are being hacked to death with machetes, one by one."

Longtime animosities between Rwanda's two major ethnic groups— Hutus, who comprise 85 percent of the population; and Tutsis, who make up 14 percent—fueled the genocide. In just three months, vicious Hutu militias killed eight hundred thousand Tutsis and moderate Hutus who wanted to avoid the clash. Two million Rwandans were driven out of the country, and another million fled their homes for safer places inside the country. After the fighting ended, Rwandans were scattered around their country and in neighboring Tanzania, Burundi, and the Congo. During my trip to the border, I saw three hundred thousand refugees at a single camp in Tanzania. In their panicked flights, husbands became separated from their wives, parents from their children.

When I returned to the region on a later trip, I encountered a remarkable program run by the Irish humanitarian organization Concern. In caring for refugees, Concern's workers noticed how many were separated from their families. The workers became particularly distressed about the many parentless children in their care. They suspected that many of these kids were not really orphans but had living parents someplace else in Rwanda or a neighboring country. Some of these children were so young and in so much shock that they couldn't tell the Concern workers what their names were, where they had come from, who their parents were, or whether they had any idea where their parents might be.

Concern recruited local mothers who could relate to the children. The mothers would spend time with the children every day, talk with them, try to

draw out information about them and their families. They'd try to get the kids to remember their names, nicknames, how old they were, what region they had lived in, what city, what town. They asked the kids what their parents looked like, what their names were. They found out whether there were particular toys the children liked to play with, particular things they liked to do. They took photos of the kids and posted them in markets all around the country, along with whatever information they had been able to elicit about the children and their families. And they had tremendous success.

I went with some workers and a child on an excursion into the mountains where they had circulated the child's picture. The child's parents, who had fled to a mountain village to escape the violence raging around their old family home, saw the picture and identified him. When we got to the village, the Concern workers participated in one of the most exciting and rewarding moments they will ever experience. Just witnessing it tore my heart out. These parents had literally run for their lives—run for miles to escape the brutality being visited upon their neighbors. In the horrific chaos, the child had been separated from his mother and father. Now these humanitarian workers were reuniting the child, who didn't think he'd ever see his parents again, with his mother and father, who believed their child was dead.

This was difficult work. Concern workers had to recruit mothers who were willing to spend a great deal of time with these kids. Then they had to distribute information about the children around a primitive country with poor roads and little in the way of modern telecommunications. To a great extent, the information had to circulate by word of mouth. But when I saw them bring a family back together, it was hard to imagine any accomplishment that could be more important.

Rwanda remains a desperately poor country, but it is possible to detect progress here.

The challenges are obvious, starting with the continuing trials of people accused in the genocide and the need to reconcile Tutsis and Hutus into lasting peaceful coexistence. Clashes persist among Tutsis, Hutus, and other ethnic groups along the borders between Burundi, Uganda, the Democratic Republic of the Congo, and Rwanda. Rwanda has the unwelcome distinction of being both predominantly rural and the most densely populated country

in Africa. Nine of ten Rwandans depend on subsistence farming for their livelihood. More than a third of the population is undernourished. Annual per capita income is $206; life expectancy is less than forty-seven years.[14]

Hope for Rwanda's future builds upon the international community's commendable, though horribly late, response to the genocide. Too late to save the eight hundred thousand killed, the United States and other countries mobilized an enormous relief effort following the genocide, and the United Nations deployed an effective peacekeeping force. Most refugees returned to Rwanda. An elected president and legislature now run the government. Corruption and crime are relatively low. The government is implementing economic reforms and is working to build an effective educational system and improve health-care programs. Crop yields are rising as more effective agricultural techniques are being adopted.

The place I always look the hardest for hope is Ethiopia, where I discovered my life's mission in 1984. And I always find hope abounding in an isolated place called Yetebon, about ninety miles south of the capital of Addis Ababa. It's there that Marta Gabre-Tsadick and her husband, Demeke Tekle-Wold, have turned absolutely nothing into the most complete private relief and development project I've ever seen.

As I discussed briefly earlier, Marta and Demeke fled Ethiopia when Communist rebels overthrew Emperor Haile Selassie in 1974. They settled as refugees in Indiana where in 1977 they founded Project Mercy with Rev. Charles Dickinson and his wife, Fran. While Marta and Demeke lived in the United States, Project Mercy offered relief and relocation assistance to African refugees. After the Communists were overthrown in 1991, Marta and Demeke returned to Ethiopia and began their work at Yetebon, a poor rural community of about seventy thousand. They do all their work with private funding, most of it raised in the United States.

When Marta and Demeke arrived, Yetebon had essentially no public facilities. On my first visit, I was struck by how they seemed to be living in the middle of nowhere. The area looked as though it might have some promise for agriculture, because the vegetation was green. The fields were surrounded by fairly big hills. There were trees, but I wouldn't really call it a forest. Except for the uncertain rain, the weather there was perfect. Yetebon lies near the equator,

but it has a fairly high elevation, so temperatures year-round tend to range from comfortably cool at night to 75 or 80 degrees during the day.

The first thing Marta and Demeke did was build a school, starting with first graders and gradually increasing the scope into high school. Children from all over the region were invited to attend, some walking three, four, even five miles a day to do so. I've watched the kids arrive in the morning, many of them barefoot. The teachers instruct these children in more than the three Rs. They teach healthy habits, cleanliness, the importance of washing their hands after going to the bathroom. If kids arrive dirty, they have to shower and put on clean clothes. They also receive two nourishing meals each day.

Next, Marta and Demeke started an agricultural project, bringing in experts from Ethiopia and the United States to teach the local farmers how to grow a greater variety of crops and how to apply better techniques to increase their yields. In a country often short of water, they ran pipes into the hills above their land to carry water from mountain springs down to the farmland. They dug a well.

Marta and Demeke are remarkably successful at recruiting help—not just donations but knowledgeable volunteers, mostly from America but also from elsewhere around the world. They've built and staffed their facilities with volunteer schoolteachers, high-tech workers, carpenters, bakers, cooks, sanitation experts, health-care professionals, and experts in the latest farming techniques.

They put up a state-of-the-art hospital—probably better than any hospital in Addis. Donors gave them all the equipment. Doctors and nurses volunteer to treat the patients.

Project Mercy once fed 250,000 people during a drought. But its primary goal is to help the people of Yetebon become self-sufficient. That's why, in addition to school classes for children, there are courses for adults in carpentry, metalworking, basket making, embroidery, spinning, and other useful skills—as well as a day-care center so both mothers and fathers can become educated and hold gainful employment.

These skills are being put to use in the construction of beautiful residential neighborhoods. The houses are simple but solid. They have indoor plumbing

with hot and cold running water—something unheard of in the past. Local carpenters build the houses' furniture.

Marta and Demeke are Christians working in a predominantly Muslim community, and early on that led to tensions. But I've met Muslim leaders in the area, and now they praise and thank these two Christians for the good they've done for the community.

Compared to most of Ethiopia, Marta and Demeke have created paradise.

Ethiopia is far better off today than when I first visited the country two decades ago, but it still has a long way to go. The people enjoy more freedom than Ethiopia has ever known, but the government doesn't meet our standards for liberty and democracy. Annual per capita income is just $116, and life expectancy is forty-nine years.[15]

When I visited in 2004 and 2005, I still encountered mothers who had to walk hours to feeding centers to get nutritious food for their underweight babies. Particularly because of AIDS, I met young orphans who were caring for even younger siblings.

While Ethiopia no longer faces mass starvation—and the government wouldn't try to hide a need for assistance—about a tenth of the population still regularly requires food assistance. And that number can double when unfavorable weather leads to low crop yields.

The key, of course, is to do as Marta and Demeke do and help Ethiopians become able to fend for themselves. That is now the Ethiopian government's policy. In dramatic contrast to the Ethiopian regime of 1984, which refused to admit the extent of famine during the great drought, the current government has acknowledged the severity of hunger there and has formed a coalition for food security with donor nations, UN agencies, and nongovernmental humanitarian organizations.

I witnessed the impact of that approach when a group of farmers showed me through fields where they were learning how to apply modern agricultural techniques to grow a wider variety of vegetables to nourish their families and to sell for cash. They were feeding themselves, and they were proud that they were able to do so.

There are days when what I do doesn't seem to produce even that drop in the ocean that Mother Teresa talked about. But then I'll discover a place where

a piece of legislation I sponsored is having a concrete effect on reducing the suffering of war, as I did when I encountered that young woman in Kinshasa who was working to end the trade in blood diamonds. Or I'll meet people who, on a small scale, make individuals' lives more worth living, as I did when Jay Nash showed me how he helps polio victims in that same city, and as I do each time I visit Marta and Demeke in Yetebon. Or I'll explore sites where organizations I support are distributing food that is keeping people alive in an emergency while also helping them learn to become self-sufficient in the future.

At times like that, I remember that what I do—what they do—saves lives and makes lives better, and that in the long run there really is hope. And I think to myself, *This is not a bad day. I'll sleep pretty good tonight.*

CHAPTER 13

NEW ORLEANS

America Discovers
Its Invisible Poor

I didn't witness firsthand the tragedy that Hurricane Katrina visited upon New Orleans at the end of August 2005. I was in Rome, as the U.S. ambassador to the UN food and agricultural agencies that are headquartered there. So, like most of the world, I watched my television set in horror as the hurricane spread destruction across parts of Louisiana, Mississippi, and Alabama, then left tens of thousands of people to fend for themselves in the cruel aftermath.

Unlike most of my fellow viewers, however, I knew exactly why the calamity unfolded as it did. And I knew there quickly would be a counterflood of help from throughout the United States.

Hurricane Katrina revealed two important truths about America. The first is that our poor are invisible, so most Americans don't even realize they're there. The second is that when Americans are exposed to people in need, they want to help.

Whatever else went wrong before, during, and after Katrina slammed into the American Southeast, most of the subsequent suffering in New Orleans stemmed from one oversight: no one made provisions to evacuate the poor who couldn't evacuate themselves. It happened because the people who were in charge—or should have been in charge—didn't think about the large number of poor people who lived in New Orleans and what it means to be poor in the inner city.

The city government gave an order to evacuate, and evacuation was no

problem for the middle and upper classes. They just packed up their cars or headed for the airport and traveled away from the hurricane zone to stay temporarily with relatives or friends or at hotels. Tens of thousands of poor New Orleans residents didn't have cars, however. Many didn't have friends or relatives outside New Orleans with whom they could stay. They certainly didn't have enough cash to pay for hotel or motel rooms for any length of time. They couldn't afford to buy airline tickets. Many didn't even have enough money to buy bus tickets to take their families away from danger.

Unlike affluent Americans, most poor people aren't mobile. They aren't used to taking vacations around the country or around the world. They live in the same neighborhood for generations. They don't own stocks and bonds. Many don't even have a bank account. Everything they own is in their homes, which they probably don't have adequately insured. So it's much more difficult for them to pack up and leave in any circumstance. Not only can they not afford it—not only do they have no place to go—but they're reluctant to leave all of their possessions behind, unprotected in neighborhoods where crime is more common than in more affluent communities.

Most Americans didn't understand this. That's why most Americans' initial reaction toward those left stranded in New Orleans was something like, how could they have been so stupid as to stay there? As the horrors of life in flooded New Orleans became clear, the reaction changed to, how can this be happening in the United States? I was asked that question many times by Europeans as well.

I wrote earlier in this book that hunger and poverty in America differ from hunger and poverty in the third world. One difference, I wrote, is that you don't find America's poor cowering in refugee camps. Yet, for a brief time in New Orleans, that's exactly what we saw. Thousands of New Orleanians fled their flooded homes and converged on the Louisiana Superdome indoor football stadium and the enormous Ernest N. Morial Convention Center. Unlike in most third world refugee camps, however, these American refugees didn't encounter humanitarian aid workers ready to give them food, shelter, clothing, and medical care. They were completely on their own—hot, wet, dirty, hungry, perhaps ill, perhaps fearing for their health and safety or for the health and safety of their children or their elderly relatives. There was no food,

no water, no electricity, no air-conditioning, no police officers, no medical personnel, no working bathrooms.

People died in these conditions, and no one was around to collect their bodies. So they were left where they died. At the convention center, one body was in a wheelchair, one on a chaise lounge, another on the ground. Other bodies were found floating in the flooded streets.

This extreme event was an aberration in America. But these people were poor before Katrina struck, and they will be poor into the future. And they have their counterparts in every big city in America and throughout rural America as well. They live on Dayton's west wide, in inner-city Detroit, in the small towns and countryside of southeastern Ohio and in the rest of Appalachia, in the southern counties of Mississippi, in central Los Angeles, on Indian reservations throughout the West, and in the shadow of the Capitol's dome in Washington, D.C., among many other places. As U.S. Senator Barack Obama of Illinois said, "The people of New Orleans weren't just abandoned during the hurricane. They were abandoned long ago—to murder and mayhem in the streets, to substandard schools, to dilapidated housing, to inadequate health care, to a pervasive sense of hopelessness." And that is true of America's other poor neighborhoods.

Nearly a quarter of New Orleans residents lived below the poverty level. In the Lower Ninth Ward, where most of the Superdome and convention center refugees had their homes, about a third were poor. In one especially hard-hit neighborhood, according to an Associated Press analysis, nearly three-quarters were poor and just one-third had a car.[1] About 120,000 residents of the New Orleans area didn't have access to a car, according to Shirley Laska of the University of New Orleans Center for Hazards Assessment, Response, and Technology.[2] Nationally, 12.7 percent of the population—thirty-seven million Americans—live in poverty, and the rate has been rising in recent years.[3] But the middle class and the rich seldom see the poor. And even when they are forced into our attention—as they were in New Orleans—we quickly forget once the drama has passed.

As much as I talked about domestic hunger while I served in Congress—as much as I called it to the attention of my constituents—even some of my best friends would say, "Tony, that can't be true. We never see many poor people."

And I'd say, "You don't see them because you don't look for them. When you drive from your home to your work, you don't see poor people on the sidewalk begging for food. You don't drive through the poorest parts of town. You don't go to the food banks and the soup kitchens. You don't talk with these people. You don't listen to these people."

When I give speeches, I tell people that nearly ten million Americans live in homes where someone frequently goes hungry, that more than twenty-five million live in homes that are at risk of hunger, that twenty to twenty-five million stave off hunger by frequenting food banks and soup kitchens. Even more disturbing, after declining during the late 1990s, these figures have been going up since 2001. My listeners scratch their heads and ask, "Where are these people? I never see these people."

To see hungry people, to see children falling asleep in class because they don't eat well, to see parents and children living on the street, you have to go look for them. And most Americans don't do that. But when you show Americans the poor and the hungry—when you connect with them and educate them and they see the problems themselves—they don't turn their backs. They want to help. They respond. We are a compassionate people, a giving people. We care. And that's the other truth about America that Hurricane Katrina revealed so dramatically.

As soon as they figured out what was happening in Katrina's wake, the American people opened their pocketbooks, their communities—even their homes—to help. Organizations all over the country raised funds for hurricane relief. Corporations contributed hundreds of millions of dollars. Other companies donated products or services of value to the relief efforts. Television networks broadcast fund-raising telethons. Employers from around the country offered jobs to the suddenly unemployed. People with potentially useful skills volunteered to travel to the affected areas to work. Communities across the country provided shelters and offered to send some of their emergency crews to help with rescue, recovery, and security efforts. Individual families invited strangers to occupy spare bedrooms in their homes.

The people also showed that they are far ahead of their political leaders when it comes to understanding what values are really important at times like this. An Associated Press survey asked where the government should find the

money to pay its share of the hurricane relief costs. Only 11 percent said it should come from cutting other domestic programs, even though that is what leaders in Congress wanted to do.[4] Another survey, by the Bendixen & Associates polling firm, found that a plurality of Americans believe our top priority as a nation should be fighting poverty.[5]

If we could sustain this level of awareness and concern beyond the immediate aftermath of the New Orleans tragedy, the goals of ending hunger and poverty really could be achieved. And it really wouldn't be that hard.

I've learned through my work over the last two decades that none of us has to take the burden of the entire world on our shoulders. None of us has to solve every problem. As Mother Teresa taught me, we just have to do the thing that's in front of us. Millions of people did that in the aftermath of Hurricane Katrina. Some did a great deal—leaving their homes, traveling to the disaster scene, working day and night for an extended time to help in the relief efforts. Others did a little bit—contributing a small amount of money to a humanitarian organization, for example. They all did what they could. Together, that amounted to a great deal.

That's all we have to do to wage an effective fight against hunger and poverty and oppression around the world—do what's in front of us. For some, that will mean joining a humanitarian organization and setting off for a strange land to work with the poor and the hungry in a place like the Congo or Rwanda. For others, it will mean leaving home to work with disadvantaged Americans in an inner city or up in an Appalachian hollow or on an Indian reservation. For yet others, it will mean volunteering close to home at a food bank, tutoring poor children in a local school, or helping at a homeless shelter a couple of nights a month. Some will join campaigns to demand that the government do more for the poor, the hungry, and the oppressed. Some will work to elect candidates who are committed to helping "the least of these." Some will run for office themselves. Others will simply visit an elderly shut-in up the street or write a check to a respected charity.

Together, they will change the world.

What will you do?

HOW TO HELP

I t's easy to join the many people who give some of their time and treasure to help the less fortunate. All you have to do is look around you, find someone with a need, and address it. It can be as simple as visiting with a lonely elderly neighbor, saying kind words to a child who is unpopular at school, or giving blood to the Red Cross. You can donate money to a good cause. You can volunteer to help out at a food bank or work in your church's clothing drive. If you see a need that isn't being addressed, you can get together with friends and neighbors and create an organization to address it. Many of the most effective humanitarian organizations in the world started out exactly that way.

It you'd rather get involved with an established national or international organization, here's a list of some of the best. All accept financial contributions. Some accept volunteers. Most employ humanitarian workers. You can learn more about them by visiting their Internet sites.

Bread for the World: Christian organization that campaigns for government programs to address hunger. Membership includes fifty-four thousand individuals and twenty-five hundred Catholic, Protestant, and Orthodox churches. Members lobby their U.S. representatives and senators. Bread for the World Institute carries out research and educational projects, including an annual report on hunger. 50 F St. NW, Suite 500, Washington, DC 20001. Phone 202-639-9400 or 800-822-7323. Fax 202-639-9401. www.bread.org.

CARE: Founded in 1945 to ship CARE Packages of relief supplies to survivors of World War II. Now runs a wide range of emergency relief and long-term development programs in more than seventy countries. Offers short-term volunteer experiences through CARE Corps Abroad. 151 Ellis St., Atlanta, GA 30303. Phone 404-681-2552 or 800-521-2273. Fax 404-589-2651. www.care.org.

Carter Center: Established in 1982 and still led by former president and first lady Jimmy and Rosalynn Carter. Operates projects around the world to advance peace and human rights, promote democracy, and fight poverty, disease, and hunger. Some volunteer opportunities at headquarters. 453 Freedom Pkwy., Atlanta, GA 30307. Phone 404-420-5100. www.cartercenter.org.

Catholic Relief Services: Official international relief and development agency of the Catholic Church in the United States. Provides emergency relief and development assistance in more than ninety countries. Offers numerous opportunities for Catholics to become involved in the agency's work. 209 W. Fayette St., Baltimore, MD 21201. Phone 410-625-2220 or 800-736-3467. www.catholicrelief.org.

Church World Service: Relief and development ministry of thirty-six Protestant, Orthodox, and Anglican denominations in the United States. Works with indigenous organizations in more than eighty countries to meet emergency needs and promote self-reliance. Offers volunteer opportunities with local affiliates in the United States. Organizes campaigns to influence U.S. government policies. 28606 Phillips St., P.O. Box 968, Elkhart, IN 46515. Phone 800-297-1516. www.churchworldservice.org.

Concern: Organized in Ireland in response to the Biafra famine in 1968. Carries out emergency relief and long-term development projects in more than twenty-five countries, most in Africa and Asia. Headquartered in Dublin, with offices in Belfast, London, and Glasgow and an affiliated organization in the United States. Offers volunteer opportunities in Ireland and the United States. 52-55 Lower Camden St., Dublin 2, Republic of Ireland. Phone 353-1-417-7700. Fax 353-1-475-7362. www.concern.net. U.S. affiliate: 104 E. 40th

St., Suite 903, New York, NY 10016. Phone 212-557-8000. Fax 212-557-8004. www.concernusa.org.

Congressional Hunger Center: Nonpartisan antihunger organization related to but independent of Congress. Develops tomorrow's humanitarian leaders through training and internship programs that place dedicated young people in internships with humanitarian organizations in the United States and around the world. 229 Pennsylvania Ave. SE, Washington, DC 20003. Phone 202-547-7022. Fax 202-547-7575. www.hungercenter.org.

Doctors without Borders: Deploys volunteer medical and support personnel, along with locally hired staff, to deliver emergency health care in more than seventy countries. Recruits volunteer doctors, nurses, midwives, laboratory technicians, logisticians, water and sanitation specialists, and financial managers. Also uses volunteers in U.S. offices. 333 7th Ave., 2nd Floor, New York, NY 10001-5004. Phone 212-679-6800. Fax 212-679-7016. www.doctorswithoutborders.org.

Feed the Children: Christian organization that distributes food, medicine, clothing, and other necessities to needy families in all fifty states and fifty-seven foreign countries. Accepts donations of food and other supplies from corporations and cash contributions from individuals. Also operates long-term programs to help people become self-sufficient. Encourages churches and other nonprofit organizations to become partner agencies to deliver food in their communities. Offers a wide range of volunteer opportunities, from conducting a small fund-raising event at home to working in the field in projects in the United States and overseas. P.O. Box 36, Oklahoma City, OK 73101-0036. Phone 800-627-4556. Fax 405-945-4177. www.feedthechildren.org.

Food for the Hungry: Christian organization that ministers to the physical and spiritual needs of the poor by providing emergency relief as well as operating child development, agriculture, clean water, health, nutrition, education, and microenterprise programs in more than forty-five countries. Offers a variety of volunteer opportunities at home and abroad. 1224 E. Washington St., Phoenix, AZ 85034-1102. Phone 480-998-310 or 800-248-6437. www.fh.org.

Global Witness: Investigative organization that exposes links between natural resource exploitation and human rights abuses—the trade in blood diamonds, for example. Gathers evidence and presents it to governments, private organizations, donors, development organizations, the media, and the general public to promote an end to the exploitation. Provides opportunities for individuals to join its lobbying campaigns. P.O. Box 6042, London, N19 5WP, United Kingdom. Phone 44-020-7272-6731. Fax 44-020-7272-9425. U.S. office: 1120 19th St. NW, 8th Floor, Washington, DC 20036. Phone 202-721-5670. Fax 202-530-0128. www.globalwitness.org.

Heifer Project International: Provides livestock, financial assistance, training, and other aid to poor families and communities in the United States and overseas to help them become self-sufficient. Heifer's unique fund-raising scheme enables individuals and organizations to purchase specific livestock (a heifer, for instance) for the poor. Also offers opportunities for individuals to volunteer and businesses to enter Heifer partnerships. P.O. Box 8058, Little Rock, AR 72203. Phone 800-422-0474. www.heifer.org.

Helen Keller International: Assists the blind and visually impaired and fights the causes of blindness in twenty-five countries. Activities include screening, education, treatment, distribution of nutritious food, agriculture development, and prenatal care. Also conducts research, advises governments, and helps establish sustainable programs. 352 Park Ave. S., 12th Floor, New York, NY 10010. Phone 212-532-0544 or 877-535-5374. Fax 212-532-6014. www.hki.org.

International Justice Mission: Works to free victims of violence, sexual exploitation, slavery, and oppression and to bring perpetrators to justice. Trains police in combating sex trafficking. Helps communities prepare to deter abuse. Assists victims in recovery. Offers internships to law students and encourages students to organize college campus chapters. P.O. Box 58147, Washington, DC 20037-8147. Phone 703-465-5495. Fax 703-465-5499. www.ijm.org.

International Polio Victims Response Committee: U.S.-registered, tax-exempt charity that raises funds for Jay Nash's Congolese Association for Orthopedic

Assistance to Young People. ACAOJH (the Congolese Association's French acronym) supplies braces to polio victims in the Congo. 10250 Harrison Rd., Loveland, OH 45140. www.congo-pages.org/ipvrc/home.htm.

Mercy Corps: Operates emergency relief and long-term development programs in thirty-five countries. Works to end and prevent conflicts by bringing together representatives of diverse groups and promoting democracy, citizen participation, and the rule of law. Offers internships for students preparing for careers in international development. Provides volunteer opportunities at headquarters in Portland. Organizes supporters to advocate government action to benefit the poor. Helps supporters conduct fund-raising events. Department W, P.O. Box 2669, Portland, OR 97208-2669. Phone 888-256-1900. www.mercycorps.org.

Opportunity International: Promotes microenterprise development by providing small loans, savings programs, insurance benefits, training and personal counseling to poor people in Africa, Asia, Eastern Europe, and Latin America. Accepts contributions and offers some volunteer opportunities. 2122 York Rd., Oak Brook, IL 60523. Phone 800-793-9455. Fax 630-645-1458. www.opportunity.org.

Operation Smile: Sends volunteer medical personnel around the world to provide reconstructive surgery and related health care to poor children and young adults. Also advocates for sustainable health-care systems. Offers volunteer opportunities for professionals with medical skills such as plastic surgery, anesthesiology, pediatrics, dentistry, and speech pathology, as well as for biomedical technicians, child life specialists, and medical students. Forms partnerships with service clubs and corporations that donate supplies and services. Helps supporters organize fund-raising events. 6435 Tidewater Dr., Norfolk, VA 23509. Phone 757-321-7645. Fax 757-321-7660. www.operationsmile.org.

Prison Fellowship International: Founded in 1976 by Charles W. Colson, former chief counsel to President Nixon, who was imprisoned for his role in the Watergate scandal. Provides support services to 100,000 volunteers in 112 prison fellowship organizations that conduct Christian missions to prisoners,

ex-prisoners, crime victims, and their families around the world. Organization's goal is to restore offenders to meaningful roles in society. Offers extensive volunteer opportunities with its affiliated fellowships. P.O. Box 17434, Washington, DC 20041. Phone 703-481-0000. www.pfi.org.

Project Mercy: Comprehensive development project to help the residents of Yetebon, Ethiopia, become self-sufficient. Has built a school, hospital, day-care center, irrigation system, and houses there. Provides adult education in agriculture, carpentry, metalworking, basket making, embroidery, spinning, and other useful skills. Uses skilled volunteers in such fields as teaching, information technology, carpentry, cooking, sanitation, and health care. Organizes volunteer expeditions with church groups. 7011 Ardmore Ave., Fort Wayne, IN 46809. Phone 260-747-2559. Fax 260-478-1361. www.projectmercy.org.

RESULTS: Grassroots advocacy organization that promotes government policies to fight hunger and poverty. Works in United States and six other countries. Lobbies public officials, conducts research, and communicates with the media and the general public. Has one hundred local chapters in the United States plus individual activists throughout the country. Volunteer opportunities range from becoming active in a local chapter to contacting public officials in response to e-mail alerts. 440 First St. NW, Suite 450, Washington, DC 20001. Phone 202-783-7100. www.results.org.

Salvation Army: Evangelical Christian movement, founded in London in 1865, that serves the poor throughout the world. Provides a wide range of emergency relief and other services in more than one hundred countries. Offers extensive volunteer opportunities. 101 Queen Victoria St., London EC4P 4EP, England. Phone 44-20-7332-0101. Fax 44-20-7236-4681. U.S. headquarters: P.O. Box 269, Alexandria, VA 22313. Phone 703-684 5500. Fax 703-684-3478. www.salvationarmy.org.

Save the Children: U.S. member of International Save the Children Alliance of 27 national organizations working in more than 110 countries. U.S. unit works in the poorest communities in 12 states and in more than 45 countries. Services,

which promote child well-being and family self-sufficiency, include literacy, physical activity, nutrition, microenterprise, agricultural development, reproductive health, newborn and child health, parent education, early childhood development, and emergency relief. Offers volunteer opportunities in U.S. projects. Organizes supporters to advocate for government programs that help children. Fosters long-term partnerships with corporations. 54 Wilton Rd., Westport, CT 06880. Phone 203-221-4030 or 800-728-3843. www.savethechildren.org. International Internet site: www.savethechildren.net.

World Vision: Christian relief and development organization focused especially on the needs of children. Operates emergency relief, education, healthcare, and economic and agricultural development programs around the world through national affiliates. U.S. affiliate offers volunteer opportunities and partnerships with churches and corporations. U.S. headquarters: P.O. Box 9716, Federal Way, WA 98063-9716. Phone 253-815-1000 or 888-511-6548. www.worldvision.org. International Internet site: www.wvi.org.

NOTES

CHAPTER 3

1. Pope John Paul II, "Letter on the Occasion of the 50th Anniversary of the Foundation of the Missionaries of Charity," October 2, 2000, www.vatican.va/holy_father/john_paul_ii/letters/2000/documents/ hf_jp-ii_let_20001017_missionaries-charity_en.html.

2. Cooper, Kenneth J., "Mother Teresa Dies at 87," *Washington Post,* September 6, 1997, A1.

3. Muhammad Yunus, "The Commonwealth Lecture," 2003, www.grameen-info.org/bank/Commonlth01.html.

4. Ibid.

5. "Grameen Bank at a Glance," Grameen Bank, September 2005, www.grameen-info.org/bank/GBGlance.htm.

6. Muhammad Yunus, "Muhammad Yunus Reflects on Working Toward Peace," Architects of Peace Project, Santa Clara University, Santa Clara, CA, www.scu.edu/ethics/architects-of-peace/Yunus/essay.html.

7. "Grameen Bank at a Glance."

8. Ibid.

9. David Bornstein, *How to Change the World* (Oxford: Oxford University Press, 2004),14.

10. Muhammad Yunus, "On the Occasion of Receiving the Planetary Consciousness Business Innovation Prize 1997 of the Club of Budapest," www.grameen-info.org/agrameen/speech.php3?speech=5.

11. Muhammad Yunus, *Banker to the Poor,* (New York: Public Affairs, 1999).

12. Ibid.

13. Lyla Bashan, "Eradicating Poverty One Loan at a Time," Global Envision, www.globalenvision.org/library/4/261/.

14. Frances Schwartzkopff, "Lending on Faith," *Atlanta Constitution,* March 14, 1993, H1. "Mini-Loans in Mini-Towns Produce Mini-Businesses," *Christian Science Monitor,* March 26, 1993.

15. Yunus, "Commonwealth Lecture."

CHAPTER 5

1. Gheorghe Calciu, "Delivered from the Lion's Den," remarks to conference sponsored by the Christian Relief Effort for the Emancipation of Dissidents, Washington, DC, November 9, 1985, www.roca.org/OA/55/55b.htm.

2. Richard Higgins, "A Sermon of Faith, Bridging Oppression," *Boston Globe,* March 12, 1990, 15.

3. "Bishop Lazlo Tokes on Spiritual Loss and Spiritual Gain," East-West Church & Ministry Report, Winter 1994, www.samford.edu/groups/global/ewcmreport/ articles/ew02112.htm.

4. Calciu, "Delivered from the Lion's Den."

CHAPTER 6

1. "Tony Hall's Fast," *Roll Call,* April 5, 1993, 4.

2. Richard Blow, "Life in the Fast Lane," *Washington Post,* April 16, 1993, B1.

3. Quoted in Tom Price, "House Welcomes Hall with Pledge of Action," *Dayton Daily News,* April 29, 1993, p.1.

4. Quoted in ibid.

5. Quoted in ibid.

CHAPTER 8

1. "Domestic Hunger and Poverty Facts," Bread for the World Institute, 2005, www.bread.org/hungerbasics/domestic.html.

2. "Household Food Security in the United States, 2003," Research Briefs, United States Department of Agriculture, www.ers.usda.gov/publications/fanrr42/ fanrr42_researchbrief.pdf.

CHAPTER 10

1. "Faith Communities Today," Hartford Institute for Religion Research, Hartford Seminary, Hartford, CT, March 2001, www.fact.hartsem.edu/research/fact2000/ Final%20FACTrpt.pdf.

2. "The Mosque in America: A National Portrait," Council on American-Islamic Relations, Washington, DC, April 25, 2001, www.cair-net.org/mosquereport/ Mosque_Community_Services.htm.

3. "USDA Conducts National Study of Food Pantries," United States Department of Agriculture, July 2003, www.pahunger.org/html/hunger/ArchPDF/ USDA_Conducts_National_Study_of_Food_Pantries.pdf.

4. "About MAZON," MAZON: A Jewish Response to Hunger, www.Mazon.org/ Who_we_Are/About_MAZON/index.asp.

5. Muhammad Yunus, *Banker to the Poor* (New York: Public Affairs, 1999), www.grameen-info.org/book/index.htm.

6. "Grameen Bank at a Glance," Grameen Bank, September 2005, www.grameen-info.org/ bank/GBGlance.htm.

7. Yunus, *Banker to the Poor.*

8. Laxminarayan, Ramdas, "Dismantling Prejudice: The Journey to a People Based Peace Strategy," Magsaysay Awardees' Lecture Series, Manila, August 27, 2004, www.rmaf.org.ph/ Awardees/Lecture/LectureRamdasLax.htm.

9. Tihomir Kukolja, posted on Web page that is no longer active.

10. "Faith Communities Today."

11. "For the Health of the Nation: An Evangelical Call to Civic Responsibiltiy," National Association of Evangelicals, October 2004, www.nae.net/images/ civic_responsibility2.pdf.

12. Ibid.

13. Ibid.

14. Ibid.

15. Quoted in Alan Cooperman "Religious Right, Left Meet in Middle," Washington Post, June 15, 2005, A1.

16. "Interview: Richard Cizik, National Association of Evangelicals," *Christian Post,* July 11, 2005, www.christianpost.com/article/church/2160/section/ interview.richard.cizik.national.association.of.evangelicals/1.htm

17. Njongonkulu W. H., Ndungane, keynote address at "Hunger No More: An Interfaith Convocation," Washington National Cathedral, Washington, DC, June 6, 2005, www.cathedral.org/cathedral/programs/hungernomore/ndunganekeynote.html.

Nominated three times for the Nobel Peace Prize, Tony Hall is widely recognized as one of the world's leading advocates for the hungry, the poor, and the oppressed. A former Democratic congressman who was appointed ambassador to the United Nations food and agricultural agencies by Republican president George W. Bush, Hall works closely with people of all political persuasions and religious faiths. He has traveled to more than one hundred countries, from Afghanistan to Zimbabwe, to investigate the needs of the poor and to urge the affluent to help.

Hall was born and reared in the Dayton, Ohio, area. He earned a bachelor of arts degree at Denison University, where he was a Little All-American football player, then served in the Peace Corps in Thailand. He was elected to the Ohio House of Representatives and the Ohio Senate before becoming Dayton's U.S. representative. In Congress from 1979 through 2002, he helped found and became chairman of the House Select Committee on Hunger and was an influential member of the powerful Rules Committee. In what began as an act of personal witness, Hall fasted for twenty-two days in 1993 to call attention to hunger and was astonished at the enormous positive public response. He has traveled to North Korea six times—more than any other elected official from the West—to investigate hunger in the reclusive Communist dictatorship. He was instrumental in bringing the United States and the Soviet Union together to combat famine in Ethiopia at the end of the Cold War in 1990. In 2004 he helped to broker a deal in which Libya opened its borders so that U.S. food could be shipped to hungry refugees in Sudan and Chad.

Hall and his wife, Janet, have reared two children, a daughter, Jyl, who is beginning a career ministering to the disadvantaged, and a son, Matt, who died of leukemia at age fifteen in 1996.

TOM PRICE

Tom Price is a veteran journalist who has written about Tony Hall since 1975, when Hall was an Ohio state senator from Dayton and Price was a reporter for the Dayton *Journal Herald*. In 1982 Price became a correspondent in the Cox Newspapers Washington Bureau, where he continued to cover Hall's congressional career. He has been a Washington-based freelance journalist since 1996. With his wife, Susan, he is coauthor of the award-winning *The Working Parents Help Book*. He also has written two Washington guidebooks. The Prices' daughter, Julie, is a student at the College of William and Mary.

**THE CAMPAIGN TO MAKE
POVERTY HISTORY
WWW.ONE.ORG**

There is a plague of biblical proportions taking place in Africa right now, but we can beat this crisis, if we each do our part. The first step is signing the ONE Declaration to join the ONE Campaign.

The ONE Campaign is a new effort to rally Americans, ONE by ONE, to fight the emergency of global AIDS and extreme poverty. We are engaging Americans everywhere we gather—in churches and synagogues, on the internet and college campuses, at community meetings and concerts.

"All we have to do to wage an effective fight against hunger, poverty, and oppression around the world—do what's in front of us. . . . Some will join campaigns to demand that the government do more for the poor, the hungry, and the oppressed. . . .Together, they will change the world. What will you do?"

—Tony Hall, *Changing the Face of Hunger*

Together, we can all make a difference in the lives of the poorest of God's children.

We invite you to join the ONE Campaign.
To learn more about ONE, please visit WWW.ONE.ORG.

**ONE Voice can make a difference.
Join the ONE Campaign now!**

This campaign is brought to you by

LaVergne, TN USA
26 February 2011
218087LV00005B/1/P